Quran Research Topics

Women- Inheritance- Divorce- Family

Sacred Months- Iman-Patience- Interest

بحث في مواضيع القرآن الكريم

ألعائلة- الطلاق - الميراث -النساء

الشهر الحرام -الايمان- الصبر- والربا

Hamza Muhammad Dakka   حمزة محمد دقة

With English Translation

copyright © 2023 by – Hamza Dakka- All Rights Reserved

بسم الله الرحمن الرحيم

Research Quranic Topics is a twin book- based on my previous book: Family Members in Holy Quran Verses – which looks mainly at **Close Family Members Quran Verses**, while in this book, I am researching **Quran Verses specific Important Topics** while keeping the Family Members Verses and Translations as they are at the first half of this book.

By doing so, reader can have more Scholar Translations of same Verse.

Default Translation of first book was **Saheeh International**, while the second part of this book (nearly half the book) is of **Hilali & Khan**.

Also used in handful number of cases **Pickhtal** Translation, and on same number of cased **Arabic Al- Jalalayn** -which I normally use for my Arabic book translation- They lived around the year 1500 (after the death of Jala Al-Mahalli, another Scolar- Jalal Al-Suyuti continues/completed the book), having said that, any scholar can get it wrong occasionally, but it is advisable to stick to a Scholars who spent all their lives researching Islamic topics.

In current/recent years, there is no clear and famous Scholars in the Muslim world due to interference from their governments as well as from foreign powers, Qaradawi - who died recently, was a distinct scholar, and while he was considered semi-extremist, US approached him to dampen Taliban approach to Indian temple, and to dampen Palestinian resistance attack against the Israeli occupation of their land having the backing of UN resolutions.

For Inheritance we know that male gets same as two female, but that can be higher depending on different situation examples are many here whether those sisters from same parents or one from different father, whether the father is married to more than one wife, etc. Quran is giving us many such verses and one can wonder why same number of people gets different share, for that reason I mentioned Calala whereby Al-Nisaa Sura 4, Verse 12 is different to verse 176.

المقدمة

الحمد لله، والصلاة والسلام على رسول الله، وعلى آله وصحبه ومن والاه.

يقول الله تعالى: "وَلَا يَأْتَلِ أُولُو الْفَضْلِ مِنكُمْ وَالسَّعَةِ أَن يُؤْتُوا أُولِي الْقُرْبَىٰ وَالْمَسَاكِينَ وَالْمُهَاجِرِينَ فِي سَبِيلِ اللَّهِ ۖ وَلْيَعْفُوا وَلْيَصْفَحُوا ۗ أَلَا تُحِبُّونَ أَن يَغْفِرَ اللَّهُ لَكُمْ ۗ وَاللَّهُ غَفُورٌ رَّحِيمٌ ﴿٢٢﴾" النور. ويقول تبارك وتعالى: ﴿٩٠﴾"النحل. "إِنَّ اللَّهَ يَأْمُرُ بِالْعَدْلِ وَالْإِحْسَانِ وَإِيتَاءِ ذِي الْقُرْبَىٰ وَيَنْهَىٰ عَنِ الْفَحْشَاءِ وَالْمُنكَرِ وَالْبَغْيِ ۚ يَعِظُكُمْ لَعَلَّكُمْ تَذَكَّرُونَ

هذا بحثٌ في مفردات القرآن الكريم بعنوان : ' القُربى والأقربون ' ، حرصت فيه على البحث في الآيات التي تتحدث عن ذوي القُربى، والأقربون، وكل من له صِلة في العائلة البشرية من الأمهات، الآباء والأنساب، فكلنا لآدم، وآدم من تراب، كما أخبر الصادق المصدوقﷺ: (الناس بنو آدم وآدم من تراب) رواه أبو داود والترمذي، فالله تعالى هو بادئ الأمم، وخالق الخلق من العدم، المتفرد بالبقاء والقدم، ومُنيرُ دروب المؤمنين في غَبَشِ الظُّلَم.

قال تعالى: "يَا أَيُّهَا النَّاسُ إِنَّا خَلَقْنَاكُم مِّن ذَكَرٍ وَأُنثَىٰ وَجَعَلْنَاكُمْ شُعُوبًا وَقَبَائِلَ لِتَعَارَفُوا ۚ إِنَّ أَكْرَمَكُمْ عِندَ اللَّهِ أَتْقَاكُمْ ۚ إِنَّ اللَّهَ عَلِيمٌ خَبِيرٌ ﴿١٣﴾"الحجرات.

وقال ﷺ في خطبة الوداع، مخاطباً الناس:

(يَا أَيُّهَا النَّاسُ، أَلَا إِنَّ رَبَّكُمْ وَاحِدٌ، وَإِنَّ أَبَاكُمْ وَاحِدٌ، أَلَا لَا فَضْلَ لِعَرَبِيٍّ عَلَى أَعْجَمِيٍّ، وَلَا لِعَجَمِيٍّ عَلَى عَرَبِيٍّ، وَلَا لِأَحْمَرَ عَلَى أَسْوَدَ، وَلَا أَسْوَدَ عَلَى أَحْمَرَ إِلَّا بِالتَّقْوَى، أَبَلَّغْتُ ؟ قَالُوا: بَلَّغَ رَسُولُ اللَّهِ صَلَّى اللَّهُ عَلَيْهِ وَسَلَّمَ، ثُمَّ قَالَ: أَيُّ يَوْمٍ هَذَا ؟ قَالُوا: يَوْمٌ حَرَامٌ، ثُمَّ قَالَ: أَيُّ شَهْرٍ هَذَا ؟ قَالَ: قَالُوا: شَهْرٌ حَرَامٌ، قَالَ: ثُمَّ قَالَ: أَيُّ بَلَدٍ هَذَا ؟ قَالُوا: بَلَدٌ حَرَامٌ، قَالَ: فَإِنَّ اللَّهَ قَدْ حَرَّمَ بَيْنَكُمْ دِمَاءَكُمْ وَأَمْوَالَكُمْ وَأَعْرَاضَكُمْ كَحُرْمَةِ يَوْمِكُمْ هَذَا، فِي شَهْرِكُمْ هَذَا، فِي بَلَدِكُمْ هَذَا، أَبَلَّغْتُ ؟ قَالُوا: بَلَّغَ رَسُولُ اللَّهِ صَلَّى اللَّهُ عَلَيْهِ وَسَلَّمَ قَالَ: لِيُبَلِّغْ الشَّاهِدُ الْغَائِبَ)رواه أحمد.

ذكرتُ في بحثي هذا بداية الأصل في القُربى من الآيات التي ذكرت الآباء، الأمهات، البنين، البنات، ثم لفظ الولد، الوِلْدان ومشتقاتها، فالاخ، الإخوة، الأخوات، ثم الأزواج.. ثم صنف المرأة ، إمرأةٌ ونساء.

ولفظ الذَّكر والذُّكران، الأنثيَيْن، والبُعُولة، وانتهيتُ ببحثي بذوي القُربى، أولو القُربى والمقربون.. .

قام بمراجعة البحث وتدقيقه فضيلة الأستاذ الشيخ محمد إبراهيم سيف، أستاذ الدراسات الإسلامية والفقه في جامعة فلسطين التقنية-خضوري، طولكرم _ فلسطين.   والله ولي التوفيق   (القسم الاول من هذا الكتاب ــ حتى ص 119)

سائلاً المولى عز وجل أن يتقبل منا هذا الجهد والعمل، وأن يجعله في ميزان حسناتنا، وأن ينفع به طلاب العلم والأئمة والخطباء والوعاظ والمهتمين بالدراسات القرآنية.

	بحث في مفردات القرآن الكريم الْقُرْبَىٰ وَالْأَقْرَبُونَ
	English Translation : Saheeh International to P119
	بسم الله الرحمن الرحيم
Father	أَبًا
12 يوسف 78	قَالُوا يَا أَيُّهَا الْعَزِيزُ إِنَّ لَهُ **أَبًا** شَيْخًا كَبِيرًا فَخُذْ أَحَدَنَا مَكَانَهُ ۖ إِنَّا نَرَاكَ مِنَ الْمُحْسِنِينَ
	They said, "O 'Azeez, indeed he has a father [who is] an old man, so take one of us in place of him. Indeed, we see you as a doer of good."
33 الأحزاب 40	مَّا كَانَ **مُحَمَّدٌ أَبَا** أَحَدٍ مِّن رِّجَالِكُمْ وَلَٰكِن رَّسُولَ اللَّهِ وَخَاتَمَ النَّبِيِّينَ ۗ وَكَانَ اللَّهُ بِكُلِّ شَيْءٍ عَلِيمًا
	Muhammad is not the father of [any] one of your men, but [he is] the Messenger of Allah and last of the prophets. And ever is Allah, of all things, Knowing.
Fathers	آباء
2 البقرة 133	أَمْ كُنتُمْ شُهَدَاءَ إِذْ حَضَرَ يَعْقُوبَ الْمَوْتُ إِذْ قَالَ لِبَنِيهِ مَا تَعْبُدُونَ مِن بَعْدِي قَالُوا نَعْبُدُ إِلَٰهَكَ وَإِلَٰهَ **آبَائِكَ** إِبْرَاهِيمَ وَإِسْمَاعِيلَ وَإِسْحَاقَ إِلَٰهًا وَاحِدًا وَنَحْنُ لَهُ مُسْلِمُونَ
	Or were you witnesses when death approached Jacob, when he said to his sons, "What will you worship after me?" They said, "We will worship your God and

		the God of your fathers, Abraham and Ishmael and Isaac - one God. And we are Muslims [in submission] to Him."
	170	وَإِذَا قِيلَ لَهُمُ اتَّبِعُوا مَا أَنزَلَ اللَّهُ قَالُوا بَلْ نَتَّبِعُ مَا أَلْفَيْنَا عَلَيْهِ آبَاءَنَا ۗ أَوَلَوْ كَانَ آبَاؤُهُمْ لَا يَعْقِلُونَ شَيْئًا وَلَا يَهْتَدُونَ
		And when it is said to them, "Follow what Allah has revealed," they say, "Rather, we will follow that which we found our fathers doing." Even though their fathers understood nothing, nor were they guided?
	200	فَإِذَا قَضَيْتُم مَّنَاسِكَكُمْ فَاذْكُرُوا اللَّهَ كَذِكْرِكُمْ آبَاءَكُمْ أَوْ أَشَدَّ ذِكْرًا ۗ فَمِنَ النَّاسِ مَن يَقُولُ رَبَّنَا آتِنَا فِي الدُّنْيَا وَمَا لَهُ فِي الْآخِرَةِ مِنْ خَلَاقٍ
		And when you have completed your rites, remember Allah like your [previous] remembrance of your fathers or with [much] greater remembrance. And among the people is he who says, "Our Lord, give us in this world," and he will have in the Hereafter no share.
4 النساء 11		يُوصِيكُمُ اللَّهُ فِي أَوْلَادِكُمْ ۖ لِلذَّكَرِ مِثْلُ حَظِّ الْأُنثَيَيْنِ ۚ فَإِن كُنَّ نِسَاءً فَوْقَ اثْنَتَيْنِ فَلَهُنَّ ثُلُثَا مَا تَرَكَ ۖ وَإِن كَانَتْ وَاحِدَةً فَلَهَا النِّصْفُ ۚ وَلِأَبَوَيْهِ لِكُلِّ وَاحِدٍ مِّنْهُمَا السُّدُسُ مِمَّا تَرَكَ إِن كَانَ لَهُ وَلَدٌ ۚ فَإِن لَّمْ يَكُن لَّهُ وَلَدٌ وَوَرِثَهُ أَبَوَاهُ فَلِأُمِّهِ الثُّلُثُ ۚ فَإِن كَانَ لَهُ إِخْوَةٌ فَلِأُمِّهِ السُّدُسُ ۚ مِن بَعْدِ وَصِيَّةٍ يُوصِي بِهَا أَوْ دَيْنٍ ۗ آبَاؤُكُمْ وَأَبْنَاؤُكُمْ لَا تَدْرُونَ أَيُّهُمْ أَقْرَبُ لَكُمْ نَفْعًا ۚ فَرِيضَةً مِّنَ اللَّهِ ۗ إِنَّ اللَّهَ كَانَ عَلِيمًا حَكِيمًا
		Allah instructs you concerning your children: for the male, what is equal to the share of two females. But if there are [only] daughters, two or more, for them is two thirds of one's estate. And if there is only one, for her is half. And for one's parents, to each one of them is a sixth of his estate if he left children. But if he had no children and the parents [alone] inherit from him, then for his mother is one third. And if he had brothers [or sisters], for his mother is a sixth, after any bequest he [may have] made or debt. Your parents or your children - you know not which of them are nearest to you in benefit. [These shares are] an obligation [imposed] by Allah. Indeed, Allah is ever Knowing and Wise.

22	وَلَا تَنكِحُوا مَا نَكَحَ آبَاؤُكُم مِّنَ النِّسَاءِ إِلَّا مَا قَدْ سَلَفَ ۚ إِنَّهُ كَانَ فَاحِشَةً وَمَقْتًا وَسَاءَ سَبِيلًا	
	And do not marry those [women] whom your fathers married, except what has already occurred. Indeed, it was an immorality and hateful [to Allah] and was evil as a way	
5 المائدة 104	وَإِذَا قِيلَ لَهُمْ تَعَالَوْا إِلَىٰ مَا أَنزَلَ اللَّهُ وَإِلَى الرَّسُولِ قَالُوا حَسْبُنَا مَا وَجَدْنَا عَلَيْهِ آبَاءَنَا ۚ أَوَلَوْ كَانَ آبَاؤُهُمْ لَا يَعْلَمُونَ شَيْئًا وَلَا يَهْتَدُونَ	
	And when it is said to them, "Come to what Allah has revealed and to the Messenger," they say, "Sufficient for us is that upon which we found our fathers." Even though their fathers knew nothing, nor were they guided?	
6 الأنعام 87	وَمِنْ آبَائِهِمْ وَذُرِّيَّاتِهِمْ وَإِخْوَانِهِمْ ۖ وَاجْتَبَيْنَاهُمْ وَهَدَيْنَاهُمْ إِلَىٰ صِرَاطٍ مُّسْتَقِيمٍ	
	And [some] among their fathers and their descendants and their brothers - and We chose them and We guided them to a straight path.	
91	وَمَا قَدَرُوا اللَّهَ حَقَّ قَدْرِهِ إِذْ قَالُوا مَا أَنزَلَ اللَّهُ عَلَىٰ بَشَرٍ مِّن شَيْءٍ ۗ قُلْ مَنْ أَنزَلَ الْكِتَابَ الَّذِي جَاءَ بِهِ مُوسَىٰ نُورًا وَهُدًى لِّلنَّاسِ ۖ تَجْعَلُونَهُ قَرَاطِيسَ تُبْدُونَهَا وَتُخْفُونَ كَثِيرًا ۖ وَعُلِّمْتُم مَّا لَمْ تَعْلَمُوا أَنتُمْ وَلَا آبَاؤُكُمْ ۖ قُلِ اللَّهُ ۖ ثُمَّ ذَرْهُمْ فِي خَوْضِهِمْ يَلْعَبُونَ	
	And they did not appraise Allah with true appraisal when they said, "Allah did not reveal to a human being anything." Say, "Who revealed the Scripture that Moses brought as light and guidance to the people? You [Jews] make it into pages, disclosing [some of] it and concealing much. And you were taught that which you knew not - neither you nor your fathers." Say, "Allah [revealed it]." Then leave them in their [empty] discourse, amusing themselves.	
148	سَيَقُولُ الَّذِينَ أَشْرَكُوا لَوْ شَاءَ اللَّهُ مَا أَشْرَكْنَا وَلَا آبَاؤُنَا وَلَا حَرَّمْنَا مِن شَيْءٍ ۚ كَذَٰلِكَ كَذَّبَ الَّذِينَ مِن قَبْلِهِمْ حَتَّىٰ ذَاقُوا بَأْسَنَا ۗ قُلْ هَلْ عِندَكُم مِّنْ عِلْمٍ فَتُخْرِجُوهُ لَنَا ۖ إِن تَتَّبِعُونَ إِلَّا الظَّنَّ وَإِنْ أَنتُمْ إِلَّا تَخْرُصُونَ	
	Those who associated with Allah will say, "If Allah had willed, we would not have associated [anything] and neither would our fathers, nor would we have prohibited anything." Likewise did those before deny until they tasted Our	

		punishment. Say, "Do you have any knowledge that you can produce for us? You follow not except assumption, and you are not but falsifying."
7 الأعراف 27		يَا بَنِي آدَمَ لَا يَفْتِنَنَّكُمُ الشَّيْطَانُ كَمَا أَخْرَجَ أَبَوَيْكُم مِّنَ الْجَنَّةِ يَنزِعُ عَنْهُمَا لِبَاسَهُمَا لِيُرِيَهُمَا سَوْآتِهِمَا ۗ إِنَّهُ يَرَاكُمْ هُوَ وَقَبِيلُهُ مِنْ حَيْثُ لَا تَرَوْنَهُمْ ۗ إِنَّا جَعَلْنَا الشَّيَاطِينَ أَوْلِيَاءَ لِلَّذِينَ لَا يُؤْمِنُونَ
		O children of Adam, let not Satan tempt you as he removed your parents from Paradise, stripping them of their clothing to show them their private parts. Indeed, he sees you, he and his tribe, from where you do not see them. Indeed, We have made the devils allies to those who do not believe.
28		وَإِذَا فَعَلُوا فَاحِشَةً قَالُوا وَجَدْنَا عَلَيْهَا آبَاءَنَا وَاللَّهُ أَمَرَنَا بِهَا ۗ قُلْ إِنَّ اللَّهَ لَا يَأْمُرُ بِالْفَحْشَاءِ ۗ أَتَقُولُونَ عَلَى اللَّهِ مَا لَا تَعْلَمُونَ
		And when they commit an immorality, they say, "We found our fathers doing it, and Allah has ordered us to do it." Say, "Indeed, Allah does not order immorality. Do you say about Allah that which you do not know?"
70		قَالُوا أَجِئْتَنَا لِنَعْبُدَ اللَّهَ وَحْدَهُ وَنَذَرَ مَا كَانَ يَعْبُدُ آبَاؤُنَا ۖ فَأْتِنَا بِمَا تَعِدُنَا إِن كُنتَ مِنَ الصَّادِقِينَ
		They said, "Have you come to us that we should worship Allah alone and leave what our fathers have worshipped? Then bring us what you promise us, if you should be of the truthful."
71		قَالَ قَدْ وَقَعَ عَلَيْكُم مِّن رَّبِّكُمْ رِجْسٌ وَغَضَبٌ ۖ أَتُجَادِلُونَنِي فِي أَسْمَاءٍ سَمَّيْتُمُوهَا أَنتُمْ وَآبَاؤُكُم مَّا نَزَّلَ اللَّهُ بِهَا مِن سُلْطَانٍ ۚ فَانتَظِرُوا إِنِّي مَعَكُم مِّنَ الْمُنتَظِرِينَ
		[Hud] said, "Already have defilement and anger fallen upon you from your Lord. Do you dispute with me concerning [mere] names you have named them, you and your fathers, for which Allah has not sent down any authority? Then wait; indeed, I am with you among those who wait."
95		ثُمَّ بَدَّلْنَا مَكَانَ السَّيِّئَةِ الْحَسَنَةَ حَتَّىٰ عَفَوا وَّقَالُوا قَدْ مَسَّ آبَاءَنَا الضَّرَّاءُ وَالسَّرَّاءُ فَأَخَذْنَاهُم بَغْتَةً وَهُمْ لَا يَشْعُرُونَ
		Then We exchanged in place of the bad [condition], good, until they increased [and prospered] and said, "Our fathers [also] were touched with hardship and ease." So We seized them suddenly while they did not perceive.

		Or [lest] you say, "It was only that our fathers associated [others in worship] with Allah before, and we were but descendants after them. Then would You destroy us for what the falsifiers have done?"
9 التوبة 23		يَا أَيُّهَا الَّذِينَ آمَنُوا لَا تَتَّخِذُوا آبَاءَكُمْ وَإِخْوَانَكُمْ أَوْلِيَاءَ إِنِ اسْتَحَبُّوا الْكُفْرَ عَلَى الْإِيمَانِ ۚ وَمَن يَتَوَلَّهُم مِّنكُمْ فَأُولَٰئِكَ هُمُ الظَّالِمُونَ
		O you who have believed, do not take your fathers or your brothers as allies if they have preferred disbelief over belief. And whoever does so among you - then it is those who are the wrongdoers.
24		قُلْ إِن كَانَ آبَاؤُكُمْ وَأَبْنَاؤُكُمْ وَإِخْوَانُكُمْ وَأَزْوَاجُكُمْ وَعَشِيرَتُكُمْ وَأَمْوَالٌ اقْتَرَفْتُمُوهَا وَتِجَارَةٌ تَخْشَوْنَ كَسَادَهَا وَمَسَاكِنُ تَرْضَوْنَهَا أَحَبَّ إِلَيْكُم مِّنَ اللَّهِ وَرَسُولِهِ وَجِهَادٍ فِي سَبِيلِهِ فَتَرَبَّصُوا حَتَّىٰ يَأْتِيَ اللَّهُ بِأَمْرِهِ ۗ وَاللَّهُ لَا يَهْدِي الْقَوْمَ الْفَاسِقِينَ
		Say, [O Muhammad], "If your fathers, your sons, your brothers, your wives, your relatives, wealth which you have obtained, commerce wherein you fear decline, and dwellings with which you are pleased are more beloved to you than Allah and His Messenger and jihad in His cause, then wait until Allah executes His command. And Allah does not guide the defiantly disobedient people."
10 يونس 78		قَالُوا أَجِئْتَنَا لِتَلْفِتَنَا عَمَّا وَجَدْنَا عَلَيْهِ آبَاءَنَا وَتَكُونَ لَكُمَا الْكِبْرِيَاءُ فِي الْأَرْضِ وَمَا نَحْنُ لَكُمَا بِمُؤْمِنِينَ
		They said, "Have you come to us to turn us away from that upon which we found our fathers and so that you two may have grandeur in the land? And we are not believers in you."
11 هود 62		قَالُوا يَا صَالِحُ قَدْ كُنتَ فِينَا مَرْجُوًّا قَبْلَ هَٰذَا ۖ أَتَنْهَانَا أَن نَّعْبُدَ مَا يَعْبُدُ آبَاؤُنَا وَإِنَّنَا لَفِي شَكٍّ مِّمَّا تَدْعُونَا إِلَيْهِ مُرِيبٍ
		They said, "O Salih, you were among us a man of promise before this. Do you forbid us to worship what our fathers worshipped? And indeed we are, about that to which you invite us, in disquieting doubt."
87		قَالُوا يَا شُعَيْبُ أَصَلَاتُكَ تَأْمُرُكَ أَن نَّتْرُكَ مَا يَعْبُدُ آبَاؤُنَا أَوْ أَن نَّفْعَلَ فِي أَمْوَالِنَا مَا نَشَاءُ ۖ إِنَّكَ لَأَنتَ الْحَلِيمُ الرَّشِيدُ

	They said, "O Shu'ayb, does your prayer command you that we should leave what our fathers worship or not do with our wealth what we please? Indeed, you are the forbearing, the discerning!"
109	فَلَا تَكُ فِي مِرْيَةٍ مِّمَّا يَعْبُدُ هَٰؤُلَاءِ ۚ مَا يَعْبُدُونَ إِلَّا كَمَا يَعْبُدُ آبَاؤُهُم مِّن قَبْلُ ۚ وَإِنَّا لَمُوَفُّوهُمْ نَصِيبَهُمْ غَيْرَ مَنقُوصٍ
	So do not be in doubt, [O Muhammad], as to what these [polytheists] are worshipping. They worship not except as their fathers worshipped before. And indeed, We will give them their share undiminished.
12 يوسف 4	إِذْ قَالَ يُوسُفُ لِأَبِيهِ يَا أَبَتِ إِنِّي رَأَيْتُ أَحَدَ عَشَرَ كَوْكَبًا وَالشَّمْسَ وَالْقَمَرَ رَأَيْتُهُمْ لِي سَاجِدِينَ
	[Of these stories mention] when Joseph said to his father, "O my father, indeed I have seen [in a dream] eleven stars and the sun and the moon; I saw them prostrating to me."
6	وَكَذَٰلِكَ يَجْتَبِيكَ رَبُّكَ وَيُعَلِّمُكَ مِن تَأْوِيلِ الْأَحَادِيثِ وَيُتِمُّ نِعْمَتَهُ عَلَيْكَ وَعَلَىٰ آلِ يَعْقُوبَ كَمَا أَتَمَّهَا عَلَىٰ أَبَوَيْكَ مِن قَبْلُ إِبْرَاهِيمَ وَإِسْحَاقَ ۚ إِنَّ رَبَّكَ عَلِيمٌ حَكِيمٌ
	And thus will your Lord choose you and teach you the interpretation of narratives and complete His favor upon you and upon the family of Jacob, as He completed it upon your fathers before, Abraham and Isaac. Indeed, your Lord is Knowing and Wise."
8	إِذْ قَالُوا لَيُوسُفُ وَأَخُوهُ أَحَبُّ إِلَىٰ أَبِينَا مِنَّا وَنَحْنُ عُصْبَةٌ إِنَّ أَبَانَا لَفِي ضَلَالٍ مُّبِينٍ
	When they said, "Joseph and his brother are more beloved to our father than we, while we are a clan. Indeed, our father is in clear error.
9	اقْتُلُوا يُوسُفَ أَوِ اطْرَحُوهُ أَرْضًا يَخْلُ لَكُمْ وَجْهُ أَبِيكُمْ وَتَكُونُوا مِن بَعْدِهِ قَوْمًا صَالِحِينَ
	Kill Joseph or cast him out to [another] land; the countenance of your father will [then] be only for you, and you will be after that a righteous people."
11	قَالُوا يَا أَبَانَا مَا لَكَ لَا تَأْمَنَّا عَلَىٰ يُوسُفَ وَإِنَّا لَهُ لَنَاصِحُونَ

	They said, "O our father, why do you not entrust us with Joseph while indeed, we are to him sincere counselors?
16	وَجَاءُوا أَبَاهُمْ عِشَاءً يَبْكُونَ
	And they came to their father at night, weeping.
17	قَالُوا يَا أَبَانَا إِنَّا ذَهَبْنَا نَسْتَبِقُ وَتَرَكْنَا يُوسُفَ عِندَ مَتَاعِنَا فَأَكَلَهُ الذِّئْبُ ۖ وَمَا أَنتَ بِمُؤْمِنٍ لَّنَا وَلَوْ كُنَّا صَادِقِينَ
	They said, "O our father, indeed we went racing each other and left Joseph with our possessions, and a wolf ate him. But you would not believe us, even if we were truthful."
38	وَاتَّبَعْتُ مِلَّةَ آبَائِي إِبْرَاهِيمَ وَإِسْحَاقَ وَيَعْقُوبَ ۚ مَا كَانَ لَنَا أَن نُّشْرِكَ بِاللَّهِ مِن شَيْءٍ ۚ ذَٰلِكَ مِن فَضْلِ اللَّهِ عَلَيْنَا وَعَلَى النَّاسِ وَلَٰكِنَّ أَكْثَرَ النَّاسِ لَا يَشْكُرُونَ
	And I have followed the religion of my fathers, Abraham, Isaac and Jacob. And it was not for us to associate anything with Allah. That is from the favor of Allah upon us and upon the people, but most of the people are not grateful.
40	مَا تَعْبُدُونَ مِن دُونِهِ إِلَّا أَسْمَاءً سَمَّيْتُمُوهَا أَنتُمْ وَآبَاؤُكُم مَّا أَنزَلَ اللَّهُ بِهَا مِن سُلْطَانٍ ۚ إِنِ الْحُكْمُ إِلَّا لِلَّهِ ۚ أَمَرَ أَلَّا تَعْبُدُوا إِلَّا إِيَّاهُ ۚ ذَٰلِكَ الدِّينُ الْقَيِّمُ وَلَٰكِنَّ أَكْثَرَ النَّاسِ لَا يَعْلَمُونَ
	You worship not besides Him except [mere] names you have named them, you and your fathers, for which Allah has sent down no authority. Legislation is not but for Allah. He has commanded that you worship not except Him. That is the correct religion, but most of the people do not know.
59	وَلَمَّا جَهَّزَهُم بِجَهَازِهِمْ قَالَ ائْتُونِي بِأَخٍ لَّكُم مِّنْ أَبِيكُمْ ۚ أَلَا تَرَوْنَ أَنِّي أُوفِي الْكَيْلَ وَأَنَا خَيْرُ الْمُنزِلِينَ
	And when he had furnished them with their supplies, he said, "Bring me a brother of yours from your father. Do not you see that I give full measure and that I am the best of accommodators?
61	قَالُوا سَنُرَاوِدُ عَنْهُ أَبَاهُ وَإِنَّا لَفَاعِلُونَ
	They said, "We will attempt to dissuade his father from [keeping] him, and indeed, we will do [it]."
63	فَلَمَّا رَجَعُوا إِلَىٰ أَبِيهِمْ قَالُوا يَا أَبَانَا مُنِعَ مِنَّا الْكَيْلُ فَأَرْسِلْ مَعَنَا أَخَانَا نَكْتَلْ وَإِنَّا لَهُ لَحَافِظُونَ

	So when they returned to their father, they said, "O our father, [further] measure has been denied to us, so send with us our brother [that] we will be given measure. And indeed, we will be his guardians."
65	وَلَمَّا فَتَحُوا مَتَاعَهُمْ وَجَدُوا بِضَاعَتَهُمْ رُدَّتْ إِلَيْهِمْ ۖ قَالُوا يَا أَبَانَا مَا نَبْغِي ۖ هَٰذِهِ بِضَاعَتُنَا رُدَّتْ إِلَيْنَا ۖ وَنَمِيرُ أَهْلَنَا وَنَحْفَظُ أَخَانَا وَنَزْدَادُ كَيْلَ بَعِيرٍ ۖ ذَٰلِكَ كَيْلٌ يَسِيرٌ
	And when they opened their baggage, they found their merchandise returned to them. They said, "O our father, what [more] could we desire? This is our merchandise returned to us. And we will obtain supplies for our family and protect our brother and obtain an increase of a camel's load; that is an easy measurement."
68	وَلَمَّا دَخَلُوا مِنْ حَيْثُ أَمَرَهُمْ أَبُوهُم مَّا كَانَ يُغْنِي عَنْهُم مِّنَ اللَّهِ مِن شَيْءٍ إِلَّا حَاجَةً فِي نَفْسِ يَعْقُوبَ قَضَاهَا ۚ وَإِنَّهُ لَذُو عِلْمٍ لِّمَا عَلَّمْنَاهُ وَلَٰكِنَّ أَكْثَرَ النَّاسِ لَا يَعْلَمُونَ
	And when they entered from where their father had ordered them, it did not avail them against Allah at all except [it was] a need within the soul of Jacob, which he satisfied. And indeed, he was a possessor of knowledge because of what We had taught him, but most of the people do not know.
78	قَالُوا يَا أَيُّهَا الْعَزِيزُ إِنَّ لَهُ أَبًا شَيْخًا كَبِيرًا فَخُذْ أَحَدَنَا مَكَانَهُ ۖ إِنَّا نَرَاكَ مِنَ الْمُحْسِنِينَ
	They said, "O 'Azeez, indeed he has a father [who is] an old man, so take one of us in place of him. Indeed, we see you as a doer of good."
80	فَلَمَّا اسْتَيْأَسُوا مِنْهُ خَلَصُوا نَجِيًّا ۖ قَالَ كَبِيرُهُمْ أَلَمْ تَعْلَمُوا أَنَّ أَبَاكُمْ قَدْ أَخَذَ عَلَيْكُم مَّوْثِقًا مِّنَ اللَّهِ وَمِن قَبْلُ مَا فَرَّطتُمْ فِي يُوسُفَ ۖ فَلَنْ أَبْرَحَ الْأَرْضَ حَتَّىٰ يَأْذَنَ لِي أَبِي أَوْ يَحْكُمَ اللَّهُ لِي ۖ وَهُوَ خَيْرُ الْحَاكِمِينَ
	So when they had despaired of him, they secluded themselves in private consultation. The eldest of them said, "Do you not know that your father has taken upon you an oath by Allah and [that] before you failed in [your duty to] Joseph? So I will never leave [this] land until my father permits me or Allah decides for me, and He is the best of judges.

81	ارْجِعُوا إِلَىٰ أَبِيكُمْ فَقُولُوا يَا أَبَانَا إِنَّ ابْنَكَ سَرَقَ وَمَا شَهِدْنَا إِلَّا بِمَا عَلِمْنَا وَمَا كُنَّا لِلْغَيْبِ حَافِظِينَ
	Return to your father and say, "O our father, indeed your son has stolen, and we did not testify except to what we knew. And we were not witnesses of the unseen,
94	وَلَمَّا فَصَلَتِ الْعِيرُ قَالَ أَبُوهُمْ إِنِّي لَأَجِدُ رِيحَ يُوسُفَ ۖ لَوْلَا أَن تُفَنِّدُونِ
	And when the caravan departed [from Egypt], their father said, "Indeed, I find the smell of Joseph [and would say that he was alive] if you did not think me weakened in mind."
97	قَالُوا يَا أَبَانَا اسْتَغْفِرْ لَنَا ذُنُوبَنَا إِنَّا كُنَّا خَاطِئِينَ
	They said, "O our father, ask for us forgiveness of our sins; indeed, we have been sinners."
99	فَلَمَّا دَخَلُوا عَلَىٰ يُوسُفَ آوَىٰ إِلَيْهِ أَبَوَيْهِ وَقَالَ ادْخُلُوا مِصْرَ إِن شَاءَ اللَّهُ آمِنِينَ
	And when they entered upon Joseph, he took his parents to himself and said, "Enter Egypt, Allah willing, safe [and secure]."
100	وَرَفَعَ أَبَوَيْهِ عَلَى الْعَرْشِ وَخَرُّوا لَهُ سُجَّدًا ۖ وَقَالَ يَا أَبَتِ هَٰذَا تَأْوِيلُ رُؤْيَايَ مِن قَبْلُ قَدْ جَعَلَهَا رَبِّي حَقًّا ۖ وَقَدْ أَحْسَنَ بِي إِذْ أَخْرَجَنِي مِنَ السِّجْنِ وَجَاءَ بِكُم مِّنَ الْبَدْوِ مِن بَعْدِ أَن نَّزَغَ الشَّيْطَانُ بَيْنِي وَبَيْنَ إِخْوَتِي ۚ إِنَّ رَبِّي لَطِيفٌ لِّمَا يَشَاءُ ۚ إِنَّهُ هُوَ الْعَلِيمُ الْحَكِيمُ
	And he raised his parents upon the throne, and they bowed to him in prostration. And he said, "O my father, this is the explanation of my vision of before. My Lord has made it reality. And He was certainly good to me when He took me out of prison and brought you [here] from bedouin life after Satan had induced [estrangement] between me and my brothers. Indeed, my Lord is Subtle in what He wills. Indeed, it is He who is the Knowing, the Wise
13 الرعد 23	جَنَّاتُ عَدْنٍ يَدْخُلُونَهَا وَمَن صَلَحَ مِنْ آبَائِهِمْ وَأَزْوَاجِهِمْ وَذُرِّيَّاتِهِمْ ۖ وَالْمَلَائِكَةُ يَدْخُلُونَ عَلَيْهِم مِّن كُلِّ بَابٍ
	Gardens of perpetual residence; they will enter them with whoever were righteous among their fathers, their spouses and their descendants. And the angels will enter upon them from every gate, [saying],

14 ابراهيم 10	قَالَتْ رُسُلُهُمْ أَفِي اللَّهِ شَكٌّ فَاطِرِ السَّمَاوَاتِ وَالْأَرْضِ ۖ يَدْعُوكُمْ لِيَغْفِرَ لَكُم مِّن ذُنُوبِكُمْ وَيُؤَخِّرَكُمْ إِلَىٰ أَجَلٍ مُّسَمًّى ۚ قَالُوا إِنْ أَنتُمْ إِلَّا بَشَرٌ مِّثْلُنَا تُرِيدُونَ أَن تَصُدُّونَا عَمَّا كَانَ يَعْبُدُ آبَاؤُنَا فَأْتُونَا بِسُلْطَانٍ مُّبِينٍ
	Their messengers said, "Can there be doubt about Allah, Creator of the heavens and earth? He invites you that He may forgive you of your sins, and He delays your death for a specified term." They said, "You are not but men like us who wish to avert us from what our fathers were worshipping. So bring us a clear authority."
16 النحل 35	وَقَالَ الَّذِينَ أَشْرَكُوا لَوْ شَاءَ اللَّهُ مَا عَبَدْنَا مِن دُونِهِ مِن شَيْءٍ نَّحْنُ وَلَا آبَاؤُنَا وَلَا حَرَّمْنَا مِن دُونِهِ مِن شَيْءٍ ۚ كَذَٰلِكَ فَعَلَ الَّذِينَ مِن قَبْلِهِمْ ۚ فَهَلْ عَلَى الرُّسُلِ إِلَّا الْبَلَاغُ الْمُبِينُ
	And those who associate others with Allah say, "If Allah had willed, we would not have worshipped anything other than Him, neither we nor our fathers, nor would we have forbidden anything through other than Him." Thus did those do before them. So is there upon the messengers except [the duty of] clear notification?
18 الكهف 5	مَّا لَهُم بِهِ مِنْ عِلْمٍ وَلَا لِآبَائِهِمْ ۚ كَبُرَتْ كَلِمَةً تَخْرُجُ مِنْ أَفْوَاهِهِمْ ۚ إِن يَقُولُونَ إِلَّا كَذِبًا
	They have no knowledge of it, nor had their fathers. Grave is the word that comes out of their mouths; they speak not except a lie
80	وَأَمَّا الْغُلَامُ فَكَانَ أَبَوَاهُ مُؤْمِنَيْنِ فَخَشِينَا أَن يُرْهِقَهُمَا طُغْيَانًا وَكُفْرًا
	And as for the **boy**, his parents were believers, and we feared that he would overburden them by transgression and disbelief
82	وَأَمَّا الْجِدَارُ فَكَانَ لِغُلَامَيْنِ يَتِيمَيْنِ فِي الْمَدِينَةِ وَكَانَ تَحْتَهُ كَنزٌ لَّهُمَا وَكَانَ أَبُوهُمَا صَالِحًا فَأَرَادَ رَبُّكَ أَن يَبْلُغَا أَشُدَّهُمَا وَيَسْتَخْرِجَا كَنزَهُمَا رَحْمَةً مِّن رَّبِّكَ ۚ وَمَا فَعَلْتُهُ عَنْ أَمْرِي ۚ ذَٰلِكَ تَأْوِيلُ مَا لَمْ تَسْطِع عَّلَيْهِ صَبْرًا

	And as for the wall, it belonged to **two** orphan **boys** in the city, and there was beneath it a treasure for them, and their father had been righteous. So your Lord intended that they reach maturity and extract their treasure, as a mercy from your Lord. And I did it not of my own accord. That is the interpretation of that about which you could not have patience."	
19 مريم 28	يَا أُخْتَ هَارُونَ مَا كَانَ أَبُوكِ امْرَأَ سَوْءٍ وَمَا كَانَتْ أُمُّكِ بَغِيًّا	
	O sister of Aaron, your father was not a man of evil, nor was your mother unchaste."	
42	إِذْ قَالَ لِأَبِيهِ يَا أَبَتِ لِمَ تَعْبُدُ مَا لَا يَسْمَعُ وَلَا يُبْصِرُ وَلَا يُغْنِي عَنكَ شَيْئًا	
	[Mention] when he said to his father, "O my father, why do you worship that which does not hear and does not see and will not benefit you at all?	
43	يَا أَبَتِ إِنِّي قَدْ جَاءَنِي مِنَ الْعِلْمِ مَا لَمْ يَأْتِكَ فَاتَّبِعْنِي أَهْدِكَ صِرَاطًا سَوِيًّا	
	O my father, indeed there has come to me of knowledge that which has not come to you, so follow me; I will guide you to an even path	
44	يَا أَبَتِ لَا تَعْبُدِ الشَّيْطَانَ ۖ إِنَّ الشَّيْطَانَ كَانَ لِلرَّحْمَٰنِ عَصِيًّا	
	O my father, do not worship Satan. Indeed Satan has ever been, to the Most Merciful, disobedient	
45	يَا أَبَتِ إِنِّي أَخَافُ أَن يَمَسَّكَ عَذَابٌ مِّنَ الرَّحْمَٰنِ فَتَكُونَ لِلشَّيْطَانِ وَلِيًّا	
	O my father, indeed I fear that there will touch you a punishment from the Most Merciful so you would be to Satan a companion [in Hellfire]."	
21 الأنبياء 44	بَلْ مَتَّعْنَا هَٰؤُلَاءِ وَآبَاءَهُمْ حَتَّىٰ طَالَ عَلَيْهِمُ الْعُمُرُ ۗ أَفَلَا يَرَوْنَ أَنَّا نَأْتِي الْأَرْضَ نَنقُصُهَا مِنْ أَطْرَافِهَا ۚ أَفَهُمُ الْغَالِبُونَ	
	But, [on the contrary], We have provided good things for these [disbelievers] and their fathers until life was prolonged for them. Then do they not see that We set upon the land, reducing it from its borders? So it is they who will overcome?	

53	قَالُوا وَجَدْنَا آبَاءَنَا لَهَا عَابِدِينَ
	They said, "We found our fathers worshippers of them."
54	قَالَ لَقَدْ كُنتُمْ أَنتُمْ وَآبَاؤُكُمْ فِي ضَلَالٍ مُّبِينٍ
	He said, "You were certainly, you and your fathers, in manifest error."
22 الحج 78	وَجَاهِدُوا فِي اللَّهِ حَقَّ جِهَادِهِ ۚ هُوَ اجْتَبَاكُمْ وَمَا جَعَلَ عَلَيْكُمْ فِي الدِّينِ مِنْ حَرَجٍ ۚ مِّلَّةَ أَبِيكُمْ إِبْرَاهِيمَ ۚ هُوَ سَمَّاكُمُ الْمُسْلِمِينَ مِن قَبْلُ وَفِي هَٰذَا لِيَكُونَ الرَّسُولُ شَهِيدًا عَلَيْكُمْ وَتَكُونُوا شُهَدَاءَ عَلَى النَّاسِ ۚ فَأَقِيمُوا الصَّلَاةَ وَآتُوا الزَّكَاةَ وَاعْتَصِمُوا بِاللَّهِ هُوَ مَوْلَاكُمْ ۖ فَنِعْمَ الْمَوْلَىٰ وَنِعْمَ النَّصِيرُ
	And strive for Allah with the striving due to Him. He has chosen you and has not placed upon you in the religion any difficulty. [It is] the religion of your father, Abraham. Allah named you "Muslims" before [in former scriptures] and in this [revelation] that the Messenger may be a witness over you and you may be witnesses over the people. So establish prayer and give zakah and hold fast to Allah. He is your protector; and excellent is the protector, and excellent is the helper.
23 المؤمنون 24	فَقَالَ الْمَلَأُ الَّذِينَ كَفَرُوا مِن قَوْمِهِ مَا هَٰذَا إِلَّا بَشَرٌ مِّثْلُكُمْ يُرِيدُ أَن يَتَفَضَّلَ عَلَيْكُمْ وَلَوْ شَاءَ اللَّهُ لَأَنزَلَ مَلَائِكَةً مَّا سَمِعْنَا بِهَٰذَا فِي آبَائِنَا الْأَوَّلِينَ
	But the eminent among those who disbelieved from his people said, "This is not but a man like yourselves who wishes to take precedence over you; and if Allah had willed [to send a messenger], He would have sent down angels. We have not heard of this among our forefathers.
68	أَفَلَمْ يَدَّبَّرُوا الْقَوْلَ أَمْ جَاءَهُم مَّا لَمْ يَأْتِ آبَاءَهُمُ الْأَوَّلِينَ
	Then have they not reflected over the Qur'an, or has there come to them that which had not come to their forefathers?
83	لَقَدْ وُعِدْنَا نَحْنُ وَآبَاؤُنَا هَٰذَا مِن قَبْلُ إِنْ هَٰذَا إِلَّا أَسَاطِيرُ الْأَوَّلِينَ

		We have been promised this, we and our forefathers, before; this is not but legends of the former peoples."
24 النور 31		وَقُل لِّلْمُؤْمِنَاتِ يَغْضُضْنَ مِنْ أَبْصَارِهِنَّ وَيَحْفَظْنَ فُرُوجَهُنَّ وَلَا يُبْدِينَ زِينَتَهُنَّ إِلَّا مَا ظَهَرَ مِنْهَا ۖ وَلْيَضْرِبْنَ بِخُمُرِهِنَّ عَلَىٰ جُيُوبِهِنَّ ۖ وَلَا يُبْدِينَ زِينَتَهُنَّ إِلَّا لِبُعُولَتِهِنَّ أَوْ آبَائِهِنَّ أَوْ آبَاءِ بُعُولَتِهِنَّ أَوْ أَبْنَائِهِنَّ أَوْ أَبْنَاءِ بُعُولَتِهِنَّ أَوْ إِخْوَانِهِنَّ أَوْ بَنِي إِخْوَانِهِنَّ أَوْ بَنِي أَخَوَاتِهِنَّ أَوْ نِسَائِهِنَّ أَوْ مَا مَلَكَتْ أَيْمَانُهُنَّ أَوِ التَّابِعِينَ غَيْرِ أُولِي الْإِرْبَةِ مِنَ الرِّجَالِ أَوِ الطِّفْلِ الَّذِينَ لَمْ يَظْهَرُوا عَلَىٰ عَوْرَاتِ النِّسَاءِ ۖ وَلَا يَضْرِبْنَ بِأَرْجُلِهِنَّ لِيُعْلَمَ مَا يُخْفِينَ مِن زِينَتِهِنَّ ۚ وَتُوبُوا إِلَى اللَّهِ جَمِيعًا أَيُّهَ الْمُؤْمِنُونَ لَعَلَّكُمْ تُفْلِحُونَ
		And tell the believing women to reduce [some] of their vision and guard their private parts and not expose their adornment except that which [necessarily] appears thereof and to wrap [a portion of] their headcovers over their chests and not expose their adornment except to their husbands, their fathers, their husbands' fathers, their sons, their husbands' sons, their brothers, their brothers' sons, their sisters' sons, their women, that which their right hands possess, or those male attendants having no physical desire, or children who are not yet aware of the private aspects of women. And let them not stamp their feet to make known what they conceal of their adornment. And turn to Allah in repentance, all of you, O believers, that you might succeed.
	61	لَّيْسَ عَلَى الْأَعْمَىٰ حَرَجٌ وَلَا عَلَى الْأَعْرَجِ حَرَجٌ وَلَا عَلَى الْمَرِيضِ حَرَجٌ وَلَا عَلَىٰ أَنفُسِكُمْ أَن تَأْكُلُوا مِن بُيُوتِكُمْ أَوْ بُيُوتِ آبَائِكُمْ أَوْ بُيُوتِ أُمَّهَاتِكُمْ أَوْ بُيُوتِ إِخْوَانِكُمْ أَوْ بُيُوتِ أَخَوَاتِكُمْ أَوْ بُيُوتِ أَعْمَامِكُمْ أَوْ بُيُوتِ عَمَّاتِكُمْ أَوْ بُيُوتِ أَخْوَالِكُمْ أَوْ بُيُوتِ خَالَاتِكُمْ أَوْ مَا مَلَكْتُم مَّفَاتِحَهُ أَوْ صَدِيقِكُمْ ۚ لَيْسَ عَلَيْكُمْ جُنَاحٌ أَن تَأْكُلُوا جَمِيعًا أَوْ أَشْتَاتًا ۚ فَإِذَا دَخَلْتُم بُيُوتًا فَسَلِّمُوا عَلَىٰ أَنفُسِكُمْ تَحِيَّةً مِّنْ عِندِ اللَّهِ مُبَارَكَةً طَيِّبَةً ۚ كَذَٰلِكَ يُبَيِّنُ اللَّهُ لَكُمُ الْآيَاتِ لَعَلَّكُمْ تَعْقِلُونَ
		There is not upon the blind [any] constraint nor upon the lame constraint nor upon the ill constraint nor upon yourselves when you eat from your [own] houses or the houses of your fathers or the houses of your mothers or the houses of your brothers or the houses of your sisters or the houses of your father's brothers or the houses of your father's sisters or the houses of your mother's brothers or the houses of your mother's sisters or [from houses] whose keys you possess or [from the house] of your friend. There is no blame upon you whether you eat together or separately. But when you enter houses, give greetings of peace upon each other - a greeting from Allah, blessed and good. Thus does Allah make clear to you the verses [of ordinance] that you may understand.

	قَالُوا سُبْحَانَكَ مَا كَانَ يَنبَغِي لَنَا أَن نَّتَّخِذَ مِن دُونِكَ مِنْ أَوْلِيَاءَ وَلَٰكِن مَّتَّعْتَهُمْ وَآبَاءَهُمْ حَتَّىٰ نَسُوا الذِّكْرَ وَكَانُوا قَوْمًا بُورًا	25 الفرقان 18
	They will say, "Exalted are You! It was not for us to take besides You any allies. But You provided comforts for them and their fathers until they forgot the message and became a people ruined."	
	قَالَ رَبُّكُمْ وَرَبُّ آبَائِكُمُ الْأَوَّلِينَ	26 الشعراء 26
	[Moses] said, "Your Lord and the Lord of your first forefathers."	
	قَالُوا بَلْ وَجَدْنَا آبَاءَنَا كَذَٰلِكَ يَفْعَلُونَ	74
	They said, "But we found our fathers doing thus."	
	أَنتُمْ وَآبَاؤُكُمُ الْأَقْدَمُونَ	76
	You and your ancient forefathers?	
	وَقَالَ الَّذِينَ كَفَرُوا أَإِذَا كُنَّا تُرَابًا وَآبَاؤُنَا أَئِنَّا لَمُخْرَجُونَ	27 النمل 67
	And those who disbelieve say, "When we have become dust as well as our forefathers, will we indeed be brought out [of the graves]?	
	لَقَدْ وُعِدْنَا هَٰذَا نَحْنُ وَآبَاؤُنَا مِن قَبْلُ إِنْ هَٰذَا إِلَّا أَسَاطِيرُ الْأَوَّلِينَ	68
	We have been promised this, we and our forefathers, before. This is not but legends of the former peoples."	
	قَالَتْ إِحْدَاهُمَا يَا أَبَتِ اسْتَأْجِرْهُ ۖ إِنَّ خَيْرَ مَنِ اسْتَأْجَرْتَ الْقَوِيُّ الْأَمِينُ	28 القصص 26
	One of the women said, "O my father, hire him. Indeed, the best one you can hire is the strong and the trustworthy."	
	فَلَمَّا جَاءَهُم مُّوسَىٰ بِآيَاتِنَا بَيِّنَاتٍ قَالُوا مَا هَٰذَا إِلَّا سِحْرٌ مُّفْتَرًى وَمَا سَمِعْنَا بِهَٰذَا فِي آبَائِنَا الْأَوَّلِينَ	36

	But when Moses came to them with Our signs as clear evidences, they said, "This is not except invented magic, and we have not heard of this [religion] among our forefathers."
31 لقمان 21	وَإِذَا قِيلَ لَهُمُ اتَّبِعُوا مَا أَنزَلَ اللَّهُ قَالُوا بَلْ نَتَّبِعُ مَا وَجَدْنَا عَلَيْهِ آبَاءَنَا ۚ أَوَلَوْ كَانَ الشَّيْطَانُ يَدْعُوهُمْ إِلَىٰ عَذَابِ السَّعِيرِ
	And when it is said to them, "Follow what Allah has revealed," they say, "Rather, we will follow that upon which we found our fathers." Even if Satan was inviting them to the punishment of the Blaze?
33 الأحزاب 5	ادْعُوهُمْ لِآبَائِهِمْ هُوَ أَقْسَطُ عِندَ اللَّهِ ۚ فَإِن لَّمْ تَعْلَمُوا آبَاءَهُمْ فَإِخْوَانُكُمْ فِي الدِّينِ وَمَوَالِيكُمْ ۚ وَلَيْسَ عَلَيْكُمْ جُنَاحٌ فِيمَا أَخْطَأْتُم بِهِ وَلَٰكِن مَّا تَعَمَّدَتْ قُلُوبُكُمْ ۚ وَكَانَ اللَّهُ غَفُورًا رَّحِيمًا
	Call them by [the names of] their fathers; it is more just in the sight of Allah. But if you do not know their fathers - then they are [still] your brothers in religion and those entrusted to you. And there is no blame upon you for that in which you have erred but [only for] what your hearts intended. And ever is Allah Forgiving and Merciful.
40	مَّا كَانَ مُحَمَّدٌ أَبَا أَحَدٍ مِّن رِّجَالِكُمْ وَلَٰكِن رَّسُولَ اللَّهِ وَخَاتَمَ النَّبِيِّينَ ۗ وَكَانَ اللَّهُ بِكُلِّ شَيْءٍ عَلِيمًا
	Muhammad is not the father of [any] one of your men, but [he is] the Messenger of Allah and last of the prophets. And ever is Allah, of all things, Knowing.
55	لَّا جُنَاحَ عَلَيْهِنَّ فِي آبَائِهِنَّ وَلَا أَبْنَائِهِنَّ وَلَا إِخْوَانِهِنَّ وَلَا أَبْنَاءِ إِخْوَانِهِنَّ وَلَا أَبْنَاءِ أَخَوَاتِهِنَّ وَلَا نِسَائِهِنَّ وَلَا مَا مَلَكَتْ أَيْمَانُهُنَّ ۗ وَاتَّقِينَ اللَّهَ ۚ إِنَّ اللَّهَ كَانَ عَلَىٰ كُلِّ شَيْءٍ شَهِيدًا
	There is no blame upon women concerning their fathers or their sons or their brothers or their brothers' sons or their sisters' sons or their women or those their right hands possess. And fear Allah. Indeed Allah is ever, over all things, Witness.
34 سبأ 43	وَإِذَا تُتْلَىٰ عَلَيْهِمْ آيَاتُنَا بَيِّنَاتٍ قَالُوا مَا هَٰذَا إِلَّا رَجُلٌ يُرِيدُ أَن يَصُدَّكُمْ عَمَّا كَانَ يَعْبُدُ آبَاؤُكُمْ وَقَالُوا مَا هَٰذَا إِلَّا إِفْكٌ مُّفْتَرًى ۚ وَقَالَ الَّذِينَ كَفَرُوا لِلْحَقِّ لَمَّا جَاءَهُمْ إِنْ هَٰذَا إِلَّا سِحْرٌ مُّبِينٌ
	And when our verses are recited to them as clear evidences, they say, "This is not but a man who wishes to avert you from that which your fathers were worshipping." And they say, "This is not except a lie invented." And those who

		disbelieve say of the truth when it has come to them, "This is not but obvious magic."
36 يس 6	لِتُنذِرَ قَوْمًا مَّا أُنذِرَ آبَاؤُهُمْ فَهُمْ غَافِلُونَ	
	That you may warn a people whose forefathers were not warned, so they are unaware	
37 الصافات 17	أَوَآبَاؤُنَا الْأَوَّلُونَ	
	And our forefathers [as well]?"	
69	إِنَّهُمْ أَلْفَوْا آبَاءَهُمْ ضَالِّينَ	
	Indeed they found their fathers astray.	
102	فَلَمَّا بَلَغَ مَعَهُ السَّعْيَ قَالَ يَا بُنَيَّ إِنِّي أَرَىٰ فِي الْمَنَامِ أَنِّي أَذْبَحُكَ فَانظُرْ مَاذَا تَرَىٰ ۚ قَالَ يَا أَبَتِ افْعَلْ مَا تُؤْمَرُ ۖ سَتَجِدُنِي إِن شَاءَ اللَّهُ مِنَ الصَّابِرِينَ	
	And when he reached with him [the age of] exertion, he said, "O my son, indeed I have seen in a dream that I [must] sacrifice you, so see what you think." He said, "O my father, do as you are commanded. You will find me, if Allah wills, of the steadfast."	
126	اللَّهَ رَبَّكُمْ وَرَبَّ آبَائِكُمُ الْأَوَّلِينَ	
	Allah, your Lord and the Lord of your first forefathers?"	
40 غافر 8	رَبَّنَا وَأَدْخِلْهُمْ جَنَّاتِ عَدْنٍ الَّتِي وَعَدتَّهُمْ وَمَن صَلَحَ مِنْ آبَائِهِمْ وَأَزْوَاجِهِمْ وَذُرِّيَّاتِهِمْ ۚ إِنَّكَ أَنتَ الْعَزِيزُ الْحَكِيمُ	
	Our Lord, and admit them to gardens of perpetual residence which You have promised them and whoever was righteous among their fathers, their spouses and their offspring. Indeed, it is You who is the Exalted in Might, the Wise.	
43 الزخرف 22	بَلْ قَالُوا إِنَّا وَجَدْنَا آبَاءَنَا عَلَىٰ أُمَّةٍ وَإِنَّا عَلَىٰ آثَارِهِم مُّهْتَدُونَ	

	Rather, they say, "Indeed, we found our fathers upon a religion, and we are in their footsteps [rightly] guided."	
23	وَكَذَٰلِكَ مَا أَرْسَلْنَا مِن قَبْلِكَ فِي قَرْيَةٍ مِّن نَّذِيرٍ إِلَّا قَالَ مُتْرَفُوهَا إِنَّا وَجَدْنَا آبَاءَنَا عَلَىٰ أُمَّةٍ وَإِنَّا عَلَىٰ آثَارِهِم مُّقْتَدُونَ	
	And similarly, We did not send before you any warner into a city except that its affluent said, "Indeed, we found our fathers upon a religion, and we are, in their footsteps, following."	
24	قَالَ أَوَلَوْ جِئْتُكُم بِأَهْدَىٰ مِمَّا وَجَدتُّمْ عَلَيْهِ آبَاءَكُمْ ۖ قَالُوا إِنَّا بِمَا أُرْسِلْتُم بِهِ كَافِرُونَ	
	[Each warner] said, "Even if I brought you better guidance than that [religion] upon which you found your fathers?" They said, "Indeed we, in that with which you were sent, are disbelievers."	
29	بَلْ مَتَّعْتُ هَٰؤُلَاءِ وَآبَاءَهُمْ حَتَّىٰ جَاءَهُمُ الْحَقُّ وَرَسُولٌ مُّبِينٌ	
	However, I gave enjoyment to these [people of Makkah] and their fathers until there came to them the truth and a clear Messenger	
44 الدخان 8	لَا إِلَٰهَ إِلَّا هُوَ يُحْيِي وَيُمِيتُ ۖ رَبُّكُمْ وَرَبُّ آبَائِكُمُ الْأَوَّلِينَ	
	There is no deity except Him; He gives life and causes death. [He is] your Lord and the Lord of your first forefathers.	
36	فَأْتُوا بِآبَائِنَا إِن كُنتُمْ صَادِقِينَ	
	Then bring [back] our forefathers, if you should be truthful."	
45 الجاثية 25	وَإِذَا تُتْلَىٰ عَلَيْهِمْ آيَاتُنَا بَيِّنَاتٍ مَّا كَانَ حُجَّتَهُمْ إِلَّا أَن قَالُوا ائْتُوا بِآبَائِنَا إِن كُنتُمْ صَادِقِينَ	
	And when Our verses are recited to them as clear evidences, their argument is only that they say, "Bring [back] our forefathers, if you should be truthful."	
53 النجم 23	إِنْ هِيَ إِلَّا أَسْمَاءٌ سَمَّيْتُمُوهَا أَنتُمْ وَآبَاؤُكُم مَّا أَنزَلَ اللَّهُ بِهَا مِن سُلْطَانٍ ۚ إِن يَتَّبِعُونَ إِلَّا الظَّنَّ وَمَا تَهْوَى الْأَنفُسُ ۖ وَلَقَدْ جَاءَهُم مِّن رَّبِّهِمُ الْهُدَىٰ	
	They are not but [mere] names you have named them - you and your forefathers - for which Allah has sent down no authority. They follow not except assumption and what [their] souls desire, and there has already come to them from their Lord guidance.	
56 الواقعة 48	أَوَآبَاؤُنَا الْأَوَّلُونَ	

	And our forefathers [as well]?"	
المجادلة 58 22	لَا تَجِدُ قَوْمًا يُؤْمِنُونَ بِاللَّهِ وَالْيَوْمِ الْآخِرِ يُوَادُّونَ مَنْ حَادَّ اللَّهَ وَرَسُولَهُ وَلَوْ كَانُوا آبَاءَهُمْ أَوْ أَبْنَاءَهُمْ أَوْ إِخْوَانَهُمْ أَوْ عَشِيرَتَهُمْ ۚ أُولَٰئِكَ كَتَبَ فِي قُلُوبِهِمُ الْإِيمَانَ وَأَيَّدَهُم بِرُوحٍ مِّنْهُ ۖ وَيُدْخِلُهُمْ جَنَّاتٍ تَجْرِي مِن تَحْتِهَا الْأَنْهَارُ خَالِدِينَ فِيهَا ۚ رَضِيَ اللَّهُ عَنْهُمْ وَرَضُوا عَنْهُ ۚ أُولَٰئِكَ حِزْبُ اللَّهِ ۚ أَلَا إِنَّ حِزْبَ اللَّهِ هُمُ الْمُفْلِحُونَ	
	You will not find a people who believe in Allah and the Last Day having affection for those who oppose Allah and His Messenger, even if they were their fathers or their sons or their brothers or their kindred. Those - He has decreed within their hearts faith and supported them with spirit from Him. And We will admit them to gardens beneath which rivers flow, wherein they abide eternally. Allah is pleased with them, and they are pleased with Him - those are the party of Allah. Unquestionably, the party of Allah - they are the successful.	
Father of ...	أبو .. (وَلِأَبَوَيْهِ/ أَبَوَاهُ/ أَبَوَيْكُمْ/ أَبَوَيْكَ/ أَبُوهُمْ/ أَبَوَيْهِ/ أَبُوهُمَا/ أَبُوكَ)	
النساء 4 11	يُوصِيكُمُ اللَّهُ فِي أَوْلَادِكُمْ ۖ لِلذَّكَرِ مِثْلُ حَظِّ الْأُنثَيَيْنِ ۚ فَإِن كُنَّ نِسَاءً فَوْقَ اثْنَتَيْنِ فَلَهُنَّ ثُلُثَا مَا تَرَكَ ۖ وَإِن كَانَتْ وَاحِدَةً فَلَهَا النِّصْفُ ۚ وَلِأَبَوَيْهِ لِكُلِّ وَاحِدٍ مِّنْهُمَا السُّدُسُ مِمَّا تَرَكَ إِن كَانَ لَهُ وَلَدٌ ۚ فَإِن لَّمْ يَكُن لَّهُ وَلَدٌ وَوَرِثَهُ أَبَوَاهُ فَلِأُمِّهِ الثُّلُثُ ۚ فَإِن كَانَ لَهُ إِخْوَةٌ فَلِأُمِّهِ السُّدُسُ ۚ مِن بَعْدِ وَصِيَّةٍ يُوصِي بِهَا أَوْ دَيْنٍ ۗ آبَاؤُكُمْ وَأَبْنَاؤُكُمْ لَا تَدْرُونَ أَيُّهُمْ أَقْرَبُ لَكُمْ نَفْعًا ۚ فَرِيضَةً مِّنَ اللَّهِ ۗ إِنَّ اللَّهَ كَانَ عَلِيمًا حَكِيمًا	
	Allah instructs you concerning your children: for the male, what is equal to the share of two females. But if there are [only] daughters, two or more, for them is two thirds of one's estate. And if there is only one, for her is half. And for one's parents, to each one of them is a sixth of his estate if he left children. But if he had no children and the parents [alone] inherit from him, then for his mother is one third. And if he had brothers [or sisters], for his mother is a sixth, after any bequest he [may have] made or debt. Your parents or your children - you know not which of them are nearest to you in benefit. [These shares are] an obligation [imposed] by Allah. Indeed, Allah is ever Knowing and Wise.	

7 الأعراف 27		يَا بَنِي آدَمَ لَا يَفْتِنَنَّكُمُ الشَّيْطَانُ كَمَا أَخْرَجَ **أَبَوَيْكُم** مِّنَ الْجَنَّةِ يَنزِعُ عَنْهُمَا لِبَاسَهُمَا لِيُرِيَهُمَا سَوْآتِهِمَا ۗ إِنَّهُ يَرَاكُمْ هُوَ وَقَبِيلُهُ مِنْ حَيْثُ لَا تَرَوْنَهُمْ ۗ إِنَّا جَعَلْنَا الشَّيَاطِينَ أَوْلِيَاءَ لِلَّذِينَ لَا يُؤْمِنُونَ
		O children of Adam, let not Satan tempt you as he removed your parents from Paradise, stripping them of their clothing to show them their private parts. Indeed, he sees you, he and his tribe, from where you do not see them. Indeed, We have made the devils allies to those who do not believe
12 يوسف 6		وَكَذَٰلِكَ يَجْتَبِيكَ رَبُّكَ وَيُعَلِّمُكَ مِن تَأْوِيلِ الْأَحَادِيثِ وَيُتِمُّ نِعْمَتَهُ عَلَيْكَ وَعَلَىٰ آلِ يَعْقُوبَ كَمَا أَتَمَّهَا عَلَىٰ **أَبَوَيْكَ** مِن قَبْلُ إِبْرَاهِيمَ وَإِسْحَاقَ ۚ إِنَّ رَبَّكَ عَلِيمٌ حَكِيمٌ
		And thus will your Lord choose you and teach you the interpretation of narratives and complete His favor upon you and upon the family of Jacob, as He completed it upon your fathers before, Abraham and Isaac. Indeed, your Lord is Knowing and Wise."
68		وَلَمَّا دَخَلُوا مِنْ حَيْثُ أَمَرَهُمْ **أَبُوهُم** مَّا كَانَ يُغْنِي عَنْهُم مِّنَ اللَّهِ مِن شَيْءٍ إِلَّا حَاجَةً فِي نَفْسِ يَعْقُوبَ قَضَاهَا ۚ وَإِنَّهُ لَذُو عِلْمٍ لِّمَا عَلَّمْنَاهُ وَلَٰكِنَّ أَكْثَرَ النَّاسِ لَا يَعْلَمُونَ
		And when they entered from where their father had ordered them, it did not avail them against Allah at all except [it was] a need within the soul of Jacob, which he satisfied. And indeed, he was a possessor of knowledge because of what We had taught him, but most of the people do not know.
94		وَلَمَّا فَصَلَتِ الْعِيرُ قَالَ **أَبُوهُمْ** إِنِّي لَأَجِدُ رِيحَ يُوسُفَ ۖ لَوْلَا أَن تُفَنِّدُونِ
		And when the caravan departed [from Egypt], their father said, "Indeed, I find the smell of Joseph [and would say that he was alive] if you did not think me weakened in mind."
99		فَلَمَّا دَخَلُوا عَلَىٰ يُوسُفَ آوَىٰ إِلَيْهِ **أَبَوَيْهِ** وَقَالَ ادْخُلُوا مِصْرَ إِن شَاءَ اللَّهُ آمِنِينَ
		And when they entered upon Joseph, he took his parents to himself and said, "Enter Egypt, Allah willing, safe [and secure]."
100		وَرَفَعَ **أَبَوَيْهِ** عَلَى الْعَرْشِ وَخَرُّوا لَهُ سُجَّدًا ۖ وَقَالَ يَا أَبَتِ هَٰذَا تَأْوِيلُ رُؤْيَايَ مِن قَبْلُ قَدْ جَعَلَهَا رَبِّي حَقًّا ۖ وَقَدْ أَحْسَنَ بِي إِذْ أَخْرَجَنِي مِنَ السِّجْنِ وَجَاءَ بِكُم مِّنَ **الْبَدْوِ** مِن بَعْدِ أَن نَّزَغَ الشَّيْطَانُ بَيْنِي وَبَيْنَ **إِخْوَتِي** ۚ إِنَّ رَبِّي لَطِيفٌ لِّمَا يَشَاءُ ۚ إِنَّهُ هُوَ الْعَلِيمُ الْحَكِيمُ

	And he raised his parents upon the throne, and they bowed to him in prostration. And he said, "O my father, this is the explanation of my vision of before. My Lord has made it reality. And He was certainly good to me when He took me out of prison and brought you [here] from bedouin life after Satan had induced [estrangement] between me and my brothers. Indeed, my Lord is Subtle in what He wills. Indeed, it is He who is the Knowing, the Wise.
18 الكهف 80	وَأَمَّا الْغُلَامُ فَكَانَ أَبَوَاهُ مُؤْمِنَيْنِ فَخَشِينَا أَن يُرْهِقَهُمَا طُغْيَانًا وَكُفْرًا
	And as for the **boy**, his parents were believers, and we feared that he would overburden them by transgression and disbelief.
82	وَأَمَّا الْجِدَارُ فَكَانَ لِغُلَامَيْنِ يَتِيمَيْنِ فِي الْمَدِينَةِ وَكَانَ تَحْتَهُ كَنزٌ لَّهُمَا وَكَانَ أَبُوهُمَا صَالِحًا فَأَرَادَ رَبُّكَ أَن يَبْلُغَا أَشُدَّهُمَا وَيَسْتَخْرِجَا كَنزَهُمَا رَحْمَةً مِّن رَّبِّكَ ۚ وَمَا فَعَلْتُهُ عَنْ أَمْرِي ۚ ذَٰلِكَ تَأْوِيلُ مَا لَمْ تَسْطِع عَّلَيْهِ صَبْرًا
	And as for the wall, it belonged to **two** orphan **boys** in the city, and there was beneath it a treasure for them, and their father had been righteous. So your Lord intended that they reach maturity and extract their treasure, as a mercy from your Lord. And I did it not of my own accord. That is the interpretation of that about which you could not have patience."
19 مريم 28	يَا أُخْتَ هَارُونَ مَا كَانَ أَبُوكِ امْرَأَ سَوْءٍ وَمَا كَانَتْ أُمُّكِ بَغِيًّا
	O sister of Aaron, your father was not a man of evil, nor was your mother unchaste."
My Father	أَبِي
6 الأنعام 74	وَإِذْ قَالَ إِبْرَاهِيمُ لِأَبِيهِ آزَرَ أَتَتَّخِذُ أَصْنَامًا آلِهَةً ۖ إِنِّي أَرَاكَ وَقَوْمَكَ فِي ضَلَالٍ مُّبِينٍ
	And [mention, O Muhammad], when Abraham said to his father Azar, "Do you take idols as deities? Indeed, I see you and your people to be in manifest error."
9 التوبة 114	وَمَا كَانَ اسْتِغْفَارُ إِبْرَاهِيمَ لِأَبِيهِ إِلَّا عَن مَّوْعِدَةٍ وَعَدَهَا إِيَّاهُ فَلَمَّا تَبَيَّنَ لَهُ أَنَّهُ عَدُوٌّ لِّلَّهِ تَبَرَّأَ مِنْهُ ۚ إِنَّ إِبْرَاهِيمَ لَأَوَّاهٌ حَلِيمٌ

		And the request of forgiveness of Abraham for his father was only because of a promise he had made to him. But when it became apparent to Abraham that his father was an enemy to Allah, he disassociated himself from him. Indeed was Abraham compassionate and patient.
12 يوسف	4	إِذْ قَالَ يُوسُفُ لِأَبِيهِ يَا أَبَتِ إِنِّي رَأَيْتُ أَحَدَ عَشَرَ كَوْكَبًا وَالشَّمْسَ وَالْقَمَرَ رَأَيْتُهُمْ لِي سَاجِدِينَ
		[Of these stories mention] when Joseph said to his father, "O my father, indeed I have seen [in a dream] eleven stars and the sun and the moon; I saw them prostrating to me."
	8	إِذْ قَالُوا لَيُوسُفُ وَأَخُوهُ أَحَبُّ إِلَىٰ أَبِينَا مِنَّا وَنَحْنُ عُصْبَةٌ إِنَّ أَبَانَا لَفِي ضَلَالٍ مُبِينٍ
		When they said, "Joseph and his brother are more beloved to our father than we, while we are a clan. Indeed, our father is in clear error.
	9	اقْتُلُوا يُوسُفَ أَوِ اطْرَحُوهُ أَرْضًا يَخْلُ لَكُمْ وَجْهُ أَبِيكُمْ وَتَكُونُوا مِنْ بَعْدِهِ قَوْمًا صَالِحِينَ
		Kill Joseph or cast him out to [another] land; the countenance of your father will [then] be only for you, and you will be after that a righteous people."
	59	وَلَمَّا جَهَّزَهُم بِجَهَازِهِمْ قَالَ ائْتُونِي بِأَخٍ لَّكُم مِّنْ أَبِيكُمْ ۚ أَلَا تَرَوْنَ أَنِّي أُوفِي الْكَيْلَ وَأَنَا خَيْرُ الْمُنزِلِينَ
		And when he had furnished them with their supplies, he said, "Bring me a brother of yours from your father. Do not you see that I give full measure and that I am the best of accommodators?
	63	فَلَمَّا رَجَعُوا إِلَىٰ أَبِيهِمْ قَالُوا يَا أَبَانَا مُنِعَ مِنَّا الْكَيْلُ فَأَرْسِلْ مَعَنَا أَخَانَا نَكْتَلْ وَإِنَّا لَهُ لَحَافِظُونَ
		So when they returned to their father, they said, "O our father, [further] measure has been denied to us, so send with us our brother [that] we will be given measure. And indeed, we will be his guardians."
	80	فَلَمَّا اسْتَيْأَسُوا مِنْهُ خَلَصُوا نَجِيًّا ۖ قَالَ كَبِيرُهُمْ أَلَمْ تَعْلَمُوا أَنَّ أَبَاكُمْ قَدْ أَخَذَ عَلَيْكُم مَّوْثِقًا مِّنَ اللَّهِ وَمِن قَبْلُ مَا فَرَّطتُمْ فِي يُوسُفَ ۖ فَلَنْ أَبْرَحَ الْأَرْضَ حَتَّىٰ يَأْذَنَ لِي أَبِي أَوْ يَحْكُمَ اللَّهُ لِي ۖ وَهُوَ خَيْرُ الْحَاكِمِينَ
		So when they had despaired of him, they secluded themselves in private consultation. The eldest of them said, "Do you not know that your father has taken upon you an oath by Allah and [that] before you failed in [your duty to] Joseph? So I will never leave [this] land until my father permits me or Allah decides for me, and He is the best of judges.

81	ارْجِعُوا إِلَىٰ أَبِيكُمْ فَقُولُوا يَا أَبَانَا إِنَّ ابْنَكَ سَرَقَ وَمَا شَهِدْنَا إِلَّا بِمَا عَلِمْنَا وَمَا كُنَّا لِلْغَيْبِ حَافِظِينَ
	Return to your father and say, "O our father, indeed your son has stolen, and we did not testify except to what we knew. And we were not witnesses of the unseen,
93	اذْهَبُوا بِقَمِيصِي هَٰذَا فَأَلْقُوهُ عَلَىٰ وَجْهِ أَبِي يَأْتِ بَصِيرًا وَأْتُونِي بِأَهْلِكُمْ أَجْمَعِينَ
	Take this, my shirt, and cast it over the face of my father; he will become seeing. And bring me your family, all together."
100	وَرَفَعَ أَبَوَيْهِ عَلَى الْعَرْشِ وَخَرُّوا لَهُ سُجَّدًا ۖ وَقَالَ يَا أَبَتِ هَٰذَا تَأْوِيلُ رُؤْيَايَ مِن قَبْلُ قَدْ جَعَلَهَا رَبِّي حَقًّا ۖ وَقَدْ أَحْسَنَ بِي إِذْ أَخْرَجَنِي مِنَ السِّجْنِ وَجَاءَ بِكُم مِّنَ الْبَدْوِ مِن بَعْدِ أَن نَّزَغَ الشَّيْطَانُ بَيْنِي وَبَيْنَ إِخْوَتِي ۚ إِنَّ رَبِّي لَطِيفٌ لِّمَا يَشَاءُ ۚ إِنَّهُ هُوَ الْعَلِيمُ الْحَكِيمُ
	And he raised his parents upon the throne, and they bowed to him in prostration. And he said, "O my father, this is the explanation of my vision of before. My Lord has made it reality. And He was certainly good to me when He took me out of prison and brought you [here] from bedouin life after Satan had induced [estrangement] between me and my brothers. Indeed, my Lord is Subtle in what He wills. Indeed, it is He who is the Knowing, the Wise.
19 مريم 42	إِذْ قَالَ لِأَبِيهِ يَا أَبَتِ لِمَ تَعْبُدُ مَا لَا يَسْمَعُ وَلَا يُبْصِرُ وَلَا يُغْنِي عَنكَ شَيْئًا
	[Mention] when he said to his father, "O my father, why do you worship that which does not hear and does not see and will not benefit you at all?
43	يَا أَبَتِ إِنِّي قَدْ جَاءَنِي مِنَ الْعِلْمِ مَا لَمْ يَأْتِكَ فَاتَّبِعْنِي أَهْدِكَ صِرَاطًا سَوِيًّا
	O my father, indeed there has come to me of knowledge that which has not come to you, so follow me; I will guide you to an even path.
44	يَا أَبَتِ لَا تَعْبُدِ الشَّيْطَانَ ۖ إِنَّ الشَّيْطَانَ كَانَ لِلرَّحْمَٰنِ عَصِيًّا
	O my father, do not worship Satan. Indeed Satan has ever been, to the Most Merciful, disobedient.

45		يَا أَبَتِ إِنِّي أَخَافُ أَن يَمَسَّكَ عَذَابٌ مِّنَ الرَّحْمَٰنِ فَتَكُونَ لِلشَّيْطَانِ وَلِيًّا
	O my father, indeed I fear that there will touch you a punishment from the Most Merciful so you would be to Satan a companion [in Hellfire]."	
21 الأنبياء 52		إِذْ قَالَ لِأَبِيهِ وَقَوْمِهِ مَا هَٰذِهِ التَّمَاثِيلُ الَّتِي أَنتُمْ لَهَا عَاكِفُونَ
	When he said to his father and his people, "What are these statues to which you are devoted?"	
22 الحج 78		وَجَاهِدُوا فِي اللَّهِ حَقَّ جِهَادِهِ ۚ هُوَ اجْتَبَاكُمْ وَمَا جَعَلَ عَلَيْكُمْ فِي الدِّينِ مِنْ حَرَجٍ ۚ مِّلَّةَ أَبِيكُمْ إِبْرَاهِيمَ ۚ هُوَ سَمَّاكُمُ الْمُسْلِمِينَ مِن قَبْلُ وَفِي هَٰذَا لِيَكُونَ الرَّسُولُ شَهِيدًا عَلَيْكُمْ وَتَكُونُوا شُهَدَاءَ عَلَى النَّاسِ ۚ فَأَقِيمُوا الصَّلَاةَ وَآتُوا الزَّكَاةَ وَاعْتَصِمُوا بِاللَّهِ هُوَ مَوْلَاكُمْ ۖ فَنِعْمَ الْمَوْلَىٰ وَنِعْمَ النَّصِيرُ
	And strive for Allah with the striving due to Him. He has chosen you and has not placed upon you in the religion any difficulty. [It is] the religion of your father, Abraham. Allah named you "Muslims" before [in former scriptures] and in this [revelation] that the Messenger may be a witness over you and you may be witnesses over the people. So establish prayer and give zakah and hold fast to Allah. He is your protector; and excellent is the protector, and excellent is the helper.	
26 الشعراء 70		إِذْ قَالَ لِأَبِيهِ وَقَوْمِهِ مَا تَعْبُدُونَ
	When he said to his father and his people, "What do you worship?"	
86		وَاغْفِرْ لِأَبِي إِنَّهُ كَانَ مِنَ الضَّالِّينَ
	And forgive my father. Indeed, he has been of those astray.	
28 القصص 25		فَجَاءَتْهُ إِحْدَاهُمَا تَمْشِي عَلَى اسْتِحْيَاءٍ قَالَتْ إِنَّ أَبِي يَدْعُوكَ لِيَجْزِيَكَ أَجْرَ مَا سَقَيْتَ لَنَا ۚ فَلَمَّا جَاءَهُ وَقَصَّ عَلَيْهِ الْقَصَصَ قَالَ لَا تَخَفْ ۖ نَجَوْتَ مِنَ الْقَوْمِ الظَّالِمِينَ

	Then one of the two women came to him walking with shyness. She said, "Indeed, my father invites you that he may reward you for having watered for us." So when he came to him and related to him the story, he said, "Fear not. You have escaped from the wrongdoing people."
26	قَالَتْ إِحْدَاهُمَا يَا أَبَتِ اسْتَأْجِرْهُ ۖ إِنَّ خَيْرَ مَنِ اسْتَأْجَرْتَ الْقَوِيُّ الْأَمِينُ
	One of the women said, "O my father, hire him. Indeed, the best one you can hire is the strong and the trustworthy."
37 الصافات 85	إِذْ قَالَ لِأَبِيهِ وَقَوْمِهِ مَاذَا تَعْبُدُونَ
	[And] when he said to his father and his people, "What do you worship?
102	فَلَمَّا بَلَغَ مَعَهُ السَّعْيَ قَالَ يَا بُنَيَّ إِنِّي أَرَىٰ فِي الْمَنَامِ أَنِّي أَذْبَحُكَ فَانْظُرْ مَاذَا تَرَىٰ ۚ قَالَ يَا أَبَتِ افْعَلْ مَا تُؤْمَرُ ۖ سَتَجِدُنِي إِنْ شَاءَ اللَّهُ مِنَ الصَّابِرِينَ
	And when he reached with him [the age of] exertion, he said, "O my son, indeed I have seen in a dream that I [must] sacrifice you, so see what you think." He said, "O my father, do as you are commanded. You will find me, if Allah wills, of the steadfast."
43 الزخرف 26	وَإِذْ قَالَ إِبْرَاهِيمُ لِأَبِيهِ وَقَوْمِهِ إِنَّنِي بَرَاءٌ مِمَّا تَعْبُدُونَ
	And [mention, O Muhammad], when Abraham said to his father and his people, "Indeed, I am disassociated from that which you worship
60 الممتحنة 4	قَدْ كَانَتْ لَكُمْ أُسْوَةٌ حَسَنَةٌ فِي إِبْرَاهِيمَ وَالَّذِينَ مَعَهُ إِذْ قَالُوا لِقَوْمِهِمْ إِنَّا بُرَآءُ مِنكُمْ وَمِمَّا تَعْبُدُونَ مِن دُونِ اللَّهِ كَفَرْنَا بِكُمْ وَبَدَا بَيْنَنَا وَبَيْنَكُمُ الْعَدَاوَةُ وَالْبَغْضَاءُ أَبَدًا حَتَّىٰ تُؤْمِنُوا بِاللَّهِ وَحْدَهُ إِلَّا قَوْلَ إِبْرَاهِيمَ لِأَبِيهِ لَأَسْتَغْفِرَنَّ لَكَ وَمَا أَمْلِكُ لَكَ مِنَ اللَّهِ مِن شَيْءٍ ۖ رَّبَّنَا عَلَيْكَ تَوَكَّلْنَا وَإِلَيْكَ أَنَبْنَا وَإِلَيْكَ الْمَصِيرُ

80 عبس 35	وَأُمِّهِ وَأَبِيهِ	
	And his mother and his father	
111 المسد 1	تَبَّتْ يَدَا أَبِي لَهَبٍ وَتَبَّ	
	May the hands of Abu Lahab be ruined, and ruined is he.	
Son/s My/yours..	ابن/ابناء/أَبْنَاءَكُمْ/أَبْنَاؤُكُمْ/أَبْنَاءَهُمْ/أَبْنَائِنَا/ابْنَيْ/بَنِيَّ/بُنَيَّ/ابْنَهَا/أَبْنَائِهِنَّ/ أَبْنَاءَ	
2 البقرة 49	وَإِذْ نَجَّيْنَاكُم مِّنْ آلِ فِرْعَوْنَ يَسُومُونَكُمْ سُوءَ الْعَذَابِ يُذَبِّحُونَ أَبْنَاءَكُمْ وَيَسْتَحْيُونَ نِسَاءَكُمْ ۚ وَفِي ذَٰلِكُم بَلَاءٌ مِّن رَّبِّكُمْ عَظِيمٌ	
	And [recall] when We saved your forefathers from the people of Pharaoh, who afflicted you with the worst torment, slaughtering your [newborn] sons and keeping your females alive. And in that was a great trial from your Lord.	
87	وَلَقَدْ آتَيْنَا مُوسَى الْكِتَابَ وَقَفَّيْنَا مِن بَعْدِهِ بِالرُّسُلِ ۖ وَآتَيْنَا عِيسَى ابْنَ مَرْيَمَ الْبَيِّنَاتِ وَأَيَّدْنَاهُ بِرُوحِ الْقُدُسِ ۗ أَفَكُلَّمَا جَاءَكُمْ رَسُولٌ بِمَا لَا تَهْوَىٰ أَنفُسُكُمُ اسْتَكْبَرْتُمْ فَفَرِيقًا كَذَّبْتُمْ وَفَرِيقًا تَقْتُلُونَ	
	And We did certainly give Moses the Torah and followed up after him with messengers. And We gave Jesus, the son of Mary, clear proofs and supported him with the Pure Spirit. But is it [not] that every time a messenger came to you, [O Children of Israel], with what your souls did not desire, you were arrogant? And a party [of messengers] you denied and another party you killed	
146	الَّذِينَ آتَيْنَاهُمُ الْكِتَابَ يَعْرِفُونَهُ كَمَا يَعْرِفُونَ أَبْنَاءَهُمْ ۖ وَإِنَّ فَرِيقًا مِّنْهُمْ لَيَكْتُمُونَ الْحَقَّ وَهُمْ يَعْلَمُونَ	
	Those to whom We gave the Scripture know him as they know their own sons. But indeed, a party of them conceal the truth while they know [it].	

177	لَّيْسَ الْبِرَّ أَن تُوَلُّوا وُجُوهَكُمْ قِبَلَ الْمَشْرِقِ وَالْمَغْرِبِ وَلَٰكِنَّ الْبِرَّ مَنْ آمَنَ بِاللَّهِ وَالْيَوْمِ الْآخِرِ وَالْمَلَائِكَةِ وَالْكِتَابِ وَالنَّبِيِّينَ وَآتَى الْمَالَ عَلَىٰ حُبِّهِ ذَوِي الْقُرْبَىٰ وَالْيَتَامَىٰ وَالْمَسَاكِينَ وَابْنَ السَّبِيلِ وَالسَّائِلِينَ وَفِي الرِّقَابِ وَأَقَامَ الصَّلَاةَ وَآتَى الزَّكَاةَ وَالْمُوفُونَ بِعَهْدِهِمْ إِذَا عَاهَدُوا ۖ وَالصَّابِرِينَ فِي الْبَأْسَاءِ وَالضَّرَّاءِ وَحِينَ الْبَأْسِ ۗ أُولَٰئِكَ الَّذِينَ صَدَقُوا ۖ وَأُولَٰئِكَ هُمُ الْمُتَّقُونَ
	Righteousness is not that you turn your faces toward the east or the west, but [true] righteousness is [in] one who believes in Allah, the Last Day, the angels, the Book, and the prophets and gives wealth, in spite of love for it, to relatives, orphans, the needy, the traveler, those who ask [for help], and for freeing slaves; [and who] establishes prayer and gives zakah; [those who] fulfill their promise when they promise; and [those who] are patient in poverty and hardship and during battle. Those are the ones who have been true, and it is those who are the righteous.
215	يَسْأَلُونَكَ مَاذَا يُنفِقُونَ ۖ قُلْ مَا أَنفَقْتُم مِّنْ خَيْرٍ فَلِلْوَالِدَيْنِ وَالْأَقْرَبِينَ وَالْيَتَامَىٰ وَالْمَسَاكِينِ وَابْنِ السَّبِيلِ ۗ وَمَا تَفْعَلُوا مِنْ خَيْرٍ فَإِنَّ اللَّهَ بِهِ عَلِيمٌ
	They ask you, [O Muhammad], what they should spend. Say, "Whatever you spend of good is [to be] for parents and relatives and orphans and the needy and the traveler. And whatever you do of good - indeed, Allah is Knowing of it."
246	أَلَمْ تَرَ إِلَى الْمَلَإِ مِن بَنِي إِسْرَائِيلَ مِن بَعْدِ مُوسَىٰ إِذْ قَالُوا لِنَبِيٍّ لَّهُمُ ابْعَثْ لَنَا مَلِكًا نُّقَاتِلْ فِي سَبِيلِ اللَّهِ ۖ قَالَ هَلْ عَسَيْتُمْ إِن كُتِبَ عَلَيْكُمُ الْقِتَالُ أَلَّا تُقَاتِلُوا ۖ قَالُوا وَمَا لَنَا أَلَّا نُقَاتِلَ فِي سَبِيلِ اللَّهِ وَقَدْ أُخْرِجْنَا مِن دِيَارِنَا وَأَبْنَائِنَا ۖ فَلَمَّا كُتِبَ عَلَيْهِمُ الْقِتَالُ تَوَلَّوْا إِلَّا قَلِيلًا مِّنْهُمْ ۗ وَاللَّهُ عَلِيمٌ بِالظَّالِمِينَ
	Have you not considered the assembly of the Children of Israel after [the time of] Moses when they said to a prophet of theirs, "Send to us a king, and we will fight in the way of Allah "? He said, "Would you perhaps refrain from fighting if fighting was prescribed for you?" They said, "And why should we not fight in the cause of Allah when we have been driven out from our homes and from our children?" But when fighting was prescribed for them, they turned away, except for a few of them. And Allah is Knowing of the wrongdoers.
253	تِلْكَ الرُّسُلُ فَضَّلْنَا بَعْضَهُمْ عَلَىٰ بَعْضٍ ۘ مِّنْهُم مَّن كَلَّمَ اللَّهُ ۖ وَرَفَعَ بَعْضَهُمْ دَرَجَاتٍ ۚ وَآتَيْنَا عِيسَى ابْنَ مَرْيَمَ الْبَيِّنَاتِ وَأَيَّدْنَاهُ بِرُوحِ الْقُدُسِ ۗ وَلَوْ شَاءَ اللَّهُ مَا اقْتَتَلَ الَّذِينَ مِن بَعْدِهِم مِّن بَعْدِ مَا

	جَاءَتْهُمُ الْبَيِّنَاتُ وَلَٰكِنِ اخْتَلَفُوا فَمِنْهُم مَّنْ آمَنَ وَمِنْهُم مَّن كَفَرَ ۚ وَلَوْ شَاءَ اللَّهُ مَا اقْتَتَلُوا وَلَٰكِنَّ اللَّهَ يَفْعَلُ مَا يُرِيدُ
	Those messengers - some of them We caused to exceed others. Among them were those to whom Allah spoke, and He raised some of them in degree. And We gave Jesus, the Son of Mary, clear proofs, and We supported him with the Pure Spirit. If Allah had willed, those [generations] succeeding them would not have fought each other after the clear proofs had come to them. But they differed, and some of them believed and some of them disbelieved. And if Allah had willed, they would not have fought each other, but Allah does what He intends
3 آل عمران 45	إِذْ قَالَتِ الْمَلَائِكَةُ يَا مَرْيَمُ إِنَّ اللَّهَ يُبَشِّرُكِ بِكَلِمَةٍ مِّنْهُ اسْمُهُ الْمَسِيحُ عِيسَى ابْنُ مَرْيَمَ وَجِيهًا فِي الدُّنْيَا وَالْآخِرَةِ وَمِنَ الْمُقَرَّبِينَ
	[And mention] when the angels said, "O Mary, indeed Allah gives you good tidings of a word from Him, whose name will be the Messiah, Jesus, the son of Mary - distinguished in this world and the Hereafter and among those brought near [to Allah].
61	فَمَنْ حَاجَّكَ فِيهِ مِن بَعْدِ مَا جَاءَكَ مِنَ الْعِلْمِ فَقُلْ تَعَالَوْا نَدْعُ أَبْنَاءَنَا وَأَبْنَاءَكُمْ وَنِسَاءَنَا وَنِسَاءَكُمْ وَأَنفُسَنَا وَأَنفُسَكُمْ ثُمَّ نَبْتَهِلْ فَنَجْعَل لَّعْنَتَ اللَّهِ عَلَى الْكَاذِبِينَ
	Then whoever argues with you about it after [this] knowledge has come to you - say, "Come, let us call our sons and your sons, our women and your women, ourselves and yourselves, then supplicate earnestly [together] and invoke the curse of Allah upon the liars [among us]."
4 النساء 11	يُوصِيكُمُ اللَّهُ فِي أَوْلَادِكُمْ ۖ لِلذَّكَرِ مِثْلُ حَظِّ الْأُنثَيَيْنِ ۚ فَإِن كُنَّ نِسَاءً فَوْقَ اثْنَتَيْنِ فَلَهُنَّ ثُلُثَا مَا تَرَكَ ۖ وَإِن كَانَتْ وَاحِدَةً فَلَهَا النِّصْفُ ۚ وَلِأَبَوَيْهِ لِكُلِّ وَاحِدٍ مِّنْهُمَا السُّدُسُ مِمَّا تَرَكَ إِن كَانَ لَهُ وَلَدٌ ۚ فَإِن لَّمْ يَكُن لَّهُ وَلَدٌ وَوَرِثَهُ أَبَوَاهُ فَلِأُمِّهِ الثُّلُثُ ۚ فَإِن كَانَ لَهُ إِخْوَةٌ فَلِأُمِّهِ السُّدُسُ ۚ مِن بَعْدِ وَصِيَّةٍ يُوصِي بِهَا أَوْ دَيْنٍ ۗ آبَاؤُكُمْ وَأَبْنَاؤُكُمْ لَا تَدْرُونَ أَيُّهُمْ أَقْرَبُ لَكُمْ نَفْعًا ۚ فَرِيضَةً مِّنَ اللَّهِ ۗ إِنَّ اللَّهَ كَانَ عَلِيمًا حَكِيمًا
	Allah instructs you concerning your children: for the male, what is equal to the share of two females. But if there are [only] daughters, two or more, for them is two thirds of one's estate. And if there is only one, for her is half. And for one's parents, to each one of them is a sixth of his estate if he left children. But if he had no children and the parents [alone] inherit from him, then for his mother is one third. And if he had brothers [or sisters], for his mother is a sixth, after any

	bequest he [may have] made or debt. Your parents or your children - you know not which of them are nearest to you in benefit. [These shares are] an obligation [imposed] by Allah. Indeed, Allah is ever Knowing and Wise.
23	حُرِّمَتْ عَلَيْكُمْ أُمَّهَاتُكُمْ وَبَنَاتُكُمْ وَأَخَوَاتُكُمْ وَعَمَّاتُكُمْ وَخَالَاتُكُمْ وَبَنَاتُ الْأَخِ وَبَنَاتُ الْأُخْتِ وَأُمَّهَاتُكُمُ اللَّاتِي أَرْضَعْنَكُمْ وَأَخَوَاتُكُم مِّنَ الرَّضَاعَةِ وَأُمَّهَاتُ نِسَائِكُمْ وَرَبَائِبُكُمُ اللَّاتِي فِي حُجُورِكُم مِّن نِّسَائِكُمُ اللَّاتِي دَخَلْتُم بِهِنَّ فَإِن لَّمْ تَكُونُوا دَخَلْتُم بِهِنَّ فَلَا جُنَاحَ عَلَيْكُمْ وَحَلَائِلُ أَبْنَائِكُمُ الَّذِينَ مِنْ أَصْلَابِكُمْ وَأَن تَجْمَعُوا بَيْنَ الْأُخْتَيْنِ إِلَّا مَا قَدْ سَلَفَ ۗ إِنَّ اللَّهَ كَانَ غَفُورًا رَّحِيمًا
	Prohibited to you [for marriage] are your mothers, your daughters, your sisters, your father's sisters, your mother's sisters, your brother's daughters, your sister's daughters, your [milk] mothers who nursed you, your sisters through nursing, your wives' mothers, and your step-daughters under your guardianship [born] of your wives unto whom you have gone in. But if you have not gone in unto them, there is no sin upon you. And [also prohibited are] the wives of your sons who are from your [own] loins, and that you take [in marriage] two sisters simultaneously, except for what has already occurred. Indeed, Allah is ever Forgiving and Merciful.
36	۞ وَاعْبُدُوا اللَّهَ وَلَا تُشْرِكُوا بِهِ شَيْئًا ۖ وَبِالْوَالِدَيْنِ إِحْسَانًا وَبِذِي الْقُرْبَىٰ وَالْيَتَامَىٰ وَالْمَسَاكِينِ وَالْجَارِ ذِي الْقُرْبَىٰ وَالْجَارِ الْجُنُبِ وَالصَّاحِبِ بِالْجَنبِ وَابْنِ السَّبِيلِ وَمَا مَلَكَتْ أَيْمَانُكُمْ ۗ إِنَّ اللَّهَ لَا يُحِبُّ مَن كَانَ مُخْتَالًا فَخُورًا
	Worship Allah and associate nothing with Him, and to parents do good, and to relatives, orphans, the needy, the near neighbor, the neighbor farther away, the companion at your side, the traveler, and those whom your right hands possess. Indeed, Allah does not like those who are self-deluding and boastful.
157	وَقَوْلِهِمْ إِنَّا قَتَلْنَا الْمَسِيحَ عِيسَى ابْنَ مَرْيَمَ رَسُولَ اللَّهِ وَمَا قَتَلُوهُ وَمَا صَلَبُوهُ وَلَٰكِن شُبِّهَ لَهُمْ ۚ وَإِنَّ الَّذِينَ اخْتَلَفُوا فِيهِ لَفِي شَكٍّ مِّنْهُ ۚ مَا لَهُم بِهِ مِنْ عِلْمٍ إِلَّا اتِّبَاعَ الظَّنِّ ۚ وَمَا قَتَلُوهُ يَقِينًا
	And [for] their saying, "Indeed, we have killed the Messiah, Jesus, the son of Mary, the messenger of Allah." And they did not kill him, nor did they crucify him; but [another] was made to resemble him to them. And indeed, those who

	differ over it are in doubt about it. They have no knowledge of it except the following of assumption. And they did not kill him, for certain.
171	يَا أَهْلَ الْكِتَابِ لَا تَغْلُوا فِي دِينِكُمْ وَلَا تَقُولُوا عَلَى اللَّهِ إِلَّا الْحَقَّ ۚ إِنَّمَا الْمَسِيحُ عِيسَى ابْنُ مَرْيَمَ رَسُولُ اللَّهِ وَكَلِمَتُهُ أَلْقَاهَا إِلَىٰ مَرْيَمَ وَرُوحٌ مِنْهُ ۖ فَآمِنُوا بِاللَّهِ وَرُسُلِهِ ۖ وَلَا تَقُولُوا ثَلَاثَةٌ ۚ انتَهُوا خَيْرًا لَكُمْ ۚ إِنَّمَا اللَّهُ إِلَٰهٌ وَاحِدٌ ۖ سُبْحَانَهُ أَن يَكُونَ لَهُ وَلَدٌ ۘ لَهُ مَا فِي السَّمَاوَاتِ وَمَا فِي الْأَرْضِ ۗ وَكَفَىٰ بِاللَّهِ وَكِيلًا
	O People of the Scripture, do not commit excess in your religion or say about Allah except the truth. The Messiah, Jesus, the son of Mary, was but a messenger of Allah and His word which He directed to Mary and a soul [created at a command] from Him. So believe in Allah and His messengers. And do not say, "Three"; desist - it is better for you. Indeed, Allah is but one God. Exalted is He above having a son. To Him belongs whatever is in the heavens and whatever is on the earth. And sufficient is Allah as Disposer of affairs.
5 المائدة 17	لَقَدْ كَفَرَ الَّذِينَ قَالُوا إِنَّ اللَّهَ هُوَ الْمَسِيحُ ابْنُ مَرْيَمَ ۚ قُلْ فَمَن يَمْلِكُ مِنَ اللَّهِ شَيْئًا إِنْ أَرَادَ أَن يُهْلِكَ الْمَسِيحَ ابْنَ مَرْيَمَ وَأُمَّهُ وَمَن فِي الْأَرْضِ جَمِيعًا ۗ وَلِلَّهِ مُلْكُ السَّمَاوَاتِ وَالْأَرْضِ وَمَا بَيْنَهُمَا ۚ يَخْلُقُ مَا يَشَاءُ ۚ وَاللَّهُ عَلَىٰ كُلِّ شَيْءٍ قَدِيرٌ
	They have certainly disbelieved who say that Allah is Christ, the son of Mary. Say, "Then who could prevent Allah at all if He had intended to destroy Christ, the son of Mary, or his mother or everyone on the earth?" And to Allah belongs the dominion of the heavens and the earth and whatever is between them. He creates what He wills, and Allah is over all things competent.
18	وَقَالَتِ الْيَهُودُ وَالنَّصَارَىٰ نَحْنُ أَبْنَاءُ اللَّهِ وَأَحِبَّاؤُهُ ۚ قُلْ فَلِمَ يُعَذِّبُكُم بِذُنُوبِكُم ۖ بَلْ أَنتُم بَشَرٌ مِّمَّنْ خَلَقَ ۚ يَغْفِرُ لِمَن يَشَاءُ وَيُعَذِّبُ مَن يَشَاءُ ۚ وَلِلَّهِ مُلْكُ السَّمَاوَاتِ وَالْأَرْضِ وَمَا بَيْنَهُمَا ۖ وَإِلَيْهِ الْمَصِيرُ
	But the Jews and the Christians say, "We are the children of Allah and His beloved." Say, "Then why does He punish you for your sins?" Rather, you are human beings from among those He has created. He forgives whom He wills, and He punishes whom He wills. And to Allah belongs the dominion of the

	heavens and the earth and whatever is between them, and to Him is the [final] destination.
27	وَاتْلُ عَلَيْهِمْ نَبَأَ ابْنَيْ آدَمَ بِالْحَقِّ إِذْ قَرَّبَا قُرْبَانًا فَتُقُبِّلَ مِنْ أَحَدِهِمَا وَلَمْ يُتَقَبَّلْ مِنَ الْآخَرِ قَالَ لَأَقْتُلَنَّكَ ۖ قَالَ إِنَّمَا يَتَقَبَّلُ اللَّهُ مِنَ الْمُتَّقِينَ
	And recite to them the story of Adam's two sons, in truth, when they both offered a sacrifice [to Allah], and it was accepted from one of them but was not accepted from the other. Said [the latter], "I will surely kill you." Said [the former], "Indeed, Allah only accepts from the righteous [who fear Him].
46	وَقَفَّيْنَا عَلَىٰ آثَارِهِم بِعِيسَى ابْنِ مَرْيَمَ مُصَدِّقًا لِّمَا بَيْنَ يَدَيْهِ مِنَ التَّوْرَاةِ ۖ وَآتَيْنَاهُ الْإِنجِيلَ فِيهِ هُدًى وَنُورٌ وَمُصَدِّقًا لِّمَا بَيْنَ يَدَيْهِ مِنَ التَّوْرَاةِ وَهُدًى وَمَوْعِظَةً لِّلْمُتَّقِينَ
	And We sent, following in their footsteps, Jesus, the son of Mary, confirming that which came before him in the Torah; and We gave him the Gospel, in which was guidance and light and confirming that which preceded it of the Torah as guidance and instruction for the righteous.
72	لَقَدْ كَفَرَ الَّذِينَ قَالُوا إِنَّ اللَّهَ هُوَ الْمَسِيحُ ابْنُ مَرْيَمَ ۖ وَقَالَ الْمَسِيحُ يَا بَنِي إِسْرَائِيلَ اعْبُدُوا اللَّهَ رَبِّي وَرَبَّكُمْ ۖ إِنَّهُ مَن يُشْرِكْ بِاللَّهِ فَقَدْ حَرَّمَ اللَّهُ عَلَيْهِ الْجَنَّةَ وَمَأْوَاهُ النَّارُ ۖ وَمَا لِلظَّالِمِينَ مِنْ أَنصَارٍ
	They have certainly disbelieved who say, "Allah is the Messiah, the son of Mary" while the Messiah has said, "O Children of Israel, worship Allah, my Lord and your Lord." Indeed, he who associates others with Allah - Allah has forbidden him Paradise, and his refuge is the Fire. And there are not for the wrongdoers any helpers.
75	مَّا الْمَسِيحُ ابْنُ مَرْيَمَ إِلَّا رَسُولٌ قَدْ خَلَتْ مِن قَبْلِهِ الرُّسُلُ وَأُمُّهُ صِدِّيقَةٌ ۖ كَانَا يَأْكُلَانِ الطَّعَامَ ۗ انظُرْ كَيْفَ نُبَيِّنُ لَهُمُ الْآيَاتِ ثُمَّ انظُرْ أَنَّىٰ يُؤْفَكُونَ
	The Messiah, son of Mary, was not but a messenger; [other] messengers have passed on before him. And his mother was a supporter of truth. They both used to eat food. Look how We make clear to them the signs; then look how they are deluded.

78	لُعِنَ الَّذِينَ كَفَرُوا مِن بَنِي إِسْرَائِيلَ عَلَىٰ لِسَانِ دَاوُودَ وَعِيسَى ابْنِ مَرْيَمَ ۚ ذَٰلِكَ بِمَا عَصَوا وَّكَانُوا يَعْتَدُونَ
	Cursed were those who disbelieved among the Children of Israel by the tongue of David and of Jesus, the son of Mary. That was because they disobeyed and [habitually] transgressed.
110	إِذْ قَالَ اللَّهُ يَا عِيسَى ابْنَ مَرْيَمَ اذْكُرْ نِعْمَتِي عَلَيْكَ وَعَلَىٰ وَالِدَتِكَ إِذْ أَيَّدتُّكَ بِرُوحِ الْقُدُسِ تُكَلِّمُ النَّاسَ فِي الْمَهْدِ وَكَهْلًا ۖ وَإِذْ عَلَّمْتُكَ الْكِتَابَ وَالْحِكْمَةَ وَالتَّوْرَاةَ وَالْإِنجِيلَ ۖ وَإِذْ تَخْلُقُ مِنَ الطِّينِ كَهَيْئَةِ الطَّيْرِ بِإِذْنِي فَتَنفُخُ فِيهَا فَتَكُونُ طَيْرًا بِإِذْنِي ۖ وَتُبْرِئُ الْأَكْمَهَ وَالْأَبْرَصَ بِإِذْنِي ۖ وَإِذْ تُخْرِجُ الْمَوْتَىٰ بِإِذْنِي ۖ وَإِذْ كَفَفْتُ بَنِي إِسْرَائِيلَ عَنكَ إِذْ جِئْتَهُم بِالْبَيِّنَاتِ فَقَالَ الَّذِينَ كَفَرُوا مِنْهُمْ إِنْ هَٰذَا إِلَّا سِحْرٌ مُّبِينٌ
	[The Day] when Allah will say, "O Jesus, Son of Mary, remember My favor upon you and upon your mother when I supported you with the Pure Spirit and you spoke to the people in the cradle and in maturity; and [remember] when I taught you writing and wisdom and the Torah and the Gospel; and when you designed from clay [what was] like the form of a bird with My permission, then you breathed into it, and it became a bird with My permission; and you healed the blind and the leper with My permission; and when you brought forth the dead with My permission; and when I restrained the Children of Israel from [killing] you when you came to them with clear proofs and those who disbelieved among them said, "This is not but obvious magic."
112	إِذْ قَالَ الْحَوَارِيُّونَ يَا عِيسَى ابْنَ مَرْيَمَ هَلْ يَسْتَطِيعُ رَبُّكَ أَن يُنَزِّلَ عَلَيْنَا مَائِدَةً مِّنَ السَّمَاءِ ۖ قَالَ اتَّقُوا اللَّهَ إِن كُنتُم مُّؤْمِنِينَ
	[And remember] when the disciples said, "O Jesus, Son of Mary, can your Lord send down to us a table [spread with food] from the heaven? [Jesus] said," Fear Allah, if you should be believers."
114	قَالَ عِيسَى ابْنُ مَرْيَمَ اللَّهُمَّ رَبَّنَا أَنزِلْ عَلَيْنَا مَائِدَةً مِّنَ السَّمَاءِ تَكُونُ لَنَا عِيدًا لِّأَوَّلِنَا وَآخِرِنَا وَآيَةً مِّنكَ ۖ وَارْزُقْنَا وَأَنتَ خَيْرُ الرَّازِقِينَ
	Said Jesus, the son of Mary, "O Allah, our Lord, send down to us a table [spread with food] from the heaven to be for us a festival for the first of us and the last of us and a sign from You. And provide for us, and You are the best of providers."

116	وَإِذْ قَالَ اللَّهُ يَا عِيسَى ابْنَ مَرْيَمَ أَأَنتَ قُلْتَ لِلنَّاسِ اتَّخِذُونِي وَأُمِّيَ إِلَٰهَيْنِ مِن دُونِ اللَّهِ ۖ قَالَ سُبْحَانَكَ مَا يَكُونُ لِي أَنْ أَقُولَ مَا لَيْسَ لِي بِحَقٍّ ۚ إِن كُنتُ قُلْتُهُ فَقَدْ عَلِمْتَهُ ۚ تَعْلَمُ مَا فِي نَفْسِي وَلَا أَعْلَمُ مَا فِي نَفْسِكَ ۚ إِنَّكَ أَنتَ عَلَّامُ الْغُيُوبِ
	And [beware the Day] when Allah will say, "O Jesus, Son of Mary, did you say to the people, 'Take me and my mother as deities besides Allah?'" He will say, "Exalted are You! It was not for me to say that to which I have no right. If I had said it, You would have known it. You know what is within myself, and I do not know what is within Yourself. Indeed, it is You who is Knower of the unseen.
6 الأنعام 20	الَّذِينَ آتَيْنَاهُمُ الْكِتَابَ يَعْرِفُونَهُ كَمَا يَعْرِفُونَ أَبْنَاءَهُمُ ۘ الَّذِينَ خَسِرُوا أَنفُسَهُمْ فَهُمْ لَا يُؤْمِنُونَ
	Those to whom We have given the Scripture recognize it as they recognize their [own] sons. Those who will lose themselves [in the Hereafter] do not believe.
7 الأعراف 127	وَقَالَ الْمَلَأُ مِن قَوْمِ فِرْعَوْنَ أَتَذَرُ مُوسَىٰ وَقَوْمَهُ لِيُفْسِدُوا فِي الْأَرْضِ وَيَذَرَكَ وَآلِهَتَكَ ۚ قَالَ سَنُقَتِّلُ أَبْنَاءَهُمْ وَنَسْتَحْيِي نِسَاءَهُمْ وَإِنَّا فَوْقَهُمْ قَاهِرُونَ
	And the eminent among the people of Pharaoh said," Will you leave Moses and his people to cause corruption in the land and abandon you and your gods?" [Pharaoh] said, "We will kill their sons and keep their women alive; and indeed, we are subjugators over them."
141	وَإِذْ أَنجَيْنَاكُم مِّنْ آلِ فِرْعَوْنَ يَسُومُونَكُمْ سُوءَ الْعَذَابِ ۖ يُقَتِّلُونَ أَبْنَاءَكُمْ وَيَسْتَحْيُونَ نِسَاءَكُمْ ۚ وَفِي ذَٰلِكُم بَلَاءٌ مِّن رَّبِّكُمْ عَظِيمٌ
	And [recall, O Children of Israel], when We saved you from the people of Pharaoh, [who were] afflicting you with the worst torment - killing your sons and keeping your women alive. And in that was a great trial from your Lord.
150	وَلَمَّا رَجَعَ مُوسَىٰ إِلَىٰ قَوْمِهِ غَضْبَانَ أَسِفًا قَالَ بِئْسَمَا خَلَفْتُمُونِي مِن بَعْدِي ۖ أَعَجِلْتُمْ أَمْرَ رَبِّكُمْ ۖ وَأَلْقَى الْأَلْوَاحَ وَأَخَذَ بِرَأْسِ أَخِيهِ يَجُرُّهُ إِلَيْهِ ۚ قَالَ ابْنَ أُمَّ إِنَّ الْقَوْمَ اسْتَضْعَفُونِي وَكَادُوا يَقْتُلُونَنِي فَلَا تُشْمِتْ بِيَ الْأَعْدَاءَ وَلَا تَجْعَلْنِي مَعَ الْقَوْمِ الظَّالِمِينَ
	And when Moses returned to his people, angry and grieved, he said, "How wretched is that by which you have replaced me after [my departure]. Were you impatient over the matter of your Lord?" And he threw down the tablets and seized his brother by [the hair of] his head, pulling him toward him. [Aaron] said, "O son of my mother, indeed the people oppressed me and were about to kill me, so let not the enemies rejoice over me and do not place me among the wrongdoing people."

8 الأنفال 41	وَاعْلَمُوا أَنَّمَا غَنِمْتُم مِّن شَيْءٍ فَأَنَّ لِلَّهِ خُمُسَهُ وَلِلرَّسُولِ وَلِذِي الْقُرْبَىٰ وَالْيَتَامَىٰ وَالْمَسَاكِينِ وَابْنِ السَّبِيلِ إِن كُنتُمْ آمَنتُم بِاللَّهِ وَمَا أَنزَلْنَا عَلَىٰ عَبْدِنَا يَوْمَ الْفُرْقَانِ يَوْمَ الْتَقَى الْجَمْعَانِ ۗ وَاللَّهُ عَلَىٰ كُلِّ شَيْءٍ قَدِيرٌ	
	And know that anything you obtain of war booty - then indeed, for Allah is one fifth of it and for the Messenger and for [his] near relatives and the orphans, the needy, and the [stranded] traveler, if you have believed in Allah and in that which We sent down to Our Servant on the day of criterion - the day when the two armies met. And Allah, over all things, is competent.	
9 التوبة 24	قُلْ إِن كَانَ آبَاؤُكُمْ وَأَبْنَاؤُكُمْ وَإِخْوَانُكُمْ وَأَزْوَاجُكُمْ وَعَشِيرَتُكُمْ وَأَمْوَالٌ اقْتَرَفْتُمُوهَا وَتِجَارَةٌ تَخْشَوْنَ كَسَادَهَا وَمَسَاكِنُ تَرْضَوْنَهَا أَحَبَّ إِلَيْكُم مِّنَ اللَّهِ وَرَسُولِهِ وَجِهَادٍ فِي سَبِيلِهِ فَتَرَبَّصُوا حَتَّىٰ يَأْتِيَ اللَّهُ بِأَمْرِهِ ۗ وَاللَّهُ لَا يَهْدِي الْقَوْمَ الْفَاسِقِينَ	
	Say, [O Muhammad], "If your fathers, your sons, your brothers, your wives, your relatives, wealth which you have obtained, commerce wherein you fear decline, and dwellings with which you are pleased are more beloved to you than Allah and His Messenger and jihad in His cause, then wait until Allah executes His command. And Allah does not guide the defiantly disobedient people."	
30	وَقَالَتِ الْيَهُودُ عُزَيْرٌ ابْنُ اللَّهِ وَقَالَتِ النَّصَارَى الْمَسِيحُ ابْنُ اللَّهِ ۖ ذَٰلِكَ قَوْلُهُم بِأَفْوَاهِهِمْ ۖ يُضَاهِئُونَ قَوْلَ الَّذِينَ كَفَرُوا مِن قَبْلُ ۚ قَاتَلَهُمُ اللَّهُ ۚ أَنَّىٰ يُؤْفَكُونَ	
	The Jews say, "Ezra is the son of Allah "; and the Christians say, "The Messiah is the son of Allah." That is their statement from their mouths; they imitate the saying of those who disbelieved [before them]. May Allah destroy them; how are they deluded?	
31	اتَّخَذُوا أَحْبَارَهُمْ وَرُهْبَانَهُمْ أَرْبَابًا مِّن دُونِ اللَّهِ وَالْمَسِيحَ ابْنَ مَرْيَمَ وَمَا أُمِرُوا إِلَّا لِيَعْبُدُوا إِلَٰهًا وَاحِدًا ۖ لَّا إِلَٰهَ إِلَّا هُوَ ۚ سُبْحَانَهُ عَمَّا يُشْرِكُونَ	
	They have taken their scholars and monks as lords besides Allah, and [also] the Messiah, the son of Mary. And they were not commanded except to worship one God; there is no deity except Him. Exalted is He above whatever they associate with Him.	

60		۞ إِنَّمَا الصَّدَقَاتُ لِلْفُقَرَاءِ وَالْمَسَاكِينِ وَالْعَامِلِينَ عَلَيْهَا وَالْمُؤَلَّفَةِ قُلُوبُهُمْ وَفِي الرِّقَابِ وَالْغَارِمِينَ وَفِي سَبِيلِ اللَّهِ وَابْنِ السَّبِيلِ ۖ فَرِيضَةً مِّنَ اللَّهِ ۗ وَاللَّهُ عَلِيمٌ حَكِيمٌ
	Zakah expenditures are only for the poor and for the needy and for those employed to collect [zakah] and for bringing hearts together [for Islam] and for freeing captives [or slaves] and for those in debt and for the cause of Allah and for the [stranded] traveler - an obligation [imposed] by Allah. And Allah is Knowing and Wise.	
11 هود 42		وَهِيَ تَجْرِي بِهِمْ فِي مَوْجٍ كَالْجِبَالِ وَنَادَىٰ نُوحٌ ابْنَهُ وَكَانَ فِي مَعْزِلٍ يَا بُنَيَّ ارْكَب مَّعَنَا وَلَا تَكُن مَّعَ الْكَافِرِينَ
	And it sailed with them through waves like mountains, and Noah called to his son who was apart [from them], "O my son, come aboard with us and be not with the disbelievers."	
45		وَنَادَىٰ نُوحٌ رَّبَّهُ فَقَالَ رَبِّ إِنَّ ابْنِي مِنْ أَهْلِي وَإِنَّ وَعْدَكَ الْحَقُّ وَأَنتَ أَحْكَمُ الْحَاكِمِينَ
	And Noah called to his Lord and said, "My Lord, indeed my son is of my family; and indeed, Your promise is true; and You are the most just of judges!"	
12 يوسف 81		ارْجِعُوا إِلَىٰ أَبِيكُمْ فَقُولُوا يَا أَبَانَا إِنَّ ابْنَكَ سَرَقَ وَمَا شَهِدْنَا إِلَّا بِمَا عَلِمْنَا وَمَا كُنَّا لِلْغَيْبِ حَافِظِينَ
	Return to your father and say, "O our father, indeed your son has stolen, and we did not testify except to what we knew. And we were not witnesses of the unseen,	
14 ابراهيم 6		وَإِذْ قَالَ مُوسَىٰ لِقَوْمِهِ اذْكُرُوا نِعْمَةَ اللَّهِ عَلَيْكُمْ إِذْ أَنجَاكُم مِّنْ آلِ فِرْعَوْنَ يَسُومُونَكُمْ سُوءَ الْعَذَابِ وَيُذَبِّحُونَ أَبْنَاءَكُمْ وَيَسْتَحْيُونَ نِسَاءَكُمْ ۚ وَفِي ذَٰلِكُم بَلَاءٌ مِّن رَّبِّكُمْ عَظِيمٌ
	And [recall, O Children of Israel], when Moses said to His people, "Remember the favor of Allah upon you when He saved you from the people of Pharaoh, who were afflicting you with the worst torment and were slaughtering your [newborn] sons and keeping your females alive. And in that was a great trial from your Lord.	
17 الإسراء 26		وَآتِ ذَا الْقُرْبَىٰ حَقَّهُ وَالْمِسْكِينَ وَابْنَ السَّبِيلِ وَلَا تُبَذِّرْ تَبْذِيرًا
	And give the relative his right, and [also] the poor and the traveler, and do not spend wastefully.	

19 مريم 34	ذَٰلِكَ عِيسَى ابْنُ مَرْيَمَ ۚ قَوْلَ الْحَقِّ الَّذِي فِيهِ يَمْتَرُونَ
	That is Jesus, the son of Mary - the word of truth about which they are in dispute.
20 طه 94	قَالَ يَا ابْنَ أُمَّ لَا تَأْخُذْ بِلِحْيَتِي وَلَا بِرَأْسِي ۖ إِنِّي خَشِيتُ أَن تَقُولَ فَرَّقْتَ بَيْنَ بَنِي إِسْرَائِيلَ وَلَمْ تَرْقُبْ قَوْلِي
	[Aaron] said, "O son of my mother, do not seize [me] by my beard or by my head. Indeed, I feared that you would say, 'You caused division among the Children of Israel, and you did not observe [or await] my word.'
21 الأنبياء 91	وَالَّتِي أَحْصَنَتْ فَرْجَهَا فَنَفَخْنَا فِيهَا مِن رُّوحِنَا وَجَعَلْنَاهَا وَابْنَهَا آيَةً لِّلْعَالَمِينَ
	And [mention] the one who guarded her chastity, so We blew into her [garment] through Our angel [Gabriel], and We made her and her son a sign for the worlds.
23 المؤمنون 50	وَجَعَلْنَا ابْنَ مَرْيَمَ وَأُمَّهُ آيَةً وَآوَيْنَاهُمَا إِلَىٰ رَبْوَةٍ ذَاتِ قَرَارٍ وَمَعِينٍ
	And We made the son of Mary and his mother a sign and sheltered them within a high ground having level [areas] and flowing water.
24 النور 31	وَقُل لِّلْمُؤْمِنَاتِ يَغْضُضْنَ مِنْ أَبْصَارِهِنَّ وَيَحْفَظْنَ فُرُوجَهُنَّ وَلَا يُبْدِينَ زِينَتَهُنَّ إِلَّا مَا ظَهَرَ مِنْهَا ۖ وَلْيَضْرِبْنَ بِخُمُرِهِنَّ عَلَىٰ جُيُوبِهِنَّ ۖ وَلَا يُبْدِينَ زِينَتَهُنَّ إِلَّا لِبُعُولَتِهِنَّ أَوْ آبَائِهِنَّ أَوْ آبَاءِ بُعُولَتِهِنَّ أَوْ أَبْنَائِهِنَّ أَوْ أَبْنَاءِ بُعُولَتِهِنَّ أَوْ إِخْوَانِهِنَّ أَوْ بَنِي إِخْوَانِهِنَّ أَوْ بَنِي أَخَوَاتِهِنَّ أَوْ نِسَائِهِنَّ أَوْ مَا مَلَكَتْ أَيْمَانُهُنَّ أَوِ التَّابِعِينَ غَيْرِ أُولِي الْإِرْبَةِ مِنَ الرِّجَالِ أَوِ الطِّفْلِ الَّذِينَ لَمْ يَظْهَرُوا عَلَىٰ عَوْرَاتِ النِّسَاءِ ۖ وَلَا يَضْرِبْنَ بِأَرْجُلِهِنَّ لِيُعْلَمَ مَا يُخْفِينَ مِن زِينَتِهِنَّ ۚ وَتُوبُوا إِلَى اللَّهِ جَمِيعًا أَيُّهَ الْمُؤْمِنُونَ لَعَلَّكُمْ تُفْلِحُونَ
	And tell the believing women to reduce [some] of their vision and guard their private parts and not expose their adornment except that which [necessarily] appears thereof and to wrap [a portion of] their headcovers over their chests and not expose their adornment except to their husbands, their fathers, their husbands' fathers, their sons, their husbands' sons, their brothers, their brothers' sons, their sisters' sons, their women, that which their right hands possess, or those male attendants having no physical desire, or children who are not yet aware of the private aspects of women. And let them not stamp their feet to make known what they conceal of their adornment. And turn to Allah in repentance, all of you, O believers, that you might succeed.

28 القصص 4	إِنَّ فِرْعَوْنَ عَلَا فِي الْأَرْضِ وَجَعَلَ أَهْلَهَا شِيَعًا يَسْتَضْعِفُ طَائِفَةً مِنْهُمْ يُذَبِّحُ أَبْنَاءَهُمْ وَيَسْتَحْيِي نِسَاءَهُمْ ۚ إِنَّهُ كَانَ مِنَ الْمُفْسِدِينَ	
	Indeed, Pharaoh exalted himself in the land and made its people into factions, oppressing a sector among them, slaughtering their [newborn] sons and keeping their females alive. Indeed, he was of the corrupters.	
30 الروم 38	فَآتِ ذَا الْقُرْبَىٰ حَقَّهُ وَالْمِسْكِينَ وَابْنَ السَّبِيلِ ۚ ذَٰلِكَ خَيْرٌ لِّلَّذِينَ يُرِيدُونَ وَجْهَ اللَّهِ ۖ وَأُولَٰئِكَ هُمُ الْمُفْلِحُونَ	
	So give the relative his right, as well as the needy and the traveler. That is best for those who desire the countenance of Allah, and it is they who will be the successful	
31 لقمان 13	وَإِذْ قَالَ لُقْمَانُ لِابْنِهِ وَهُوَ يَعِظُهُ يَا بُنَيَّ لَا تُشْرِكْ بِاللَّهِ ۖ إِنَّ الشِّرْكَ لَظُلْمٌ عَظِيمٌ	
	And [mention, O Muhammad], when Luqman said to his son while he was instructing him, "O my son, do not associate [anything] with Allah. Indeed, association [with him] is great injustice."	
33 الأحزاب 4	مَّا جَعَلَ اللَّهُ لِرَجُلٍ مِّن قَلْبَيْنِ فِي جَوْفِهِ ۚ وَمَا جَعَلَ أَزْوَاجَكُمُ اللَّائِي تُظَاهِرُونَ مِنْهُنَّ أُمَّهَاتِكُمْ ۚ وَمَا جَعَلَ أَدْعِيَاءَكُمْ أَبْنَاءَكُمْ ۚ ذَٰلِكُمْ قَوْلُكُم بِأَفْوَاهِكُمْ ۖ وَاللَّهُ يَقُولُ الْحَقَّ وَهُوَ يَهْدِي السَّبِيلَ	
	Allah has not made for a man two hearts in his interior. And He has not made your wives whom you declare unlawful your mothers. And he has not made your adopted sons your [true] sons. That is [merely] your saying by your mouths, but Allah says the truth, and He guides to the [right] way.	
7	وَإِذْ أَخَذْنَا مِنَ النَّبِيِّينَ مِيثَاقَهُمْ وَمِنكَ وَمِن نُّوحٍ وَإِبْرَاهِيمَ وَمُوسَىٰ وَعِيسَى ابْنِ مَرْيَمَ ۖ وَأَخَذْنَا مِنْهُم مِّيثَاقًا غَلِيظًا	

	And [mention, O Muhammad], when We took from the prophets their covenant and from you and from Noah and Abraham and Moses and Jesus, the son of Mary; and We took from them a solemn covenant.
55	لَّا جُنَاحَ عَلَيْهِنَّ فِي آبَائِهِنَّ وَلَا أَبْنَائِهِنَّ وَلَا إِخْوَانِهِنَّ وَلَا أَبْنَاءِ إِخْوَانِهِنَّ وَلَا أَبْنَاءِ أَخَوَاتِهِنَّ وَلَا نِسَائِهِنَّ وَلَا مَا مَلَكَتْ أَيْمَانُهُنَّ ۗ وَاتَّقِينَ اللَّهَ ۚ إِنَّ اللَّهَ كَانَ عَلَىٰ كُلِّ شَيْءٍ شَهِيدًا
	There is no blame upon women concerning their fathers or their sons or their brothers or their brothers' sons or their sisters' sons or their women or those their right hands possess. And fear Allah. Indeed Allah is ever, over all things, Witness.
40 غافر 25	فَلَمَّا جَاءَهُم بِالْحَقِّ مِنْ عِندِنَا قَالُوا اقْتُلُوا أَبْنَاءَ الَّذِينَ آمَنُوا مَعَهُ وَاسْتَحْيُوا نِسَاءَهُمْ ۚ وَمَا كَيْدُ الْكَافِرِينَ إِلَّا فِي ضَلَالٍ
	And when he brought them the truth from Us, they said, "Kill the sons of those who have believed with him and keep their women alive." But the plan of the disbelievers is not except in error.
43 الزخرف 57	۞ وَلَمَّا ضُرِبَ ابْنُ مَرْيَمَ مَثَلًا إِذَا قَوْمُكَ مِنْهُ يَصِدُّونَ
	And when the son of Mary was presented as an example, immediately your people laughed aloud.
57 الحديد 27	ثُمَّ قَفَّيْنَا عَلَىٰ آثَارِهِم بِرُسُلِنَا وَقَفَّيْنَا بِعِيسَى ابْنِ مَرْيَمَ وَآتَيْنَاهُ الْإِنجِيلَ وَجَعَلْنَا فِي قُلُوبِ الَّذِينَ اتَّبَعُوهُ رَأْفَةً وَرَحْمَةً وَرَهْبَانِيَّةً ابْتَدَعُوهَا مَا كَتَبْنَاهَا عَلَيْهِمْ إِلَّا ابْتِغَاءَ رِضْوَانِ اللَّهِ فَمَا رَعَوْهَا حَقَّ رِعَايَتِهَا ۖ فَآتَيْنَا الَّذِينَ آمَنُوا مِنْهُمْ أَجْرَهُمْ ۖ وَكَثِيرٌ مِّنْهُمْ فَاسِقُونَ
	Then We sent following their footsteps Our messengers and followed [them] with Jesus, the son of Mary, and gave him the Gospel. And We placed in the hearts of those who followed him compassion and mercy and monasticism, which they innovated; We did not prescribe it for them except [that they did so] seeking the approval of Allah. But they did not observe it with due observance. So We gave the ones who believed among them their reward, but many of them are defiantly disobedient.
58 المجادلة 22	لَّا تَجِدُ قَوْمًا يُؤْمِنُونَ بِاللَّهِ وَالْيَوْمِ الْآخِرِ يُوَادُّونَ مَنْ حَادَّ اللَّهَ وَرَسُولَهُ وَلَوْ كَانُوا آبَاءَهُمْ أَوْ أَبْنَاءَهُمْ أَوْ إِخْوَانَهُمْ أَوْ عَشِيرَتَهُمْ ۚ أُولَٰئِكَ كَتَبَ فِي قُلُوبِهِمُ الْإِيمَانَ وَأَيَّدَهُم بِرُوحٍ مِّنْهُ ۖ وَيُدْخِلُهُمْ جَنَّاتٍ تَجْرِي مِن تَحْتِهَا الْأَنْهَارُ خَالِدِينَ فِيهَا ۚ رَضِيَ اللَّهُ عَنْهُمْ وَرَضُوا عَنْهُ ۚ أُولَٰئِكَ حِزْبُ اللَّهِ ۚ أَلَا إِنَّ حِزْبَ اللَّهِ هُمُ الْمُفْلِحُونَ

		You will not find a people who believe in Allah and the Last Day having affection for those who oppose Allah and His Messenger, even if they were their fathers or their sons or their brothers or their kindred. Those - He has decreed within their hearts faith and supported them with spirit from Him. And We will admit them to gardens beneath which rivers flow, wherein they abide eternally. Allah is pleased with them, and they are pleased with Him - those are the party of Allah. Unquestionably, the party of Allah - they are the successful.
59 الحشر 7		مَّا أَفَاءَ اللَّهُ عَلَىٰ رَسُولِهِ مِنْ أَهْلِ الْقُرَىٰ فَلِلَّهِ وَلِلرَّسُولِ وَلِذِي الْقُرْبَىٰ وَالْيَتَامَىٰ وَالْمَسَاكِينِ وَابْنِ السَّبِيلِ كَيْ لَا يَكُونَ دُولَةً بَيْنَ الْأَغْنِيَاءِ مِنكُمْ ۚ وَمَا آتَاكُمُ الرَّسُولُ فَخُذُوهُ وَمَا نَهَاكُمْ عَنْهُ فَانتَهُوا ۚ وَاتَّقُوا اللَّهَ ۖ إِنَّ اللَّهَ شَدِيدُ الْعِقَابِ
		And what Allah restored to His Messenger from the people of the towns - it is for Allah and for the Messenger and for [his] near relatives and orphans and the [stranded] traveler - so that it will not be a perpetual distribution among the rich from among you. And whatever the Messenger has given you - take; and what he has forbidden you - refrain from. And fear Allah; indeed, Allah is severe in penalty.
61 الصف 6		وَإِذْ قَالَ عِيسَى ابْنُ مَرْيَمَ يَا بَنِي إِسْرَائِيلَ إِنِّي رَسُولُ اللَّهِ إِلَيْكُم مُّصَدِّقًا لِّمَا بَيْنَ يَدَيَّ مِنَ التَّوْرَاةِ وَمُبَشِّرًا بِرَسُولٍ يَأْتِي مِن بَعْدِي اسْمُهُ أَحْمَدُ ۖ فَلَمَّا جَاءَهُم بِالْبَيِّنَاتِ قَالُوا هَٰذَا سِحْرٌ مُّبِينٌ
		And [mention] when Jesus, the son of Mary, said, "O children of Israel, indeed I am the messenger of Allah to you confirming what came before me of the Torah and bringing good tidings of a messenger to come after me, whose name is Ahmad." But when he came to them with clear evidences, they said, "This is obvious magic."
14		يَا أَيُّهَا الَّذِينَ آمَنُوا كُونُوا أَنصَارَ اللَّهِ كَمَا قَالَ عِيسَى ابْنُ مَرْيَمَ لِلْحَوَارِيِّينَ مَنْ أَنصَارِي إِلَى اللَّهِ ۖ قَالَ الْحَوَارِيُّونَ نَحْنُ أَنصَارُ اللَّهِ ۖ فَآمَنَت طَّائِفَةٌ مِّن بَنِي إِسْرَائِيلَ وَكَفَرَت طَّائِفَةٌ ۖ فَأَيَّدْنَا الَّذِينَ آمَنُوا عَلَىٰ عَدُوِّهِمْ فَأَصْبَحُوا ظَاهِرِينَ
		O you who have believed, be supporters of Allah, as when Jesus, the son of Mary, said to the disciples, "Who are my supporters for Allah?" The disciples said, "We are supporters of Allah." And a faction of the Children of Israel believed and a faction disbelieved. So We supported those who believed against their enemy, and they became dominant

The Sons	الْبَنُونَ	
18 الكهف 46	الْمَالُ وَالْبَنُونَ زِينَةُ الْحَيَاةِ الدُّنْيَا ۖ وَالْبَاقِيَاتُ الصَّالِحَاتُ خَيْرٌ عِندَ رَبِّكَ ثَوَابًا وَخَيْرٌ أَمَلًا	
	Wealth and children are [but] adornment of the worldly life. But the enduring good deeds are better to your Lord for reward and better for [one's] hope.	
26 الشعراء 88	يَوْمَ لَا يَنفَعُ مَالٌ وَلَا بَنُونَ	
	The Day when there will not benefit [anyone] wealth or children	
37 الصافات 149	فَاسْتَفْتِهِمْ أَلِرَبِّكَ الْبَنَاتُ وَلَهُمُ الْبَنُونَ	
	So inquire of them, [O Muhammad], "Does your Lord have daughters while they have sons?	
52 الطور 39	أَمْ لَهُ الْبَنَاتُ وَلَكُمُ الْبَنُونَ	
	Or has He daughters while you have sons?	
Sons	بَنِينَ	
3 آل عمران 14	زُيِّنَ لِلنَّاسِ حُبُّ الشَّهَوَاتِ مِنَ النِّسَاءِ وَالْبَنِينَ وَالْقَنَاطِيرِ الْمُقَنطَرَةِ مِنَ الذَّهَبِ وَالْفِضَّةِ وَالْخَيْلِ الْمُسَوَّمَةِ وَالْأَنْعَامِ وَالْحَرْثِ ۗ ذَٰلِكَ مَتَاعُ الْحَيَاةِ الدُّنْيَا ۖ وَاللَّهُ عِندَهُ حُسْنُ الْمَآبِ	
	Beautified for people is the love of that which they desire - of women and sons, heaped-up sums of gold and silver, fine branded horses, and cattle and tilled land. That is the enjoyment of worldly life, but Allah has with Him the best return.	
6 الأنعام 100	وَجَعَلُوا لِلَّهِ شُرَكَاءَ الْجِنَّ وَخَلَقَهُمْ ۖ وَخَرَقُوا لَهُ بَنِينَ وَبَنَاتٍ بِغَيْرِ عِلْمٍ ۚ سُبْحَانَهُ وَتَعَالَىٰ عَمَّا يَصِفُونَ	
	But they have attributed to Allah partners - the jinn, while He has created them - and have fabricated for Him sons and daughters. Exalted is He and high above what they describe	

16 النحل 72	وَاللَّهُ جَعَلَ لَكُم مِّنْ أَنفُسِكُمْ أَزْوَاجًا وَجَعَلَ لَكُم مِّنْ أَزْوَاجِكُم بَنِينَ وَحَفَدَةً وَرَزَقَكُم مِّنَ الطَّيِّبَاتِ ۚ أَفَبِالْبَاطِلِ يُؤْمِنُونَ وَبِنِعْمَتِ اللَّهِ هُمْ يَكْفُرُونَ	
	And Allah has made for you from yourselves mates and has made for you from your mates sons and grandchildren and has provided for you from the good things. Then in falsehood do they believe and in the favor of Allah they disbelieve?	
17 الإسراء 6	ثُمَّ رَدَدْنَا لَكُمُ الْكَرَّةَ عَلَيْهِمْ وَأَمْدَدْنَاكُم بِأَمْوَالٍ وَبَنِينَ وَجَعَلْنَاكُمْ أَكْثَرَ نَفِيرًا	
	Then We gave back to you a return victory over them. And We reinforced you with wealth and sons and made you more numerous in manpower	
40	أَفَأَصْفَاكُمْ رَبُّكُم بِالْبَنِينَ وَاتَّخَذَ مِنَ الْمَلَائِكَةِ إِنَاثًا ۚ إِنَّكُمْ لَتَقُولُونَ قَوْلًا عَظِيمًا	
	Then, has your Lord chosen you for [having] sons and taken from among the angels daughters? Indeed, you say a grave saying.	
23 المؤمنون 55	أَيَحْسَبُونَ أَنَّمَا نُمِدُّهُم بِهِ مِن مَّالٍ وَبَنِينَ	
	Do they think that what We extend to them of wealth and children	
26 الشعراء 133	أَمَدَّكُم بِأَنْعَامٍ وَبَنِينَ	
	Provided you with grazing livestock and children	
37 الصافات 153	أَصْطَفَى الْبَنَاتِ عَلَى الْبَنِينَ	
	Has He chosen daughters over sons?	
43 الزخرف 16	أَمِ اتَّخَذَ مِمَّا يَخْلُقُ بَنَاتٍ وَأَصْفَاكُم بِالْبَنِينَ	
	Or has He taken, out of what He has created, daughters and chosen you for [having] sons?	
68 القلم 14	أَن كَانَ ذَا مَالٍ وَبَنِينَ	
	Because he is a possessor of wealth and children,	

71 نوح 12	وَيُمْدِدْكُم بِأَمْوَالٍ وَبَنِينَ وَيَجْعَل لَّكُمْ جَنَّاتٍ وَيَجْعَل لَّكُمْ أَنْهَارًا	
	And give you increase in wealth and children and provide for you gardens and provide for you rivers	
74 المدثر 13	وَبَنِينَ شُهُودًا	
	And children present [with him]	
Daughter of	ابْنَتَ	
28 القصص 27	قَالَ إِنِّي أُرِيدُ أَنْ أُنكِحَكَ إِحْدَى ابْنَتَيَّ هَاتَيْنِ عَلَى أَن تَأْجُرَنِي ثَمَانِيَ حِجَجٍ ۖ فَإِنْ أَتْمَمْتَ عَشْرًا فَمِنْ عِندِكَ ۖ وَمَا أُرِيدُ أَنْ أَشُقَّ عَلَيْكَ ۚ سَتَجِدُنِي إِن شَاءَ اللَّهُ مِنَ الصَّالِحِينَ	
	He said, "Indeed, I wish to wed you one of these, my two daughters, on [the condition] that you serve me for eight years; but if you complete ten, it will be [as a favor] from you. And I do not wish to put you in difficulty. You will find me, if Allah wills, from among the righteous."	
66 التحريم 12	وَمَرْيَمَ ابْنَتَ عِمْرَانَ الَّتِي أَحْصَنَتْ فَرْجَهَا فَنَفَخْنَا فِيهِ مِن رُّوحِنَا وَصَدَّقَتْ بِكَلِمَاتِ رَبِّهَا وَكُتُبِهِ وَكَانَتْ مِنَ الْقَانِتِينَ	
	And [the example of] Mary, the daughter of 'Imran, who guarded her chastity, so We blew into [her garment] through Our angel, and she believed in the words of her Lord and His scriptures and was of the devoutly obedient.	
Daughters	بنات	
4 النساء 23	حُرِّمَتْ عَلَيْكُمْ أُمَّهَاتُكُمْ وَبَنَاتُكُمْ وَأَخَوَاتُكُمْ وَعَمَّاتُكُمْ وَخَالَاتُكُمْ وَبَنَاتُ الْأَخِ وَبَنَاتُ الْأُخْتِ وَأُمَّهَاتُكُمُ اللَّاتِي أَرْضَعْنَكُمْ وَأَخَوَاتُكُم مِّنَ الرَّضَاعَةِ وَأُمَّهَاتُ نِسَائِكُمْ وَرَبَائِبُكُمُ اللَّاتِي فِي حُجُورِكُم مِّن نِّسَائِكُمُ اللَّاتِي دَخَلْتُم بِهِنَّ فَإِن لَّمْ تَكُونُوا دَخَلْتُم بِهِنَّ فَلَا جُنَاحَ عَلَيْكُمْ وَحَلَائِلُ أَبْنَائِكُمُ الَّذِينَ مِنْ أَصْلَابِكُمْ وَأَن تَجْمَعُوا بَيْنَ الْأُخْتَيْنِ إِلَّا مَا قَدْ سَلَفَ ۗ إِنَّ اللَّهَ كَانَ غَفُورًا رَّحِيمًا	
	Prohibited to you [for marriage] are your mothers, your daughters, your sisters, your father's sisters, your mother's sisters, your brother's daughters, your sister's	

		daughters, your [milk] mothers who nursed you, your sisters through nursing, your wives' mothers, and your step-daughters under your guardianship [born] of your wives unto whom you have gone in. But if you have not gone in unto them, there is no sin upon you. And [also prohibited are] the wives of your sons who are from your [own] loins, and that you take [in marriage] two sisters simultaneously, except for what has already occurred. Indeed, Allah is ever Forgiving and Merciful.
6 الأنعام	100	وَجَعَلُوا لِلَّهِ شُرَكَاءَ الْجِنَّ وَخَلَقَهُمْ ۖ وَخَرَقُوا لَهُ بَنِينَ وَبَنَاتٍ بِغَيْرِ عِلْمٍ ۚ سُبْحَانَهُ وَتَعَالَىٰ عَمَّا يَصِفُونَ
		But they have attributed to Allah partners - the jinn, while He has created them - and have fabricated for Him sons and daughters. Exalted is He and high above what they describe
11 هود	78	وَجَاءَهُ قَوْمُهُ يُهْرَعُونَ إِلَيْهِ وَمِن قَبْلُ كَانُوا يَعْمَلُونَ السَّيِّئَاتِ ۚ قَالَ يَا قَوْمِ هَٰؤُلَاءِ بَنَاتِي هُنَّ أَطْهَرُ لَكُمْ ۖ فَاتَّقُوا اللَّهَ وَلَا تُخْزُونِ فِي ضَيْفِي ۖ أَلَيْسَ مِنكُمْ رَجُلٌ رَّشِيدٌ
		And his people came hastening to him, and before [this] they had been doing evil deeds. He said, "O my people, these are my daughters; they are purer for you. So fear Allah and do not disgrace me concerning my guests. Is there not among you a man of reason?"
	79	قَالُوا لَقَدْ عَلِمْتَ مَا لَنَا فِي بَنَاتِكَ مِنْ حَقٍّ وَإِنَّكَ لَتَعْلَمُ مَا نُرِيدُ
		They said, "You have already known that we have not concerning your daughters any claim, and indeed, you know what we want."
15 الحجر	71	قَالَ هَٰؤُلَاءِ بَنَاتِي إِن كُنتُمْ فَاعِلِينَ
		[Lot] said, "These are my daughters - if you would be doers [of lawful marriage]."
16 النحل	57	وَيَجْعَلُونَ لِلَّهِ الْبَنَاتِ سُبْحَانَهُ ۙ وَلَهُم مَّا يَشْتَهُونَ
		And they attribute to Allah daughters - exalted is He - and for them is what they desire.
33 الأحزاب	50	يَا أَيُّهَا النَّبِيُّ إِنَّا أَحْلَلْنَا لَكَ أَزْوَاجَكَ اللَّاتِي آتَيْتَ أُجُورَهُنَّ وَمَا مَلَكَتْ يَمِينُكَ مِمَّا أَفَاءَ اللَّهُ عَلَيْكَ وَبَنَاتِ عَمِّكَ وَبَنَاتِ عَمَّاتِكَ وَبَنَاتِ خَالِكَ وَبَنَاتِ خَالَاتِكَ اللَّاتِي هَاجَرْنَ مَعَكَ وَامْرَأَةً مُّؤْمِنَةً إِن

	وَهَبَتْ نَفْسَهَا لِلنَّبِيِّ إِنْ أَرَادَ النَّبِيُّ أَن يَسْتَنكِحَهَا خَالِصَةً لَّكَ مِن دُونِ الْمُؤْمِنِينَ ۗ قَدْ عَلِمْنَا مَا فَرَضْنَا عَلَيْهِمْ فِي أَزْوَاجِهِمْ وَمَا مَلَكَتْ أَيْمَانُهُمْ لِكَيْلَا يَكُونَ عَلَيْكَ حَرَجٌ ۗ وَكَانَ اللَّهُ غَفُورًا رَّحِيمًا
	O Prophet, indeed We have made lawful to you your wives to whom you have given their due compensation and those your right hand possesses from what Allah has returned to you [of captives] and the daughters of your paternal uncles and the daughters of your paternal aunts and the daughters of your maternal uncles and the daughters of your maternal aunts who emigrated with you and a believing woman if she gives herself to the Prophet [and] if the Prophet wishes to marry her, [this is] only for you, excluding the [other] believers. We certainly know what We have made obligatory upon them concerning their wives and those their right hands possess, [but this is for you] in order that there will be upon you no discomfort. And ever is Allah Forgiving and Merciful.
59	يَا أَيُّهَا النَّبِيُّ قُل لِّأَزْوَاجِكَ وَبَنَاتِكَ وَنِسَاءِ الْمُؤْمِنِينَ يُدْنِينَ عَلَيْهِنَّ مِن جَلَابِيبِهِنَّ ۚ ذَٰلِكَ أَدْنَىٰ أَن يُعْرَفْنَ فَلَا يُؤْذَيْنَ ۗ وَكَانَ اللَّهُ غَفُورًا رَّحِيمًا
	O Prophet, tell your wives and your daughters and the women of the believers to bring down over themselves [part] of their outer garments. That is more suitable that they will be known and not be abused. And ever is Allah Forgiving and Merciful.
37 الصافات 149	فَاسْتَفْتِهِمْ أَلِرَبِّكَ الْبَنَاتُ وَلَهُمُ الْبَنُونَ
	So inquire of them, [O Muhammad], "Does your Lord have daughters while they have sons?
153	أَصْطَفَى الْبَنَاتِ عَلَى الْبَنِينَ
	Has He chosen daughters over sons?
52 الطور 39	أَمْ لَهُ الْبَنَاتُ وَلَكُمُ الْبَنُونَ
	Or has He daughters while you have sons?.

	أُمٌّ	Mother
3 آل عمران 7	هُوَ الَّذِي أَنزَلَ عَلَيْكَ الْكِتَابَ مِنْهُ آيَاتٌ مُّحْكَمَاتٌ هُنَّ أُمُّ الْكِتَابِ وَأُخَرُ مُتَشَابِهَاتٌ ۖ فَأَمَّا الَّذِينَ فِي قُلُوبِهِمْ زَيْغٌ فَيَتَّبِعُونَ مَا تَشَابَهَ مِنْهُ ابْتِغَاءَ الْفِتْنَةِ وَابْتِغَاءَ تَأْوِيلِهِ ۗ وَمَا يَعْلَمُ تَأْوِيلَهُ إِلَّا اللَّهُ ۗ وَالرَّاسِخُونَ فِي الْعِلْمِ يَقُولُونَ آمَنَّا بِهِ كُلٌّ مِّنْ عِندِ رَبِّنَا ۗ وَمَا يَذَّكَّرُ إِلَّا أُولُو الْأَلْبَابِ	
	It is He who has sent down to you, [O Muhammad], the Book; in it are verses [that are] precise - they are the foundation of the Book - and others unspecific. As for those in whose hearts is deviation [from truth], they will follow that of it which is unspecific, seeking discord and seeking an interpretation [suitable to them]. And no one knows its [true] interpretation except Allah. But those firm in knowledge say, "We believe in it. All [of it] is from our Lord." And no one will be reminded except those of understanding.	
6 الأنعام 92	وَهَٰذَا كِتَابٌ أَنزَلْنَاهُ مُبَارَكٌ مُّصَدِّقُ الَّذِي بَيْنَ يَدَيْهِ وَلِتُنذِرَ أُمَّ الْقُرَىٰ وَمَنْ حَوْلَهَا ۚ وَالَّذِينَ يُؤْمِنُونَ بِالْآخِرَةِ يُؤْمِنُونَ بِهِ ۖ وَهُمْ عَلَىٰ صَلَاتِهِمْ يُحَافِظُونَ	
	And this is a Book which We have sent down, blessed and confirming what was before it, that you may warn the Mother of Cities and those around it. Those who believe in the Hereafter believe in it, and they are maintaining their prayers.	
13 الرعد 39	يَمْحُو اللَّهُ مَا يَشَاءُ وَيُثْبِتُ ۖ وَعِندَهُ أُمُّ الْكِتَابِ	
	Allah eliminates what He wills or confirms, and with Him is the Mother of the Book.	
20 طه 94	قَالَ يَا ابْنَ أُمَّ لَا تَأْخُذْ بِلِحْيَتِي وَلَا بِرَأْسِي ۖ إِنِّي خَشِيتُ أَن تَقُولَ فَرَّقْتَ بَيْنَ بَنِي إِسْرَائِيلَ وَلَمْ تَرْقُبْ قَوْلِي	
	[Aaron] said, "O son of my mother, do not seize [me] by my beard or by my head. Indeed, I feared that you would say, 'You caused division among the Children of Israel, and you did not observe [or await] my word.'	

28 القصص 7	وَأَوْحَيْنَا إِلَىٰ أُمِّ مُوسَىٰ أَنْ أَرْضِعِيهِ ۖ فَإِذَا خِفْتِ عَلَيْهِ فَأَلْقِيهِ فِي الْيَمِّ وَلَا تَخَافِي وَلَا تَحْزَنِي ۖ إِنَّا رَادُّوهُ إِلَيْكِ وَجَاعِلُوهُ مِنَ الْمُرْسَلِينَ	
	And We inspired to the mother of Moses, "Suckle him; but when you fear for him, cast him into the river and do not fear and do not grieve. Indeed, We will return him to you and will make him [one] of the messengers."	
10	وَأَصْبَحَ فُؤَادُ أُمِّ مُوسَىٰ فَارِغًا ۖ إِنْ كَادَتْ لَتُبْدِي بِهِ لَوْلَا أَنْ رَبَطْنَا عَلَىٰ قَلْبِهَا لِتَكُونَ مِنَ الْمُؤْمِنِينَ	
	And the heart of Moses' mother became empty [of all else]. She was about to disclose [the matter concerning] him had We not bound fast her heart that she would be of the believers.	
43 الزخرف 4	وَإِنَّهُ فِي أُمِّ الْكِتَابِ لَدَيْنَا لَعَلِيٌّ حَكِيمٌ	
	And indeed it is, in the Mother of the Book with Us, exalted and full of wisdom.	
Your Mother	أُمك	
19 مريم 28	يَا أُخْتَ هَارُونَ مَا كَانَ أَبُوكِ امْرَأَ سَوْءٍ وَمَا كَانَتْ أُمُّكِ بَغِيًّا	
	O sister of Aaron, your father was not a man of evil, nor was your mother unchaste."	
20 طه 38	إِذْ أَوْحَيْنَا إِلَىٰ أُمِّكَ مَا يُوحَىٰ	
	When We inspired to your mother what We inspired,	

40	إِذْ تَمْشِي **أُخْتُكَ** فَتَقُولُ هَلْ أَدُلُّكُمْ عَلَىٰ مَن يَكْفُلُهُ ۖ فَرَجَعْنَاكَ إِلَىٰ **أُمِّكَ** كَيْ تَقَرَّ عَيْنُهَا وَلَا تَحْزَنَ ۚ وَقَتَلْتَ نَفْسًا فَنَجَّيْنَاكَ مِنَ الْغَمِّ وَفَتَنَّاكَ فُتُونًا ۚ فَلَبِثْتَ سِنِينَ فِي **أَهْلِ** مَدْيَنَ ثُمَّ جِئْتَ عَلَىٰ قَدَرٍ يَا مُوسَىٰ
	[And We favored you] when your sister went and said, 'Shall I direct you to someone who will be responsible for him?' So We restored you to your mother that she might be content and not grieve. And you killed someone, but We saved you from retaliation and tried you with a [severe] trial. And you remained [some] years among the people of Madyan. Then you came [here] at the decreed time, O Moses.
His/Her Mother/s-....	فَلِأُمِّهِ/أُمَّهُ/أُمِّهَا/أُمَّهَاتُ
4 النساء 11	يُوصِيكُمُ اللَّهُ فِي **أَوْلَادِكُمْ** ۖ **لِلذَّكَرِ** مِثْلُ حَظِّ **الْأُنثَيَيْنِ** ۚ فَإِن كُنَّ نِسَاءً فَوْقَ اثْنَتَيْنِ فَلَهُنَّ ثُلُثَا مَا تَرَكَ ۖ وَإِن كَانَتْ وَاحِدَةً فَلَهَا النِّصْفُ ۚ **وَلِأَبَوَيْهِ** لِكُلِّ وَاحِدٍ مِّنْهُمَا السُّدُسُ مِمَّا تَرَكَ إِن كَانَ لَهُ **وَلَدٌ** ۚ فَإِن لَّمْ يَكُن لَّهُ **وَلَدٌ** وَوَرِثَهُ **أَبَوَاهُ فَلِأُمِّهِ** الثُّلُثُ ۚ فَإِن كَانَ لَهُ إِخْوَةٌ **فَلِأُمِّهِ** السُّدُسُ ۚ مِن بَعْدِ وَصِيَّةٍ يُوصِي بِهَا أَوْ دَيْنٍ ۗ **آبَاؤُكُمْ وَأَبْنَاؤُكُمْ** لَا تَدْرُونَ أَيُّهُمْ أَقْرَبُ لَكُمْ نَفْعًا ۚ فَرِيضَةً مِّنَ اللَّهِ ۗ إِنَّ اللَّهَ كَانَ عَلِيمًا حَكِيمًا
	Allah instructs you concerning your children: for the male, what is equal to the share of two females. But if there are [only] daughters, two or more, for them is two thirds of one's estate. And if there is only one, for her is half. And for one's parents, to each one of them is a sixth of his estate if he left children. But if he had no children and the parents [alone] inherit from him, then for his mother is one third. And if he had brothers [or sisters], for his mother is a sixth, after any bequest he [may have] made or debt. Your parents or your children - you know not which of them are nearest to you in benefit. [These shares are] an obligation [imposed] by Allah. Indeed, Allah is ever Knowing and Wise.
23	حُرِّمَتْ عَلَيْكُمْ **أُمَّهَاتُكُمْ** وَبَنَاتُكُمْ وَأَخَوَاتُكُمْ وَعَمَّاتُكُمْ وَخَالَاتُكُمْ وَبَنَاتُ الْأَخِ وَبَنَاتُ الْأُخْتِ **وَأُمَّهَاتُكُمُ** اللَّاتِي أَرْضَعْنَكُمْ وَأَخَوَاتُكُم مِّنَ الرَّضَاعَةِ **وَأُمَّهَاتُ** نِسَائِكُمْ وَرَبَائِبُكُمُ اللَّاتِي فِي حُجُورِكُم مِّن نِّسَائِكُمُ اللَّاتِي دَخَلْتُم بِهِنَّ فَإِن لَّمْ تَكُونُوا دَخَلْتُم بِهِنَّ فَلَا جُنَاحَ عَلَيْكُمْ وَحَلَائِلُ **أَبْنَائِكُمُ** الَّذِينَ مِنْ أَصْلَابِكُمْ وَأَن تَجْمَعُوا بَيْنَ الْأُخْتَيْنِ إِلَّا مَا قَدْ سَلَفَ ۗ إِنَّ اللَّهَ كَانَ غَفُورًا رَّحِيمًا

	Prohibited to you [for marriage] are your mothers, your daughters, your sisters, your father's sisters, your mother's sisters, your brother's daughters, your sister's daughters, your [milk] mothers who nursed you, your sisters through nursing, your wives' mothers, and your step-daughters under your guardianship [born] of your wives unto whom you have gone in. But if you have not gone in unto them, there is no sin upon you. And [also prohibited are] the wives of your sons who are from your [own] loins, and that you take [in marriage] two sisters simultaneously, except for what has already occurred. Indeed, Allah is ever Forgiving and Merciful.
5 المائدة 17	لَقَدْ كَفَرَ الَّذِينَ قَالُوا إِنَّ اللَّهَ هُوَ الْمَسِيحُ ابْنُ مَرْيَمَ ۚ قُلْ فَمَن يَمْلِكُ مِنَ اللَّهِ شَيْئًا إِنْ أَرَادَ أَن يُهْلِكَ الْمَسِيحَ ابْنَ مَرْيَمَ وَأُمَّهُ وَمَن فِي الْأَرْضِ جَمِيعًا ۗ وَلِلَّهِ مُلْكُ السَّمَاوَاتِ وَالْأَرْضِ وَمَا بَيْنَهُمَا ۚ يَخْلُقُ مَا يَشَاءُ ۚ وَاللَّهُ عَلَىٰ كُلِّ شَيْءٍ قَدِيرٌ
	They have certainly disbelieved who say that Allah is Christ, the son of Mary. Say, "Then who could prevent Allah at all if He had intended to destroy Christ, the son of Mary, or his mother or everyone on the earth?" And to Allah belongs the dominion of the heavens and the earth and whatever is between them. He creates what He wills, and Allah is over all things competent.
75	مَّا الْمَسِيحُ ابْنُ مَرْيَمَ إِلَّا رَسُولٌ قَدْ خَلَتْ مِن قَبْلِهِ الرُّسُلُ وَأُمُّهُ صِدِّيقَةٌ ۖ كَانَا يَأْكُلَانِ الطَّعَامَ ۗ انظُرْ كَيْفَ نُبَيِّنُ لَهُمُ الْآيَاتِ ثُمَّ انظُرْ أَنَّىٰ يُؤْفَكُونَ
	The Messiah, son of Mary, was not but a messenger; [other] messengers have passed on before him. And his mother was a supporter of truth. They both used to eat food. Look how We make clear to them the signs; then look how they are deluded.
23 المؤمنون 50	وَجَعَلْنَا ابْنَ مَرْيَمَ وَأُمَّهُ آيَةً وَآوَيْنَاهُمَا إِلَىٰ رَبْوَةٍ ذَاتِ قَرَارٍ وَمَعِينٍ
	And We made the son of Mary and his mother a sign and sheltered them within a high ground having level [areas] and flowing water
28 القصص 13	فَرَدَدْنَاهُ إِلَىٰ أُمِّهِ كَيْ تَقَرَّ عَيْنُهَا وَلَا تَحْزَنَ وَلِتَعْلَمَ أَنَّ وَعْدَ اللَّهِ حَقٌّ وَلَٰكِنَّ أَكْثَرَهُمْ لَا يَعْلَمُونَ
	So We restored him to his mother that she might be content and not grieve and that she would know that the promise of Allah is true. But most of the people do not know.

59	وَمَا كَانَ رَبُّكَ مُهْلِكَ الْقُرَىٰ حَتَّىٰ يَبْعَثَ فِي أُمِّهَا رَسُولًا يَتْلُو عَلَيْهِمْ آيَاتِنَا ۚ وَمَا كُنَّا مُهْلِكِي الْقُرَىٰ إِلَّا وَأَهْلُهَا ظَالِمُونَ
	And never would your Lord have destroyed the cities until He had sent to their mother a messenger reciting to them Our verses. And We would not destroy the cities except while their people were wrongdoers.
31 لقمان 14	وَوَصَّيْنَا الْإِنسَانَ بِوَالِدَيْهِ حَمَلَتْهُ أُمُّهُ وَهْنًا عَلَىٰ وَهْنٍ وَفِصَالُهُ فِي عَامَيْنِ أَنِ اشْكُرْ لِي وَلِوَالِدَيْكَ إِلَيَّ الْمَصِيرُ
	And We have enjoined upon man [care] for his parents. His mother carried him, [increasing her] in weakness upon weakness, and his weaning is in two years. Be grateful to Me and to your parents; to Me is the [final] destination.
46 الأحقاف 15	وَوَصَّيْنَا الْإِنسَانَ بِوَالِدَيْهِ إِحْسَانًا ۖ حَمَلَتْهُ أُمُّهُ كُرْهًا وَوَضَعَتْهُ كُرْهًا ۖ وَحَمْلُهُ وَفِصَالُهُ ثَلَاثُونَ شَهْرًا ۚ حَتَّىٰ إِذَا بَلَغَ أَشُدَّهُ وَبَلَغَ أَرْبَعِينَ سَنَةً قَالَ رَبِّ أَوْزِعْنِي أَنْ أَشْكُرَ نِعْمَتَكَ الَّتِي أَنْعَمْتَ عَلَيَّ وَعَلَىٰ وَالِدَيَّ وَأَنْ أَعْمَلَ صَالِحًا تَرْضَاهُ وَأَصْلِحْ لِي فِي ذُرِّيَّتِي ۖ إِنِّي تُبْتُ إِلَيْكَ وَإِنِّي مِنَ الْمُسْلِمِينَ
	And We have enjoined upon man, to his parents, good treatment. His mother carried him with hardship and gave birth to him with hardship, and his gestation and weaning [period] is thirty months. [He grows] until, when he reaches maturity and reaches [the age of] forty years, he says, "My Lord, enable me to be grateful for Your favor which You have bestowed upon me and upon my parents and to work righteousness of which You will approve and make righteous for me my offspring. Indeed, I have repented to You, and indeed, I am of the Muslims."
80 عبس 35	وَأُمِّهِ وَأَبِيهِ
	And his mother and his father
101 القارعة 9	فَأُمُّهُ هَاوِيَةٌ
	His refuge will be an abyss

Your Mothers	أُمَّهَاتُكُم
4 النساء 23	حُرِّمَتْ عَلَيْكُمْ أُمَّهَاتُكُمْ وَبَنَاتُكُمْ وَأَخَوَاتُكُمْ وَعَمَّاتُكُمْ وَخَالَاتُكُمْ وَبَنَاتُ الْأَخِ وَبَنَاتُ الْأُخْتِ وَأُمَّهَاتُكُمُ اللَّاتِي أَرْضَعْنَكُمْ وَأَخَوَاتُكُم مِّنَ الرَّضَاعَةِ وَأُمَّهَاتُ نِسَائِكُمْ وَرَبَائِبُكُمُ اللَّاتِي فِي حُجُورِكُم مِّن نِّسَائِكُمُ اللَّاتِي دَخَلْتُم بِهِنَّ فَإِن لَّمْ تَكُونُوا دَخَلْتُم بِهِنَّ فَلَا جُنَاحَ عَلَيْكُمْ وَحَلَائِلُ أَبْنَائِكُمُ الَّذِينَ مِنْ أَصْلَابِكُمْ وَأَن تَجْمَعُوا بَيْنَ الْأُخْتَيْنِ إِلَّا مَا قَدْ سَلَفَ ۗ إِنَّ اللَّهَ كَانَ غَفُورًا رَّحِيمًا
	Prohibited to you [for marriage] are your mothers, your daughters, your sisters, your father's sisters, your mother's sisters, your brother's daughters, your sister's daughters, your [milk] mothers who nursed you, your sisters through nursing, your wives' mothers, and your step-daughters under your guardianship [born] of your wives unto whom you have gone in. But if you have not gone in unto them, there is no sin upon you. And [also prohibited are] the wives of your sons who are from your [own] loins, and that you take [in marriage] two sisters simultaneously, except for what has already occurred. Indeed, Allah is ever Forgiving and Merciful.
16 النحل 78	وَاللَّهُ أَخْرَجَكُم مِّن بُطُونِ أُمَّهَاتِكُمْ لَا تَعْلَمُونَ شَيْئًا وَجَعَلَ لَكُمُ السَّمْعَ وَالْأَبْصَارَ وَالْأَفْئِدَةَ ۙ لَعَلَّكُمْ تَشْكُرُونَ
	And Allah has extracted you from the wombs of your mothers not knowing a thing, and He made for you hearing and vision and intellect that perhaps you would be grateful.
24 النور 61	لَّيْسَ عَلَى الْأَعْمَىٰ حَرَجٌ وَلَا عَلَى الْأَعْرَجِ حَرَجٌ وَلَا عَلَى الْمَرِيضِ حَرَجٌ وَلَا عَلَىٰ أَنفُسِكُمْ أَن تَأْكُلُوا مِن بُيُوتِكُمْ أَوْ بُيُوتِ آبَائِكُمْ أَوْ بُيُوتِ أُمَّهَاتِكُمْ أَوْ بُيُوتِ إِخْوَانِكُمْ أَوْ بُيُوتِ أَخَوَاتِكُمْ أَوْ بُيُوتِ أَعْمَامِكُمْ أَوْ بُيُوتِ عَمَّاتِكُمْ أَوْ بُيُوتِ أَخْوَالِكُمْ أَوْ بُيُوتِ خَالَاتِكُمْ أَوْ مَا مَلَكْتُم مَّفَاتِحَهُ أَوْ صَدِيقِكُمْ ۚ لَيْسَ عَلَيْكُمْ جُنَاحٌ أَن تَأْكُلُوا جَمِيعًا أَوْ أَشْتَاتًا ۚ فَإِذَا دَخَلْتُم بُيُوتًا فَسَلِّمُوا عَلَىٰ أَنفُسِكُمْ تَحِيَّةً مِّنْ عِندِ اللَّهِ مُبَارَكَةً طَيِّبَةً ۚ كَذَٰلِكَ يُبَيِّنُ اللَّهُ لَكُمُ الْآيَاتِ لَعَلَّكُمْ تَعْقِلُونَ
	There is not upon the blind [any] constraint nor upon the lame constraint nor upon the ill constraint nor upon yourselves when you eat from your [own] houses or the houses of your fathers or the houses of your mothers or the houses of your brothers or the houses of your sisters or the houses of your father's brothers or the houses of your father's sisters or the houses of your mother's brothers or the houses of your mother's sisters or [from houses] whose keys you possess or [from the house] of your friend. There is no blame upon you whether you eat together or separately. But when you enter houses, give greetings of peace upon each other - a greeting from Allah, blessed and

		good. Thus does Allah make clear to you the verses [of ordinance] that you may understand.
	33 الأحزاب 4	مَّا جَعَلَ اللَّهُ لِرَجُلٍ مِّن قَلْبَيْنِ فِي جَوْفِهِ ۚ وَمَا جَعَلَ أَزْوَاجَكُمُ اللَّائِي تُظَاهِرُونَ مِنْهُنَّ أُمَّهَاتِكُمْ ۚ وَمَا جَعَلَ أَدْعِيَاءَكُمْ أَبْنَاءَكُمْ ۚ ذَٰلِكُمْ قَوْلُكُم بِأَفْوَاهِكُمْ ۖ وَاللَّهُ يَقُولُ الْحَقَّ وَهُوَ يَهْدِي السَّبِيلَ
		Allah has not made for a man two hearts in his interior. And He has not made your wives whom you declare unlawful your mothers. And he has not made your adopted sons your [true] sons. That is [merely] your saying by your mouths, but Allah says the truth, and He guides to the [right] way.
	39 الزمر 6	خَلَقَكُم مِّن نَّفْسٍ وَاحِدَةٍ ثُمَّ جَعَلَ مِنْهَا زَوْجَهَا وَأَنزَلَ لَكُم مِّنَ الْأَنْعَامِ ثَمَانِيَةَ أَزْوَاجٍ ۚ يَخْلُقُكُمْ فِي بُطُونِ أُمَّهَاتِكُمْ خَلْقًا مِّن بَعْدِ خَلْقٍ فِي ظُلُمَاتٍ ثَلَاثٍ ۚ ذَٰلِكُمُ اللَّهُ رَبُّكُمْ لَهُ الْمُلْكُ ۖ لَا إِلَٰهَ إِلَّا هُوَ ۖ فَأَنَّىٰ تُصْرَفُونَ
		He created you from one soul. Then He made from it its mate, and He produced for you from the grazing livestock eight mates. He creates you in the wombs of your mothers, creation after creation, within three darknesses. That is Allah, your Lord; to Him belongs dominion. There is no deity except Him, so how are you averted?
	53 النجم 32	الَّذِينَ يَجْتَنِبُونَ كَبَائِرَ الْإِثْمِ وَالْفَوَاحِشَ إِلَّا اللَّمَمَ ۚ إِنَّ رَبَّكَ وَاسِعُ الْمَغْفِرَةِ ۚ هُوَ أَعْلَمُ بِكُمْ إِذْ أَنشَأَكُم مِّنَ الْأَرْضِ وَإِذْ أَنتُمْ أَجِنَّةٌ فِي بُطُونِ أُمَّهَاتِكُمْ ۖ فَلَا تُزَكُّوا أَنفُسَكُمْ ۖ هُوَ أَعْلَمُ بِمَنِ اتَّقَىٰ
		Those who avoid the major sins and immoralities, only [committing] slight ones. Indeed, your Lord is vast in forgiveness. He was most knowing of you when He produced you from the earth and when you were fetuses in the wombs of your mothers. So do not claim yourselves to be pure; He is most knowing of who fears Him.

Their Mothers	أُمَّهَاتُهُمْ
33 الأحزاب 6	النَّبِيُّ أَوْلَىٰ بِالْمُؤْمِنِينَ مِنْ أَنفُسِهِمْ ۖ وَأَزْوَاجُهُ أُمَّهَاتُهُمْ ۗ وَأُولُو الْأَرْحَامِ بَعْضُهُمْ أَوْلَىٰ بِبَعْضٍ فِي كِتَابِ اللَّهِ مِنَ الْمُؤْمِنِينَ وَالْمُهَاجِرِينَ إِلَّا أَن تَفْعَلُوا إِلَىٰ أَوْلِيَائِكُم مَّعْرُوفًا ۚ كَانَ ذَٰلِكَ فِي الْكِتَابِ مَسْطُورًا
	The Prophet is more worthy of the believers than themselves, and his wives are [in the position of] their mothers. And those of [blood] relationship are more entitled [to inheritance] in the decree of Allah than the [other] believers and the emigrants, except that you may do to your close associates a kindness [through bequest]. That was in the Book inscribed.
58 المجادلة 2	الَّذِينَ يُظَاهِرُونَ مِنكُم مِّن نِّسَائِهِم مَّا هُنَّ أُمَّهَاتِهِمْ ۖ إِنْ أُمَّهَاتُهُمْ إِلَّا اللَّائِي وَلَدْنَهُمْ ۚ وَإِنَّهُمْ لَيَقُولُونَ مُنكَرًا مِّنَ الْقَوْلِ وَزُورًا ۚ وَإِنَّ اللَّهَ لَعَفُوٌّ غَفُورٌ
	Those who pronounce thihar among you [to separate] from their wives - they are not [consequently] their mothers. Their mothers are none but those who gave birth to them. And indeed, they are saying an objectionable statement and a falsehood. But indeed, Allah is Pardoning and Forgiving.

Give Birth	**Shall I bear a child when !** أَأَلِدُ
11 هود 72	قَالَتْ يَا وَيْلَتَىٰ أَأَلِدُ وَأَنَا عَجُوزٌ وَهَٰذَا بَعْلِي شَيْخًا ۖ إِنَّ هَٰذَا لَشَيْءٌ عَجِيبٌ
	She said, "Woe to me! Shall I give birth while I am an old woman and this, my husband, is an old man? Indeed, this is an amazing thing!"
P	She said: Oh woe is me! Shall I bear a child when I am an old woman, and this my husband is an old man? Lo! this is a strange thing! **(Pickthall)**

The Father	مَوْلُودٌ لَهُ
2 البقرة 233	وَالْوَالِدَاتُ يُرْضِعْنَ أَوْلَادَهُنَّ حَوْلَيْنِ كَامِلَيْنِ ۖ لِمَنْ أَرَادَ أَن يُتِمَّ الرَّضَاعَةَ ۚ وَعَلَى الْمَوْلُودِ لَهُ رِزْقُهُنَّ وَكِسْوَتُهُنَّ بِالْمَعْرُوفِ ۚ لَا تُكَلَّفُ نَفْسٌ إِلَّا وُسْعَهَا ۚ لَا تُضَارَّ وَالِدَةٌ بِوَلَدِهَا وَلَا مَوْلُودٌ لَّهُ بِوَلَدِهِ ۚ وَعَلَى الْوَارِثِ مِثْلُ ذَٰلِكَ ۗ فَإِنْ أَرَادَا فِصَالًا عَن تَرَاضٍ مِّنْهُمَا وَتَشَاوُرٍ فَلَا جُنَاحَ عَلَيْهِمَا ۗ وَإِنْ أَرَدتُّمْ أَن تَسْتَرْضِعُوا أَوْلَادَكُمْ فَلَا جُنَاحَ عَلَيْكُمْ إِذَا سَلَّمْتُم مَّا آتَيْتُم بِالْمَعْرُوفِ ۗ وَاتَّقُوا اللَّهَ وَاعْلَمُوا أَنَّ اللَّهَ بِمَا تَعْمَلُونَ بَصِيرٌ
	Mothers may breastfeed their children two complete years for whoever wishes to complete the nursing [period]. Upon the father is the mothers' provision and their clothing according to what is acceptable. No person is charged with more than his capacity. No mother should be harmed through her child, and no father through his child. And upon the [father's] heir is [a duty] like that [of the father]. And if they both desire weaning through mutual consent from both of them and consultation, there is no blame upon either of them. And if you wish to have your children nursed by a substitute, there is no blame upon you as long as you give payment according to what is acceptable. And fear Allah and know that Allah is Seeing of what you do.
A child	وليدا
26 الشعراء 18	قَالَ أَلَمْ نُرَبِّكَ فِينَا وَلِيدًا وَلَبِثْتَ فِينَا مِنْ عُمُرِكَ سِنِينَ
	[Pharaoh] said, "Did we not raise you among us as a child, and you remained among us for years of your life?
Child/born/ His/her/ Gave birth	وَلَدٌ/وُلِدَ/وَلَدًا/مَوْلُودٌ/وَلَدِهِ/الْوَلَدَانِ/وِلْدَانٌ/وَلْدَهُمْ
2 البقرة 116	وَقَالُوا اتَّخَذَ اللَّهُ وَلَدًا ۗ سُبْحَانَهُ ۖ بَل لَّهُ مَا فِي السَّمَاوَاتِ وَالْأَرْضِ ۖ كُلٌّ لَّهُ قَانِتُونَ
	They say, "Allah has taken a son." Exalted is He! Rather, to Him belongs whatever is in the heavens and the earth. All are devoutly obedient to Him,

233	وَالْوَالِدَاتُ يُرْضِعْنَ **أَوْلَادَهُنَّ** حَوْلَيْنِ كَامِلَيْنِ ۖ لِمَنْ أَرَادَ أَن يُتِمَّ الرَّضَاعَةَ ۚ وَعَلَى **الْمَوْلُودِ** **لَهُ** رِزْقُهُنَّ وَكِسْوَتُهُنَّ بِالْمَعْرُوفِ ۚ لَا تُكَلَّفُ نَفْسٌ إِلَّا وُسْعَهَا ۚ لَا تُضَارَّ **وَالِدَةٌ بِوَلَدِهَا** وَلَا **مَوْلُودٌ لَّهُ بِوَلَدِهِ** ۚ وَعَلَى الْوَارِثِ مِثْلُ ذَٰلِكَ ۗ فَإِنْ أَرَادَا فِصَالًا عَن تَرَاضٍ مِّنْهُمَا وَتَشَاوُرٍ فَلَا جُنَاحَ عَلَيْهِمَا ۗ وَإِنْ أَرَدتُّمْ أَن تَسْتَرْضِعُوا **أَوْلَادَكُمْ** فَلَا جُنَاحَ عَلَيْكُمْ إِذَا سَلَّمْتُم مَّا آتَيْتُم بِالْمَعْرُوفِ ۗ وَاتَّقُوا اللَّهَ وَاعْلَمُوا أَنَّ اللَّهَ بِمَا تَعْمَلُونَ بَصِيرٌ	
	Mothers may breastfeed their children two complete years for whoever wishes to complete the nursing [period]. Upon the father is the mothers' provision and their clothing according to what is acceptable. No person is charged with more than his capacity. No mother should be harmed through her child, and no father through his child. And upon the [father's] heir is [a duty] like that [of the father]. And if they both desire weaning through mutual consent from both of them and consultation, there is no blame upon either of them. And if you wish to have your children nursed by a substitute, there is no blame upon you as long as you give payment according to what is acceptable. And fear Allah and know that Allah is Seeing of what you do.	
3 آل عمران 47	قَالَتْ رَبِّ أَنَّىٰ يَكُونُ لِي **وَلَدٌ** وَلَمْ يَمْسَسْنِي **بَشَرٌ** ۖ قَالَ كَذَٰلِكِ اللَّهُ يَخْلُقُ مَا يَشَاءُ ۚ إِذَا **قَضَىٰ** أَمْرًا فَإِنَّمَا يَقُولُ لَهُ كُن فَيَكُونُ	
	She said, "My Lord, how will I have a child when no man has touched me?" [The angel] said, "Such is Allah; He creates what He wills. When He decrees a matter, He only says to it, 'Be,' and it is.	
4 النساء 11	يُوصِيكُمُ اللَّهُ فِي **أَوْلَادِكُمْ** ۖ لِلذَّكَرِ مِثْلُ حَظِّ **الْأُنثَيَيْنِ** ۚ فَإِن كُنَّ نِسَاءً فَوْقَ اثْنَتَيْنِ فَلَهُنَّ ثُلُثَا مَا تَرَكَ ۖ وَإِن كَانَتْ وَاحِدَةً فَلَهَا النِّصْفُ ۚ **وَلِأَبَوَيْهِ** لِكُلِّ وَاحِدٍ مِّنْهُمَا السُّدُسُ مِمَّا تَرَكَ إِن كَانَ لَهُ **وَلَدٌ** ۚ فَإِن لَّمْ يَكُن لَّهُ **وَلَدٌ** وَوَرِثَهُ أَبَوَاهُ فَلِأُمِّهِ الثُّلُثُ ۚ فَإِن كَانَ لَهُ **إِخْوَةٌ** فَلِأُمِّهِ السُّدُسُ ۚ مِن بَعْدِ وَصِيَّةٍ يُوصِي بِهَا أَوْ دَيْنٍ ۗ **آبَاؤُكُمْ وَأَبْنَاؤُكُمْ** لَا تَدْرُونَ أَيُّهُمْ أَقْرَبُ لَكُمْ نَفْعًا ۚ فَرِيضَةً مِّنَ اللَّهِ ۗ إِنَّ اللَّهَ كَانَ عَلِيمًا حَكِيمًا	
	Allah instructs you concerning your children: for the male, what is equal to the share of two females. But if there are [only] daughters, two or more, for them is two thirds of one's estate. And if there is only one, for her is half. And for one's parents, to each one of them is a sixth of his estate if he left children. But if he had no children and the parents [alone] inherit from him, then for his mother is one third. And if he had brothers [or sisters], for his mother is a sixth, after any bequest he [may have] made or debt. Your parents or your children - you know not which of them are nearest to you in benefit. [These shares are] an obligation [imposed] by Allah. Indeed, Allah is ever Knowing and Wise.	

12	وَلَكُمْ نِصْفُ مَا تَرَكَ أَزْوَاجُكُمْ إِن لَّمْ يَكُن لَّهُنَّ وَلَدٌ ۚ فَإِن كَانَ لَهُنَّ وَلَدٌ فَلَكُمُ الرُّبُعُ مِمَّا تَرَكْنَ ۚ مِن بَعْدِ وَصِيَّةٍ يُوصِينَ بِهَا أَوْ دَيْنٍ ۚ وَلَهُنَّ الرُّبُعُ مِمَّا تَرَكْتُمْ إِن لَّمْ يَكُن لَّكُمْ وَلَدٌ ۚ فَإِن كَانَ لَكُمْ وَلَدٌ فَلَهُنَّ الثُّمُنُ مِمَّا تَرَكْتُم ۚ مِّن بَعْدِ وَصِيَّةٍ تُوصُونَ بِهَا أَوْ دَيْنٍ ۗ وَإِن كَانَ رَجُلٌ يُورَثُ كَلَالَةً أَوِ امْرَأَةٌ وَلَهُ أَخٌ أَوْ أُخْتٌ فَلِكُلِّ وَاحِدٍ مِّنْهُمَا السُّدُسُ ۚ فَإِن كَانُوا أَكْثَرَ مِن ذَٰلِكَ فَهُمْ شُرَكَاءُ فِي الثُّلُثِ ۚ مِن بَعْدِ وَصِيَّةٍ يُوصَىٰ بِهَا أَوْ دَيْنٍ غَيْرَ مُضَارٍّ ۚ وَصِيَّةً مِّنَ اللَّهِ ۗ وَاللَّهُ عَلِيمٌ حَلِيمٌ
	And for you is half of what your wives leave if they have no child. But if they have a child, for you is one fourth of what they leave, after any bequest they [may have] made or debt. And for the wives is one fourth if you leave no child. But if you leave a child, then for them is an eighth of what you leave, after any bequest you [may have] made or debt. And if a man or woman leaves neither ascendants nor descendants but has a brother or a sister, then for each one of them is a sixth. But if they are more than two, they share a third, after any bequest which was made or debt, as long as there is no detriment [caused]. [This is] an ordinance from Allah, and Allah is Knowing and Forbearing.
75	وَمَا لَكُمْ لَا تُقَاتِلُونَ فِي سَبِيلِ اللَّهِ وَالْمُسْتَضْعَفِينَ مِنَ الرِّجَالِ وَالنِّسَاءِ وَالْوِلْدَانِ الَّذِينَ يَقُولُونَ رَبَّنَا أَخْرِجْنَا مِنْ هَٰذِهِ الْقَرْيَةِ الظَّالِمِ أَهْلُهَا وَاجْعَل لَّنَا مِن لَّدُنكَ وَلِيًّا وَاجْعَل لَّنَا مِن لَّدُنكَ نَصِيرًا
	And what is [the matter] with you that you fight not in the cause of Allah and [for] the oppressed among men, women, and children who say, "Our Lord, take us out of this city of oppressive people and appoint for us from Yourself a protector and appoint for us from Yourself a helper?"
98	إِلَّا الْمُسْتَضْعَفِينَ مِنَ الرِّجَالِ وَالنِّسَاءِ وَالْوِلْدَانِ لَا يَسْتَطِيعُونَ حِيلَةً وَلَا يَهْتَدُونَ سَبِيلًا
	Except for the oppressed among men, women and children who cannot devise a plan nor are they directed to a way –

127	وَيَسْتَفْتُونَكَ فِي النِّسَاءِ ۖ قُلِ اللَّهُ يُفْتِيكُمْ فِيهِنَّ وَمَا يُتْلَىٰ عَلَيْكُمْ فِي الْكِتَابِ فِي يَتَامَى النِّسَاءِ اللَّاتِي لَا تُؤْتُونَهُنَّ مَا كُتِبَ لَهُنَّ وَتَرْغَبُونَ أَن تَنكِحُوهُنَّ وَالْمُسْتَضْعَفِينَ مِنَ الْوِلْدَانِ وَأَن تَقُومُوا لِلْيَتَامَىٰ بِالْقِسْطِ ۚ وَمَا تَفْعَلُوا مِنْ خَيْرٍ فَإِنَّ اللَّهَ كَانَ بِهِ عَلِيمًا
	And they request from you, [O Muhammad], a [legal] ruling concerning women. Say, "Allah gives you a ruling about them and [about] what has been recited to you in the Book concerning the orphan girls to whom you do not give what is decreed for them - and [yet] you desire to marry them - and concerning the oppressed among children and that you maintain for orphans [their rights] in justice." And whatever you do of good - indeed, Allah is ever Knowing of it.
171	يَا أَهْلَ الْكِتَابِ لَا تَغْلُوا فِي دِينِكُمْ وَلَا تَقُولُوا عَلَى اللَّهِ إِلَّا الْحَقَّ ۚ إِنَّمَا الْمَسِيحُ عِيسَى ابْنُ مَرْيَمَ رَسُولُ اللَّهِ وَكَلِمَتُهُ أَلْقَاهَا إِلَىٰ مَرْيَمَ وَرُوحٌ مِّنْهُ ۖ فَآمِنُوا بِاللَّهِ وَرُسُلِهِ ۖ وَلَا تَقُولُوا ثَلَاثَةٌ ۚ انتَهُوا خَيْرًا لَّكُمْ ۚ إِنَّمَا اللَّهُ إِلَٰهٌ وَاحِدٌ ۖ سُبْحَانَهُ أَن يَكُونَ لَهُ وَلَدٌ ۘ لَّهُ مَا فِي السَّمَاوَاتِ وَمَا فِي الْأَرْضِ ۗ وَكَفَىٰ بِاللَّهِ وَكِيلًا
	O People of the Scripture, do not commit excess in your religion or say about Allah except the truth. The Messiah, Jesus, the son of Mary, was but a messenger of Allah and His word which He directed to Mary and a soul [created at a command] from Him. So believe in Allah and His messengers. And do not say, "Three"; desist - it is better for you. Indeed, Allah is but one God. Exalted is He above having a son. To Him belongs whatever is in the heavens and whatever is on the earth. And sufficient is Allah as Disposer of affairs.
176	يَسْتَفْتُونَكَ قُلِ اللَّهُ يُفْتِيكُمْ فِي الْكَلَالَةِ ۚ إِنِ امْرُؤٌ هَلَكَ لَيْسَ لَهُ وَلَدٌ وَلَهُ أُخْتٌ فَلَهَا نِصْفُ مَا تَرَكَ ۚ وَهُوَ يَرِثُهَا إِن لَّمْ يَكُن لَّهَا وَلَدٌ ۚ فَإِن كَانَتَا اثْنَتَيْنِ فَلَهُمَا الثُّلُثَانِ مِمَّا تَرَكَ ۚ وَإِن كَانُوا إِخْوَةً رِّجَالًا وَنِسَاءً فَلِلذَّكَرِ مِثْلُ حَظِّ الْأُنثَيَيْنِ ۗ يُبَيِّنُ اللَّهُ لَكُمْ أَن تَضِلُّوا ۗ وَاللَّهُ بِكُلِّ شَيْءٍ عَلِيمٌ
	They request from you a [legal] ruling. Say, "Allah gives you a ruling concerning one having neither descendants nor ascendants [as heirs]." If a man dies, leaving no child but [only] a sister, she will have half of what he left. And he inherits from her if she [dies and] has no child. But if there are two sisters [or more], they will have two-thirds of what he left. If there are both brothers and sisters, the male will have the share of two females. Allah makes clear to you [His law], lest you go astray. And Allah is Knowing of all things.

6 الأنعام 101	بَدِيعُ السَّمَاوَاتِ وَالْأَرْضِ ۖ أَنَّىٰ يَكُونُ لَهُ وَلَدٌ وَلَمْ تَكُن لَّهُ صَاحِبَةٌ ۖ وَخَلَقَ كُلَّ شَيْءٍ ۖ وَهُوَ بِكُلِّ شَيْءٍ عَلِيمٌ
	[He is] Originator of the heavens and the earth. How could He have a son when He does not have a companion and He created all things? And He is, of all things, Knowing.
10 يونس 68	قَالُوا اتَّخَذَ اللَّهُ وَلَدًا ۗ سُبْحَانَهُ ۖ هُوَ الْغَنِيُّ ۖ لَهُ مَا فِي السَّمَاوَاتِ وَمَا فِي الْأَرْضِ ۚ إِنْ عِندَكُم مِّن سُلْطَانٍ بِهَٰذَا ۚ أَتَقُولُونَ عَلَى اللَّهِ مَا لَا تَعْلَمُونَ
	They have said, "Allah has taken a son." Exalted is He; He is the [one] Free of need. To Him belongs whatever is in the heavens and whatever is in the earth. You have no authority for this [claim]. Do you say about Allah that which you do not know?
12 يوسف 21	وَقَالَ الَّذِي اشْتَرَاهُ مِن مِّصْرَ لِامْرَأَتِهِ أَكْرِمِي مَثْوَاهُ عَسَىٰ أَن يَنفَعَنَا أَوْ نَتَّخِذَهُ وَلَدًا ۚ وَكَذَٰلِكَ مَكَّنَّا لِيُوسُفَ فِي الْأَرْضِ وَلِنُعَلِّمَهُ مِن تَأْوِيلِ الْأَحَادِيثِ ۚ وَاللَّهُ غَالِبٌ عَلَىٰ أَمْرِهِ وَلَٰكِنَّ أَكْثَرَ النَّاسِ لَا يَعْلَمُونَ
	And the one from Egypt who bought him said to his wife, "Make his residence comfortable. Perhaps he will benefit us, or we will adopt him as a son." And thus, We established Joseph in the land that We might teach him the interpretation of events. And Allah is predominant over His affair, but most of the people do not know.
17 الإسراء 111	وَقُلِ الْحَمْدُ لِلَّهِ الَّذِي لَمْ يَتَّخِذْ وَلَدًا وَلَمْ يَكُن لَّهُ شَرِيكٌ فِي الْمُلْكِ وَلَمْ يَكُن لَّهُ وَلِيٌّ مِّنَ الذُّلِّ ۖ وَكَبِّرْهُ تَكْبِيرًا
	And say, "Praise to Allah, who has not taken a son and has had no partner in [His] dominion and has no [need of a] protector out of weakness; and glorify Him with [great] glorification."
18 الكهف 4	وَيُنذِرَ الَّذِينَ قَالُوا اتَّخَذَ اللَّهُ وَلَدًا
	And to warn those who say, "Allah has taken a son."
39	وَلَوْلَا إِذْ دَخَلْتَ جَنَّتَكَ قُلْتَ مَا شَاءَ اللَّهُ لَا قُوَّةَ إِلَّا بِاللَّهِ ۚ إِن تَرَنِ أَنَا أَقَلَّ مِنكَ مَالًا وَوَلَدًا

		And why did you, when you entered your garden, not say, 'What Allah willed [has occurred]; there is no power except in Allah'? Although you see me less than you in wealth and children,
19 مريم	15	وَسَلَامٌ عَلَيْهِ يَوْمَ وُلِدَ وَيَوْمَ يَمُوتُ وَيَوْمَ يُبْعَثُ حَيًّا
		And peace be upon him the day he was born and the day he dies and the day he is raised alive.
	33	وَالسَّلَامُ عَلَيَّ يَوْمَ وُلِدتُّ وَيَوْمَ أَمُوتُ وَيَوْمَ أُبْعَثُ حَيًّا
		And peace is on me the day I was born and the day I will die and the day I am raised alive."
	35	مَا كَانَ لِلَّهِ أَن يَتَّخِذَ مِن وَلَدٍ ۖ سُبْحَانَهُ ۚ إِذَا قَضَىٰ أَمْرًا فَإِنَّمَا يَقُولُ لَهُ كُن فَيَكُونُ
		It is not [befitting] for Allah to take a son; exalted is He! When He decrees an affair, He only says to it, "Be," and it is.
	77	أَفَرَأَيْتَ الَّذِي كَفَرَ بِآيَاتِنَا وَقَالَ لَأُوتَيَنَّ مَالًا وَوَلَدًا
		Then, have you seen he who disbelieved in Our verses and said, "I will surely be given wealth and children [in the next life]?"
	88	وَقَالُوا اتَّخَذَ الرَّحْمَٰنُ وَلَدًا
		And they say, "The Most Merciful has taken [for Himself] a son."
	91	أَن دَعَوْا لِلرَّحْمَٰنِ وَلَدًا
		That they attribute to the Most Merciful a son.
	92	وَمَا يَنبَغِي لِلرَّحْمَٰنِ أَن يَتَّخِذَ وَلَدًا
		And it is not appropriate for the Most Merciful that He should take a son.
21 الأنبياء	26	وَقَالُوا اتَّخَذَ الرَّحْمَٰنُ وَلَدًا ۗ سُبْحَانَهُ ۚ بَلْ عِبَادٌ مُّكْرَمُونَ
		And they say, "The Most Merciful has taken a son." Exalted is He! Rather, they are [but] honored servants.

ما اتَّخَذَ اللَّهُ مِن وَلَدٍ وَمَا كَانَ مَعَهُ مِنْ إِلَٰهٍ ۚ إِذًا لَّذَهَبَ كُلُّ إِلَٰهٍ بِمَا خَلَقَ وَلَعَلَا بَعْضُهُمْ عَلَىٰ بَعْضٍ ۚ سُبْحَانَ اللَّهِ عَمَّا يَصِفُونَ	23 المؤمنون 91	
Allah has not taken any son, nor has there ever been with Him any deity. [If there had been], then each deity would have taken what it created, and some of them would have sought to overcome others. Exalted is Allah above what they describe [concerning Him].		
الَّذِي لَهُ مُلْكُ السَّمَاوَاتِ وَالْأَرْضِ وَلَمْ يَتَّخِذْ وَلَدًا وَلَمْ يَكُن لَّهُ شَرِيكٌ فِي الْمُلْكِ وَخَلَقَ كُلَّ شَيْءٍ فَقَدَّرَهُ تَقْدِيرًا	25 الفرقان 2	
He to whom belongs the dominion of the heavens and the earth and who has not taken a son and has not had a partner in dominion and has created each thing and determined it with [precise] determination.		
وَقَالَتِ امْرَأَتُ فِرْعَوْنَ قُرَّتُ عَيْنٍ لِّي وَلَكَ ۖ لَا تَقْتُلُوهُ عَسَىٰ أَن يَنفَعَنَا أَوْ نَتَّخِذَهُ وَلَدًا وَهُمْ لَا يَشْعُرُونَ	28 القصص 9	
And the wife of Pharaoh said, "[He will be] a comfort of the eye for me and for you. Do not kill him; perhaps he may benefit us, or we may adopt him as a son." And they perceived not		
يَا أَيُّهَا النَّاسُ اتَّقُوا رَبَّكُمْ وَاخْشَوْا يَوْمًا لَّا يَجْزِي وَالِدٌ عَن وَلَدِهِ وَلَا مَوْلُودٌ هُوَ جَازٍ عَن وَالِدِهِ شَيْئًا ۚ إِنَّ وَعْدَ اللَّهِ حَقٌّ ۖ فَلَا تَغُرَّنَّكُمُ الْحَيَاةُ الدُّنْيَا وَلَا يَغُرَّنَّكُم بِاللَّهِ الْغَرُورُ	31 لقمان 33	
O mankind, fear your Lord and fear a Day when no father will avail his son, nor will a son avail his father at all. Indeed, the promise of Allah is truth, so let not the worldly life delude you and be not deceived about Allah by the Deceiver.		
وَلَدَ اللَّهُ وَإِنَّهُمْ لَكَاذِبُونَ	37 الصافات 152	
" Allah has begotten," and indeed, they are liars.		
لَّوْ أَرَادَ اللَّهُ أَن يَتَّخِذَ وَلَدًا لَّاصْطَفَىٰ مِمَّا يَخْلُقُ مَا يَشَاءُ ۚ سُبْحَانَهُ ۖ هُوَ اللَّهُ الْوَاحِدُ الْقَهَّارُ	39 الزمر 4	
If Allah had intended to take a son, He could have chosen from what He creates whatever He willed. Exalted is He; He is Allah, the One, the Prevailing.		

43 الزخرف 81	قُلْ إِن كَانَ لِلرَّحْمَٰنِ وَلَدٌ فَأَنَا أَوَّلُ الْعَابِدِينَ
	Say, [O Muhammad], "If the Most Merciful had a son, then I would be the first of [his] worshippers."
56 الواقعة 17	يَطُوفُ عَلَيْهِمْ وِلْدَانٌ مُّخَلَّدُونَ
	There will circulate among them young boys made eternal
58 المجادلة 2	الَّذِينَ يُظَاهِرُونَ مِنكُم مِّن نِّسَائِهِم مَّا هُنَّ أُمَّهَاتِهِمْ ۖ إِنْ أُمَّهَاتُهُمْ إِلَّا اللَّائِي وَلَدْنَهُمْ ۚ وَإِنَّهُمْ لَيَقُولُونَ مُنكَرًا مِّنَ الْقَوْلِ وَزُورًا ۚ وَإِنَّ اللَّهَ لَعَفُوٌّ غَفُورٌ
	Those who pronounce thihar among you [to separate] from their wives - they are not [consequently] their mothers. Their mothers are none but those who gave birth to them. And indeed, they are saying an objectionable statement and a falsehood. But indeed, Allah is Pardoning and Forgiving.
71 نوح 21	قَالَ نُوحٌ رَّبِّ إِنَّهُمْ عَصَوْنِي وَاتَّبَعُوا مَن لَّمْ يَزِدْهُ مَالُهُ وَوَلَدُهُ إِلَّا خَسَارًا
	Noah said, "My Lord, indeed they have disobeyed me and followed him whose wealth and children will not increase him except in loss.
72 الجن 3	وَأَنَّهُ تَعَالَىٰ جَدُّ رَبِّنَا مَا اتَّخَذَ صَاحِبَةً وَلَا وَلَدًا
	And [it teaches] that exalted is the nobleness of our Lord; He has not taken a wife or a son
73 المزمل 17	فَكَيْفَ تَتَّقُونَ إِن كَفَرْتُمْ يَوْمًا يَجْعَلُ الْوِلْدَانَ شِيبًا
	Then how can you fear, if you disbelieve, a Day that will make the children white-haired?
76 الانسان 19	۞ وَيَطُوفُ عَلَيْهِمْ وِلْدَانٌ مُّخَلَّدُونَ إِذَا رَأَيْتَهُمْ حَسِبْتَهُمْ لُؤْلُؤًا مَّنثُورًا
	There will circulate among them young boys made eternal. When you see them, you would think them [as beautiful as] scattered pearls

وَوَالِدٍ وَمَا وَلَدَ		البلد 90 3
And [by] the father and that which was born [of him],		
لَمْ يَلِدْ وَلَمْ يُولَدْ		الإخلاص 112 3
He neither begets nor is born,		
أَوْلَادِكُمْ		Your children
۞ وَالْوَالِدَاتُ يُرْضِعْنَ **أَوْلَادَهُنَّ** حَوْلَيْنِ كَامِلَيْنِ ۖ لِمَنْ أَرَادَ أَن يُتِمَّ الرَّضَاعَةَ ۚ وَعَلَى **الْمَوْلُودِ** لَهُ رِزْقُهُنَّ وَكِسْوَتُهُنَّ بِالْمَعْرُوفِ ۚ لَا تُكَلَّفُ نَفْسٌ إِلَّا وُسْعَهَا ۚ لَا تُضَارَّ **وَالِدَةٌ بِوَلَدِهَا** وَلَا **مَوْلُودٌ لَّهُ بِوَلَدِهِ** ۚ وَعَلَى الْوَارِثِ مِثْلُ ذَٰلِكَ ۗ فَإِنْ أَرَادَا فِصَالًا عَن تَرَاضٍ مِّنْهُمَا وَتَشَاوُرٍ فَلَا جُنَاحَ عَلَيْهِمَا ۗ وَإِنْ أَرَدتُّمْ أَن تَسْتَرْضِعُوا **أَوْلَادَكُمْ** فَلَا جُنَاحَ عَلَيْكُمْ إِذَا سَلَّمْتُم مَّا آتَيْتُم بِالْمَعْرُوفِ ۗ وَاتَّقُوا اللَّهَ وَاعْلَمُوا أَنَّ اللَّهَ بِمَا تَعْمَلُونَ بَصِيرٌ		البقرة 2 233
Mothers may breastfeed their children two complete years for whoever wishes to complete the nursing [period]. Upon the father is the mothers' provision and their clothing according to what is acceptable. No person is charged with more than his capacity. No mother should be harmed through her child, and no father through his child. And upon the [father's] heir is [a duty] like that [of the father]. And if they both desire weaning through mutual consent from both of them and consultation, there is no blame upon either of them. And if you wish to have your children nursed by a substitute, there is no blame upon you as long as you give payment according to what is acceptable. And fear Allah and know that Allah is Seeing of what you do.		
يُوصِيكُمُ اللَّهُ فِي **أَوْلَادِكُمْ** ۖ لِلذَّكَرِ مِثْلُ حَظِّ **الْأُنثَيَيْنِ** ۚ فَإِن كُنَّ نِسَاءً فَوْقَ اثْنَتَيْنِ فَلَهُنَّ ثُلُثَا مَا تَرَكَ ۖ وَإِن كَانَتْ وَاحِدَةً فَلَهَا النِّصْفُ ۚ **وَلِأَبَوَيْهِ** لِكُلِّ وَاحِدٍ مِّنْهُمَا السُّدُسُ مِمَّا تَرَكَ إِن كَانَ لَهُ **وَلَدٌ** ۚ فَإِن لَّمْ يَكُن لَّهُ **وَلَدٌ** وَوَرِثَهُ **أَبَوَاهُ فَلِأُمِّهِ** الثُّلُثُ ۚ فَإِن كَانَ لَهُ **إِخْوَةٌ فَلِأُمِّهِ**		النساء 4 11

	السُّدُسُ ۚ مِن بَعْدِ وَصِيَّةٍ يُوصِي بِهَا أَوْ دَيْنٍ ۗ آبَاؤُكُمْ وَأَبْنَاؤُكُمْ لَا تَدْرُونَ أَيُّهُمْ أَقْرَبُ لَكُمْ نَفْعًا ۚ فَرِيضَةً مِّنَ اللَّهِ ۗ إِنَّ اللَّهَ كَانَ عَلِيمًا حَكِيمًا	
	Allah instructs you concerning your children: for the male, what is equal to the share of two females. But if there are [only] daughters, two or more, for them is two thirds of one's estate. And if there is only one, for her is half. And for one's parents, to each one of them is a sixth of his estate if he left children. But if he had no children and the parents [alone] inherit from him, then for his mother is one third. And if he had brothers [or sisters], for his mother is a sixth, after any bequest he [may have] made or debt. Your parents or your children - you know not which of them are nearest to you in benefit. [These shares are] an obligation [imposed] by Allah. Indeed, Allah is ever Knowing and Wise.	
6 الأنعام 151	قُلْ تَعَالَوْا أَتْلُ مَا حَرَّمَ رَبُّكُمْ عَلَيْكُمْ ۖ أَلَّا تُشْرِكُوا بِهِ شَيْئًا ۖ وَبِالْوَالِدَيْنِ إِحْسَانًا ۖ وَلَا تَقْتُلُوا أَوْلَادَكُم مِّنْ إِمْلَاقٍ ۖ نَّحْنُ نَرْزُقُكُمْ وَإِيَّاهُمْ ۖ وَلَا تَقْرَبُوا الْفَوَاحِشَ مَا ظَهَرَ مِنْهَا وَمَا بَطَنَ ۖ وَلَا تَقْتُلُوا النَّفْسَ الَّتِي حَرَّمَ اللَّهُ إِلَّا بِالْحَقِّ ۚ ذَٰلِكُمْ وَصَّاكُم بِهِ لَعَلَّكُمْ تَعْقِلُونَ	
	Say, "Come, I will recite what your Lord has prohibited to you. [He commands] that you not associate anything with Him, and to parents, good treatment, and do not kill your children out of poverty; We will provide for you and them. And do not approach immoralities - what is apparent of them and what is concealed. And do not kill the soul which Allah has forbidden [to be killed] except by [legal] right. This has He instructed you that you may use reason."	
8 الأنفال 28	وَاعْلَمُوا أَنَّمَا أَمْوَالُكُمْ وَأَوْلَادُكُمْ فِتْنَةٌ وَأَنَّ اللَّهَ عِندَهُ أَجْرٌ عَظِيمٌ	
	And know that your properties and your children are but a trial and that Allah has with Him a great reward.	
17 الإسراء 31	وَلَا تَقْتُلُوا أَوْلَادَكُمْ خَشْيَةَ إِمْلَاقٍ ۖ نَّحْنُ نَرْزُقُهُمْ وَإِيَّاكُمْ ۚ إِنَّ قَتْلَهُمْ كَانَ خِطْئًا كَبِيرًا	
	And do not kill your children for fear of poverty. We provide for them and for you. Indeed, their killing is ever a great sin.	
34 سبأ 37	وَمَا أَمْوَالُكُمْ وَلَا أَوْلَادُكُم بِالَّتِي تُقَرِّبُكُمْ عِندَنَا زُلْفَىٰ إِلَّا مَنْ آمَنَ وَعَمِلَ صَالِحًا فَأُولَٰئِكَ لَهُمْ جَزَاءُ الضِّعْفِ بِمَا عَمِلُوا وَهُمْ فِي الْغُرُفَاتِ آمِنُونَ	
	And it is not your wealth or your children that bring you nearer to Us in position, but it is [by being] one who has believed and done righteousness. For	

		them there will be the double reward for what they did, and they will be in the upper chambers [of Paradise], safe [and secure].
60 الممتحنة 3	لَن تَنفَعَكُمْ أَرْحَامُكُمْ وَلَا **أَوْلَادُكُمْ** ۚ يَوْمَ الْقِيَامَةِ يَفْصِلُ بَيْنَكُمْ ۚ وَاللَّهُ بِمَا تَعْمَلُونَ بَصِيرٌ	
	Never will your relatives or your children benefit you; the Day of Resurrection He will judge between you. And Allah, of what you do, is Seeing.	
63 المنافقون 9	يَا أَيُّهَا الَّذِينَ آمَنُوا لَا تُلْهِكُمْ **أَمْوَالُكُمْ** وَلَا **أَوْلَادُكُمْ** عَن ذِكْرِ اللَّهِ ۚ وَمَن يَفْعَلْ ذَٰلِكَ فَأُولَٰئِكَ هُمُ الْخَاسِرُونَ	
	O you who have believed, let not your wealth and your children divert you from remembrance of Allah. And whoever does that - then those are the losers.	
64 التغابن 14	يَا أَيُّهَا الَّذِينَ آمَنُوا إِنَّ مِنْ أَزْوَاجِكُمْ وَأَوْلَادِكُمْ **عَدُوًّا** لَّكُمْ فَاحْذَرُوهُمْ ۚ وَإِن تَعْفُوا وَتَصْفَحُوا وَتَغْفِرُوا فَإِنَّ اللَّهَ غَفُورٌ رَّحِيمٌ	
	O you who have believed, indeed, among your wives and your children are enemies to you, so beware of them. But if you pardon and overlook and forgive - then indeed, Allah is Forgiving and Merciful.	
15	إِنَّمَا أَمْوَالُكُمْ وَأَوْلَادُكُمْ **فِتْنَةٌ** ۚ وَاللَّهُ عِندَهُ أَجْرٌ عَظِيمٌ	
	Your wealth and your children are but a trial, and Allah has with Him a great reward.	
Children ...	أَوْلَادًا/ الْأَوْلَادِ/ أَوْلَادَهُنَّ/ أَوْلَادُهُم	
2 البقرة 233	وَالْوَالِدَاتُ يُرْضِعْنَ **أَوْلَادَهُنَّ** حَوْلَيْنِ كَامِلَيْنِ ۖ لِمَنْ أَرَادَ أَن يُتِمَّ الرَّضَاعَةَ ۚ وَعَلَى **الْمَوْلُودِ** لَهُ رِزْقُهُنَّ وَكِسْوَتُهُنَّ بِالْمَعْرُوفِ ۚ لَا تُكَلَّفُ نَفْسٌ إِلَّا وُسْعَهَا ۚ لَا تُضَارَّ وَالِدَةٌ **بِوَلَدِهَا** وَلَا **مَوْلُودٌ** لَّهُ **بِوَلَدِهِ** ۚ وَعَلَى الْوَارِثِ مِثْلُ ذَٰلِكَ ۗ فَإِنْ أَرَادَا فِصَالًا عَن تَرَاضٍ مِّنْهُمَا وَتَشَاوُرٍ فَلَا جُنَاحَ	

	عَلَيْهِمَا ۗ وَإِنْ أَرَدتُّمْ أَن تَسْتَرْضِعُوا **أَوْلَادَكُمْ** فَلَا جُنَاحَ عَلَيْكُمْ إِذَا سَلَّمْتُم مَّا آتَيْتُم بِالْمَعْرُوفِ ۗ وَاتَّقُوا اللَّهَ وَاعْلَمُوا أَنَّ اللَّهَ بِمَا تَعْمَلُونَ بَصِيرٌ
	Mothers may breastfeed their children two complete years for whoever wishes to complete the nursing [period]. Upon the father is the mothers' provision and their clothing according to what is acceptable. No person is charged with more than his capacity. No mother should be harmed through her child, and no father through his child. And upon the [father's] heir is [a duty] like that [of the father]. And if they both desire weaning through mutual consent from both of them and consultation, there is no blame upon either of them. And if you wish to have your children nursed by a substitute, there is no blame upon you as long as you give payment according to what is acceptable. And fear Allah and know that Allah is Seeing of what you do.
3 آل عمران 10	إِنَّ الَّذِينَ كَفَرُوا لَن تُغْنِيَ عَنْهُمْ أَمْوَالُهُمْ وَلَا **أَوْلَادُهُم** مِّنَ اللَّهِ شَيْئًا ۖ وَأُولَٰئِكَ هُمْ وَقُودُ النَّارِ
	Indeed, those who disbelieve - never will their wealth or their children avail them against Allah at all. And it is they who are fuel for the Fire.
116	إِنَّ الَّذِينَ كَفَرُوا لَن تُغْنِيَ عَنْهُمْ أَمْوَالُهُمْ وَلَا **أَوْلَادُهُم** مِّنَ اللَّهِ شَيْئًا ۖ وَأُولَٰئِكَ أَصْحَابُ النَّارِ ۚ هُمْ فِيهَا خَالِدُونَ
	Indeed, those who disbelieve - never will their wealth or their children avail them against Allah at all, and those are the companions of the Fire; they will abide therein eternally.
6 الأنعام 137	وَكَذَٰلِكَ زَيَّنَ لِكَثِيرٍ مِّنَ الْمُشْرِكِينَ قَتْلَ **أَوْلَادِهِمْ** شُرَكَاؤُهُمْ لِيُرْدُوهُمْ وَلِيَلْبِسُوا عَلَيْهِمْ دِينَهُمْ ۖ وَلَوْ شَاءَ اللَّهُ مَا فَعَلُوهُ ۖ فَذَرْهُمْ وَمَا يَفْتَرُونَ
	And likewise, to many of the polytheists their partners have made [to seem] pleasing the killing of their children in order to bring about their destruction and to cover them with confusion in their religion. And if Allah had willed, they would not have done so. So leave them and that which they invent.

140	قَدْ خَسِرَ الَّذِينَ قَتَلُوا أَوْلَادَهُمْ سَفَهًا بِغَيْرِ عِلْمٍ وَحَرَّمُوا مَا رَزَقَهُمُ اللَّهُ افْتِرَاءً عَلَى اللَّهِ ۚ قَدْ ضَلُّوا وَمَا كَانُوا مُهْتَدِينَ
	And likewise, to many of the polytheists their partners have made [to seem] pleasing the killing of their children in order to bring about their destruction and to cover them with confusion in their religion. And if Allah had willed, they would not have done so. So leave them and that which they invent.
9 التوبة 55	فَلَا تُعْجِبْكَ أَمْوَالُهُمْ وَلَا أَوْلَادُهُمْ ۚ إِنَّمَا يُرِيدُ اللَّهُ لِيُعَذِّبَهُم بِهَا فِي الْحَيَاةِ الدُّنْيَا وَتَزْهَقَ أَنفُسُهُمْ وَهُمْ كَافِرُونَ
	So let not their wealth or their children impress you. Allah only intends to punish them through them in worldly life and that their souls should depart [at death] while they are disbelievers.
85	وَلَا تُعْجِبْكَ أَمْوَالُهُمْ وَأَوْلَادُهُمْ ۚ إِنَّمَا يُرِيدُ اللَّهُ أَن يُعَذِّبَهُم بِهَا فِي الدُّنْيَا وَتَزْهَقَ أَنفُسُهُمْ وَهُمْ كَافِرُونَ
	And let not their wealth and their children impress you. Allah only intends to punish them through them in this world and that their souls should depart [at death] while they are disbelievers.
17 الإسراء 64	وَاسْتَفْزِزْ مَنِ اسْتَطَعْتَ مِنْهُم بِصَوْتِكَ وَأَجْلِبْ عَلَيْهِم بِخَيْلِكَ وَرَجِلِكَ وَشَارِكْهُمْ فِي الْأَمْوَالِ وَالْأَوْلَادِ وَعِدْهُمْ ۚ وَمَا يَعِدُهُمُ الشَّيْطَانُ إِلَّا غُرُورًا
	And incite [to senselessness] whoever you can among them with your voice and assault them with your horses and foot soldiers and become a partner in their wealth and their children and promise them." But Satan does not promise them except delusion.
34 سبأ 35	وَقَالُوا نَحْنُ أَكْثَرُ أَمْوَالًا وَأَوْلَادًا وَمَا نَحْنُ بِمُعَذَّبِينَ
	And they said, "We are more [than the believers] in wealth and children, and we are not to be punished."

57 الحديد 20	اعْلَمُوا أَنَّمَا الْحَيَاةُ الدُّنْيَا لَعِبٌ وَلَهْوٌ وَزِينَةٌ وَتَفَاخُرٌ بَيْنَكُمْ وَتَكَاثُرٌ فِي الْأَمْوَالِ وَالْأَوْلَادِ ۖ كَمَثَلِ غَيْثٍ أَعْجَبَ الْكُفَّارَ نَبَاتُهُ ثُمَّ يَهِيجُ فَتَرَاهُ مُصْفَرًّا ثُمَّ يَكُونُ حُطَامًا ۖ وَفِي الْآخِرَةِ عَذَابٌ شَدِيدٌ وَمَغْفِرَةٌ مِّنَ اللَّهِ وَرِضْوَانٌ ۚ وَمَا الْحَيَاةُ الدُّنْيَا إِلَّا مَتَاعُ الْغُرُورِ	
	Know that the life of this world is but amusement and diversion and adornment and boasting to one another and competition in increase of wealth and children - like the example of a rain whose [resulting] plant growth pleases the tillers; then it dries and you see it turned yellow; then it becomes [scattered] debris. And in the Hereafter is severe punishment and forgiveness from Allah and approval. And what is the worldly life except the enjoyment of delusion.	
58 المجادلة 17	لَّن تُغْنِيَ عَنْهُمْ أَمْوَالُهُمْ وَلَا أَوْلَادُهُم مِّنَ اللَّهِ شَيْئًا ۚ أُولَٰئِكَ أَصْحَابُ النَّارِ ۖ هُمْ فِيهَا خَالِدُونَ	
	Never will their wealth or their children avail them against Allah at all. Those are the companions of the Fire; they will abide therein eternally	
60 الممتحنة 12	يَا أَيُّهَا النَّبِيُّ إِذَا جَاءَكَ الْمُؤْمِنَاتُ يُبَايِعْنَكَ عَلَىٰ أَن لَّا يُشْرِكْنَ بِاللَّهِ شَيْئًا وَلَا يَسْرِقْنَ وَلَا يَزْنِينَ وَلَا يَقْتُلْنَ أَوْلَادَهُنَّ وَلَا يَأْتِينَ بِبُهْتَانٍ يَفْتَرِينَهُ بَيْنَ أَيْدِيهِنَّ وَأَرْجُلِهِنَّ وَلَا يَعْصِينَكَ فِي مَعْرُوفٍ ۙ فَبَايِعْهُنَّ وَاسْتَغْفِرْ لَهُنَّ اللَّهَ ۖ إِنَّ اللَّهَ غَفُورٌ رَّحِيمٌ	
	O Prophet, when the believing women come to you pledging to you that they will not associate anything with Allah, nor will they steal, nor will they commit unlawful sexual intercourse, nor will they kill their children, nor will they bring forth a slander they have invented between their arms and legs, nor will they disobey you in what is right - then accept their pledge and ask forgiveness for them of Allah. Indeed, Allah is Forgiving and Merciful.	
Parent	والد	
2 البقرة 83	وَإِذْ أَخَذْنَا مِيثَاقَ بَنِي إِسْرَائِيلَ لَا تَعْبُدُونَ إِلَّا اللَّهَ وَبِالْوَالِدَيْنِ إِحْسَانًا وَذِي الْقُرْبَىٰ وَالْيَتَامَىٰ وَالْمَسَاكِينِ وَقُولُوا لِلنَّاسِ حُسْنًا وَأَقِيمُوا الصَّلَاةَ وَآتُوا الزَّكَاةَ ثُمَّ تَوَلَّيْتُمْ إِلَّا قَلِيلًا مِّنكُمْ وَأَنتُم مُّعْرِضُونَ	

	And [recall] when We took the covenant from the Children of Israel, [enjoining upon them], "Do not worship except Allah; and to parents do good and to relatives, orphans, and the needy. And speak to people good [words] and establish prayer and give zakah." Then you turned away, except a few of you, and you were refusing.
180	كُتِبَ عَلَيْكُمْ إِذَا حَضَرَ أَحَدَكُمُ الْمَوْتُ إِن تَرَكَ خَيْرًا الْوَصِيَّةُ **لِلْوَالِدَيْنِ وَالْأَقْرَبِينَ** بِالْمَعْرُوفِ ۖ حَقًّا عَلَى الْمُتَّقِينَ
	Prescribed for you when death approaches [any] one of you if he leaves wealth [is that he should make] a bequest for the parents and near relatives according to what is acceptable - a duty upon the righteous.
215	يَسْأَلُونَكَ مَاذَا يُنفِقُونَ ۖ قُلْ مَا أَنفَقْتُم مِّنْ خَيْرٍ فَ**لِلْوَالِدَيْنِ وَالْأَقْرَبِينَ** وَالْيَتَامَىٰ وَالْمَسَاكِينِ وَابْنِ السَّبِيلِ ۗ وَمَا تَفْعَلُوا مِنْ خَيْرٍ فَإِنَّ اللَّهَ بِهِ عَلِيمٌ
	They ask you, [O Muhammad], what they should spend. Say, "Whatever you spend of good is [to be] for parents and relatives and orphans and the needy and the traveler. And whatever you do of good - indeed, Allah is Knowing of it."
233	۞ **وَالْوَالِدَاتُ** يُرْضِعْنَ **أَوْلَادَهُنَّ** حَوْلَيْنِ كَامِلَيْنِ ۖ لِمَنْ أَرَادَ أَن يُتِمَّ الرَّضَاعَةَ ۚ وَعَلَى **الْمَوْلُودِ لَهُ** رِزْقُهُنَّ وَكِسْوَتُهُنَّ بِالْمَعْرُوفِ ۚ لَا تُكَلَّفُ نَفْسٌ إِلَّا وُسْعَهَا ۚ لَا تُضَارَّ **وَالِدَةٌ بِوَلَدِهَا وَلَا مَوْلُودٌ لَّهُ بِوَلَدِهِ** ۚ وَعَلَى الْوَارِثِ مِثْلُ ذَٰلِكَ ۗ فَإِنْ أَرَادَا فِصَالًا عَن تَرَاضٍ مِّنْهُمَا وَتَشَاوُرٍ فَلَا جُنَاحَ عَلَيْهِمَا ۗ وَإِنْ أَرَدتُّمْ أَن تَسْتَرْضِعُوا **أَوْلَادَكُمْ** فَلَا جُنَاحَ عَلَيْكُمْ إِذَا سَلَّمْتُم مَّا آتَيْتُم بِالْمَعْرُوفِ ۗ وَاتَّقُوا اللَّهَ وَاعْلَمُوا أَنَّ اللَّهَ بِمَا تَعْمَلُونَ بَصِيرٌ
	Mothers may breastfeed their children two complete years for whoever wishes to complete the nursing [period]. Upon the father is the mothers' provision and their clothing according to what is acceptable. No person is charged with more than his capacity. No mother should be harmed through her child, and no father through his child. And upon the [father's] heir is [a duty] like that [of the father]. And if they both desire weaning through mutual consent from both of them and consultation, there is no blame upon either of them. And if you wish to have your children nursed by a substitute, there is no blame upon you as long as you give payment according to what is acceptable. And fear Allah and know that Allah is Seeing of what you do.

4 النساء 7	لِلرِّجَالِ نَصِيبٌ مِّمَّا تَرَكَ **الْوَالِدَانِ وَالْأَقْرَبُونَ** وَلِلنِّسَاءِ نَصِيبٌ مِّمَّا تَرَكَ **الْوَالِدَانِ وَالْأَقْرَبُونَ** مِمَّا قَلَّ مِنْهُ أَوْ كَثُرَ ۚ نَصِيبًا مَّفْرُوضًا	
	For men is a share of what the parents and close relatives leave, and for women is a share of what the parents and close relatives leave, be it little or much - an obligatory share.	
33	وَلِكُلٍّ جَعَلْنَا مَوَالِيَ مِمَّا تَرَكَ **الْوَالِدَانِ وَالْأَقْرَبُونَ** ۚ وَالَّذِينَ عَقَدَتْ أَيْمَانُكُمْ فَآتُوهُمْ نَصِيبَهُمْ ۚ إِنَّ اللَّهَ كَانَ عَلَىٰ كُلِّ شَيْءٍ شَهِيدًا	
	And for all, We have made heirs to what is left by parents and relatives. And to those whom your oaths have bound [to you] - give them their share. Indeed Allah is ever, over all things, a Witness.	
36	وَاعْبُدُوا اللَّهَ وَلَا تُشْرِكُوا بِهِ شَيْئًا ۖ **وَبِالْوَالِدَيْنِ** إِحْسَانًا وَبِذِي **الْقُرْبَىٰ** وَالْيَتَامَىٰ وَالْمَسَاكِينِ وَالْجَارِ ذِي **الْقُرْبَىٰ** وَالْجَارِ الْجُنُبِ وَالصَّاحِبِ بِالْجَنبِ وَابْنِ السَّبِيلِ وَمَا مَلَكَتْ أَيْمَانُكُمْ ۗ إِنَّ اللَّهَ لَا يُحِبُّ مَن كَانَ مُخْتَالًا فَخُورًا	
	Worship Allah and associate nothing with Him, and to parents do good, and to relatives, orphans, the needy, the near neighbor, the neighbor farther away, the companion at your side, the traveler, and those whom your right hands possess. Indeed, Allah does not like those who are self-deluding and boastful	
135	يَا أَيُّهَا الَّذِينَ آمَنُوا كُونُوا قَوَّامِينَ **بِالْقِسْطِ** شُهَدَاءَ لِلَّهِ وَلَوْ عَلَىٰ أَنفُسِكُمْ أَوِ **الْوَالِدَيْنِ وَالْأَقْرَبِينَ** ۚ إِن يَكُنْ **غَنِيًّا** أَوْ **فَقِيرًا** فَاللَّهُ أَوْلَىٰ بِهِمَا ۖ فَلَا تَتَّبِعُوا **الْهَوَىٰ** أَن تَعْدِلُوا ۚ وَإِن تَلْوُوا أَوْ تُعْرِضُوا فَإِنَّ اللَّهَ كَانَ بِمَا تَعْمَلُونَ خَبِيرًا	
	O you who have believed, be persistently standing firm in justice, witnesses for Allah, even if it be against yourselves or parents and relatives. Whether one is rich or poor, Allah is more worthy of both. So follow not [personal] inclination, lest you not be just. And if you distort [your testimony] or refuse [to give it], then indeed Allah is ever, with what you do, Acquainted.	
5 المائدة 110	إِذْ قَالَ اللَّهُ يَا عِيسَى **ابْنَ** مَرْيَمَ اذْكُرْ نِعْمَتِي عَلَيْكَ وَعَلَىٰ **وَالِدَتِكَ** إِذْ أَيَّدتُّكَ بِرُوحِ الْقُدُسِ تُكَلِّمُ النَّاسَ فِي الْمَهْدِ وَكَهْلًا ۖ وَإِذْ عَلَّمْتُكَ الْكِتَابَ وَالْحِكْمَةَ وَالتَّوْرَاةَ وَالْإِنجِيلَ ۖ وَإِذْ تَخْلُقُ مِنَ الطِّينِ كَهَيْئَةِ الطَّيْرِ بِإِذْنِي فَتَنفُخُ فِيهَا فَتَكُونُ طَيْرًا بِإِذْنِي ۖ وَتُبْرِئُ الْأَكْمَهَ وَالْأَبْرَصَ بِإِذْنِي ۖ وَإِذْ تُخْرِجُ الْمَوْتَىٰ بِإِذْنِي ۖ وَإِذْ كَفَفْتُ **بَنِي** إِسْرَائِيلَ عَنكَ إِذْ جِئْتَهُم بِالْبَيِّنَاتِ فَقَالَ الَّذِينَ كَفَرُوا مِنْهُمْ إِنْ هَٰذَا إِلَّا سِحْرٌ مُّبِينٌ	

	[The Day] when Allah will say, "O Jesus, Son of Mary, remember My favor upon you and upon your mother when I supported you with the Pure Spirit and you spoke to the people in the cradle and in maturity; and [remember] when I taught you writing and wisdom and the Torah and the Gospel; and when you designed from clay [what was] like the form of a bird with My permission, then you breathed into it, and it became a bird with My permission; and you healed the blind and the leper with My permission; and when you brought forth the dead with My permission; and when I restrained the Children of Israel from [killing] you when you came to them with clear proofs and those who disbelieved among them said, "This is not but obvious magic."
6 الأنعام 151	﴿ قُلْ تَعَالَوْا أَتْلُ مَا حَرَّمَ رَبُّكُمْ عَلَيْكُمْ ۖ أَلَّا تُشْرِكُوا بِهِ شَيْئًا ۖ وَبِالْوَالِدَيْنِ إِحْسَانًا ۖ وَلَا تَقْتُلُوا أَوْلَادَكُم مِّنْ إِمْلَاقٍ ۖ نَّحْنُ نَرْزُقُكُمْ وَإِيَّاهُمْ ۖ وَلَا تَقْرَبُوا الْفَوَاحِشَ مَا ظَهَرَ مِنْهَا وَمَا بَطَنَ ۖ وَلَا تَقْتُلُوا النَّفْسَ الَّتِي حَرَّمَ اللَّهُ إِلَّا بِالْحَقِّ ۚ ذَٰلِكُمْ وَصَّاكُم بِهِ لَعَلَّكُمْ تَعْقِلُونَ ﴾
	Say, "Come, I will recite what your Lord has prohibited to you. [He commands] that you not associate anything with Him, and to parents, good treatment, and do not kill your children out of poverty; We will provide for you and them. And do not approach immoralities - what is apparent of them and what is concealed. And do not kill the soul which Allah has forbidden [to be killed] except by [legal] right. This has He instructed you that you may use reason."
14 ابراهيم 41	رَبَّنَا اغْفِرْ لِي وَلِوَالِدَيَّ وَلِلْمُؤْمِنِينَ يَوْمَ يَقُومُ الْحِسَابُ
	Our Lord, forgive me and my parents and the believers the Day the account is established."
17 الإسراء 23	﴿ وَقَضَىٰ رَبُّكَ أَلَّا تَعْبُدُوا إِلَّا إِيَّاهُ وَبِالْوَالِدَيْنِ إِحْسَانًا ۚ إِمَّا يَبْلُغَنَّ عِندَكَ الْكِبَرَ أَحَدُهُمَا أَوْ كِلَاهُمَا فَلَا تَقُل لَّهُمَا أُفٍّ وَلَا تَنْهَرْهُمَا وَقُل لَّهُمَا قَوْلًا كَرِيمًا ﴾
	And your Lord has decreed that you not worship except Him, and to parents, good treatment. Whether one or both of them reach old age [while] with you, say not to them [so much as], "uff," and do not repel them but speak to them a noble word.

19 مريم 14	وَبَرًّا بِوَالِدَيْهِ وَلَمْ يَكُن جَبَّارًا عَصِيًّا	
	And dutiful to his parents, and he was not a disobedient tyrant.	
32	وَبَرًّا بِوَالِدَتِي وَلَمْ يَجْعَلْنِي جَبَّارًا شَقِيًّا	
	And [made me] dutiful to my mother, and He has not made me a wretched tyrant.	
27 النمل 19	فَتَبَسَّمَ ضَاحِكًا مِّن قَوْلِهَا وَقَالَ رَبِّ أَوْزِعْنِي أَنْ أَشْكُرَ نِعْمَتَكَ الَّتِي أَنْعَمْتَ عَلَيَّ وَعَلَىٰ وَالِدَيَّ وَأَنْ أَعْمَلَ صَالِحًا تَرْضَاهُ وَأَدْخِلْنِي بِرَحْمَتِكَ فِي عِبَادِكَ الصَّالِحِينَ	
	So [Solomon] smiled, amused at her speech, and said, "My Lord, enable me to be grateful for Your favor which You have bestowed upon me and upon my parents and to do righteousness of which You approve. And admit me by Your mercy into [the ranks of] Your righteous servants."	
29 العنكبوت 8	وَوَصَّيْنَا الْإِنسَانَ بِوَالِدَيْهِ حُسْنًا ۖ وَإِن جَاهَدَاكَ لِتُشْرِكَ بِي مَا لَيْسَ لَكَ بِهِ عِلْمٌ فَلَا تُطِعْهُمَا ۚ إِلَيَّ مَرْجِعُكُمْ فَأُنَبِّئُكُم بِمَا كُنتُمْ تَعْمَلُونَ	
	And We have enjoined upon man goodness to parents. But if they endeavor to make you associate with Me that of which you have no knowledge, do not obey them. To Me is your return, and I will inform you about what you used to do.	
31 لقمان 14	وَوَصَّيْنَا الْإِنسَانَ بِوَالِدَيْهِ حَمَلَتْهُ أُمُّهُ وَهْنًا عَلَىٰ وَهْنٍ وَفِصَالُهُ فِي عَامَيْنِ أَنِ اشْكُرْ لِي وَلِوَالِدَيْكَ إِلَيَّ الْمَصِيرُ	
	And We have enjoined upon man [care] for his parents. His mother carried him, [increasing her] in weakness upon weakness, and his weaning is in two years. Be grateful to Me and to your parents; to Me is the [final] destination.	
33	يَا أَيُّهَا النَّاسُ اتَّقُوا رَبَّكُمْ وَاخْشَوْا يَوْمًا لَّا يَجْزِي وَالِدٌ عَن وَلَدِهِ وَلَا مَوْلُودٌ هُوَ جَازٍ عَن وَالِدِهِ شَيْئًا ۚ إِنَّ وَعْدَ اللَّهِ حَقٌّ ۖ فَلَا تَغُرَّنَّكُمُ الْحَيَاةُ الدُّنْيَا وَلَا يَغُرَّنَّكُم بِاللَّهِ الْغَرُورُ	
	O mankind, fear your Lord and fear a Day when no father will avail his son, nor will a son avail his father at all. Indeed, the promise of Allah is truth, so let not the worldly life delude you and be not deceived about Allah by the Deceiver.	

46 الأحقاف 15	وَوَصَّيْنَا الْإِنسَانَ بِوَالِدَيْهِ إِحْسَانًا ۖ حَمَلَتْهُ أُمُّهُ كُرْهًا وَوَضَعَتْهُ كُرْهًا ۖ وَحَمْلُهُ وَفِصَالُهُ ثَلَاثُونَ شَهْرًا ۚ حَتَّىٰ إِذَا بَلَغَ أَشُدَّهُ وَبَلَغَ أَرْبَعِينَ سَنَةً قَالَ رَبِّ أَوْزِعْنِي أَنْ أَشْكُرَ نِعْمَتَكَ الَّتِي أَنْعَمْتَ عَلَيَّ وَعَلَىٰ وَالِدَيَّ وَأَنْ أَعْمَلَ صَالِحًا تَرْضَاهُ وَأَصْلِحْ لِي فِي ذُرِّيَّتِي ۖ إِنِّي تُبْتُ إِلَيْكَ وَإِنِّي مِنَ الْمُسْلِمِينَ	
	And We have enjoined upon man, to his parents, good treatment. His mother carried him with hardship and gave birth to him with hardship, and his gestation and weaning [period] is thirty months. [He grows] until, when he reaches maturity and reaches [the age of] forty years, he says, "My Lord, enable me to be grateful for Your favor which You have bestowed upon me and upon my parents and to work righteousness of which You will approve and make righteous for me my offspring. Indeed, I have repented to You, and indeed, I am of the Muslims."	
17	وَالَّذِي قَالَ لِوَالِدَيْهِ أُفٍّ لَّكُمَا أَتَعِدَانِنِي أَنْ أُخْرَجَ وَقَدْ خَلَتِ الْقُرُونُ مِن قَبْلِي وَهُمَا يَسْتَغِيثَانِ اللَّهَ وَيْلَكَ آمِنْ إِنَّ وَعْدَ اللَّهِ حَقٌّ فَيَقُولُ مَا هَٰذَا إِلَّا أَسَاطِيرُ الْأَوَّلِينَ	
	But one who says to his parents, "Uff to you; do you promise me that I will be brought forth [from the earth] when generations before me have already passed on [into oblivion]?" while they call to Allah for help [and to their son], "Woe to you! Believe! Indeed, the promise of Allah is truth." But he says, "This is not but legends of the former people"	
71 نوح 28	رَبِّ اغْفِرْ لِي وَلِوَالِدَيَّ وَلِمَن دَخَلَ بَيْتِيَ مُؤْمِنًا وَلِلْمُؤْمِنِينَ وَالْمُؤْمِنَاتِ وَلَا تَزِدِ الظَّالِمِينَ إِلَّا تَبَارًا	
	My Lord, forgive me and my parents and whoever enters my house a believer and the believing men and believing women. And do not increase the wrongdoers except in destruction."	
90 البلد 3	وَوَالِدٍ وَمَا وَلَدَ	
	And [by] the father and that which was born [of him],	

The Brother/his	الأَخ / أَخِيهِ	
2 البقرة 178	يَا أَيُّهَا الَّذِينَ آمَنُوا كُتِبَ عَلَيْكُمُ الْقِصَاصُ فِي الْقَتْلَى ۖ الْحُرُّ بِالْحُرِّ وَالْعَبْدُ بِالْعَبْدِ وَالْأُنثَىٰ بِالْأُنثَىٰ ۚ فَمَنْ عُفِيَ لَهُ مِنْ أَخِيهِ شَيْءٌ فَاتِّبَاعٌ بِالْمَعْرُوفِ وَأَدَاءٌ إِلَيْهِ بِإِحْسَانٍ ۗ ذَٰلِكَ تَخْفِيفٌ مِّن رَّبِّكُمْ وَرَحْمَةٌ ۗ فَمَنِ اعْتَدَىٰ بَعْدَ ذَٰلِكَ فَلَهُ عَذَابٌ أَلِيمٌ	
	O you who have believed, prescribed for you is legal retribution for those murdered - the free for the free, the slave for the slave, and the female for the female. But whoever overlooks from his brother anything, then there should be a suitable follow-up and payment to him with good conduct. This is an alleviation from your Lord and a mercy. But whoever transgresses after that will have a painful punishment.	
4 النساء 11	يُوصِيكُمُ اللَّهُ فِي أَوْلَادِكُمْ ۖ لِلذَّكَرِ مِثْلُ حَظِّ الْأُنثَيَيْنِ ۚ فَإِن كُنَّ نِسَاءً فَوْقَ اثْنَتَيْنِ فَلَهُنَّ ثُلُثَا مَا تَرَكَ ۖ وَإِن كَانَتْ وَاحِدَةً فَلَهَا النِّصْفُ ۚ وَلِأَبَوَيْهِ لِكُلِّ وَاحِدٍ مِّنْهُمَا السُّدُسُ مِمَّا تَرَكَ إِن كَانَ لَهُ وَلَدٌ ۚ فَإِن لَّمْ يَكُن لَّهُ وَلَدٌ وَوَرِثَهُ أَبَوَاهُ فَلِأُمِّهِ الثُّلُثُ ۚ فَإِن كَانَ لَهُ إِخْوَةٌ فَلِأُمِّهِ السُّدُسُ ۚ مِن بَعْدِ وَصِيَّةٍ يُوصِي بِهَا أَوْ دَيْنٍ ۗ آبَاؤُكُمْ وَأَبْنَاؤُكُمْ لَا تَدْرُونَ أَيُّهُمْ أَقْرَبُ لَكُمْ نَفْعًا ۚ فَرِيضَةً مِّنَ اللَّهِ ۗ إِنَّ اللَّهَ كَانَ عَلِيمًا حَكِيمًا	
	Allah instructs you concerning your children: for the male, what is equal to the share of two females. But if there are [only] daughters, two or more, for them is two thirds of one's estate. And if there is only one, for her is half. And for one's parents, to each one of them is a sixth of his estate if he left children. But if he had no children and the parents [alone] inherit from him, then for his mother is one third. And if he had brothers [or sisters], for his mother is a sixth, after any bequest he [may have] made or debt. Your parents or your children - you know not which of them are nearest to you in benefit. [These shares are] an obligation [imposed] by Allah. Indeed, Allah is ever Knowing and Wise.	
12	وَلَكُمْ نِصْفُ مَا تَرَكَ أَزْوَاجُكُمْ إِن لَّمْ يَكُن لَّهُنَّ وَلَدٌ ۚ فَإِن كَانَ لَهُنَّ وَلَدٌ فَلَكُمُ الرُّبُعُ مِمَّا تَرَكْنَ ۚ مِن بَعْدِ وَصِيَّةٍ يُوصِينَ بِهَا أَوْ دَيْنٍ ۚ وَلَهُنَّ الرُّبُعُ مِمَّا تَرَكْتُمْ إِن لَّمْ يَكُن لَّكُمْ وَلَدٌ ۚ فَإِن كَانَ لَكُمْ وَلَدٌ فَلَهُنَّ الثُّمُنُ مِمَّا تَرَكْتُم ۚ مِّن بَعْدِ وَصِيَّةٍ تُوصُونَ بِهَا أَوْ دَيْنٍ ۗ وَإِن كَانَ رَجُلٌ يُورَثُ كَلَالَةً أَوِ امْرَأَةٌ وَلَهُ أَخٌ أَوْ أُخْتٌ فَلِكُلِّ وَاحِدٍ مِّنْهُمَا السُّدُسُ ۚ فَإِن كَانُوا أَكْثَرَ مِن ذَٰلِكَ فَهُمْ شُرَكَاءُ فِي الثُّلُثِ ۚ مِن بَعْدِ وَصِيَّةٍ يُوصَىٰ بِهَا أَوْ دَيْنٍ غَيْرَ مُضَارٍّ ۚ وَصِيَّةً مِّنَ اللَّهِ ۗ وَاللَّهُ عَلِيمٌ حَلِيمٌ	
	And for you is half of what your wives leave if they have no child. But if they have a child, for you is one fourth of what they leave, after any bequest they	

	[may have] made or debt. And for the wives is one fourth if you leave no child. But if you leave a child, then for them is an eighth of what you leave, after any bequest you [may have] made or debt. And if a man or woman leaves neither ascendants nor descendants but has a brother or a sister, then for each one of them is a sixth. But if they are more than two, they share a third, after any bequest which was made or debt, as long as there is no detriment [caused]. [This is] an ordinance from Allah, and Allah is Knowing and Forbearing.
23	حُرِّمَتْ عَلَيْكُمْ أُمَّهَاتُكُمْ وَبَنَاتُكُمْ وَأَخَوَاتُكُمْ وَعَمَّاتُكُمْ وَخَالَاتُكُمْ وَبَنَاتُ الْأَخِ وَبَنَاتُ الْأُخْتِ وَأُمَّهَاتُكُمُ اللَّاتِي أَرْضَعْنَكُمْ وَأَخَوَاتُكُم مِّنَ الرَّضَاعَةِ وَأُمَّهَاتُ نِسَائِكُمْ وَرَبَائِبُكُمُ اللَّاتِي فِي حُجُورِكُم مِّن نِّسَائِكُمُ اللَّاتِي دَخَلْتُم بِهِنَّ فَإِن لَّمْ تَكُونُوا دَخَلْتُم بِهِنَّ فَلَا جُنَاحَ عَلَيْكُمْ وَحَلَائِلُ أَبْنَائِكُمُ الَّذِينَ مِنْ أَصْلَابِكُمْ وَأَن تَجْمَعُوا بَيْنَ الْأُخْتَيْنِ إِلَّا مَا قَدْ سَلَفَ ۗ إِنَّ اللَّهَ كَانَ غَفُورًا رَّحِيمًا
	Prohibited to you [for marriage] are your mothers, your daughters, your sisters, your father's sisters, your mother's sisters, your brother's daughters, your sister's daughters, your [milk] mothers who nursed you, your sisters through nursing, your wives' mothers, and your step-daughters under your guardianship [born] of your wives unto whom you have gone in. But if you have not gone in unto them, there is no sin upon you. And [also prohibited are] the wives of your sons who are from your [own] loins, and that you take [in marriage] two sisters simultaneously, except for what has already occurred. Indeed, Allah is ever Forgiving and Merciful.
176	يَسْتَفْتُونَكَ قُلِ اللَّهُ يُفْتِيكُمْ فِي الْكَلَالَةِ ۚ إِنِ امْرُؤٌ هَلَكَ لَيْسَ لَهُ وَلَدٌ وَلَهُ أُخْتٌ فَلَهَا نِصْفُ مَا تَرَكَ ۚ وَهُوَ يَرِثُهَا إِن لَّمْ يَكُن لَّهَا وَلَدٌ ۚ فَإِن كَانَتَا اثْنَتَيْنِ فَلَهُمَا الثُّلُثَانِ مِمَّا تَرَكَ ۚ وَإِن كَانُوا إِخْوَةً رِّجَالًا وَنِسَاءً فَلِلذَّكَرِ مِثْلُ حَظِّ الْأُنثَيَيْنِ ۗ يُبَيِّنُ اللَّهُ لَكُمْ أَن تَضِلُّوا ۗ وَاللَّهُ بِكُلِّ شَيْءٍ عَلِيمٌ
	They request from you a [legal] ruling. Say, "Allah gives you a ruling concerning one having neither descendants nor ascendants [as heirs]." If a man dies, leaving no child but [only] a sister, she will have half of what he left. And he inherits from her if she [dies and] has no child. But if there are two sisters [or more], they will have two-thirds of what he left. If there are both brothers and sisters, the male will have the share of two females. Allah makes clear to you [His law], lest you go astray. And Allah is Knowing of all things.

5 المائدة 25	قَالَ رَبِّ إِنِّي لَا أَمْلِكُ إِلَّا نَفْسِي وَأَخِي ۖ فَافْرُقْ بَيْنَنَا وَبَيْنَ الْقَوْمِ الْفَاسِقِينَ
	[Moses] said, "My Lord, indeed I do not possess except myself and my brother, so part us from the defiantly disobedient people."
30	فَطَوَّعَتْ لَهُ نَفْسُهُ قَتْلَ أَخِيهِ فَقَتَلَهُ فَأَصْبَحَ مِنَ الْخَاسِرِينَ
	And his soul permitted to him the murder of his brother, so he killed him and became among the losers.
31	فَبَعَثَ اللَّهُ غُرَابًا يَبْحَثُ فِي الْأَرْضِ لِيُرِيَهُ كَيْفَ يُوَارِي سَوْءَةَ أَخِيهِ ۚ قَالَ يَا وَيْلَتَىٰ أَعَجَزْتُ أَنْ أَكُونَ مِثْلَ هَٰذَا الْغُرَابِ فَأُوَارِيَ سَوْءَةَ أَخِي ۖ فَأَصْبَحَ مِنَ النَّادِمِينَ
	Then Allah sent a crow searching in the ground to show him how to hide the disgrace of his brother. He said, "O woe to me! Have I failed to be like this crow and hide the body of my brother?" And he became of the regretful.
6 الأنعام 87	وَمِنْ آبَائِهِمْ وَذُرِّيَّاتِهِمْ وَإِخْوَانِهِمْ ۖ وَاجْتَبَيْنَاهُمْ وَهَدَيْنَاهُمْ إِلَىٰ صِرَاطٍ مُّسْتَقِيمٍ
	And [some] among their fathers and their descendants and their brothers - and We chose them and We guided them to a straight path.
Sister/s	أُخْتٌ/ الأُخْتِ/ الأُخْتَيْنِ/ أُخْتَهَا
4 النساء 12	وَلَكُمْ نِصْفُ مَا تَرَكَ أَزْوَاجُكُمْ إِن لَّمْ يَكُن لَّهُنَّ وَلَدٌ ۚ فَإِن كَانَ لَهُنَّ وَلَدٌ فَلَكُمُ الرُّبُعُ مِمَّا تَرَكْنَ ۚ مِن بَعْدِ وَصِيَّةٍ يُوصِينَ بِهَا أَوْ دَيْنٍ ۚ وَلَهُنَّ الرُّبُعُ مِمَّا تَرَكْتُمْ إِن لَّمْ يَكُن لَّكُمْ وَلَدٌ ۚ فَإِن كَانَ لَكُمْ وَلَدٌ فَلَهُنَّ الثُّمُنُ مِمَّا تَرَكْتُم ۚ مِّن بَعْدِ وَصِيَّةٍ تُوصُونَ بِهَا أَوْ دَيْنٍ ۗ وَإِن كَانَ رَجُلٌ يُورَثُ كَلَالَةً أَوِ امْرَأَةٌ وَلَهُ أَخٌ أَوْ أُخْتٌ فَلِكُلِّ وَاحِدٍ مِّنْهُمَا السُّدُسُ ۚ فَإِن كَانُوا أَكْثَرَ مِن ذَٰلِكَ فَهُمْ شُرَكَاءُ فِي الثُّلُثِ ۚ مِن بَعْدِ وَصِيَّةٍ يُوصَىٰ بِهَا أَوْ دَيْنٍ غَيْرَ مُضَارٍّ ۚ وَصِيَّةً مِّنَ اللَّهِ ۗ وَاللَّهُ عَلِيمٌ حَلِيمٌ
	And for you is half of what your wives leave if they have no child. But if they have a child, for you is one fourth of what they leave, after any bequest they [may have] made or debt. And for the wives is one fourth if you leave no child. But if you leave a child, then for them is an eighth of what you leave, after any bequest you [may have] made or debt. And if a man or woman leaves neither ascendants nor descendants but has a brother or a sister, then for each one of them is a sixth. But if they are more than two, they share a third, after

	any bequest which was made or debt, as long as there is no detriment [caused]. [This is] an ordinance from Allah, and Allah is Knowing and Forbearing.
23	حُرِّمَتْ عَلَيْكُمْ أُمَّهَاتُكُمْ وَبَنَاتُكُمْ وَأَخَوَاتُكُمْ وَعَمَّاتُكُمْ وَخَالَاتُكُمْ وَبَنَاتُ الْأَخِ وَبَنَاتُ الْأُخْتِ وَأُمَّهَاتُكُمُ اللَّاتِي أَرْضَعْنَكُمْ وَأَخَوَاتُكُم مِّنَ الرَّضَاعَةِ وَأُمَّهَاتُ نِسَائِكُمْ وَرَبَائِبُكُمُ اللَّاتِي فِي حُجُورِكُم مِّن نِّسَائِكُمُ اللَّاتِي دَخَلْتُم بِهِنَّ فَإِن لَّمْ تَكُونُوا دَخَلْتُم بِهِنَّ فَلَا جُنَاحَ عَلَيْكُمْ وَحَلَائِلُ أَبْنَائِكُمُ الَّذِينَ مِنْ أَصْلَابِكُمْ وَأَن تَجْمَعُوا بَيْنَ الْأُخْتَيْنِ إِلَّا مَا قَدْ سَلَفَ ۗ إِنَّ اللَّهَ كَانَ غَفُورًا رَّحِيمًا
	Prohibited to you [for marriage] are your mothers, your daughters, your sisters, your father's sisters, your mother's sisters, your brother's daughters, your sister's daughters, your [milk] mothers who nursed you, your sisters through nursing, your wives' mothers, and your step-daughters under your guardianship [born] of your wives unto whom you have gone in. But if you have not gone in unto them, there is no sin upon you. And [also prohibited are] the wives of your sons who are from your [own] loins, and that you take [in marriage] two sisters simultaneously, except for what has already occurred. Indeed, Allah is ever Forgiving and Merciful.
176	يَسْتَفْتُونَكَ قُلِ اللَّهُ يُفْتِيكُمْ فِي الْكَلَالَةِ ۚ إِنِ امْرُؤٌ هَلَكَ لَيْسَ لَهُ وَلَدٌ وَلَهُ أُخْتٌ فَلَهَا نِصْفُ مَا تَرَكَ ۚ وَهُوَ يَرِثُهَا إِن لَّمْ يَكُن لَّهَا وَلَدٌ ۚ فَإِن كَانَتَا اثْنَتَيْنِ فَلَهُمَا الثُّلُثَانِ مِمَّا تَرَكَ ۚ وَإِن كَانُوا إِخْوَةً رِّجَالًا وَنِسَاءً فَلِلذَّكَرِ مِثْلُ حَظِّ الْأُنثَيَيْنِ ۗ يُبَيِّنُ اللَّهُ لَكُمْ أَن تَضِلُّوا ۗ وَاللَّهُ بِكُلِّ شَيْءٍ عَلِيمٌ
	They request from you a [legal] ruling. Say, "Allah gives you a ruling concerning one having neither descendants nor ascendants [as heirs]." If a man dies, leaving no child but [only] a sister, she will have half of what he left. And he inherits from her if she [dies and] has no child. But if there are two sisters [or more], they will have two-thirds of what he left. If there are both brothers and sisters, the male will have the share of two females. Allah makes clear to you [His law], lest you go astray. And Allah is Knowing of all things.

6 الأنعام 87	وَمِنْ آبَائِهِمْ وَذُرِّيَّاتِهِمْ وَإِخْوَانِهِمْ ۖ وَاجْتَبَيْنَاهُمْ وَهَدَيْنَاهُمْ إِلَىٰ صِرَاطٍ مُّسْتَقِيمٍ	
	And [some] among their fathers and their descendants and their brothers - and We chose them and We guided them to a straight path.	
7 الأعراف 38	قَالَ ادْخُلُوا فِي أُمَمٍ قَدْ خَلَتْ مِن قَبْلِكُم مِّنَ الْجِنِّ وَالْإِنسِ فِي النَّارِ ۖ كُلَّمَا دَخَلَتْ أُمَّةٌ لَّعَنَتْ أُخْتَهَا ۖ حَتَّىٰ إِذَا ادَّارَكُوا فِيهَا جَمِيعًا قَالَتْ أُخْرَاهُمْ لِأُولَاهُمْ رَبَّنَا هَٰؤُلَاءِ أَضَلُّونَا فَآتِهِمْ عَذَابًا ضِعْفًا مِّنَ النَّارِ ۖ قَالَ لِكُلٍّ ضِعْفٌ وَلَٰكِن لَّا تَعْلَمُونَ	
	[Allah] will say, "Enter among nations which had passed on before you of jinn and mankind into the Fire." Every time a nation enters, it will curse its sister until, when they have all overtaken one another therein, the last of them will say about the first of them "Our Lord, these had misled us, so give them a double punishment of the Fire. He will say, "For each is double, but you do not know."	
Your Sisters	أَخَوَاتُكُمْ	
4 النساء 23	حُرِّمَتْ عَلَيْكُمْ أُمَّهَاتُكُمْ وَبَنَاتُكُمْ وَأَخَوَاتُكُمْ وَعَمَّاتُكُمْ وَخَالَاتُكُمْ وَبَنَاتُ الْأَخِ وَبَنَاتُ الْأُخْتِ وَأُمَّهَاتُكُمُ اللَّاتِي أَرْضَعْنَكُمْ وَأَخَوَاتُكُم مِّنَ الرَّضَاعَةِ وَأُمَّهَاتُ نِسَائِكُمْ وَرَبَائِبُكُمُ اللَّاتِي فِي حُجُورِكُم مِّن نِّسَائِكُمُ اللَّاتِي دَخَلْتُم بِهِنَّ فَإِن لَّمْ تَكُونُوا دَخَلْتُم بِهِنَّ فَلَا جُنَاحَ عَلَيْكُمْ وَحَلَائِلُ أَبْنَائِكُمُ الَّذِينَ مِنْ أَصْلَابِكُمْ وَأَن تَجْمَعُوا بَيْنَ الْأُخْتَيْنِ إِلَّا مَا قَدْ سَلَفَ ۗ إِنَّ اللَّهَ كَانَ غَفُورًا رَّحِيمًا	
	Prohibited to you [for marriage] are your mothers, your daughters, your sisters, your father's sisters, your mother's sisters, your brother's daughters, your sister's daughters, your [milk] mothers who nursed you, your sisters through nursing, your wives' mothers, and your step-daughters under your guardianship [born] of your wives unto whom you have gone in. But if you have not gone in unto them, there is no sin upon you. And [also prohibited are] the wives of your sons who are from your [own] loins, and that you take [in marriage] two sisters simultaneously, except for what has already occurred. Indeed, Allah is ever Forgiving and Merciful.	

24 النور 61	لَيْسَ عَلَى الْأَعْمَىٰ حَرَجٌ وَلَا عَلَى الْأَعْرَجِ حَرَجٌ وَلَا عَلَى الْمَرِيضِ حَرَجٌ وَلَا عَلَىٰ أَنفُسِكُمْ أَن تَأْكُلُوا مِن بُيُوتِكُمْ أَوْ بُيُوتِ آبَائِكُمْ أَوْ بُيُوتِ أُمَّهَاتِكُمْ أَوْ بُيُوتِ إِخْوَانِكُمْ أَوْ بُيُوتِ أَخَوَاتِكُمْ أَوْ بُيُوتِ أَعْمَامِكُمْ أَوْ بُيُوتِ عَمَّاتِكُمْ أَوْ بُيُوتِ أَخْوَالِكُمْ أَوْ بُيُوتِ خَالَاتِكُمْ أَوْ مَا مَلَكْتُم مَّفَاتِحَهُ أَوْ صَدِيقِكُمْ ۚ لَيْسَ عَلَيْكُمْ جُنَاحٌ أَن تَأْكُلُوا جَمِيعًا أَوْ أَشْتَاتًا ۚ فَإِذَا دَخَلْتُم بُيُوتًا فَسَلِّمُوا عَلَىٰ أَنفُسِكُمْ تَحِيَّةً مِّنْ عِندِ اللَّهِ مُبَارَكَةً طَيِّبَةً ۚ كَذَٰلِكَ يُبَيِّنُ اللَّهُ لَكُمُ الْآيَاتِ لَعَلَّكُمْ تَعْقِلُونَ	
	There is not upon the blind [any] constraint nor upon the lame constraint nor upon the ill constraint nor upon yourselves when you eat from your [own] houses or the houses of your fathers or the houses of your mothers or the houses of your brothers or the houses of your sisters or the houses of your father's brothers or the houses of your father's sisters or the houses of your mother's brothers or the houses of your mother's sisters or [from houses] whose keys you possess or [from the house] of your friend. There is no blame upon you whether you eat together or separately. But when you enter houses, give greetings of peace upon each other - a greeting from Allah, blessed and good. Thus does Allah make clear to you the verses [of ordinance] that you may understand.	
Brothers	إِخْوَانًا /إِخْوَانِهِمْ /لِإِخْوَانِهِمْ	
3 آل عمران 103	وَاعْتَصِمُوا بِحَبْلِ اللَّهِ جَمِيعًا وَلَا تَفَرَّقُوا ۚ وَاذْكُرُوا نِعْمَتَ اللَّهِ عَلَيْكُمْ إِذْ كُنتُمْ أَعْدَاءً فَأَلَّفَ بَيْنَ قُلُوبِكُمْ فَأَصْبَحْتُم بِنِعْمَتِهِ إِخْوَانًا وَكُنتُمْ عَلَىٰ شَفَا حُفْرَةٍ مِّنَ النَّارِ فَأَنقَذَكُم مِّنْهَا ۗ كَذَٰلِكَ يُبَيِّنُ اللَّهُ لَكُمْ آيَاتِهِ لَعَلَّكُمْ تَهْتَدُونَ	
	And hold firmly to the rope of Allah all together and do not become divided. And remember the favor of Allah upon you - when you were enemies and He brought your hearts together and you became, by His favor, brothers. And you were on the edge of a pit of the Fire, and He saved you from it. Thus does Allah make clear to you His verses that you may be guided.	

168	الَّذِينَ قَالُوا لِإِخْوَانِهِمْ وَقَعَدُوا لَوْ أَطَاعُونَا مَا قُتِلُوا ۗ قُلْ فَادْرَءُوا عَنْ أَنْفُسِكُمُ الْمَوْتَ إِنْ كُنْتُمْ صَادِقِينَ
	Those who said about their brothers while sitting [at home], "If they had obeyed us, they would not have been killed." Say, "Then prevent death from yourselves, if you should be truthful."
6 الأنعام 87	وَمِنْ آبَائِهِمْ وَذُرِّيَّاتِهِمْ وَإِخْوَانِهِمْ ۖ وَاجْتَبَيْنَاهُمْ وَهَدَيْنَاهُمْ إِلَىٰ صِرَاطٍ مُسْتَقِيمٍ
	And [some] among their fathers and their descendants and their brothers - and We chose them and We guided them to a straight path.
7 الأعراف 202	وَإِخْوَانُهُمْ يَمُدُّونَهُمْ فِي الْغَيِّ ثُمَّ لَا يُقْصِرُونَ
	But their brothers - the devils increase them in error; then they do not stop short.
33 الأحزاب 18	قَدْ يَعْلَمُ اللَّهُ الْمُعَوِّقِينَ مِنْكُمْ وَالْقَائِلِينَ لِإِخْوَانِهِمْ هَلُمَّ إِلَيْنَا ۖ وَلَا يَأْتُونَ الْبَأْسَ إِلَّا قَلِيلًا
	Already Allah knows the hinderers among you and those [hypocrites] who say to their brothers, "Come to us," and do not go to battle, except for a few,
58 المجادلة 22	لَا تَجِدُ قَوْمًا يُؤْمِنُونَ بِاللَّهِ وَالْيَوْمِ الْآخِرِ يُوَادُّونَ مَنْ حَادَّ اللَّهَ وَرَسُولَهُ وَلَوْ كَانُوا آبَاءَهُمْ أَوْ أَبْنَاءَهُمْ أَوْ إِخْوَانَهُمْ أَوْ عَشِيرَتَهُمْ ۚ أُولَٰئِكَ كَتَبَ فِي قُلُوبِهِمُ الْإِيمَانَ وَأَيَّدَهُمْ بِرُوحٍ مِنْهُ ۖ وَيُدْخِلُهُمْ جَنَّاتٍ تَجْرِي مِنْ تَحْتِهَا الْأَنْهَارُ خَالِدِينَ فِيهَا ۚ رَضِيَ اللَّهُ عَنْهُمْ وَرَضُوا عَنْهُ ۚ أُولَٰئِكَ حِزْبُ اللَّهِ ۚ أَلَا إِنَّ حِزْبَ اللَّهِ هُمُ الْمُفْلِحُونَ
	You will not find a people who believe in Allah and the Last Day having affection for those who oppose Allah and His Messenger, even if they were their fathers or their sons or their brothers or their kindred. Those - He has decreed within their hearts faith and supported them with spirit from Him. And We will admit them to gardens beneath which rivers flow, wherein they abide eternally. Allah is pleased with them, and they are pleased with Him - those are the party of Allah. Unquestionably, the party of Allah - they are the successful.

59 الحشر 11	۞ أَلَمْ تَرَ إِلَى الَّذِينَ نَافَقُوا يَقُولُونَ لِإِخْوَانِهِمُ الَّذِينَ كَفَرُوا مِنْ أَهْلِ الْكِتَابِ لَئِنْ أُخْرِجْتُمْ لَنَخْرُجَنَّ مَعَكُمْ وَلَا نُطِيعُ فِيكُمْ أَحَدًا أَبَدًا وَإِنْ قُوتِلْتُمْ لَنَنْصُرَنَّكُمْ وَاللَّهُ يَشْهَدُ إِنَّهُمْ لَكَاذِبُونَ
	Have you not considered those who practice hypocrisy, saying to their brothers who have disbelieved among the People of the Scripture, "If you are expelled, we will surely leave with you, and we will not obey, in regard to you, anyone - ever; and if you are fought, we will surely aid you." But Allah testifies that they are liars.

Her/its Sister	أُخْتَهَا
7 الأعراف 38	قَالَ ادْخُلُوا فِي أُمَمٍ قَدْ خَلَتْ مِنْ قَبْلِكُمْ مِنَ الْجِنِّ وَالْإِنْسِ فِي النَّارِ ۖ كُلَّمَا دَخَلَتْ أُمَّةٌ لَعَنَتْ أُخْتَهَا ۖ حَتَّىٰ إِذَا ادَّارَكُوا فِيهَا جَمِيعًا قَالَتْ أُخْرَاهُمْ لِأُولَاهُمْ رَبَّنَا هَٰؤُلَاءِ أَضَلُّونَا فَآتِهِمْ عَذَابًا ضِعْفًا مِنَ النَّارِ ۖ قَالَ لِكُلٍّ ضِعْفٌ وَلَٰكِنْ لَا تَعْلَمُونَ
	[Allah] will say, "Enter among nations which had passed on before you of jinn and mankind into the Fire." Every time a nation enters, it will curse its sister until, when they have all overtaken one another therein, the last of them will say about the first of them "Our Lord, these had misled us, so give them a double punishment of the Fire. He will say, "For each is double, but you do not know."
43 الزخرف 48	وَمَا نُرِيهِمْ مِنْ آيَةٍ إِلَّا هِيَ أَكْبَرُ مِنْ أُخْتِهَا ۖ وَأَخَذْنَاهُمْ بِالْعَذَابِ لَعَلَّهُمْ يَرْجِعُونَ
	And We showed them not a sign except that it was greater than its sister, and We seized them with affliction that perhaps they might return [to faith].

Our Brother	أَخَانَا
12 يوسف 63	فَلَمَّا رَجَعُوا إِلَىٰ أَبِيهِمْ قَالُوا يَا أَبَانَا مُنِعَ مِنَّا الْكَيْلُ فَأَرْسِلْ مَعَنَا أَخَانَا نَكْتَلْ وَإِنَّا لَهُ لَحَافِظُونَ
	So when they returned to their father, they said, "O our father, [further] measure has been denied to us, so send with us our brother [that] we will be given measure. And indeed, we will be his guardians."

65	وَلَمَّا فَتَحُوا مَتَاعَهُمْ وَجَدُوا بِضَاعَتَهُمْ رُدَّتْ إِلَيْهِمْ ۖ قَالُوا يَا أَبَانَا مَا نَبْغِي ۖ هَٰذِهِ بِضَاعَتُنَا رُدَّتْ إِلَيْنَا ۖ وَنَمِيرُ أَهْلَنَا وَنَحْفَظُ أَخَانَا وَنَزْدَادُ كَيْلَ بَعِيرٍ ۖ ذَٰلِكَ كَيْلٌ يَسِيرٌ	
	And when they opened their baggage, they found their merchandise returned to them. They said, "O our father, what [more] could we desire? This is our merchandise returned to us. And we will obtain supplies for our family and protect our brother and obtain an increase of a camel's load; that is an easy measurement."	
	Father's Brothers/Sisters أَخَوَاتُكُمْ/ إِخْوَانُكُمْ/ أَخْوَالِكُمْ/ خَالَاتِكُمْ	
24 النور 61	لَّيْسَ عَلَى الْأَعْمَىٰ حَرَجٌ وَلَا عَلَى الْأَعْرَجِ حَرَجٌ وَلَا عَلَى الْمَرِيضِ حَرَجٌ وَلَا عَلَىٰ أَنفُسِكُمْ أَن تَأْكُلُوا مِن بُيُوتِكُمْ أَوْ بُيُوتِ آبَائِكُمْ أَوْ بُيُوتِ أُمَّهَاتِكُمْ أَوْ بُيُوتِ إِخْوَانِكُمْ أَوْ بُيُوتِ أَخَوَاتِكُمْ أَوْ بُيُوتِ أَعْمَامِكُمْ أَوْ بُيُوتِ عَمَّاتِكُمْ أَوْ بُيُوتِ أَخْوَالِكُمْ أَوْ بُيُوتِ خَالَاتِكُمْ أَوْ مَا مَلَكْتُم مَّفَاتِحَهُ أَوْ صَدِيقِكُمْ ۚ لَيْسَ عَلَيْكُمْ جُنَاحٌ أَن تَأْكُلُوا جَمِيعًا أَوْ أَشْتَاتًا ۚ فَإِذَا دَخَلْتُم بُيُوتًا فَسَلِّمُوا عَلَىٰ أَنفُسِكُمْ تَحِيَّةً مِّنْ عِندِ اللَّهِ مُبَارَكَةً طَيِّبَةً ۚ كَذَٰلِكَ يُبَيِّنُ اللَّهُ لَكُمُ الْآيَاتِ لَعَلَّكُمْ تَعْقِلُونَ	
	There is not upon the blind [any] constraint nor upon the lame constraint nor upon the ill constraint nor upon yourselves when you eat from your [own] houses or the houses of your fathers or the houses of your mothers or the houses of your brothers or the houses of your sisters or the houses of your father's brothers or the houses of your father's sisters or the houses of your mother's brothers or the houses of your mother's sisters or [from houses] whose keys you possess or [from the house] of your friend. There is no blame upon you whether you eat together or separately. But when you enter houses, give greetings of peace upon each other - a greeting from Allah, blessed and good. Thus does Allah make clear to you the verses [of ordinance] that you may understand.	

Your Brothers	إِخْوَانُكُمْ	
2 البقرة 220	فِي الدُّنْيَا وَالْآخِرَةِ ۗ وَيَسْأَلُونَكَ عَنِ الْيَتَامَىٰ ۖ قُلْ إِصْلَاحٌ لَّهُمْ خَيْرٌ ۖ وَإِن تُخَالِطُوهُمْ فَإِخْوَانُكُمْ ۚ وَاللَّهُ يَعْلَمُ الْمُفْسِدَ مِنَ الْمُصْلِحِ ۚ وَلَوْ شَاءَ اللَّهُ لَأَعْنَتَكُمْ ۚ إِنَّ اللَّهَ عَزِيزٌ حَكِيمٌ	
	To this world and the Hereafter. And they ask you about orphans. Say, "Improvement for them is best. And if you mix your affairs with theirs - they are your brothers. And Allah knows the corrupter from the amender. And if Allah had willed, He could have put you in difficulty. Indeed, Allah is Exalted in Might and Wise.	
9 التوبة 11	فَإِن تَابُوا وَأَقَامُوا الصَّلَاةَ وَآتَوُا الزَّكَاةَ فَإِخْوَانُكُمْ فِي الدِّينِ ۗ وَنُفَصِّلُ الْآيَاتِ لِقَوْمٍ يَعْلَمُونَ	
	But if they repent, establish prayer, and give zakah, then they are your brothers in religion; and We detail the verses for a people who know.	
9 التوبة 23	يَا أَيُّهَا الَّذِينَ آمَنُوا لَا تَتَّخِذُوا آبَاءَكُمْ وَإِخْوَانَكُمْ أَوْلِيَاءَ إِنِ اسْتَحَبُّوا الْكُفْرَ عَلَى الْإِيمَانِ ۚ وَمَن يَتَوَلَّهُم مِّنكُمْ فَأُولَٰئِكَ هُمُ الظَّالِمُونَ	
	O you who have believed, do not take your fathers or your brothers as allies if they have preferred disbelief over belief. And whoever does so among you - then it is those who are the wrongdoers.	
24	قُلْ إِن كَانَ آبَاؤُكُمْ وَأَبْنَاؤُكُمْ وَإِخْوَانُكُمْ وَأَزْوَاجُكُمْ وَعَشِيرَتُكُمْ وَأَمْوَالٌ اقْتَرَفْتُمُوهَا وَتِجَارَةٌ تَخْشَوْنَ كَسَادَهَا وَمَسَاكِنُ تَرْضَوْنَهَا أَحَبَّ إِلَيْكُم مِّنَ اللَّهِ وَرَسُولِهِ وَجِهَادٍ فِي سَبِيلِهِ فَتَرَبَّصُوا حَتَّىٰ يَأْتِيَ اللَّهُ بِأَمْرِهِ ۗ وَاللَّهُ لَا يَهْدِي الْقَوْمَ الْفَاسِقِينَ	
	Say, [O Muhammad], "If your fathers, your sons, your brothers, your wives, your relatives, wealth which you have obtained, commerce wherein you fear decline, and dwellings with which you are pleased are more beloved to you than Allah and His Messenger and jihad in His cause, then wait until Allah executes His command. And Allah does not guide the defiantly disobedient people."	

24 النور 61	لَّيْسَ عَلَى الْأَعْمَىٰ حَرَجٌ وَلَا عَلَى الْأَعْرَجِ حَرَجٌ وَلَا عَلَى الْمَرِيضِ حَرَجٌ وَلَا عَلَىٰ أَنفُسِكُمْ أَن تَأْكُلُوا مِن بُيُوتِكُمْ أَوْ بُيُوتِ آبَائِكُمْ أَوْ بُيُوتِ أُمَّهَاتِكُمْ أَوْ بُيُوتِ إِخْوَانِكُمْ أَوْ بُيُوتِ أَخَوَاتِكُمْ أَوْ بُيُوتِ أَعْمَامِكُمْ أَوْ بُيُوتِ عَمَّاتِكُمْ أَوْ بُيُوتِ أَخْوَالِكُمْ أَوْ بُيُوتِ خَالَاتِكُمْ أَوْ مَا مَلَكْتُم مَّفَاتِحَهُ أَوْ صَدِيقِكُمْ ۚ لَيْسَ عَلَيْكُمْ جُنَاحٌ أَن تَأْكُلُوا جَمِيعًا أَوْ أَشْتَاتًا ۚ فَإِذَا دَخَلْتُم بُيُوتًا فَسَلِّمُوا عَلَىٰ أَنفُسِكُمْ تَحِيَّةً مِّنْ عِندِ اللَّهِ مُبَارَكَةً طَيِّبَةً ۚ كَذَٰلِكَ يُبَيِّنُ اللَّهُ لَكُمُ الْآيَاتِ لَعَلَّكُمْ تَعْقِلُونَ
	There is not upon the blind [any] constraint nor upon the lame constraint nor upon the ill constraint nor upon yourselves when you eat from your [own] houses or the houses of your fathers or the houses of your mothers or the houses of your brothers or the houses of your sisters or the houses of your father's brothers or the houses of your father's sisters or the houses of your mother's brothers or the houses of your mother's sisters or [from houses] whose keys you possess or [from the house] of your friend. There is no blame upon you whether you eat together or separately. But when you enter houses, give greetings of peace upon each other - a greeting from Allah, blessed and good. Thus does Allah make clear to you the verses [of ordinance] that you may understand.
33 الأحزاب 5	ادْعُوهُمْ لِآبَائِهِمْ هُوَ أَقْسَطُ عِندَ اللَّهِ ۚ فَإِن لَّمْ تَعْلَمُوا آبَاءَهُمْ فَإِخْوَانُكُمْ فِي الدِّينِ وَمَوَالِيكُمْ ۚ وَلَيْسَ عَلَيْكُمْ جُنَاحٌ فِيمَا أَخْطَأْتُم بِهِ وَلَٰكِن مَّا تَعَمَّدَتْ قُلُوبُكُمْ ۚ وَكَانَ اللَّهُ غَفُورًا رَّحِيمًا
	Call them by [the names of] their fathers; it is more just in the sight of Allah. But if you do not know their fathers - then they are [still] your brothers in religion and those entrusted to you. And there is no blame upon you for that in which you have erred but [only for] what your hearts intended. And ever is Allah Forgiving and Merciful.

Couple/two in a type	أَزْوَاجٍ أَزْوَاجُهُنَّ أَزْوَاجًا لِأَزْوَاجِهِم أَزْوَاجِنَا أَزْوَاجِكُم أَزْوَاجُهُ لِأَزْوَاجِكَ
Husband or wife	زَوْجَكَ أَزْوَاجُهُ الْأَزْوَاجَ زَوْجَانِ /زَوْجَهَا /زَوْجَهُ/ زَوْجَيْنِ
2 البقرة 25	وَبَشِّرِ الَّذِينَ آمَنُوا وَعَمِلُوا الصَّالِحَاتِ أَنَّ لَهُمْ جَنَّاتٍ تَجْرِي مِن تَحْتِهَا الْأَنْهَارُ ۖ كُلَّمَا رُزِقُوا مِنْهَا مِن ثَمَرَةٍ رِّزْقًا ۙ قَالُوا هَٰذَا الَّذِي رُزِقْنَا مِن قَبْلُ ۖ وَأُتُوا بِهِ مُتَشَابِهًا ۖ وَلَهُمْ فِيهَا أَزْوَاجٌ مُّطَهَّرَةٌ ۖ وَهُمْ فِيهَا خَالِدُونَ
	And give good tidings to those who believe and do righteous deeds that they will have gardens [in Paradise] beneath which rivers flow. Whenever they are provided with a provision of fruit therefrom, they will say, "This is what we were provided with before." And it is given to them in likeness. And they will have therein purified spouses, and they will abide therein eternally.
232	وَإِذَا طَلَّقْتُمُ النِّسَاءَ فَبَلَغْنَ أَجَلَهُنَّ فَلَا تَعْضُلُوهُنَّ أَن يَنكِحْنَ أَزْوَاجَهُنَّ إِذَا تَرَاضَوْا بَيْنَهُم بِالْمَعْرُوفِ ۗ ذَٰلِكَ يُوعَظُ بِهِ مَن كَانَ مِنكُمْ يُؤْمِنُ بِاللَّهِ وَالْيَوْمِ الْآخِرِ ۗ ذَٰلِكُمْ أَزْكَىٰ لَكُمْ وَأَطْهَرُ ۗ وَاللَّهُ يَعْلَمُ وَأَنتُمْ لَا تَعْلَمُونَ
	And when you divorce women and they have fulfilled their term, do not prevent them from remarrying their [former] husbands if they agree among themselves on an acceptable basis. That is instructed to whoever of you believes in Allah and the Last Day. That is better for you and purer, and Allah knows and you know not
234	وَالَّذِينَ يُتَوَفَّوْنَ مِنكُمْ وَيَذَرُونَ أَزْوَاجًا يَتَرَبَّصْنَ بِأَنفُسِهِنَّ أَرْبَعَةَ أَشْهُرٍ وَعَشْرًا ۖ فَإِذَا بَلَغْنَ أَجَلَهُنَّ فَلَا جُنَاحَ عَلَيْكُمْ فِيمَا فَعَلْنَ فِي أَنفُسِهِنَّ بِالْمَعْرُوفِ ۗ وَاللَّهُ بِمَا تَعْمَلُونَ خَبِيرٌ
	And those who are taken in death among you and leave wives behind - they, [the wives, shall] wait four months and ten [days]. And when they have fulfilled their term, then there is no blame upon you for what they do with themselves in an acceptable manner. And Allah is [fully] Acquainted with what you do.
240	وَالَّذِينَ يُتَوَفَّوْنَ مِنكُمْ وَيَذَرُونَ أَزْوَاجًا وَصِيَّةً لِّأَزْوَاجِهِم مَّتَاعًا إِلَى الْحَوْلِ غَيْرَ إِخْرَاجٍ ۚ فَإِنْ خَرَجْنَ فَلَا جُنَاحَ عَلَيْكُمْ فِي مَا فَعَلْنَ فِي أَنفُسِهِنَّ مِن مَّعْرُوفٍ ۗ وَاللَّهُ عَزِيزٌ حَكِيمٌ
	And those who are taken in death among you and leave wives behind - for their wives is a bequest: maintenance for one year without turning [them] out. But if they leave [of their own accord], then there is no blame upon you for what they do with themselves in an acceptable way. And Allah is Exalted in Might and Wise.

3 آل عمران 15	۞ قُلْ أَؤُنَبِّئُكُم بِخَيْرٍ مِّن ذَٰلِكُمْ ۚ لِلَّذِينَ اتَّقَوْا عِندَ رَبِّهِمْ جَنَّاتٌ تَجْرِي مِن تَحْتِهَا الْأَنْهَارُ خَالِدِينَ فِيهَا وَأَزْوَاجٌ مُّطَهَّرَةٌ وَرِضْوَانٌ مِّنَ اللَّهِ ۗ وَاللَّهُ بَصِيرٌ بِالْعِبَادِ	
	Say, "Shall I inform you of [something] better than that? For those who fear Allah will be gardens in the presence of their Lord beneath which rivers flow, wherein they abide eternally, and purified spouses and approval from Allah. And Allah is Seeing of [His] servants -	
4 النساء 1	يَا أَيُّهَا النَّاسُ اتَّقُوا رَبَّكُمُ الَّذِي خَلَقَكُم مِّن نَّفْسٍ وَاحِدَةٍ وَخَلَقَ مِنْهَا زَوْجَهَا وَبَثَّ مِنْهُمَا رِجَالًا كَثِيرًا وَنِسَاءً ۚ وَاتَّقُوا اللَّهَ الَّذِي تَسَاءَلُونَ بِهِ وَالْأَرْحَامَ ۚ إِنَّ اللَّهَ كَانَ عَلَيْكُمْ رَقِيبًا	
4 النساء 57	وَالَّذِينَ آمَنُوا وَعَمِلُوا الصَّالِحَاتِ سَنُدْخِلُهُمْ جَنَّاتٍ تَجْرِي مِن تَحْتِهَا الْأَنْهَارُ خَالِدِينَ فِيهَا أَبَدًا ۖ لَّهُمْ فِيهَا أَزْوَاجٌ مُّطَهَّرَةٌ ۖ وَنُدْخِلُهُمْ ظِلًّا ظَلِيلًا	
6 الأنعام 139	وَقَالُوا مَا فِي بُطُونِ هَٰذِهِ الْأَنْعَامِ خَالِصَةٌ لِّذُكُورِنَا وَمُحَرَّمٌ عَلَىٰ أَزْوَاجِنَا ۖ وَإِن يَكُن مَّيْتَةً فَهُمْ فِيهِ شُرَكَاءُ ۚ سَيَجْزِيهِمْ وَصْفَهُمْ ۚ إِنَّهُ حَكِيمٌ عَلِيمٌ	
143	ثَمَانِيَةَ أَزْوَاجٍ ۖ مِّنَ الضَّأْنِ اثْنَيْنِ وَمِنَ الْمَعْزِ اثْنَيْنِ ۗ قُلْ آلذَّكَرَيْنِ حَرَّمَ أَمِ الْأُنثَيَيْنِ أَمَّا اشْتَمَلَتْ عَلَيْهِ أَرْحَامُ الْأُنثَيَيْنِ ۖ نَبِّئُونِي بِعِلْمٍ إِن كُنتُمْ صَادِقِينَ	
	[They are] eight mates - of the sheep, two and of the goats, two. Say, "Is it the two males He has forbidden or the two females or that which the wombs of the two females contain? Inform me with knowledge, if you should be truthful	
7 الأعراف 189	هُوَ الَّذِي خَلَقَكُم مِّن نَّفْسٍ وَاحِدَةٍ وَجَعَلَ مِنْهَا زَوْجَهَا لِيَسْكُنَ إِلَيْهَا ۖ فَلَمَّا تَغَشَّاهَا حَمَلَتْ حَمْلًا خَفِيفًا فَمَرَّتْ بِهِ ۖ فَلَمَّا أَثْقَلَت دَّعَوَا اللَّهَ رَبَّهُمَا لَئِنْ آتَيْتَنَا صَالِحًا لَّنَكُونَنَّ مِنَ الشَّاكِرِينَ	
11 هود 40	حَتَّىٰ إِذَا جَاءَ أَمْرُنَا وَفَارَ التَّنُّورُ قُلْنَا احْمِلْ فِيهَا مِن كُلٍّ زَوْجَيْنِ اثْنَيْنِ وَأَهْلَكَ إِلَّا مَن سَبَقَ عَلَيْهِ الْقَوْلُ وَمَنْ آمَنَ ۚ وَمَا آمَنَ مَعَهُ إِلَّا قَلِيلٌ	
13 الرعد 3	وَهُوَ الَّذِي مَدَّ الْأَرْضَ وَجَعَلَ فِيهَا رَوَاسِيَ وَأَنْهَارًا ۖ وَمِن كُلِّ الثَّمَرَاتِ جَعَلَ فِيهَا زَوْجَيْنِ اثْنَيْنِ ۖ يُغْشِي اللَّيْلَ النَّهَارَ ۚ إِنَّ فِي ذَٰلِكَ لَآيَاتٍ لِّقَوْمٍ يَتَفَكَّرُونَ	
13 الرعد 23	جَنَّاتُ عَدْنٍ يَدْخُلُونَهَا وَمَن صَلَحَ مِنْ آبَائِهِمْ وَأَزْوَاجِهِمْ وَذُرِّيَّاتِهِمْ ۖ وَالْمَلَائِكَةُ يَدْخُلُونَ عَلَيْهِم مِّن كُلِّ بَابٍ	
38	وَلَقَدْ أَرْسَلْنَا رُسُلًا مِّن قَبْلِكَ وَجَعَلْنَا لَهُمْ أَزْوَاجًا وَذُرِّيَّةً ۚ وَمَا كَانَ لِرَسُولٍ أَن يَأْتِيَ بِآيَةٍ إِلَّا بِإِذْنِ اللَّهِ ۗ لِكُلِّ أَجَلٍ كِتَابٌ	
	And We have already sent messengers before you and assigned to them wives and descendants. And it was not for a messenger to come with a sign except by permission of Allah. For every term is a decree.	

	لَا تَمُدَّنَّ عَيْنَيْكَ إِلَىٰ مَا مَتَّعْنَا بِهِ **أَزْوَاجًا** مِّنْهُمْ وَلَا تَحْزَنْ عَلَيْهِمْ وَاخْفِضْ **جَنَاحَكَ** لِلْمُؤْمِنِينَ	15 الحجر 88
	Do not extend your eyes toward that by which We have given enjoyment to [certain] categories of the disbelievers, and do not grieve over them. And lower your wing to the believers	
	وَاللَّهُ جَعَلَ لَكُم مِّنْ أَنفُسِكُمْ **أَزْوَاجًا** وَجَعَلَ لَكُم مِّنْ **أَزْوَاجِكُم** بَنِينَ وَحَفَدَةً وَرَزَقَكُم مِّنَ الطَّيِّبَاتِ ۚ أَفَبِالْبَاطِلِ يُؤْمِنُونَ وَبِنِعْمَتِ اللَّهِ هُمْ يَكْفُرُونَ	16 النحل 72
	And Allah has made for you from yourselves mates and has made for you from your mates sons and grandchildren and has provided for you from the good things. Then in falsehood do they believe and in the favor of Allah they disbelieve?	
	الَّذِي جَعَلَ لَكُمُ الْأَرْضَ مَهْدًا وَسَلَكَ لَكُمْ فِيهَا سُبُلًا وَأَنزَلَ مِنَ السَّمَاءِ مَاءً فَأَخْرَجْنَا بِهِ **أَزْوَاجًا** مِّن نَّبَاتٍ شَتَّىٰ	20 طه 53
	[It is He] who has made for you the earth as a bed [spread out] and inserted therein for you roadways and sent down from the sky, rain and produced thereby categories of various plants.	
	وَلَا تَمُدَّنَّ عَيْنَيْكَ إِلَىٰ مَا مَتَّعْنَا بِهِ **أَزْوَاجًا** مِّنْهُمْ زَهْرَةَ الْحَيَاةِ الدُّنْيَا لِنَفْتِنَهُمْ فِيهِ ۚ وَرِزْقُ رَبِّكَ خَيْرٌ وَأَبْقَىٰ	131
	فَاسْتَجَبْنَا لَهُ وَوَهَبْنَا لَهُ يَحْيَىٰ وَأَصْلَحْنَا لَهُ **زَوْجَهُ** ۚ إِنَّهُمْ كَانُوا يُسَارِعُونَ فِي الْخَيْرَاتِ وَيَدْعُونَنَا رَغَبًا وَرَهَبًا ۖ وَكَانُوا لَنَا خَاشِعِينَ	21 الأنبياء 90
	إِلَّا عَلَىٰ **أَزْوَاجِهِمْ** أَوْ مَا مَلَكَتْ أَيْمَانُهُمْ فَإِنَّهُمْ غَيْرُ مَلُومِينَ	23 المؤمنون 6
	فَأَوْحَيْنَا إِلَيْهِ أَنِ اصْنَعِ الْفُلْكَ بِأَعْيُنِنَا وَوَحْيِنَا فَإِذَا جَاءَ أَمْرُنَا وَفَارَ التَّنُّورُ ۙ فَاسْلُكْ فِيهَا مِن كُلٍّ **زَوْجَيْنِ** اثْنَيْنِ وَأَهْلَكَ إِلَّا مَن سَبَقَ عَلَيْهِ الْقَوْلُ مِنْهُمْ ۖ وَلَا تُخَاطِبْنِي فِي الَّذِينَ ظَلَمُوا ۖ إِنَّهُم مُّغْرَقُونَ	23 المؤمنون 27
	وَالَّذِينَ يَرْمُونَ **أَزْوَاجَهُمْ** وَلَمْ يَكُن لَّهُمْ شُهَدَاءُ إِلَّا أَنفُسُهُمْ فَشَهَادَةُ أَحَدِهِمْ أَرْبَعُ **شَهَادَاتٍ** بِاللَّهِ ۙ إِنَّهُ لَمِنَ الصَّادِقِينَ	24 النور 6

	And those who accuse their wives [of adultery] and have no witnesses except themselves - then the witness of one of them [shall be] four testimonies [swearing] by Allah that indeed, he is of the truthful
25 الفرقان 74	وَالَّذِينَ يَقُولُونَ رَبَّنَا هَبْ لَنَا مِنْ **أَزْوَاجِنَا** وَ**ذُرِّيَّاتِنَا** قُرَّةَ أَعْيُنٍ وَاجْعَلْنَا لِلْمُتَّقِينَ إِمَامًا
	And those who say, "Our Lord, grant us from among our wives and offspring comfort to our eyes and make us an example for the righteous."
30 الروم 21	وَمِنْ آيَاتِهِ أَنْ خَلَقَ لَكُم مِّنْ أَنفُسِكُمْ **أَزْوَاجًا** لِّتَسْكُنُوا إِلَيْهَا وَجَعَلَ بَيْنَكُم مَّوَدَّةً وَرَحْمَةً ۚ إِنَّ فِي ذَٰلِكَ لَآيَاتٍ لِّقَوْمٍ يَتَفَكَّرُونَ
	And of His signs is that He created for you from yourselves mates that you may find tranquillity in them; and He placed between you affection and mercy. Indeed in that are signs for a people who give thought.
33 الأحزاب 6	النَّبِيُّ أَوْلَىٰ بِالْمُؤْمِنِينَ مِنْ أَنفُسِهِمْ ۖ وَ**أَزْوَاجُهُ** **أُمَّهَاتُهُمْ** ۗ وَأُولُو الْأَرْحَامِ بَعْضُهُمْ أَوْلَىٰ بِبَعْضٍ فِي كِتَابِ اللَّهِ مِنَ الْمُؤْمِنِينَ وَالْمُهَاجِرِينَ إِلَّا أَن تَفْعَلُوا إِلَىٰ أَوْلِيَائِكُم مَّعْرُوفًا ۚ كَانَ ذَٰلِكَ فِي الْكِتَابِ مَسْطُورًا
	The Prophet is more worthy of the believers than themselves, and his wives are [in the position of] their mothers. And those of [blood] relationship are more entitled [to inheritance] in the decree of Allah than the [other] believers and the emigrants, except that you may do to your close associates a kindness [through bequest]. That was in the Book inscribed.
28	يَا أَيُّهَا النَّبِيُّ قُل لِّ**أَزْوَاجِكَ** إِن كُنتُنَّ تُرِدْنَ الْحَيَاةَ الدُّنْيَا وَزِينَتَهَا فَتَعَالَيْنَ أُمَتِّعْكُنَّ وَأُسَرِّحْكُنَّ سَرَاحًا جَمِيلًا
	O Prophet, say to your wives, "If you should desire the worldly life and its adornment, then come, I will provide for you and give you a gracious release.
37	وَإِذْ تَقُولُ لِلَّذِي أَنْعَمَ اللَّهُ عَلَيْهِ وَأَنْعَمْتَ عَلَيْهِ أَمْسِكْ عَلَيْكَ **زَوْجَكَ** وَاتَّقِ اللَّهَ وَتُخْفِي فِي نَفْسِكَ مَا اللَّهُ مُبْدِيهِ وَتَخْشَى النَّاسَ وَاللَّهُ أَحَقُّ أَن تَخْشَاهُ ۖ فَلَمَّا قَضَىٰ **زَيْدٌ** مِّنْهَا وَطَرًا **زَوَّجْنَاكَهَا** لِكَيْ لَا يَكُونَ عَلَى الْمُؤْمِنِينَ حَرَجٌ فِي **أَزْوَاجِ** أَدْعِيَائِهِمْ إِذَا **قَضَوْا** مِنْهُنَّ وَطَرًا ۚ وَكَانَ أَمْرُ اللَّهِ مَفْعُولًا
	And [remember, O Muhammad], when you said to the one on whom Allah bestowed favor and you bestowed favor, "Keep your wife and fear Allah," while you concealed within yourself that which Allah is to disclose. And you feared the people, while Allah has more right that you fear Him. So when Zayd

	had no longer any need for her, We married her to you in order that there not be upon the believers any discomfort concerning the wives of their adopted sons when they no longer have need of them. And ever is the command of Allah accomplished.
50	يَا أَيُّهَا النَّبِيُّ إِنَّا أَحْلَلْنَا لَكَ أَزْوَاجَكَ اللَّاتِي آتَيْتَ أُجُورَهُنَّ وَمَا مَلَكَتْ يَمِينُكَ مِمَّا أَفَاءَ اللَّهُ عَلَيْكَ وَبَنَاتِ عَمِّكَ وَبَنَاتِ عَمَّاتِكَ وَبَنَاتِ خَالِكَ وَبَنَاتِ خَالَاتِكَ اللَّاتِي هَاجَرْنَ مَعَكَ وَامْرَأَةً مُؤْمِنَةً إِنْ وَهَبَتْ نَفْسَهَا لِلنَّبِيِّ إِنْ أَرَادَ النَّبِيُّ أَنْ يَسْتَنْكِحَهَا خَالِصَةً لَكَ مِنْ دُونِ الْمُؤْمِنِينَ ۗ قَدْ عَلِمْنَا مَا فَرَضْنَا عَلَيْهِمْ فِي أَزْوَاجِهِمْ وَمَا مَلَكَتْ أَيْمَانُهُمْ لِكَيْلَا يَكُونَ عَلَيْكَ حَرَجٌ ۗ وَكَانَ اللَّهُ غَفُورًا رَحِيمًا
	O Prophet, indeed We have made lawful to you your wives to whom you have given their due compensation and those your right hand possesses from what Allah has returned to you [of captives] and the daughters of your paternal uncles and the daughters of your paternal aunts and the daughters of your maternal uncles and the daughters of your maternal aunts who emigrated with you and a believing woman if she gives herself to the Prophet [and] if the Prophet wishes to marry her, [this is] only for you, excluding the [other] believers. We certainly know what We have made obligatory upon them concerning their wives and those their right hands possess, [but this is for you] in order that there will be upon you no discomfort. And ever is Allah Forgiving and Merciful.
52	لَا يَحِلُّ لَكَ النِّسَاءُ مِنْ بَعْدُ وَلَا أَنْ تَبَدَّلَ بِهِنَّ مِنْ أَزْوَاجٍ وَلَوْ أَعْجَبَكَ حُسْنُهُنَّ إِلَّا مَا مَلَكَتْ يَمِينُكَ ۗ وَكَانَ اللَّهُ عَلَىٰ كُلِّ شَيْءٍ رَقِيبًا
	Not lawful to you, [O Muhammad], are [any additional] women after [this], nor [is it] for you to exchange them for [other] wives, even if their beauty were to please you, except what your right hand possesses. And ever is Allah, over all things, an Observer.
53	يَا أَيُّهَا الَّذِينَ آمَنُوا لَا تَدْخُلُوا بُيُوتَ النَّبِيِّ إِلَّا أَنْ يُؤْذَنَ لَكُمْ إِلَىٰ طَعَامٍ غَيْرَ نَاظِرِينَ إِنَاهُ وَلَٰكِنْ إِذَا دُعِيتُمْ فَادْخُلُوا فَإِذَا طَعِمْتُمْ فَانْتَشِرُوا وَلَا مُسْتَأْنِسِينَ لِحَدِيثٍ ۚ إِنَّ ذَٰلِكُمْ كَانَ يُؤْذِي النَّبِيَّ فَيَسْتَحْيِي مِنْكُمْ ۖ وَاللَّهُ لَا يَسْتَحْيِي مِنَ الْحَقِّ ۚ وَإِذَا سَأَلْتُمُوهُنَّ مَتَاعًا فَاسْأَلُوهُنَّ مِنْ وَرَاءِ حِجَابٍ ۚ ذَٰلِكُمْ أَطْهَرُ لِقُلُوبِكُمْ وَقُلُوبِهِنَّ ۚ وَمَا كَانَ لَكُمْ أَنْ تُؤْذُوا رَسُولَ اللَّهِ وَلَا أَنْ تَنْكِحُوا أَزْوَاجَهُ مِنْ بَعْدِهِ أَبَدًا ۚ إِنَّ ذَٰلِكُمْ كَانَ عِنْدَ اللَّهِ عَظِيمًا
	O you who have believed, do not enter the houses of the Prophet except when you are permitted for a meal, without awaiting its readiness. But when you are invited, then enter; and when you have eaten, disperse without seeking to remain for conversation. Indeed, that [behavior] was troubling the Prophet, and he is shy of [dismissing] you. But Allah is not shy of the truth. And when you ask [his wives] for something, ask them from behind a partition. That is purer

	for your hearts and their hearts. And it is not [conceivable or lawful] for you to harm the Messenger of Allah or to marry his wives after him, ever. Indeed, that would be in the sight of Allah an enormity.
59	يَا أَيُّهَا النَّبِيُّ قُل لِّأَزْوَاجِكَ وَبَنَاتِكَ وَنِسَاءِ الْمُؤْمِنِينَ يُدْنِينَ عَلَيْهِنَّ مِن جَلَابِيبِهِنَّ ۚ ذَٰلِكَ أَدْنَىٰ أَن يُعْرَفْنَ فَلَا يُؤْذَيْنَ ۗ وَكَانَ اللَّهُ غَفُورًا رَّحِيمًا
	O Prophet, tell your wives and your daughters and the women of the believers to bring down over themselves [part] of their outer garments. That is more suitable that they will be known and not be abused. And ever is Allah Forgiving and Merciful.
35 فاطر 11	وَاللَّهُ خَلَقَكُم مِّن تُرَابٍ ثُمَّ مِن نُّطْفَةٍ ثُمَّ جَعَلَكُمْ أَزْوَاجًا ۚ وَمَا تَحْمِلُ مِنْ أُنثَىٰ وَلَا تَضَعُ إِلَّا بِعِلْمِهِ ۚ وَمَا يُعَمَّرُ مِن مُّعَمَّرٍ وَلَا يُنقَصُ مِنْ عُمُرِهِ إِلَّا فِي كِتَابٍ ۚ إِنَّ ذَٰلِكَ عَلَى اللَّهِ يَسِيرٌ
	And Allah created you from dust, then from a sperm-drop; then He made you mates. And no female conceives nor does she give birth except with His knowledge. And no aged person is granted [additional] life nor is his lifespan lessened but that it is in a register. Indeed, that for Allah is easy.
36 يس 36	سُبْحَانَ الَّذِي خَلَقَ الْأَزْوَاجَ كُلَّهَا مِمَّا تُنبِتُ الْأَرْضُ وَمِنْ أَنفُسِهِمْ وَمِمَّا لَا يَعْلَمُونَ
	Exalted is He who created all pairs - from what the earth grows and from themselves and from that which they do not know.
56	هُمْ وَأَزْوَاجُهُمْ فِي ظِلَالٍ عَلَى الْأَرَائِكِ مُتَّكِئُونَ
	They and their spouses – in shade, reclining on adorned couches.
37 الصافات 22	احْشُرُوا الَّذِينَ ظَلَمُوا وَأَزْوَاجَهُمْ وَمَا كَانُوا يَعْبُدُونَ
	[The angels will be ordered], "Gather those who committed wrong, their kinds, and what they used to worship
38 ص 58	وَآخَرُ مِن شَكْلِهِ أَزْوَاجٌ
	And other [punishments] of its type [in various] kinds.

39 الزمر 6	خَلَقَكُم مِّن نَّفْسٍ وَاحِدَةٍ ثُمَّ جَعَلَ مِنْهَا **زَوْجَهَا** وَأَنزَلَ لَكُم مِّنَ الْأَنْعَامِ ثَمَانِيَةَ **أَزْوَاجٍ** ۚ يَخْلُقُكُمْ فِي بُطُونِ أُمَّهَاتِكُمْ خَلْقًا مِّن بَعْدِ خَلْقٍ فِي ظُلُمَاتٍ ثَلَاثٍ ۚ ذَٰلِكُمُ اللَّهُ رَبُّكُمْ لَهُ الْمُلْكُ ۖ لَا إِلَٰهَ إِلَّا هُوَ ۖ فَأَنَّىٰ تُصْرَفُونَ
	He created you from one soul. Then He made from it its mate, and He produced for you from the grazing livestock eight mates. He creates you in the wombs of your mothers, creation after creation, within three darknesses. That is Allah, your Lord; to Him belongs dominion. There is no deity except Him, so how are you averted?
40 غافر 8	رَبَّنَا وَأَدْخِلْهُمْ جَنَّاتِ عَدْنٍ الَّتِي وَعَدتَّهُم وَمَن صَلَحَ مِنْ آبَائِهِمْ **وَأَزْوَاجِهِمْ** وَذُرِّيَّاتِهِمْ ۚ إِنَّكَ أَنتَ الْعَزِيزُ الْحَكِيمُ
	Our Lord, and admit them to gardens of perpetual residence which You have promised them and whoever was righteous among their fathers, their spouses and their offspring. Indeed, it is You who is the Exalted in Might, the Wise.
42 الشورى 11	فَاطِرُ السَّمَاوَاتِ وَالْأَرْضِ ۚ جَعَلَ لَكُم مِّنْ أَنفُسِكُمْ **أَزْوَاجًا** وَمِنَ الْأَنْعَامِ **أَزْوَاجًا** ۖ يَذْرَؤُكُمْ فِيهِ ۚ لَيْسَ كَمِثْلِهِ شَيْءٌ ۖ وَهُوَ السَّمِيعُ الْبَصِيرُ
43 الزخرف 12	وَالَّذِي خَلَقَ **الْأَزْوَاجَ** كُلَّهَا وَجَعَلَ لَكُم مِّنَ الْفُلْكِ وَالْأَنْعَامِ مَا تَرْكَبُونَ
51 الذاريات 49	وَمِن كُلِّ شَيْءٍ خَلَقْنَا **زَوْجَيْنِ** لَعَلَّكُمْ تَذَكَّرُونَ
53 النجم 45	وَأَنَّهُ خَلَقَ **الزَّوْجَيْنِ** الذَّكَرَ وَالْأُنثَىٰ
55 الرحمن 52	فِيهِمَا مِن كُلِّ فَاكِهَةٍ **زَوْجَانِ**
56 الواقعة 7	وَكُنتُمْ **أَزْوَاجًا** ثَلَاثَةً
60 الممتحنة 11	وَإِن فَاتَكُمْ شَيْءٌ مِّنْ **أَزْوَاجِكُمْ** إِلَى الْكُفَّارِ فَعَاقَبْتُمْ فَآتُوا الَّذِينَ ذَهَبَتْ **أَزْوَاجُهُم** مِّثْلَ مَا أَنفَقُوا ۚ وَاتَّقُوا اللَّهَ الَّذِي أَنتُم بِهِ مُؤْمِنُونَ
	And if you have lost any of your wives to the disbelievers and you subsequently obtain [something], then give those whose wives have gone the equivalent of what they had spent. And fear Allah, in whom you are believers.
66 التحريم 1	يَا أَيُّهَا النَّبِيُّ لِمَ تُحَرِّمُ مَا أَحَلَّ اللَّهُ لَكَ ۖ تَبْتَغِي مَرْضَاتَ **أَزْوَاجِكَ** ۚ وَاللَّهُ غَفُورٌ رَّحِيمٌ
	O Prophet, why do you prohibit [yourself from] what Allah has made lawful for you, seeking the approval of your wives? And Allah is Forgiving and Merciful.

3	وَإِذْ أَسَرَّ النَّبِيُّ إِلَىٰ بَعْضِ **أَزْوَاجِهِ** حَدِيثًا فَلَمَّا نَبَّأَتْ بِهِ وَأَظْهَرَهُ اللَّهُ عَلَيْهِ عَرَّفَ بَعْضَهُ وَأَعْرَضَ عَن بَعْضٍ ۖ فَلَمَّا نَبَّأَهَا بِهِ قَالَتْ مَنْ أَنبَأَكَ هَٰذَا ۖ قَالَ نَبَّأَنِيَ الْعَلِيمُ الْخَبِيرُ	
	And [remember] when the Prophet confided to one of his wives a statement; and when she informed [another] of it and Allah showed it to him, he made known part of it and ignored a part. And when he informed her about it, she said, "Who told you this?" He said, "I was informed by the Knowing, the Acquainted."	
5	عَسَىٰ رَبُّهُ إِن طَلَّقَكُنَّ أَن يُبْدِلَهُ **أَزْوَاجًا** خَيْرًا مِّنكُنَّ مُسْلِمَاتٍ مُّؤْمِنَاتٍ قَانِتَاتٍ تَائِبَاتٍ عَابِدَاتٍ سَائِحَاتٍ ثَيِّبَاتٍ وَأَبْكَارًا	
	Perhaps his Lord, if he divorced you [all], would substitute for him wives better than you - submitting [to Allah], believing, devoutly obedient, repentant, worshipping, and traveling - [ones] previously married and virgins.	
70 المعارج 30	إِلَّا عَلَىٰ **أَزْوَاجِهِمْ** أَوْ مَا مَلَكَتْ أَيْمَانُهُمْ فَإِنَّهُمْ غَيْرُ مَلُومِينَ	
	Except from their wives or those their right hands possess, for indeed, they are not to be blamed -	
75 القيامة 39	فَجَعَلَ مِنْهُ **الزَّوْجَيْنِ** الذَّكَرَ وَالْأُنثَىٰ	
78 النبأ 8	وَخَلَقْنَاكُمْ **أَزْوَاجًا**	
	And We created you in pairs	

Your wives	**أَزْوَاجُكُمْ**
4 النساء 12	وَلَكُمْ نِصْفُ مَا تَرَكَ **أَزْوَاجُكُمْ** إِن لَّمْ يَكُن لَّهُنَّ وَلَدٌ ۚ فَإِن كَانَ لَهُنَّ وَلَدٌ فَلَكُمُ الرُّبُعُ مِمَّا تَرَكْنَ ۚ مِن بَعْدِ وَصِيَّةٍ يُوصِينَ بِهَا أَوْ دَيْنٍ ۚ وَلَهُنَّ الرُّبُعُ مِمَّا تَرَكْتُمْ إِن لَّمْ يَكُن لَّكُمْ وَلَدٌ ۚ فَإِن كَانَ لَكُمْ وَلَدٌ فَلَهُنَّ الثُّمُنُ مِمَّا تَرَكْتُم ۚ مِّن بَعْدِ وَصِيَّةٍ تُوصُونَ بِهَا أَوْ دَيْنٍ ۗ وَإِن كَانَ رَجُلٌ يُورَثُ كَلَالَةً أَوِ امْرَأَةٌ وَلَهُ أَخٌ أَوْ أُخْتٌ فَلِكُلِّ وَاحِدٍ مِّنْهُمَا السُّدُسُ ۚ فَإِن كَانُوا أَكْثَرَ مِن ذَٰلِكَ فَهُمْ شُرَكَاءُ فِي الثُّلُثِ ۚ مِن بَعْدِ وَصِيَّةٍ يُوصَىٰ بِهَا أَوْ دَيْنٍ غَيْرَ مُضَارٍّ ۚ وَصِيَّةً مِّنَ اللَّهِ ۗ وَاللَّهُ عَلِيمٌ حَلِيمٌ

		And for you is half of what your wives leave if they have no child. But if they have a child, for you is one fourth of what they leave, after any bequest they [may have] made or debt. And for the wives is one fourth if you leave no child. But if you leave a child, then for them is an eighth of what you leave, after any bequest you [may have] made or debt. And if a man or woman leaves neither ascendants nor descendants but has a brother or a sister, then for each one of them is a sixth. But if they are more than two, they share a third, after any bequest which was made or debt, as long as there is no detriment [caused]. [This is] an ordinance from Allah, and Allah is Knowing and Forbearing.
9 التوبة 24		قُلْ إِن كَانَ آبَاؤُكُمْ وَأَبْنَاؤُكُمْ وَإِخْوَانُكُمْ وَأَزْوَاجُكُمْ وَعَشِيرَتُكُمْ وَأَمْوَالٌ اقْتَرَفْتُمُوهَا وَتِجَارَةٌ تَخْشَوْنَ كَسَادَهَا وَمَسَاكِنُ تَرْضَوْنَهَا أَحَبَّ إِلَيْكُم مِّنَ اللَّهِ وَرَسُولِهِ وَجِهَادٍ فِي سَبِيلِهِ فَتَرَبَّصُوا حَتَّىٰ يَأْتِيَ اللَّهُ بِأَمْرِهِ ۗ وَاللَّهُ لَا يَهْدِي الْقَوْمَ الْفَاسِقِينَ
		Say, [O Muhammad], "If your fathers, your sons, your brothers, your wives, your relatives, wealth which you have obtained, commerce wherein you fear decline, and dwellings with which you are pleased are more beloved to you than Allah and His Messenger and jihad in His cause, then wait until Allah executes His command. And Allah does not guide the defiantly disobedient people."
16 النحل 72		وَاللَّهُ جَعَلَ لَكُم مِّنْ أَنفُسِكُمْ أَزْوَاجًا وَجَعَلَ لَكُم مِّنْ أَزْوَاجِكُم بَنِينَ وَحَفَدَةً وَرَزَقَكُم مِّنَ الطَّيِّبَاتِ ۚ أَفَبِالْبَاطِلِ يُؤْمِنُونَ وَبِنِعْمَتِ اللَّهِ هُمْ يَكْفُرُونَ
		And Allah has made for you from yourselves mates and has made for you from your mates sons and grandchildren and has provided for you from the good things. Then in falsehood do they believe and in the favor of Allah they disbelieve?
26 الشعراء 166		وَتَذَرُونَ مَا خَلَقَ لَكُمْ رَبُّكُم مِّنْ أَزْوَاجِكُم ۚ بَلْ أَنتُمْ قَوْمٌ عَادُونَ
		And leave what your Lord has created for you as mates? But you are a people transgressing."
33 الأحزاب 4		مَّا جَعَلَ اللَّهُ لِرَجُلٍ مِّن قَلْبَيْنِ فِي جَوْفِهِ ۚ وَمَا جَعَلَ أَزْوَاجَكُمُ اللَّائِي تُظَاهِرُونَ مِنْهُنَّ أُمَّهَاتِكُمْ ۚ وَمَا جَعَلَ أَدْعِيَاءَكُمْ أَبْنَاءَكُمْ ۚ ذَٰلِكُمْ قَوْلُكُم بِأَفْوَاهِكُمْ ۖ وَاللَّهُ يَقُولُ الْحَقَّ وَهُوَ يَهْدِي السَّبِيلَ
		Allah has not made for a man two hearts in his interior. And He has not made your wives whom you declare unlawful your mothers. And he has not made your adopted sons your [true] sons. That is [merely] your saying by your mouths, but Allah says the truth, and He guides to the [right] way.

43 الزخرف 70	ادْخُلُوا الْجَنَّةَ أَنتُمْ وَأَزْوَاجُكُمْ تُحْبَرُونَ	
	Enter Paradise, you and your kinds, delighted."	
60 الممتحنة 11	وَإِن فَاتَكُمْ شَيْءٌ مِّنْ أَزْوَاجِكُمْ إِلَى الْكُفَّارِ فَعَاقَبْتُمْ فَآتُوا الَّذِينَ ذَهَبَتْ أَزْوَاجُهُم مِّثْلَ مَا أَنفَقُوا ۚ وَاتَّقُوا اللَّهَ الَّذِي أَنتُم بِهِ مُؤْمِنُونَ	
	And if you have lost any of your wives to the disbelievers and you subsequently obtain [something], then give those whose wives have gone the equivalent of what they had spent. And fear Allah, in whom you are believers.	
64 التغابن 14	يَا أَيُّهَا الَّذِينَ آمَنُوا إِنَّ مِنْ أَزْوَاجِكُمْ وَأَوْلَادِكُمْ عَدُوًّا لَّكُمْ فَاحْذَرُوهُمْ ۚ وَإِن تَعْفُوا وَتَصْفَحُوا وَتَغْفِرُوا فَإِنَّ اللَّهَ غَفُورٌ رَّحِيمٌ	
	O you who have believed, indeed, among your wives and your children are enemies to you, so beware of them. But if you pardon and overlook and forgive - then indeed, Allah is Forgiving and Merciful.	
Woman	امْرَأَةٌ	
4 النساء 12	۞ وَلَكُمْ نِصْفُ مَا تَرَكَ أَزْوَاجُكُمْ إِن لَّمْ يَكُن لَّهُنَّ وَلَدٌ ۚ فَإِن كَانَ لَهُنَّ وَلَدٌ فَلَكُمُ الرُّبُعُ مِمَّا تَرَكْنَ ۚ مِن بَعْدِ وَصِيَّةٍ يُوصِينَ بِهَا أَوْ دَيْنٍ ۚ وَلَهُنَّ الرُّبُعُ مِمَّا تَرَكْتُمْ إِن لَّمْ يَكُن لَّكُمْ وَلَدٌ ۚ فَإِن كَانَ لَكُمْ وَلَدٌ فَلَهُنَّ الثُّمُنُ مِمَّا تَرَكْتُم ۚ مِّن بَعْدِ وَصِيَّةٍ تُوصُونَ بِهَا أَوْ دَيْنٍ ۗ وَإِن كَانَ رَجُلٌ يُورَثُ كَلَالَةً أَوِ امْرَأَةٌ وَلَهُ أَخٌ أَوْ أُخْتٌ فَلِكُلِّ وَاحِدٍ مِّنْهُمَا السُّدُسُ ۚ فَإِن كَانُوا أَكْثَرَ مِن ذَٰلِكَ فَهُمْ شُرَكَاءُ فِي الثُّلُثِ ۚ مِن بَعْدِ وَصِيَّةٍ يُوصَىٰ بِهَا أَوْ دَيْنٍ غَيْرَ مُضَارٍّ ۚ وَصِيَّةً مِّنَ اللَّهِ ۗ وَاللَّهُ عَلِيمٌ حَلِيمٌ	
	And for you is half of what your wives leave if they have no child. But if they have a child, for you is one fourth of what they leave, after any bequest they [may have] made or debt. And for the wives is one fourth if you leave no child. But if you leave a child, then for them is an eighth of what you leave, after any bequest you [may have] made or debt. And if a man or woman leaves neither ascendants nor descendants but has a brother or a sister, then for each one of them is a sixth. But if they are more than two, they share a third, after any bequest which was made or debt, as long as there is no detriment [caused]. [This is] an ordinance from Allah, and Allah is Knowing and Forbearing.	

128	وَإِنِ امْرَأَةٌ خَافَتْ مِن بَعْلِهَا نُشُوزًا أَوْ إِعْرَاضًا فَلَا جُنَاحَ عَلَيْهِمَا أَن يُصْلِحَا بَيْنَهُمَا صُلْحًا ۚ وَالصُّلْحُ خَيْرٌ ۗ وَأُحْضِرَتِ الْأَنفُسُ الشُّحَّ ۚ وَإِن تُحْسِنُوا وَتَتَّقُوا فَإِنَّ اللَّهَ كَانَ بِمَا تَعْمَلُونَ خَبِيرًا
	And if a woman fears from her husband contempt or evasion, there is no sin upon them if they make terms of settlement between them - and settlement is best. And present in [human] souls is stinginess. But if you do good and fear Allah - then indeed Allah is ever, with what you do, Acquainted.
27 النمل 23	إِنِّي وَجَدتُّ امْرَأَةً تَمْلِكُهُمْ وَأُوتِيَتْ مِن كُلِّ شَيْءٍ وَلَهَا عَرْشٌ عَظِيمٌ
	Indeed, I found [there] a woman ruling them, and she has been given of all things, and she has a great throne.
33 الأحزاب 50	يَا أَيُّهَا النَّبِيُّ إِنَّا أَحْلَلْنَا لَكَ أَزْوَاجَكَ اللَّاتِي آتَيْتَ أُجُورَهُنَّ وَمَا مَلَكَتْ يَمِينُكَ مِمَّا أَفَاءَ اللَّهُ عَلَيْكَ وَبَنَاتِ عَمِّكَ وَبَنَاتِ عَمَّاتِكَ وَبَنَاتِ خَالِكَ وَبَنَاتِ خَالَاتِكَ اللَّاتِي هَاجَرْنَ مَعَكَ وَامْرَأَةً مُّؤْمِنَةً إِن وَهَبَتْ نَفْسَهَا لِلنَّبِيِّ إِنْ أَرَادَ النَّبِيُّ أَن يَسْتَنكِحَهَا خَالِصَةً لَّكَ مِن دُونِ الْمُؤْمِنِينَ ۗ قَدْ عَلِمْنَا مَا فَرَضْنَا عَلَيْهِمْ فِي أَزْوَاجِهِمْ وَمَا مَلَكَتْ أَيْمَانُهُمْ لِكَيْلَا يَكُونَ عَلَيْكَ حَرَجٌ ۗ وَكَانَ اللَّهُ غَفُورًا رَّحِيمًا
	O Prophet, indeed We have made lawful to you your wives to whom you have given their due compensation and those your right hand possesses from what Allah has returned to you [of captives] and the daughters of your paternal uncles and the daughters of your paternal aunts and the daughters of your maternal uncles and the daughters of your maternal aunts who emigrated with you and a believing woman if she gives herself to the Prophet [and] if the Prophet wishes to marry her, [this is] only for you, excluding the [other] believers. We certainly know what We have made obligatory upon them concerning their wives and those their right hands possess, [but this is for you] in order that there will be upon you no discomfort. And ever is Allah Forgiving and Merciful.

The women	النِّسَاءَ
2 البقرة 49	وَإِذْ نَجَّيْنَاكُم مِّنْ آلِ فِرْعَوْنَ يَسُومُونَكُمْ سُوءَ الْعَذَابِ يُذَبِّحُونَ أَبْنَاءَكُمْ وَيَسْتَحْيُونَ نِسَاءَكُمْ ۚ وَفِي ذَٰلِكُم بَلَاءٌ مِّن رَّبِّكُمْ عَظِيمٌ
	And [recall] when We saved your forefathers from the people of Pharaoh, who afflicted you with the worst torment, slaughtering your [newborn] sons and keeping your females alive. And in that was a great trial from your Lord.
222	وَيَسْأَلُونَكَ عَنِ الْمَحِيضِ ۖ قُلْ هُوَ أَذًى فَاعْتَزِلُوا النِّسَاءَ فِي الْمَحِيضِ ۖ وَلَا تَقْرَبُوهُنَّ حَتَّىٰ يَطْهُرْنَ ۖ فَإِذَا تَطَهَّرْنَ فَأْتُوهُنَّ مِنْ حَيْثُ أَمَرَكُمُ اللَّهُ ۚ إِنَّ اللَّهَ يُحِبُّ التَّوَّابِينَ وَيُحِبُّ الْمُتَطَهِّرِينَ
	And they ask you about menstruation. Say, "It is harm, so keep away from wives during menstruation. And do not approach them until they are pure. And when they have purified themselves, then come to them from where Allah has ordained for you. Indeed, Allah loves those who are constantly repentant and loves those who purify themselves."
231	وَإِذَا طَلَّقْتُمُ النِّسَاءَ فَبَلَغْنَ أَجَلَهُنَّ فَأَمْسِكُوهُنَّ بِمَعْرُوفٍ أَوْ سَرِّحُوهُنَّ بِمَعْرُوفٍ ۚ وَلَا تُمْسِكُوهُنَّ ضِرَارًا لِّتَعْتَدُوا ۚ وَمَن يَفْعَلْ ذَٰلِكَ فَقَدْ ظَلَمَ نَفْسَهُ ۚ وَلَا تَتَّخِذُوا آيَاتِ اللَّهِ هُزُوًا ۚ وَاذْكُرُوا نِعْمَتَ اللَّهِ عَلَيْكُمْ وَمَا أَنزَلَ عَلَيْكُم مِّنَ الْكِتَابِ وَالْحِكْمَةِ يَعِظُكُم بِهِ ۚ وَاتَّقُوا اللَّهَ وَاعْلَمُوا أَنَّ اللَّهَ بِكُلِّ شَيْءٍ عَلِيمٌ
	And when you divorce women and they have [nearly] fulfilled their term, either retain them according to acceptable terms or release them according to acceptable terms, and do not keep them, intending harm, to transgress [against them]. And whoever does that has certainly wronged himself. And do not take the verses of Allah in jest. And remember the favor of Allah upon you and what has been revealed to you of the Book and wisdom by which He instructs you. And fear Allah and know that Allah is Knowing of all things.
232	وَإِذَا طَلَّقْتُمُ النِّسَاءَ فَبَلَغْنَ أَجَلَهُنَّ فَلَا تَعْضُلُوهُنَّ أَن يَنكِحْنَ أَزْوَاجَهُنَّ إِذَا تَرَاضَوْا بَيْنَهُم بِالْمَعْرُوفِ ۗ ذَٰلِكَ يُوعَظُ بِهِ مَن كَانَ مِنكُمْ يُؤْمِنُ بِاللَّهِ وَالْيَوْمِ الْآخِرِ ۗ ذَٰلِكُمْ أَزْكَىٰ لَكُمْ وَأَطْهَرُ ۗ وَاللَّهُ يَعْلَمُ وَأَنتُمْ لَا تَعْلَمُونَ
	And when you divorce women and they have fulfilled their term, do not prevent them from remarrying their [former] husbands if they agree among themselves on an acceptable basis. That is instructed to whoever of you

	believes in Allah and the Last Day. That is better for you and purer, and Allah knows and you know not.
235	وَلَا جُنَاحَ عَلَيْكُمْ فِيمَا عَرَّضْتُم بِهِ مِنْ خِطْبَةِ النِّسَاءِ أَوْ أَكْنَنتُمْ فِي أَنفُسِكُمْ ۚ عَلِمَ اللَّهُ أَنَّكُمْ سَتَذْكُرُونَهُنَّ وَلَٰكِن لَّا تُوَاعِدُوهُنَّ سِرًّا إِلَّا أَن تَقُولُوا قَوْلًا مَّعْرُوفًا ۚ وَلَا تَعْزِمُوا عُقْدَةَ النِّكَاحِ حَتَّىٰ يَبْلُغَ الْكِتَابُ أَجَلَهُ ۚ وَاعْلَمُوا أَنَّ اللَّهَ يَعْلَمُ مَا فِي أَنفُسِكُمْ فَاحْذَرُوهُ ۚ وَاعْلَمُوا أَنَّ اللَّهَ غَفُورٌ حَلِيمٌ
	There is no blame upon you for that to which you [indirectly] allude concerning a proposal to women or for what you conceal within yourselves. Allah knows that you will have them in mind. But do not promise them secretly except for saying a proper saying. And do not determine to undertake a marriage contract until the decreed period reaches its end. And know that Allah knows what is within yourselves, so beware of Him. And know that Allah is Forgiving and Forbearing.
236	لَّا جُنَاحَ عَلَيْكُمْ إِن طَلَّقْتُمُ النِّسَاءَ مَا لَمْ تَمَسُّوهُنَّ أَوْ تَفْرِضُوا لَهُنَّ فَرِيضَةً ۚ وَمَتِّعُوهُنَّ عَلَى الْمُوسِعِ قَدَرُهُ وَعَلَى الْمُقْتِرِ قَدَرُهُ مَتَاعًا بِالْمَعْرُوفِ ۖ حَقًّا عَلَى الْمُحْسِنِينَ
	There is no blame upon you if you divorce women you have not touched nor specified for them an obligation. But give them [a gift of] compensation - the wealthy according to his capability and the poor according to his capability - a provision according to what is acceptable, a duty upon the doers of good.
3 آل عمران 14	زُيِّنَ لِلنَّاسِ حُبُّ الشَّهَوَاتِ مِنَ النِّسَاءِ وَالْبَنِينَ وَالْقَنَاطِيرِ الْمُقَنطَرَةِ مِنَ الذَّهَبِ وَالْفِضَّةِ وَالْخَيْلِ الْمُسَوَّمَةِ وَالْأَنْعَامِ وَالْحَرْثِ ۗ ذَٰلِكَ مَتَاعُ الْحَيَاةِ الدُّنْيَا ۖ وَاللَّهُ عِندَهُ حُسْنُ الْمَآبِ
	Beautified for people is the love of that which they desire - of women and sons, heaped-up sums of gold and silver, fine branded horses, and cattle and tilled land. That is the enjoyment of worldly life, but Allah has with Him the best return.
42	وَإِذْ قَالَتِ الْمَلَائِكَةُ يَا مَرْيَمُ إِنَّ اللَّهَ اصْطَفَاكِ وَطَهَّرَكِ وَاصْطَفَاكِ عَلَىٰ نِسَاءِ الْعَالَمِينَ
	And [mention] when the angels said, "O Mary, indeed Allah has chosen you and purified you and chosen you above the women of the worlds.
61	فَمَنْ حَاجَّكَ فِيهِ مِن بَعْدِ مَا جَاءَكَ مِنَ الْعِلْمِ فَقُلْ تَعَالَوْا نَدْعُ أَبْنَاءَنَا وَأَبْنَاءَكُمْ وَنِسَاءَنَا وَنِسَاءَكُمْ وَأَنفُسَنَا وَأَنفُسَكُمْ ثُمَّ نَبْتَهِلْ فَنَجْعَل لَّعْنَتَ اللَّهِ عَلَى الْكَاذِبِينَ

		Then whoever argues with you about it after [this] knowledge has come to you - say, "Come, let us call our sons and your sons, our women and your women, ourselves and yourselves, then supplicate earnestly [together] and invoke the curse of Allah upon the liars [among us]."
4 النساء 1		يَا أَيُّهَا النَّاسُ اتَّقُوا رَبَّكُمُ الَّذِي خَلَقَكُم مِّن نَّفْسٍ وَاحِدَةٍ وَخَلَقَ مِنْهَا زَوْجَهَا وَبَثَّ مِنْهُمَا رِجَالًا كَثِيرًا وَنِسَاءً ۚ وَاتَّقُوا اللَّهَ الَّذِي تَسَاءَلُونَ بِهِ وَالْأَرْحَامَ ۚ إِنَّ اللَّهَ كَانَ عَلَيْكُمْ رَقِيبًا
		O mankind, fear your Lord, who created you from one soul and created from it its mate and dispersed from both of them many men and women. And fear Allah, through whom you ask one another, and the wombs. Indeed Allah is ever, over you, an Observer.
3		وَإِنْ خِفْتُمْ أَلَّا تُقْسِطُوا فِي الْيَتَامَىٰ فَانكِحُوا مَا طَابَ لَكُم مِّنَ النِّسَاءِ مَثْنَىٰ وَثُلَاثَ وَرُبَاعَ ۖ فَإِنْ خِفْتُمْ أَلَّا تَعْدِلُوا فَوَاحِدَةً أَوْ مَا مَلَكَتْ أَيْمَانُكُمْ ۚ ذَٰلِكَ أَدْنَىٰ أَلَّا تَعُولُوا
		And if you fear that you will not deal justly with the orphan girls, then marry those that please you of [other] women, two or three or four. But if you fear that you will not be just, then [marry only] one or those your right hand possesses. That is more suitable that you may not incline [to injustice].
4		وَآتُوا النِّسَاءَ صَدُقَاتِهِنَّ نِحْلَةً ۚ فَإِن طِبْنَ لَكُمْ عَن شَيْءٍ مِّنْهُ نَفْسًا فَكُلُوهُ هَنِيئًا مَّرِيئًا
		And give the women [upon marriage] their [bridal] gifts graciously. But if they give up willingly to you anything of it, then take it in satisfaction and ease.
7		لِّلرِّجَالِ نَصِيبٌ مِّمَّا تَرَكَ الْوَالِدَانِ وَالْأَقْرَبُونَ وَلِلنِّسَاءِ نَصِيبٌ مِّمَّا تَرَكَ الْوَالِدَانِ وَالْأَقْرَبُونَ مِمَّا قَلَّ مِنْهُ أَوْ كَثُرَ ۚ نَصِيبًا مَّفْرُوضًا
		For men is a share of what the parents and close relatives leave, and for women is a share of what the parents and close relatives leave, be it little or much - an obligatory share.
11		يُوصِيكُمُ اللَّهُ فِي أَوْلَادِكُمْ ۖ لِلذَّكَرِ مِثْلُ حَظِّ الْأُنثَيَيْنِ ۚ فَإِن كُنَّ نِسَاءً فَوْقَ اثْنَتَيْنِ فَلَهُنَّ ثُلُثَا مَا تَرَكَ ۖ وَإِن كَانَتْ وَاحِدَةً فَلَهَا النِّصْفُ ۚ وَلِأَبَوَيْهِ لِكُلِّ وَاحِدٍ مِّنْهُمَا السُّدُسُ مِمَّا تَرَكَ إِن كَانَ لَهُ وَلَدٌ ۚ فَإِن لَّمْ يَكُن لَّهُ وَلَدٌ وَوَرِثَهُ أَبَوَاهُ فَلِأُمِّهِ الثُّلُثُ ۚ فَإِن كَانَ لَهُ إِخْوَةٌ فَلِأُمِّهِ السُّدُسُ ۚ مِن بَعْدِ وَصِيَّةٍ يُوصِي بِهَا أَوْ دَيْنٍ ۗ آبَاؤُكُمْ وَأَبْنَاؤُكُمْ لَا تَدْرُونَ أَيُّهُمْ أَقْرَبُ لَكُمْ نَفْعًا ۚ فَرِيضَةً مِّنَ اللَّهِ ۗ إِنَّ اللَّهَ كَانَ عَلِيمًا حَكِيمًا

	Allah instructs you concerning your children: for the male, what is equal to the share of two females. But if there are [only] daughters, two or more, for them is two thirds of one's estate. And if there is only one, for her is half. And for one's parents, to each one of them is a sixth of his estate if he left children. But if he had no children and the parents [alone] inherit from him, then for his mother is one third. And if he had brothers [or sisters], for his mother is a sixth, after any bequest he [may have] made or debt. Your parents or your children - you know not which of them are nearest to you in benefit. [These shares are] an obligation [imposed] by Allah. Indeed, Allah is ever Knowing and Wise.
19	يَا أَيُّهَا الَّذِينَ آمَنُوا لَا يَحِلُّ لَكُمْ أَن تَرِثُوا النِّسَاءَ كَرْهًا ۖ وَلَا تَعْضُلُوهُنَّ لِتَذْهَبُوا بِبَعْضِ مَا آتَيْتُمُوهُنَّ إِلَّا أَن يَأْتِينَ بِفَاحِشَةٍ مُّبَيِّنَةٍ ۚ وَعَاشِرُوهُنَّ بِالْمَعْرُوفِ ۚ فَإِن كَرِهْتُمُوهُنَّ فَعَسَىٰ أَن تَكْرَهُوا شَيْئًا وَيَجْعَلَ اللَّهُ فِيهِ خَيْرًا كَثِيرًا
	O you who have believed, it is not lawful for you to inherit women by compulsion. And do not make difficulties for them in order to take [back] part of what you gave them unless they commit a clear immorality. And live with them in kindness. For if you dislike them - perhaps you dislike a thing and Allah makes therein much good.
22	وَلَا تَنكِحُوا مَا نَكَحَ آبَاؤُكُم مِّنَ النِّسَاءِ إِلَّا مَا قَدْ سَلَفَ ۚ إِنَّهُ كَانَ فَاحِشَةً وَمَقْتًا وَسَاءَ سَبِيلًا
	And do not marry those [women] whom your fathers married, except what has already occurred. Indeed, it was an immorality and hateful [to Allah] and was evil as a way.
24	وَالْمُحْصَنَاتُ مِنَ النِّسَاءِ إِلَّا مَا مَلَكَتْ أَيْمَانُكُمْ ۖ كِتَابَ اللَّهِ عَلَيْكُمْ ۚ وَأُحِلَّ لَكُم مَّا وَرَاءَ ذَٰلِكُمْ أَن تَبْتَغُوا بِأَمْوَالِكُم مُّحْصِنِينَ غَيْرَ مُسَافِحِينَ ۚ فَمَا اسْتَمْتَعْتُم بِهِ مِنْهُنَّ فَآتُوهُنَّ أُجُورَهُنَّ فَرِيضَةً ۚ وَلَا جُنَاحَ عَلَيْكُمْ فِيمَا تَرَاضَيْتُم بِهِ مِن بَعْدِ الْفَرِيضَةِ ۚ إِنَّ اللَّهَ كَانَ عَلِيمًا حَكِيمًا
	And [also prohibited to you are all] married women except those your right hands possess. [This is] the decree of Allah upon you. And lawful to you are [all others] beyond these, [provided] that you seek them [in marriage] with [gifts from] your property, desiring chastity, not unlawful sexual intercourse. So for whatever you enjoy [of marriage] from them, give them their due compensation as an obligation. And there is no blame upon you for what you mutually agree to beyond the obligation. Indeed, Allah is ever Knowing and Wise.

32	وَلَا تَتَمَنَّوْا مَا فَضَّلَ اللَّهُ بِهِ بَعْضَكُمْ عَلَىٰ بَعْضٍ ۚ لِّلرِّجَالِ نَصِيبٌ مِّمَّا اكْتَسَبُوا ۖ وَلِلنِّسَاءِ نَصِيبٌ مِّمَّا اكْتَسَبْنَ ۚ وَاسْأَلُوا اللَّهَ مِن فَضْلِهِ ۗ إِنَّ اللَّهَ كَانَ بِكُلِّ شَيْءٍ عَلِيمًا
	And do not wish for that by which Allah has made some of you exceed others. For men is a share of what they have earned, and for women is a share of what they have earned. And ask Allah of his bounty. Indeed Allah is ever, of all things, Knowing.
34	الرِّجَالُ قَوَّامُونَ عَلَى النِّسَاءِ بِمَا فَضَّلَ اللَّهُ بَعْضَهُمْ عَلَىٰ بَعْضٍ وَبِمَا أَنفَقُوا مِنْ أَمْوَالِهِمْ ۚ فَالصَّالِحَاتُ قَانِتَاتٌ حَافِظَاتٌ لِّلْغَيْبِ بِمَا حَفِظَ اللَّهُ ۚ وَاللَّاتِي تَخَافُونَ نُشُوزَهُنَّ فَعِظُوهُنَّ وَاهْجُرُوهُنَّ فِي الْمَضَاجِعِ وَاضْرِبُوهُنَّ ۖ فَإِنْ أَطَعْنَكُمْ فَلَا تَبْغُوا عَلَيْهِنَّ سَبِيلًا ۗ إِنَّ اللَّهَ كَانَ عَلِيًّا كَبِيرًا
	Men are in charge of women by [right of] what Allah has given one over the other and what they spend [for maintenance] from their wealth. So righteous women are devoutly obedient, guarding in [the husband's] absence what Allah would have them guard. But those [wives] from whom you fear arrogance - [first] advise them; [then if they persist], forsake them in bed; and [finally], strike them. But if they obey you [once more], seek no means against them. Indeed, Allah is ever Exalted and Grand.
43	يَا أَيُّهَا الَّذِينَ آمَنُوا لَا تَقْرَبُوا الصَّلَاةَ وَأَنتُمْ سُكَارَىٰ حَتَّىٰ تَعْلَمُوا مَا تَقُولُونَ وَلَا جُنُبًا إِلَّا عَابِرِي سَبِيلٍ حَتَّىٰ تَغْتَسِلُوا ۚ وَإِن كُنتُم مَّرْضَىٰ أَوْ عَلَىٰ سَفَرٍ أَوْ جَاءَ أَحَدٌ مِّنكُم مِّنَ الْغَائِطِ أَوْ لَامَسْتُمُ النِّسَاءَ فَلَمْ تَجِدُوا مَاءً فَتَيَمَّمُوا صَعِيدًا طَيِّبًا فَامْسَحُوا بِوُجُوهِكُمْ وَأَيْدِيكُمْ ۗ إِنَّ اللَّهَ كَانَ عَفُوًّا غَفُورًا
	O you who have believed, do not approach prayer while you are intoxicated until you know what you are saying or in a state of janabah, except those passing through [a place of prayer], until you have washed [your whole body].

	And if you are ill or on a journey or one of you comes from the place of relieving himself or you have contacted women and find no water, then seek clean earth and wipe over your faces and your hands [with it]. Indeed, Allah is ever Pardoning and Forgiving.
75	وَمَا لَكُمْ لَا تُقَاتِلُونَ فِي سَبِيلِ اللَّهِ وَالْمُسْتَضْعَفِينَ مِنَ الرِّجَالِ وَالنِّسَاءِ وَالْوِلْدَانِ الَّذِينَ يَقُولُونَ رَبَّنَا أَخْرِجْنَا مِنْ هَٰذِهِ الْقَرْيَةِ الظَّالِمِ أَهْلُهَا وَاجْعَل لَّنَا مِن لَّدُنكَ وَلِيًّا وَاجْعَل لَّنَا مِن لَّدُنكَ نَصِيرًا
	And what is [the matter] with you that you fight not in the cause of Allah and [for] the oppressed among men, women, and children who say, "Our Lord, take us out of this city of oppressive people and appoint for us from Yourself a protector and appoint for us from Yourself a helper?"
98	إِلَّا الْمُسْتَضْعَفِينَ مِنَ الرِّجَالِ وَالنِّسَاءِ وَالْوِلْدَانِ لَا يَسْتَطِيعُونَ حِيلَةً وَلَا يَهْتَدُونَ سَبِيلًا
	Except for the oppressed among men, women and children who cannot devise a plan nor are they directed to a way
127	وَيَسْتَفْتُونَكَ فِي النِّسَاءِ ۖ قُلِ اللَّهُ يُفْتِيكُمْ فِيهِنَّ وَمَا يُتْلَىٰ عَلَيْكُمْ فِي الْكِتَابِ فِي يَتَامَى النِّسَاءِ اللَّاتِي لَا تُؤْتُونَهُنَّ مَا كُتِبَ لَهُنَّ وَتَرْغَبُونَ أَن تَنكِحُوهُنَّ وَالْمُسْتَضْعَفِينَ مِنَ الْوِلْدَانِ وَأَن تَقُومُوا لِلْيَتَامَىٰ بِالْقِسْطِ ۚ وَمَا تَفْعَلُوا مِنْ خَيْرٍ فَإِنَّ اللَّهَ كَانَ بِهِ عَلِيمًا
	And they request from you, [O Muhammad], a [legal] ruling concerning women. Say, "Allah gives you a ruling about them and [about] what has been recited to you in the Book concerning the orphan girls to whom you do not give what is decreed for them - and [yet] you desire to marry them - and concerning the oppressed among children and that you maintain for orphans [their rights] in justice." And whatever you do of good - indeed, Allah is ever Knowing of it.
129	وَلَن تَسْتَطِيعُوا أَن تَعْدِلُوا بَيْنَ النِّسَاءِ وَلَوْ حَرَصْتُمْ ۖ فَلَا تَمِيلُوا كُلَّ الْمَيْلِ فَتَذَرُوهَا كَالْمُعَلَّقَةِ ۚ وَإِن تُصْلِحُوا وَتَتَّقُوا فَإِنَّ اللَّهَ كَانَ غَفُورًا رَّحِيمًا
	And you will never be able to be equal [in feeling] between wives, even if you should strive [to do so]. So do not incline completely [toward one] and leave another hanging. And if you amend [your affairs] and fear Allah - then indeed, Allah is ever Forgiving and Merciful.

176	يَسْتَفْتُونَكَ قُلِ اللَّهُ يُفْتِيكُمْ فِي الْكَلَالَةِ ۚ إِنِ امْرُؤٌ هَلَكَ لَيْسَ لَهُ وَلَدٌ وَلَهُ أُخْتٌ فَلَهَا نِصْفُ مَا تَرَكَ ۚ وَهُوَ يَرِثُهَا إِن لَّمْ يَكُن لَّهَا وَلَدٌ ۚ فَإِن كَانَتَا اثْنَتَيْنِ فَلَهُمَا الثُّلُثَانِ مِمَّا تَرَكَ ۚ وَإِن كَانُوا إِخْوَةً رِّجَالًا وَنِسَاءً فَلِلذَّكَرِ مِثْلُ حَظِّ الْأُنثَيَيْنِ ۗ يُبَيِّنُ اللَّهُ لَكُمْ أَن تَضِلُّوا ۗ وَاللَّهُ بِكُلِّ شَيْءٍ عَلِيمٌ	
	They request from you a [legal] ruling. Say, "Allah gives you a ruling concerning one having neither descendants nor ascendants [as heirs]." If a man dies, leaving no child but [only] a sister, she will have half of what he left. And he inherits from her if she [dies and] has no child. But if there are two sisters [or more], they will have two-thirds of what he left. If there are both brothers and sisters, the male will have the share of two females. Allah makes clear to you [His law], lest you go astray. And Allah is Knowing of all things.	
5 المائدة 6	يَا أَيُّهَا الَّذِينَ آمَنُوا إِذَا قُمْتُمْ إِلَى الصَّلَاةِ فَاغْسِلُوا وُجُوهَكُمْ وَأَيْدِيَكُمْ إِلَى الْمَرَافِقِ وَامْسَحُوا بِرُءُوسِكُمْ وَأَرْجُلَكُمْ إِلَى الْكَعْبَيْنِ ۚ وَإِن كُنتُمْ جُنُبًا فَاطَّهَّرُوا ۚ وَإِن كُنتُم مَّرْضَىٰ أَوْ عَلَىٰ سَفَرٍ أَوْ جَاءَ أَحَدٌ مِّنكُم مِّنَ الْغَائِطِ أَوْ لَامَسْتُمُ النِّسَاءَ فَلَمْ تَجِدُوا مَاءً فَتَيَمَّمُوا صَعِيدًا طَيِّبًا فَامْسَحُوا بِوُجُوهِكُمْ وَأَيْدِيكُم مِّنْهُ ۚ مَا يُرِيدُ اللَّهُ لِيَجْعَلَ عَلَيْكُم مِّنْ حَرَجٍ وَلَٰكِن يُرِيدُ لِيُطَهِّرَكُمْ وَلِيُتِمَّ نِعْمَتَهُ عَلَيْكُمْ لَعَلَّكُمْ تَشْكُرُونَ	
	O you who have believed, when you rise to [perform] prayer, wash your faces and your forearms to the elbows and wipe over your heads and wash your feet to the ankles. And if you are in a state of janabah, then purify yourselves. But if you are ill or on a journey or one of you comes from the place of relieving himself or you have contacted women and do not find water, then seek clean earth and wipe over your faces and hands with it. Allah does not intend to make difficulty for you, but He intends to purify you and complete His favor upon you that you may be grateful.	
7 الأعراف 81	إِنَّكُمْ لَتَأْتُونَ الرِّجَالَ شَهْوَةً مِّن دُونِ النِّسَاءِ ۚ بَلْ أَنتُمْ قَوْمٌ مُّسْرِفُونَ	

	Indeed, you approach men with desire, instead of women. Rather, you are a transgressing people."	
127	وَقَالَ الْمَلَأُ مِن قَوْمِ فِرْعَوْنَ أَتَذَرُ مُوسَىٰ وَقَوْمَهُ لِيُفْسِدُوا فِي الْأَرْضِ وَيَذَرَكَ وَآلِهَتَكَ ۚ قَالَ سَنُقَتِّلُ أَبْنَاءَهُمْ وَنَسْتَحْيِي نِسَاءَهُمْ وَإِنَّا فَوْقَهُمْ قَاهِرُونَ	
	And the eminent among the people of Pharaoh said," Will you leave Moses and his people to cause corruption in the land and abandon you and your gods?" [Pharaoh] said, "We will kill their sons and keep their women alive; and indeed, we are subjugators over them."	
141	وَإِذْ أَنجَيْنَاكُم مِّنْ آلِ فِرْعَوْنَ يَسُومُونَكُمْ سُوءَ الْعَذَابِ ۖ يُقَتِّلُونَ أَبْنَاءَكُمْ وَيَسْتَحْيُونَ نِسَاءَكُمْ ۚ وَفِي ذَٰلِكُم بَلَاءٌ مِّن رَّبِّكُمْ عَظِيمٌ	
	And [recall, O Children of Israel], when We saved you from the people of Pharaoh, [who were] afflicting you with the worst torment - killing your sons and keeping your women alive. And in that was a great trial from your Lord.	
14 ابراهيم 6	وَإِذْ قَالَ مُوسَىٰ لِقَوْمِهِ اذْكُرُوا نِعْمَةَ اللَّهِ عَلَيْكُمْ إِذْ أَنجَاكُم مِّنْ آلِ فِرْعَوْنَ يَسُومُونَكُمْ سُوءَ الْعَذَابِ وَيُذَبِّحُونَ أَبْنَاءَكُمْ وَيَسْتَحْيُونَ نِسَاءَكُمْ ۚ وَفِي ذَٰلِكُم بَلَاءٌ مِّن رَّبِّكُمْ عَظِيمٌ	
	And [recall, O Children of Israel], when Moses said to His people, "Remember the favor of Allah upon you when He saved you from the people of Pharaoh, who were afflicting you with the worst torment and were slaughtering your [newborn] sons and keeping your females alive. And in that was a great trial from your Lord.	
24 النور 31	وَقُل لِّلْمُؤْمِنَاتِ يَغْضُضْنَ مِنْ أَبْصَارِهِنَّ وَيَحْفَظْنَ فُرُوجَهُنَّ وَلَا يُبْدِينَ زِينَتَهُنَّ إِلَّا مَا ظَهَرَ مِنْهَا ۖ وَلْيَضْرِبْنَ بِخُمُرِهِنَّ عَلَىٰ جُيُوبِهِنَّ ۖ وَلَا يُبْدِينَ زِينَتَهُنَّ إِلَّا لِبُعُولَتِهِنَّ أَوْ آبَائِهِنَّ أَوْ آبَاءِ بُعُولَتِهِنَّ أَوْ أَبْنَائِهِنَّ أَوْ أَبْنَاءِ بُعُولَتِهِنَّ أَوْ إِخْوَانِهِنَّ أَوْ بَنِي إِخْوَانِهِنَّ أَوْ بَنِي أَخَوَاتِهِنَّ أَوْ نِسَائِهِنَّ أَوْ مَا مَلَكَتْ أَيْمَانُهُنَّ أَوِ التَّابِعِينَ غَيْرِ أُولِي الْإِرْبَةِ مِنَ الرِّجَالِ أَوِ الطِّفْلِ الَّذِينَ لَمْ يَظْهَرُوا عَلَىٰ عَوْرَاتِ النِّسَاءِ ۖ وَلَا يَضْرِبْنَ بِأَرْجُلِهِنَّ لِيُعْلَمَ مَا يُخْفِينَ مِن زِينَتِهِنَّ ۚ وَتُوبُوا إِلَى اللَّهِ جَمِيعًا أَيُّهَ الْمُؤْمِنُونَ لَعَلَّكُمْ تُفْلِحُونَ	

		And tell the believing women to reduce [some] of their vision and guard their private parts and not expose their adornment except that which [necessarily] appears thereof and to wrap [a portion of] their headcovers over their chests and not expose their adornment except to their husbands, their fathers, their husbands' fathers, their sons, their husbands' sons, their brothers, their brothers' sons, their sisters' sons, their women, that which their right hands possess, or those male attendants having no physical desire, or children who are not yet aware of the private aspects of women. And let them not stamp their feet to make known what they conceal of their adornment. And turn to Allah in repentance, all of you, O believers, that you might succeed.
60		وَالْقَوَاعِدُ مِنَ النِّسَاءِ اللَّاتِي لَا يَرْجُونَ نِكَاحًا فَلَيْسَ عَلَيْهِنَّ جُنَاحٌ أَن يَضَعْنَ ثِيَابَهُنَّ غَيْرَ مُتَبَرِّجَاتٍ بِزِينَةٍ ۖ وَأَن يَسْتَعْفِفْنَ خَيْرٌ لَّهُنَّ ۗ وَاللَّهُ سَمِيعٌ عَلِيمٌ
		And women of post-menstrual age who have no desire for marriage - there is no blame upon them for putting aside their outer garments [but] not displaying adornment. But to modestly refrain [from that] is better for them. And Allah is Hearing and Knowing.
27 النمل 55		أَئِنَّكُمْ لَتَأْتُونَ الرِّجَالَ شَهْوَةً مِّن دُونِ النِّسَاءِ ۚ بَلْ أَنتُمْ قَوْمٌ تَجْهَلُونَ
		Do you indeed approach men with desire instead of women? Rather, you are a people behaving ignorantly."
28 القصص 4		إِنَّ فِرْعَوْنَ عَلَا فِي الْأَرْضِ وَجَعَلَ أَهْلَهَا شِيَعًا يَسْتَضْعِفُ طَائِفَةً مِّنْهُمْ يُذَبِّحُ أَبْنَاءَهُمْ وَيَسْتَحْيِي نِسَاءَهُمْ ۚ إِنَّهُ كَانَ مِنَ الْمُفْسِدِينَ
		Indeed, Pharaoh exalted himself in the land and made its people into factions, oppressing a sector among them, slaughtering their [newborn] sons and keeping their females alive. Indeed, he was of the corrupters.
33 الأحزاب 30		يَا نِسَاءَ النَّبِيِّ مَن يَأْتِ مِنكُنَّ بِفَاحِشَةٍ مُّبَيِّنَةٍ يُضَاعَفْ لَهَا الْعَذَابُ ضِعْفَيْنِ ۚ وَكَانَ ذَٰلِكَ عَلَى اللَّهِ يَسِيرًا
		O wives of the Prophet, whoever of you should commit a clear immorality - for her the punishment would be doubled two fold, and ever is that, for Allah, easy.

32	يَا نِسَاءَ النَّبِيِّ لَسْتُنَّ كَأَحَدٍ مِّنَ النِّسَاءِ ۚ إِنِ اتَّقَيْتُنَّ فَلَا تَخْضَعْنَ بِالْقَوْلِ فَيَطْمَعَ الَّذِي فِي قَلْبِهِ مَرَضٌ وَقُلْنَ قَوْلًا مَّعْرُوفًا	
	O wives of the Prophet, you are not like anyone among women. If you fear Allah, then do not be soft in speech [to men], lest he in whose heart is disease should covet, but speak with appropriate speech.	
52	لَّا يَحِلُّ لَكَ النِّسَاءُ مِن بَعْدُ وَلَا أَن تَبَدَّلَ بِهِنَّ مِنْ أَزْوَاجٍ وَلَوْ أَعْجَبَكَ حُسْنُهُنَّ إِلَّا مَا مَلَكَتْ يَمِينُكَ ۗ وَكَانَ اللَّهُ عَلَىٰ كُلِّ شَيْءٍ رَّقِيبًا	
	Not lawful to you, [O Muhammad], are [any additional] women after [this], nor [is it] for you to exchange them for [other] wives, even if their beauty were to please you, except what your right hand possesses. And ever is Allah, over all things, an Observer.	
59	يَا أَيُّهَا النَّبِيُّ قُل لِّأَزْوَاجِكَ وَبَنَاتِكَ وَنِسَاءِ الْمُؤْمِنِينَ يُدْنِينَ عَلَيْهِنَّ مِن جَلَابِيبِهِنَّ ۚ ذَٰلِكَ أَدْنَىٰ أَن يُعْرَفْنَ فَلَا يُؤْذَيْنَ ۗ وَكَانَ اللَّهُ غَفُورًا رَّحِيمًا	
	O Prophet, tell your wives and your daughters and the women of the believers to bring down over themselves [part] of their outer garments. That is more suitable that they will be known and not be abused. And ever is Allah Forgiving and Merciful.	
40 غافر 25	فَلَمَّا جَاءَهُم بِالْحَقِّ مِنْ عِندِنَا قَالُوا اقْتُلُوا أَبْنَاءَ الَّذِينَ آمَنُوا مَعَهُ وَاسْتَحْيُوا نِسَاءَهُمْ ۚ وَمَا كَيْدُ الْكَافِرِينَ إِلَّا فِي ضَلَالٍ	
	And when he brought them the truth from Us, they said, "Kill the sons of those who have believed with him and keep their women alive." But the plan of the disbelievers is not except in error.	
48 الفتح 25	هُمُ الَّذِينَ كَفَرُوا وَصَدُّوكُمْ عَنِ الْمَسْجِدِ الْحَرَامِ وَالْهَدْيَ مَعْكُوفًا أَن يَبْلُغَ مَحِلَّهُ ۚ وَلَوْلَا رِجَالٌ مُّؤْمِنُونَ وَنِسَاءٌ مُّؤْمِنَاتٌ لَّمْ تَعْلَمُوهُمْ أَن تَطَئُوهُمْ فَتُصِيبَكُم مِّنْهُم مَّعَرَّةٌ بِغَيْرِ عِلْمٍ ۖ لِّيُدْخِلَ اللَّهُ فِي رَحْمَتِهِ مَن يَشَاءُ ۚ لَوْ تَزَيَّلُوا لَعَذَّبْنَا الَّذِينَ كَفَرُوا مِنْهُمْ عَذَابًا أَلِيمًا	
	They are the ones who disbelieved and obstructed you from al-Masjid al-Haram while the offering was prevented from reaching its place of sacrifice. And if not for believing men and believing women whom you did not know - that you might trample them and there would befall you because of them dishonor without [your] knowledge - [you would have been permitted to enter Makkah]. [This was so] that Allah might admit to His mercy whom He willed.	

	If they had been apart [from them], We would have punished those who disbelieved among them with painful punishment
49 الحجرات 11	يَا أَيُّهَا الَّذِينَ آمَنُوا لَا يَسْخَرْ قَوْمٌ مِّن قَوْمٍ عَسَىٰ أَن يَكُونُوا خَيْرًا مِّنْهُمْ وَلَا نِسَاءٌ مِّن نِّسَاءٍ عَسَىٰ أَن يَكُنَّ خَيْرًا مِّنْهُنَّ ۖ وَلَا تَلْمِزُوا أَنفُسَكُمْ وَلَا تَنَابَزُوا بِالْأَلْقَابِ ۖ بِئْسَ الِاسْمُ الْفُسُوقُ بَعْدَ الْإِيمَانِ ۚ وَمَن لَّمْ يَتُبْ فَأُولَٰئِكَ هُمُ الظَّالِمُونَ
	O you who have believed, let not a people ridicule [another] people; perhaps they may be better than them; nor let women ridicule [other] women; perhaps they may be better than them. And do not insult one another and do not call each other by [offensive] nicknames. Wretched is the name of disobedience after [one's] faith. And whoever does not repent - then it is those who are the wrongdoers.
65 الطلاق 1	يَا أَيُّهَا النَّبِيُّ إِذَا طَلَّقْتُمُ النِّسَاءَ فَطَلِّقُوهُنَّ لِعِدَّتِهِنَّ وَأَحْصُوا الْعِدَّةَ ۖ وَاتَّقُوا اللَّهَ رَبَّكُمْ ۖ لَا تُخْرِجُوهُنَّ مِن بُيُوتِهِنَّ وَلَا يَخْرُجْنَ إِلَّا أَن يَأْتِينَ بِفَاحِشَةٍ مُّبَيِّنَةٍ ۚ وَتِلْكَ حُدُودُ اللَّهِ ۚ وَمَن يَتَعَدَّ حُدُودَ اللَّهِ فَقَدْ ظَلَمَ نَفْسَهُ ۚ لَا تَدْرِي لَعَلَّ اللَّهَ يُحْدِثُ بَعْدَ ذَٰلِكَ أَمْرًا
	O Prophet, when you [Muslims] divorce women, divorce them for [the commencement of] their waiting period and keep count of the waiting period, and fear Allah, your Lord. Do not turn them out of their [husbands'] houses, nor should they [themselves] leave [during that period] unless they are committing a clear immorality. And those are the limits [set by] Allah. And whoever transgresses the limits of Allah has certainly wronged himself. You know not; perhaps Allah will bring about after that a [different] matter.

Women	نِسْوَةٌ
12 يوسف 30	وَقَالَ نِسْوَةٌ فِي الْمَدِينَةِ امْرَأَتُ الْعَزِيزِ تُرَاوِدُ فَتَاهَا عَن نَّفْسِهِ ۖ قَدْ شَغَفَهَا حُبًّا ۖ إِنَّا لَنَرَاهَا فِي ضَلَالٍ مُّبِينٍ
	And women in the city said, "The wife of al-'Azeez is seeking to seduce her slave boy; he has impassioned her with love. Indeed, we see her [to be] in clear error."
50	وَقَالَ الْمَلِكُ ائْتُونِي بِهِ ۖ فَلَمَّا جَاءَهُ الرَّسُولُ قَالَ ارْجِعْ إِلَىٰ رَبِّكَ فَاسْأَلْهُ مَا بَالُ النِّسْوَةِ اللَّاتِي قَطَّعْنَ أَيْدِيَهُنَّ ۚ إِنَّ رَبِّي بِكَيْدِهِنَّ عَلِيمٌ
	And the king said, "Bring him to me." But when the messenger came to him, [Joseph] said, "Return to your master and ask him what is the case of the women who cut their hands. Indeed, my Lord is Knowing of their plan."
Male/ Female	أُنثَىٰ/ الْأُنثَىٰ/ ذَكَرٍ/ الذَّكَرُ
2 البقرة 178	يَا أَيُّهَا الَّذِينَ آمَنُوا كُتِبَ عَلَيْكُمُ الْقِصَاصُ فِي الْقَتْلَى ۖ الْحُرُّ بِالْحُرِّ وَالْعَبْدُ بِالْعَبْدِ وَالْأُنثَىٰ بِالْأُنثَىٰ ۚ فَمَنْ عُفِيَ لَهُ مِنْ أَخِيهِ شَيْءٌ فَاتِّبَاعٌ بِالْمَعْرُوفِ وَأَدَاءٌ إِلَيْهِ بِإِحْسَانٍ ۗ ذَٰلِكَ تَخْفِيفٌ مِّن رَّبِّكُمْ وَرَحْمَةٌ ۗ فَمَنِ اعْتَدَىٰ بَعْدَ ذَٰلِكَ فَلَهُ عَذَابٌ أَلِيمٌ
	O you who have believed, prescribed for you is legal retribution for those murdered - the free for the free, the slave for the slave, and the female for the female. But whoever overlooks from his brother anything, then there should be a suitable follow-up and payment to him with good conduct. This is an alleviation from your Lord and a mercy. But whoever transgresses after that will have a painful punishment.
3 آل عمران 36	فَلَمَّا وَضَعَتْهَا قَالَتْ رَبِّ إِنِّي وَضَعْتُهَا أُنثَىٰ وَاللَّهُ أَعْلَمُ بِمَا وَضَعَتْ وَلَيْسَ الذَّكَرُ كَالْأُنثَىٰ ۖ وَإِنِّي سَمَّيْتُهَا مَرْيَمَ وَإِنِّي أُعِيذُهَا بِكَ وَذُرِّيَّتَهَا مِنَ الشَّيْطَانِ الرَّجِيمِ
	But when she delivered her, she said, "My Lord, I have delivered a female." And Allah was most knowing of what she delivered, "And the male is not like the female. And I have named her Mary, and I seek refuge for her in You and [for] her descendants from Satan, the expelled [from the mercy of Allah]."

195	فَاسْتَجَابَ لَهُمْ رَبُّهُمْ أَنِّي لَا أُضِيعُ عَمَلَ عَامِلٍ مِّنكُم مِّن **ذَكَرٍ أَوْ أُنثَىٰ** ۖ بَعْضُكُم مِّن بَعْضٍ ۖ فَالَّذِينَ هَاجَرُوا وَأُخْرِجُوا مِن دِيَارِهِمْ وَأُوذُوا فِي سَبِيلِي وَقَاتَلُوا وَقُتِلُوا لَأُكَفِّرَنَّ عَنْهُمْ سَيِّئَاتِهِمْ وَلَأُدْخِلَنَّهُمْ جَنَّاتٍ تَجْرِي مِن تَحْتِهَا الْأَنْهَارُ ثَوَابًا مِّنْ عِندِ اللَّهِ ۗ وَاللَّهُ عِندَهُ حُسْنُ الثَّوَابِ	
	And their Lord responded to them, "Never will I allow to be lost the work of [any] worker among you, whether male or female; you are of one another. So those who emigrated or were evicted from their homes or were harmed in My cause or fought or were killed - I will surely remove from them their misdeeds, and I will surely admit them to gardens beneath which rivers flow as reward from Allah, and Allah has with Him the best reward."	
4 النساء 124	وَمَن يَعْمَلْ مِنَ الصَّالِحَاتِ مِن **ذَكَرٍ أَوْ أُنثَىٰ** وَهُوَ مُؤْمِنٌ فَأُولَٰئِكَ يَدْخُلُونَ الْجَنَّةَ وَلَا يُظْلَمُونَ نَقِيرًا	
	And whoever does righteous deeds, whether male or female, while being a believer - those will enter Paradise and will not be wronged, [even as much as] the speck on a date seed.	
13 الرعد 8	اللَّهُ يَعْلَمُ مَا تَحْمِلُ كُلُّ **أُنثَىٰ** وَمَا تَغِيضُ الْأَرْحَامُ وَمَا تَزْدَادُ ۖ وَكُلُّ شَيْءٍ عِندَهُ بِمِقْدَارٍ	
	Allah knows what every female carries and what the wombs lose [prematurely] or exceed. And everything with Him is by due measure.	
16 النحل 58	وَإِذَا بُشِّرَ أَحَدُهُم بِالْأُنثَىٰ ظَلَّ وَجْهُهُ مُسْوَدًّا وَهُوَ كَظِيمٌ	
	And when one of them is informed of [the birth of] a female, his face becomes dark, and he suppresses grief.	
97	مَنْ عَمِلَ صَالِحًا مِّن **ذَكَرٍ أَوْ أُنثَىٰ** وَهُوَ مُؤْمِنٌ فَلَنُحْيِيَنَّهُ حَيَاةً طَيِّبَةً ۖ وَلَنَجْزِيَنَّهُمْ أَجْرَهُم بِأَحْسَنِ مَا كَانُوا يَعْمَلُونَ	
	Whoever does righteousness, whether male or female, while he is a believer - We will surely cause him to live a good life, and We will surely give them their reward [in the Hereafter] according to the best of what they used to do.	

35 فاطر 11	وَاللَّهُ خَلَقَكُم مِّن تُرَابٍ ثُمَّ مِن نُّطْفَةٍ ثُمَّ جَعَلَكُمْ أَزْوَاجًا ۚ وَمَا تَحْمِلُ مِنْ أُنثَىٰ وَلَا تَضَعُ إِلَّا بِعِلْمِهِ ۚ وَمَا يُعَمَّرُ مِن مُّعَمَّرٍ وَلَا يُنقَصُ مِنْ عُمُرِهِ إِلَّا فِي كِتَابٍ ۚ إِنَّ ذَٰلِكَ عَلَى اللَّهِ يَسِيرٌ
	And Allah created you from dust, then from a sperm-drop; then He made you mates. And no female conceives nor does she give birth except with His knowledge. And no aged person is granted [additional] life nor is his lifespan lessened but that it is in a register. Indeed, that for Allah is easy.
40 غافر 40	مَنْ عَمِلَ سَيِّئَةً فَلَا يُجْزَىٰ إِلَّا مِثْلَهَا ۖ وَمَنْ عَمِلَ صَالِحًا مِّن ذَكَرٍ أَوْ أُنثَىٰ وَهُوَ مُؤْمِنٌ فَأُولَٰئِكَ يَدْخُلُونَ الْجَنَّةَ يُرْزَقُونَ فِيهَا بِغَيْرِ حِسَابٍ
	Whoever does an evil deed will not be recompensed except by the like thereof; but whoever does righteousness, whether male or female, while he is a believer - those will enter Paradise, being given provision therein without account.
41 فصلت 47	۞ إِلَيْهِ يُرَدُّ عِلْمُ السَّاعَةِ ۚ وَمَا تَخْرُجُ مِن ثَمَرَاتٍ مِّنْ أَكْمَامِهَا وَمَا تَحْمِلُ مِنْ أُنثَىٰ وَلَا تَضَعُ إِلَّا بِعِلْمِهِ ۚ وَيَوْمَ يُنَادِيهِمْ أَيْنَ شُرَكَائِي قَالُوا آذَنَّاكَ مَا مِنَّا مِن شَهِيدٍ
	To him [alone] is attributed knowledge of the Hour. And fruits emerge not from their coverings nor does a female conceive or give birth except with His knowledge. And the Day He will call to them, "Where are My 'partners'?" they will say, "We announce to You that there is [no longer] among us any witness [to that]."
49 الحجرات 13	يَا أَيُّهَا النَّاسُ إِنَّا خَلَقْنَاكُم مِّن ذَكَرٍ وَأُنثَىٰ وَجَعَلْنَاكُمْ شُعُوبًا وَقَبَائِلَ لِتَعَارَفُوا ۚ إِنَّ أَكْرَمَكُمْ عِندَ اللَّهِ أَتْقَاكُمْ ۚ إِنَّ اللَّهَ عَلِيمٌ خَبِيرٌ

النجم 53 21	أَلَكُمُ الذَّكَرُ وَلَهُ الْأُنثَىٰ	
	Is the male for you and for Him the female?	
27	إِنَّ الَّذِينَ لَا يُؤْمِنُونَ بِالْآخِرَةِ لَيُسَمُّونَ الْمَلَائِكَةَ تَسْمِيَةَ الْأُنثَىٰ	
	Indeed, those who do not believe in the Hereafter name the angels female names,	
45	وَأَنَّهُ خَلَقَ الزَّوْجَيْنِ الذَّكَرَ وَالْأُنثَىٰ	
	And that He creates the two mates - the male and female -	
القيامة 75 39	فَجَعَلَ مِنْهُ الزَّوْجَيْنِ الذَّكَرَ وَالْأُنثَىٰ	
	And made of him two mates, the male and the female.	
الليل 92 3	وَمَا خَلَقَ الذَّكَرَ وَالْأُنثَىٰ	
	And [by] He who created the male and female,	
The two Males/ Females	آلذَّكَرَيْنِ/الذُّكْرَانَ /الْأُنثَيَيْنِ	
6 الأنعام 143	ثَمَانِيَةَ أَزْوَاجٍ ۖ مِّنَ الضَّأْنِ اثْنَيْنِ وَمِنَ الْمَعْزِ اثْنَيْنِ ۗ قُلْ آلذَّكَرَيْنِ حَرَّمَ أَمِ الْأُنثَيَيْنِ أَمَّا اشْتَمَلَتْ عَلَيْهِ أَرْحَامُ الْأُنثَيَيْنِ ۖ نَبِّئُونِي بِعِلْمٍ إِن كُنتُمْ صَادِقِينَ	
	[They are] eight mates - of the sheep, two and of the goats, two. Say, "Is it the two males He has forbidden or the two females or that which the wombs of the two females contain? Inform me with knowledge, if you should be truthful."	

144	وَمِنَ الْإِبِلِ اثْنَيْنِ وَمِنَ الْبَقَرِ اثْنَيْنِ ۗ قُلْ آلذَّكَرَيْنِ حَرَّمَ أَمِ الْأُنثَيَيْنِ أَمَّا اشْتَمَلَتْ عَلَيْهِ أَرْحَامُ الْأُنثَيَيْنِ ۖ أَمْ كُنتُمْ شُهَدَاءَ إِذْ وَصَّاكُمُ اللَّهُ بِهَٰذَا ۚ فَمَنْ أَظْلَمُ مِمَّنِ افْتَرَىٰ عَلَى اللَّهِ كَذِبًا لِّيُضِلَّ النَّاسَ بِغَيْرِ عِلْمٍ ۗ إِنَّ اللَّهَ لَا يَهْدِي الْقَوْمَ الظَّالِمِينَ	
	And of the camels, two and of the cattle, two. Say, "Is it the two males He has forbidden or the two females or that which the wombs of the two females contain? Or were you witnesses when Allah charged you with this? Then who is more unjust than one who invents a lie about Allah to mislead the people by [something] other than knowledge? Indeed, Allah does not guide the wrongdoing people."	
26 الشعراء 165	أَتَأْتُونَ الذُّكْرَانَ مِنَ الْعَالَمِينَ	
	Do you approach males among the worlds	
Husbands	بُعُولَتِهِنَّ	
24 النور 31	وَقُل لِّلْمُؤْمِنَاتِ يَغْضُضْنَ مِنْ أَبْصَارِهِنَّ وَيَحْفَظْنَ فُرُوجَهُنَّ وَلَا يُبْدِينَ زِينَتَهُنَّ إِلَّا مَا ظَهَرَ مِنْهَا ۖ وَلْيَضْرِبْنَ بِخُمُرِهِنَّ عَلَىٰ جُيُوبِهِنَّ ۖ وَلَا يُبْدِينَ زِينَتَهُنَّ إِلَّا لِبُعُولَتِهِنَّ أَوْ آبَائِهِنَّ أَوْ آبَاءِ بُعُولَتِهِنَّ أَوْ أَبْنَائِهِنَّ أَوْ أَبْنَاءِ بُعُولَتِهِنَّ أَوْ إِخْوَانِهِنَّ أَوْ بَنِي إِخْوَانِهِنَّ أَوْ بَنِي أَخَوَاتِهِنَّ أَوْ نِسَائِهِنَّ أَوْ مَا مَلَكَتْ أَيْمَانُهُنَّ أَوِ التَّابِعِينَ غَيْرِ أُولِي الْإِرْبَةِ مِنَ الرِّجَالِ أَوِ الطِّفْلِ الَّذِينَ لَمْ يَظْهَرُوا عَلَىٰ عَوْرَاتِ النِّسَاءِ ۖ وَلَا يَضْرِبْنَ بِأَرْجُلِهِنَّ لِيُعْلَمَ مَا يُخْفِينَ مِن زِينَتِهِنَّ ۚ وَتُوبُوا إِلَى اللَّهِ جَمِيعًا أَيُّهَ الْمُؤْمِنُونَ لَعَلَّكُمْ تُفْلِحُونَ	
	And tell the believing women to reduce [some] of their vision and guard their private parts and not expose their adornment except that which [necessarily] appears thereof and to wrap [a portion of] their headcovers over their chests and not expose their adornment except to their husbands, their fathers, their husbands' fathers, their sons, their husbands' sons, their brothers, their brothers' sons, their sisters' sons, their women, that which their right hands possess, or those male attendants having no physical desire, or children who are not yet aware of the private aspects of women. And let them not stamp their feet to make known what they conceal of their adornment. And turn to Allah in repentance, all of you, O believers, that you might succeed	

Who is a Relative	وَذِي الْقُرْبَىٰ
2 البقرة 83	وَإِذْ أَخَذْنَا مِيثَاقَ بَنِي إِسْرَائِيلَ لَا تَعْبُدُونَ إِلَّا اللَّهَ وَبِالْوَالِدَيْنِ إِحْسَانًا وَذِي الْقُرْبَىٰ وَالْيَتَامَىٰ وَالْمَسَاكِينِ وَقُولُوا لِلنَّاسِ حُسْنًا وَأَقِيمُوا الصَّلَاةَ وَآتُوا الزَّكَاةَ ثُمَّ تَوَلَّيْتُمْ إِلَّا قَلِيلًا مِّنكُمْ وَأَنتُم مُّعْرِضُونَ
	And [recall] when We took the covenant from the Children of Israel, [enjoining upon them], "Do not worship except Allah; and to parents do good and to relatives, orphans, and the needy. And speak to people good [words] and establish prayer and give zakah." Then you turned away, except a few of you, and you were refusing.
Whom are Relatives	ذَوِي الْقُرْبَىٰ
2 البقرة 177	لَّيْسَ الْبِرَّ أَن تُوَلُّوا وُجُوهَكُمْ قِبَلَ الْمَشْرِقِ وَالْمَغْرِبِ وَلَٰكِنَّ الْبِرَّ مَنْ آمَنَ بِاللَّهِ وَالْيَوْمِ الْآخِرِ وَالْمَلَائِكَةِ وَالْكِتَابِ وَالنَّبِيِّينَ وَآتَى الْمَالَ عَلَىٰ حُبِّهِ ذَوِي الْقُرْبَىٰ وَالْيَتَامَىٰ وَالْمَسَاكِينَ وَابْنَ السَّبِيلِ وَالسَّائِلِينَ وَفِي الرِّقَابِ وَأَقَامَ الصَّلَاةَ وَآتَى الزَّكَاةَ وَالْمُوفُونَ بِعَهْدِهِمْ إِذَا عَاهَدُوا ۖ وَالصَّابِرِينَ فِي الْبَأْسَاءِ وَالضَّرَّاءِ وَحِينَ الْبَأْسِ ۗ أُولَٰئِكَ الَّذِينَ صَدَقُوا ۖ وَأُولَٰئِكَ هُمُ الْمُتَّقُونَ
	Righteousness is not that you turn your faces toward the east or the west, but [true] righteousness is [in] one who believes in Allah, the Last Day, the angels, the Book, and the prophets and gives wealth, in spite of love for it, to relatives, orphans, the needy, the traveler, those who ask [for help], and for freeing slaves; [and who] establishes prayer and gives zakah; [those who] fulfill their promise when they promise; and [those who] are patient in poverty and hardship and during battle. Those are the ones who have been true, and it is those who are the righteous.

Near/close Neighbor	وَبِذِي الْقُرْبَىٰ / ذِي الْقُرْبَىٰ	
4 النساء 36	۞ وَاعْبُدُوا اللَّهَ وَلَا تُشْرِكُوا بِهِ شَيْئًا ۖ وَبِالْوَالِدَيْنِ إِحْسَانًا وَبِذِي الْقُرْبَىٰ وَالْيَتَامَىٰ وَالْمَسَاكِينِ وَالْجَارِ ذِي الْقُرْبَىٰ وَالْجَارِ الْجُنُبِ وَالصَّاحِبِ بِالْجَنْبِ وَابْنِ السَّبِيلِ وَمَا مَلَكَتْ أَيْمَانُكُمْ ۗ إِنَّ اللَّهَ لَا يُحِبُّ مَن كَانَ مُخْتَالًا فَخُورًا	
	Worship Allah and associate nothing with Him, and to parents do good, and to relatives, orphans, the needy, the near neighbor, the neighbor farther away, the companion at your side, the traveler, and those whom your right hands possess. Indeed, Allah does not like those who are self-deluding and boastful	
The Relative	ذِي الْقُرْبَىٰ	
16 النحل 90	إِنَّ اللَّهَ يَأْمُرُ بِالْعَدْلِ وَالْإِحْسَانِ وَإِيتَاءِ ذِي الْقُرْبَىٰ وَيَنْهَىٰ عَنِ الْفَحْشَاءِ وَالْمُنكَرِ وَالْبَغْيِ ۚ يَعِظُكُمْ لَعَلَّكُمْ تَذَكَّرُونَ	
	Indeed, Allah orders justice and good conduct and giving to relatives and forbids immorality and bad conduct and oppression. He admonishes you that perhaps you will be reminded.	
Near Relatives	وَالْأَقْرَبِينَ / الْأَقْرَبِينَ	
2 البقرة 180	كُتِبَ عَلَيْكُمْ إِذَا حَضَرَ أَحَدَكُمُ الْمَوْتُ إِن تَرَكَ خَيْرًا الْوَصِيَّةُ لِلْوَالِدَيْنِ وَالْأَقْرَبِينَ بِالْمَعْرُوفِ ۖ حَقًّا عَلَى الْمُتَّقِينَ	
	Prescribed for you when death approaches [any] one of you if he leaves wealth [is that he should make] a bequest for the parents and near relatives according to what is acceptable - a duty upon the righteous.	
215	يَسْأَلُونَكَ مَاذَا يُنفِقُونَ ۖ قُلْ مَا أَنفَقْتُم مِّنْ خَيْرٍ فَلِلْوَالِدَيْنِ وَالْأَقْرَبِينَ وَالْيَتَامَىٰ وَالْمَسَاكِينِ وَابْنِ السَّبِيلِ ۗ وَمَا تَفْعَلُوا مِنْ خَيْرٍ فَإِنَّ اللَّهَ بِهِ عَلِيمٌ	

		They ask you, [O Muhammad], what they should spend. Say, "Whatever you spend of good is [to be] for parents and relatives and orphans and the needy and the traveler. And whatever you do of good - indeed, Allah is Knowing of it."
26 الشعراء 214	وَأَنذِرْ عَشِيرَتَكَ الْأَقْرَبِينَ	
		And warn, [O Muhammad], your closest kindred.
4 النساء 135	يَا أَيُّهَا الَّذِينَ آمَنُوا كُونُوا قَوَّامِينَ بِالْقِسْطِ شُهَدَاءَ لِلَّهِ وَلَوْ عَلَىٰ أَنفُسِكُمْ أَوِ الْوَالِدَيْنِ وَالْأَقْرَبِينَ إِن يَكُنْ غَنِيًّا أَوْ فَقِيرًا فَاللَّهُ أَوْلَىٰ بِهِمَا فَلَا تَتَّبِعُوا الْهَوَىٰ أَن تَعْدِلُوا وَإِن تَلْوُوا أَوْ تُعْرِضُوا فَإِنَّ اللَّهَ كَانَ بِمَا تَعْمَلُونَ خَبِيرًا	
		O you who have believed, be persistently standing firm in justice, witnesses for Allah, even if it be against yourselves or parents and relatives. Whether one is rich or poor, Allah is more worthy of both. So follow not [personal] inclination, lest you not be just. And if you distort [your testimony] or refuse [to give it], then indeed Allah is ever, with what you do, Acquainted.
Close Relatives	وَالْأَقْرَبُونَ	
4 النساء 7	لِّلرِّجَالِ نَصِيبٌ مِّمَّا تَرَكَ الْوَالِدَانِ وَالْأَقْرَبُونَ وَلِلنِّسَاءِ نَصِيبٌ مِّمَّا تَرَكَ الْوَالِدَانِ وَالْأَقْرَبُونَ مِمَّا قَلَّ مِنْهُ أَوْ كَثُرَ نَصِيبًا مَّفْرُوضًا	
		For men is a share of what the parents and close relatives leave, and for women is a share of what the parents and close relatives leave, be it little or much - an obligatory share.
33	وَلِكُلٍّ جَعَلْنَا مَوَالِيَ مِمَّا تَرَكَ الْوَالِدَانِ وَالْأَقْرَبُونَ وَالَّذِينَ عَقَدَتْ أَيْمَانُكُمْ فَآتُوهُمْ نَصِيبَهُمْ إِنَّ اللَّهَ كَانَ عَلَىٰ كُلِّ شَيْءٍ شَهِيدًا	
		And for all, We have made heirs to what is left by parents and relatives. And to those whom your oaths have bound [to you] - give them their share. Indeed Allah is ever, over all things, a Witness.
Those who are Relatives	أُولُو الْقُرْبَىٰ	
4 النساء 8	وَإِذَا حَضَرَ الْقِسْمَةَ أُولُو الْقُرْبَىٰ وَالْيَتَامَىٰ وَالْمَسَاكِينُ فَارْزُقُوهُم مِّنْهُ وَقُولُوا لَهُمْ قَوْلًا مَّعْرُوفًا	
		And when [other] relatives and orphans and the needy are present at the [time of] division, then provide for them [something] out of the estate and speak to them words of appropriate kindness.

Nearest	أَقْرَبُ
4 النساء 11	يُوصِيكُمُ اللَّهُ فِي أَوْلَادِكُمْ لِلذَّكَرِ مِثْلُ حَظِّ الْأُنثَيَيْنِ فَإِن كُنَّ نِسَاءً فَوْقَ اثْنَتَيْنِ فَلَهُنَّ ثُلُثَا مَا تَرَكَ وَإِن كَانَتْ وَاحِدَةً فَلَهَا النِّصْفُ وَلِأَبَوَيْهِ لِكُلِّ وَاحِدٍ مِّنْهُمَا السُّدُسُ مِمَّا تَرَكَ إِن كَانَ لَهُ وَلَدٌ فَإِن لَّمْ يَكُن لَّهُ وَلَدٌ وَوَرِثَهُ أَبَوَاهُ فَلِأُمِّهِ الثُّلُثُ فَإِن كَانَ لَهُ إِخْوَةٌ فَلِأُمِّهِ السُّدُسُ مِن بَعْدِ وَصِيَّةٍ يُوصِي بِهَا أَوْ دَيْنٍ ۗ آبَاؤُكُمْ وَأَبْنَاؤُكُمْ لَا تَدْرُونَ أَيُّهُمْ **أَقْرَبُ** لَكُمْ نَفْعًا ۚ فَرِيضَةً مِّنَ اللَّهِ ۗ إِنَّ اللَّهَ كَانَ عَلِيمًا حَكِيمًا
	Allah instructs you concerning your children: for the male, what is equal to the share of two females. But if there are [only] daughters, two or more, for them is two thirds of one's estate. And if there is only one, for her is half. And for one's parents, to each one of them is a sixth of his estate if he left children. But if he had no children and the parents [alone] inherit from him, then for his mother is one third. And if he had brothers [or sisters], for his mother is a sixth, after any bequest he [may have] made or debt. Your parents or your children - you know not which of them are nearest to you in benefit. [These shares are] an obligation [imposed] by Allah. Indeed, Allah is ever Knowing and Wise.
Near Relative	ذَا قُرْبَىٰ
5 المائدة 106	يَا أَيُّهَا الَّذِينَ آمَنُوا شَهَادَةُ بَيْنِكُمْ إِذَا حَضَرَ أَحَدَكُمُ الْمَوْتُ حِينَ الْوَصِيَّةِ اثْنَانِ ذَوَا عَدْلٍ مِّنكُمْ أَوْ آخَرَانِ مِنْ غَيْرِكُمْ إِنْ أَنتُمْ ضَرَبْتُمْ فِي الْأَرْضِ فَأَصَابَتْكُم مُّصِيبَةُ الْمَوْتِ ۚ تَحْبِسُونَهُمَا مِن بَعْدِ الصَّلَاةِ فَيُقْسِمَانِ بِاللَّهِ إِنِ ارْتَبْتُمْ لَا نَشْتَرِي بِهِ ثَمَنًا وَلَوْ كَانَ **ذَا قُرْبَىٰ** ۙ وَلَا نَكْتُمُ شَهَادَةَ اللَّهِ إِنَّا إِذًا لَّمِنَ الْآثِمِينَ
	O you who have believed, testimony [should be taken] among you when death approaches one of you at the time of bequest - [that of] two just men from among you or two others from outside if you are traveling through the land and the disaster of death should strike you. Detain them after the prayer and let them both swear by Allah if you doubt [their testimony, saying], "We will not exchange our oath for a price, even if he should be a near relative, and we will not withhold the testimony of Allah. Indeed, we would then be of the sinful."

35 فاطر 18	وَلَا تَزِرُ وَازِرَةٌ وِزْرَ أُخْرَىٰ ۚ وَإِن تَدْعُ مُثْقَلَةٌ إِلَىٰ حِمْلِهَا لَا يُحْمَلْ مِنْهُ شَيْءٌ وَلَوْ كَانَ **ذَا قُرْبَىٰ** ۗ إِنَّمَا تُنذِرُ الَّذِينَ يَخْشَوْنَ رَبَّهُم بِالْغَيْبِ وَأَقَامُوا الصَّلَاةَ ۚ وَمَن تَزَكَّىٰ فَإِنَّمَا يَتَزَكَّىٰ لِنَفْسِهِ ۚ وَإِلَى اللَّهِ الْمَصِيرُ	
	And no bearer of burdens will bear the burden of another. And if a heavily laden soul calls [another] to [carry some of] its load, nothing of it will be carried, even if he should be a close relative. You can only warn those who fear their Lord unseen and have established prayer. And whoever purifies himself only purifies himself for [the benefit of] his soul. And to Allah is the [final] destination	
The Relative	ذَا الْقُرْبَىٰ	
17 الإسراء 26	وَآتِ **ذَا الْقُرْبَىٰ** حَقَّهُ وَالْمِسْكِينَ وَابْنَ السَّبِيلِ وَلَا تُبَذِّرْ تَبْذِيرًا	
	And give the relative his right, and [also] the poor and the traveler, and do not spend wastefully.	
30 الروم 38	فَآتِ **ذَا الْقُرْبَىٰ** حَقَّهُ وَالْمِسْكِينَ وَابْنَ السَّبِيلِ ۚ ذَٰلِكَ خَيْرٌ لِّلَّذِينَ يُرِيدُونَ وَجْهَ اللَّهِ ۖ وَأُولَٰئِكَ هُمُ الْمُفْلِحُونَ	
	So give the relative his right, as well as the needy and the traveler. That is best for those who desire the countenance of Allah, and it is they who will be the successful.	
And to the near Relatives	وَلِذِي الْقُرْبَىٰ	
8 الأنفال 41	وَاعْلَمُوا أَنَّمَا غَنِمْتُم مِّن شَيْءٍ فَأَنَّ لِلَّهِ خُمُسَهُ وَلِلرَّسُولِ **وَلِذِي الْقُرْبَىٰ** وَالْيَتَامَىٰ وَالْمَسَاكِينِ وَابْنِ السَّبِيلِ إِن كُنتُمْ آمَنتُم بِاللَّهِ وَمَا أَنزَلْنَا عَلَىٰ عَبْدِنَا يَوْمَ الْفُرْقَانِ يَوْمَ الْتَقَى الْجَمْعَانِ ۗ وَاللَّهُ عَلَىٰ كُلِّ شَيْءٍ قَدِيرٌ	
	And know that anything you obtain of war booty - then indeed, for Allah is one fifth of it and for the Messenger and for [his] near relatives and the orphans, the needy, and the [stranded] traveler, if you have believed in Allah and in that which We sent down to Our Servant on the day of criterion - the day when the two armies met. And Allah, over all things, is competent.	

The Relative	ذِي الْقُرْبَىٰ	
4 النساء 36	وَاعْبُدُوا اللَّهَ وَلَا تُشْرِكُوا بِهِ شَيْئًا ۖ وَبِالْوَالِدَيْنِ إِحْسَانًا وَبِذِي الْقُرْبَىٰ وَالْيَتَامَىٰ وَالْمَسَاكِينِ وَالْجَارِ ذِي الْقُرْبَىٰ وَالْجَارِ الْجُنُبِ وَالصَّاحِبِ بِالْجَنبِ وَابْنِ السَّبِيلِ وَمَا مَلَكَتْ أَيْمَانُكُمْ ۗ إِنَّ اللَّهَ لَا يُحِبُّ مَن كَانَ مُخْتَالًا فَخُورًا	
	Worship Allah and associate nothing with Him, and to parents do good, and to relatives, orphans, the needy, the near neighbor, the neighbor farther away, the companion at your side, the traveler, and those whom your right hands possess. Indeed, Allah does not like those who are self-deluding and boastful	
16 النحل 90	إِنَّ اللَّهَ يَأْمُرُ بِالْعَدْلِ وَالْإِحْسَانِ وَإِيتَاءِ ذِي الْقُرْبَىٰ وَيَنْهَىٰ عَنِ الْفَحْشَاءِ وَالْمُنكَرِ وَالْبَغْيِ ۚ يَعِظُكُمْ لَعَلَّكُمْ تَذَكَّرُونَ	
	Indeed, Allah orders justice and good conduct and giving to relatives and forbids immorality and bad conduct and oppression. He admonishes you that perhaps you will be reminded.	
To the near /close Relatives	وَلِذِي الْقُرْبَىٰ	
59 الحشر 7	مَّا أَفَاءَ اللَّهُ عَلَىٰ رَسُولِهِ مِنْ أَهْلِ الْقُرَىٰ فَلِلَّهِ وَلِلرَّسُولِ وَلِذِي الْقُرْبَىٰ وَالْيَتَامَىٰ وَالْمَسَاكِينِ وَابْنِ السَّبِيلِ كَيْ لَا يَكُونَ دُولَةً بَيْنَ الْأَغْنِيَاءِ مِنكُمْ ۚ وَمَا آتَاكُمُ الرَّسُولُ فَخُذُوهُ وَمَا نَهَاكُمْ عَنْهُ فَانتَهُوا ۚ وَاتَّقُوا اللَّهَ ۖ إِنَّ اللَّهَ شَدِيدُ الْعِقَابِ	
	And what Allah restored to His Messenger from the people of the towns - it is for Allah and for the Messenger and for [his] near relatives and orphans and the [stranded] traveler - so that it will not be a perpetual distribution among the rich from among you. And whatever the Messenger has given you - take; and what he has forbidden you - refrain from. And fear Allah; indeed, Allah is severe in penalty.	
Relatives	أُولِي قُرْبَىٰ	
9 التوبة 113	مَا كَانَ لِلنَّبِيِّ وَالَّذِينَ آمَنُوا أَن يَسْتَغْفِرُوا لِلْمُشْرِكِينَ وَلَوْ كَانُوا أُولِي قُرْبَىٰ مِن بَعْدِ مَا تَبَيَّنَ لَهُمْ أَنَّهُمْ أَصْحَابُ الْجَحِيمِ	
	It is not for the Prophet and those who have believed to ask forgiveness for the polytheists, even if they were relatives, after it has become clear to them that they are companions of Hellfire.	
24 النور 22	وَلَا يَأْتَلِ أُولُو الْفَضْلِ مِنكُمْ وَالسَّعَةِ أَن يُؤْتُوا أُولِي الْقُرْبَىٰ وَالْمَسَاكِينَ وَالْمُهَاجِرِينَ فِي سَبِيلِ اللَّهِ ۖ وَلْيَعْفُوا وَلْيَصْفَحُوا ۗ أَلَا تُحِبُّونَ أَن يَغْفِرَ اللَّهُ لَكُمْ ۗ وَاللَّهُ غَفُورٌ رَّحِيمٌ	

	And let not those of virtue among you and wealth swear not to give [aid] to their relatives and the needy and the emigrants for the cause of Allah, and let them pardon and overlook. Would you not like that Allah should forgive you? And Allah is Forgiving and Merciful.
Being Relative	الْقُرْبَىٰ
42 الشورى 23	ذَٰلِكَ الَّذِي يُبَشِّرُ اللَّهُ عِبَادَهُ الَّذِينَ آمَنُوا وَعَمِلُوا الصَّالِحَاتِ ۗ قُل لَّا أَسْأَلُكُمْ عَلَيْهِ أَجْرًا إِلَّا الْمَوَدَّةَ فِي الْقُرْبَىٰ ۗ وَمَن يَقْتَرِفْ حَسَنَةً نَّزِدْ لَهُ فِيهَا حُسْنًا ۚ إِنَّ اللَّهَ غَفُورٌ شَكُورٌ
	It is that of which Allah gives good tidings to His servants who believe and do righteous deeds. Say, [O Muhammad], "I do not ask you for this message any payment [but] only good will through kinship." And whoever commits a good deed - We will increase for him good therein. Indeed, Allah is Forgiving and Appreciative.
Brought near	الْمُقَرَّبُونَ
56 الواقعة 11	أُولَٰئِكَ الْمُقَرَّبُونَ
	Those are the ones brought near [to Allah]
Near Relationship	مَقْرَبَةٍ
90 البلد 15	يَتِيمًا ذَا مَقْرَبَةٍ
	An orphan of near relationship

[blood] relationship الْأَرْحَام

3 آل عمران 6	هُوَ الَّذِي يُصَوِّرُكُمْ فِي الْأَرْحَامِ كَيْفَ يَشَاءُ ۚ لَا إِلَٰهَ إِلَّا هُوَ الْعَزِيزُ الْحَكِيمُ
H&K	He it is Who shapes you in the wombs as He pleases. La ilaha illa Huwa (none has the right to be worshipped but He), the All-Mighty, the All-Wise.
4 النساء 1	يَا أَيُّهَا النَّاسُ اتَّقُوا رَبَّكُمُ الَّذِي خَلَقَكُم مِّن نَّفْسٍ وَاحِدَةٍ وَخَلَقَ مِنْهَا زَوْجَهَا وَبَثَّ مِنْهُمَا رِجَالًا كَثِيرًا وَنِسَاءً ۚ وَاتَّقُوا اللَّهَ الَّذِي تَسَاءَلُونَ بِهِ وَالْأَرْحَامَ ۚ إِنَّ اللَّهَ كَانَ عَلَيْكُمْ رَقِيبًا
H&K	O mankind! Be dutiful to your Lord, Who created you from a single person (Adam), and from him (Adam) He created his wife [Hawwa (Eve)], and from them both He created many men and women and fear Allah through Whom you demand your mutual (rights), and (do not cut the relations of) the wombs (kinship). Surely, Allah is Ever an All-Watcher over you.
8 الأنفال 75	وَالَّذِينَ آمَنُوا مِن بَعْدُ وَهَاجَرُوا وَجَاهَدُوا مَعَكُمْ فَأُولَٰئِكَ مِنكُمْ ۚ وَأُولُو الْأَرْحَامِ بَعْضُهُمْ أَوْلَىٰ بِبَعْضٍ فِي كِتَابِ اللَّهِ ۗ إِنَّ اللَّهَ بِكُلِّ شَيْءٍ عَلِيمٌ
H&K	And those who believed afterwards, and emigrated and strove hard along with you, (in the Cause of Allah) they are of you. But kindred by blood are nearer to one another regarding inheritance in the decree ordained by Allah. Verily, Allah is the All-Knower of everything.
13 الرعد 8	اللَّهُ يَعْلَمُ مَا تَحْمِلُ كُلُّ أُنثَىٰ وَمَا تَغِيضُ الْأَرْحَامُ وَمَا تَزْدَادُ ۖ وَكُلُّ شَيْءٍ عِندَهُ بِمِقْدَارٍ
H&K	Allah knows what every female bears, and by how much the wombs fall short (of their time or number) or exceed. Everything with Him is in (due) proportion.
22 الحج 5	يَا أَيُّهَا النَّاسُ إِن كُنتُمْ فِي رَيْبٍ مِّنَ الْبَعْثِ فَإِنَّا خَلَقْنَاكُم مِّن تُرَابٍ ثُمَّ مِن نُّطْفَةٍ ثُمَّ مِنْ مُّضْغَةٍ مُّخَلَّقَةٍ وَغَيْرِ مُخَلَّقَةٍ لِّنُبَيِّنَ لَكُمْ ۚ وَنُقِرُّ فِي الْأَرْحَامِ مَا نَشَاءُ إِلَىٰ أَجَلٍ مُّسَمًّى ثُمَّ نُخْرِجُكُمْ طِفْلًا ثُمَّ لِتَبْلُغُوا أَشُدَّكُمْ ۖ وَمِنكُم مَّن يُتَوَفَّىٰ وَمِنكُم مَّن يُرَدُّ إِلَىٰ أَرْذَلِ الْعُمُرِ لِكَيْلَا يَعْلَمَ مِن بَعْدِ عِلْمٍ شَيْئًا ۚ وَتَرَى الْأَرْضَ هَامِدَةً فَإِذَا أَنزَلْنَا عَلَيْهَا الْمَاءَ اهْتَزَّتْ وَرَبَتْ وَأَنبَتَتْ مِن كُلِّ زَوْجٍ بَهِيجٍ

Sahih	O People, if you should be in doubt about the Resurrection, then [consider that] indeed, We created you from dust, then from a sperm-drop, then from a clinging clot, and then from a lump of flesh, formed and unformed - that We may show you. And We settle in the wombs whom We will for a specified term, then We bring you out as a child, and then [We develop you] that you may reach your [time of] maturity. And among you is he who is taken in [early] death, and among you is he who is returned to the most decrepit [old] age so that he knows, after [once having] knowledge, nothing. And you see the earth barren, but when We send down upon it rain, it quivers and swells and grows [something] of every beautiful kind
H&K	O mankind! If you are in doubt about the Resurrection, then verily! We have created you (i.e. Adam) from dust, then from a Nutfah (mixed drops of male and female sexual discharge i.e. offspring of Adam), then from a clot (a piece of thick coagulated blood) then from a little lump of flesh, some formed and some unformed (miscarriage), that We may make (it) clear to you (i.e. to show you Our Power and Ability to do what We will). And We cause whom We will to remain in the wombs for an appointed term, then We bring you out as infants, then (give you growth) that you may reach your age of full strength. And among you there is he who dies (young), and among you there is he who is brought back to the miserable old age, so that he knows nothing after having known. And you see the earth barren, but when We send down water (rain) on it, it is stirred (to life), it swells and puts forth every lovely kind (of growth).
31 لقمان 34	إِنَّ اللَّهَ عِندَهُ عِلْمُ السَّاعَةِ وَيُنَزِّلُ الْغَيْثَ وَيَعْلَمُ مَا فِي الْأَرْحَامِ ۖ وَمَا تَدْرِي نَفْسٌ مَّاذَا تَكْسِبُ غَدًا ۖ وَمَا تَدْرِي نَفْسٌ بِأَيِّ أَرْضٍ تَمُوتُ ۚ إِنَّ اللَّهَ عَلِيمٌ خَبِيرٌ
Sahih	Indeed, Allah [alone] has knowledge of the Hour and sends down the rain and knows what is in the wombs. And no soul perceives what it will earn tomorrow, and no soul perceives in what land it will die. Indeed, Allah is Knowing and Acquainted.
33 الأحزاب 6	النَّبِيُّ أَوْلَىٰ بِالْمُؤْمِنِينَ مِنْ أَنفُسِهِمْ ۖ وَأَزْوَاجُهُ أُمَّهَاتُهُمْ ۗ وَأُولُو الْأَرْحَامِ بَعْضُهُمْ أَوْلَىٰ بِبَعْضٍ فِي كِتَابِ اللَّهِ مِنَ الْمُؤْمِنِينَ وَالْمُهَاجِرِينَ إِلَّا أَن تَفْعَلُوا إِلَىٰ أَوْلِيَائِكُم مَّعْرُوفًا ۚ كَانَ ذَٰلِكَ فِي الْكِتَابِ مَسْطُورًا
Sahih	The Prophet is more worthy of the believers than themselves, and his wives are [in the position of] their mothers. And those of [blood] relationship are more entitled [to inheritance] in the decree of Allah than the [other] believers and the emigrants, except that you may do to your close associates a kindness [through bequest]. That was in the Book inscribed.
H&K	The Prophet is closer to the believers than their ownselves, and his wives are their (believers') mothers (as regards respect and marriage). And blood relations among each other have closer personal ties in the Decree of Allah (regarding inheritance) than (the brotherhood of) the believers and the Muhajirun (emigrants from Makkah, etc.), except that you do kindness to those brothers (when the Prophet SAW joined them in brotherhood ties). This has been written in the (Allah's Book of Divine) Decrees (AlLauh AlMahfuz)."

	ذُرِّيَّةٌ	
2 البقرة 124	وَإِذِ ابْتَلَىٰ إِبْرَاهِيمَ رَبُّهُ بِكَلِمَاتٍ فَأَتَمَّهُنَّ ۖ قَالَ إِنِّي جَاعِلُكَ لِلنَّاسِ إِمَامًا ۖ قَالَ وَمِن ذُرِّيَّتِي ۖ قَالَ لَا يَنَالُ عَهْدِي الظَّالِمِينَ	
H&K	And (remember) when the Lord of Ibrahim (Abraham) [i.e., Allah] tried him with (certain) Commands, which he fulfilled. He (Allah) said (to him), "Verily, I am going to make you a leader (Prophet) of mankind." [Ibrahim (Abraham)] said, "And of my offspring (to make leaders)." (Allah) said, "My Covenant (Prophethood, etc.) includes not Zalimun (polytheists and wrong-doers)."	
128	رَبَّنَا وَاجْعَلْنَا مُسْلِمَيْنِ لَكَ وَمِن ذُرِّيَّتِنَا أُمَّةً مُّسْلِمَةً لَّكَ وَأَرِنَا مَنَاسِكَنَا وَتُبْ عَلَيْنَا ۖ إِنَّكَ أَنتَ التَّوَّابُ الرَّحِيمُ	
H&K	"Our Lord! And make us submissive unto You and of our offspring a nation submissive unto You, and show us our Manasik (all the ceremonies of pilgrimage - Hajj and 'Umrah, etc.), and accept our repentance. Truly, You are the One Who accepts repentance, the Most Merciful.	
266	أَيَوَدُّ أَحَدُكُمْ أَن تَكُونَ لَهُ جَنَّةٌ مِّن نَّخِيلٍ وَأَعْنَابٍ تَجْرِي مِن تَحْتِهَا الْأَنْهَارُ لَهُ فِيهَا مِن كُلِّ الثَّمَرَاتِ وَأَصَابَهُ الْكِبَرُ وَلَهُ ذُرِّيَّةٌ ضُعَفَاءُ فَأَصَابَهَا إِعْصَارٌ فِيهِ نَارٌ فَاحْتَرَقَتْ ۗ كَذَٰلِكَ يُبَيِّنُ اللَّهُ لَكُمُ الْآيَاتِ لَعَلَّكُمْ تَتَفَكَّرُونَ	
H&K	Would any of you wish to have a garden with date-palms and vines, with rivers flowing underneath, and all kinds of fruits for him therein, while he is striken with old age, and his children are weak (not able to look after themselves), then it is struck with a fiery whirlwind, so that it is burnt? Thus does Allah make clear His Ayat (proofs, evidences, verses) to you that you may give thought.	
3 آل عمران 34	ذُرِّيَّةً بَعْضُهَا مِن بَعْضٍ ۗ وَاللَّهُ سَمِيعٌ عَلِيمٌ	
H&K	Offspring, one of the other, and Allah is the All-Hearer, All-Knower.	
3 آل عمران 36	فَلَمَّا وَضَعَتْهَا قَالَتْ رَبِّ إِنِّي وَضَعْتُهَا أُنثَىٰ وَاللَّهُ أَعْلَمُ بِمَا وَضَعَتْ وَلَيْسَ الذَّكَرُ كَالْأُنثَىٰ ۖ وَإِنِّي سَمَّيْتُهَا مَرْيَمَ وَإِنِّي أُعِيذُهَا بِكَ وَذُرِّيَّتَهَا مِنَ الشَّيْطَانِ الرَّجِيمِ	
H&K	Then when she delivered her [child Maryam (Mary)], she said: "O my Lord! I have delivered a female child," - and Allah knew better what she delivered, - "And the male is not like the female, and I have named her Maryam (Mary),	

	and I seek refuge with You (Allah) for her and for her offspring from Shaitan (Satan), the outcast."
3 آل عمران 38	هُنَالِكَ دَعَا زَكَرِيَّا رَبَّهُ ۖ قَالَ رَبِّ هَبْ لِي مِن لَّدُنكَ ذُرِّيَّةً طَيِّبَةً ۖ إِنَّكَ سَمِيعُ الدُّعَاءِ
H&K	At that time Zakariya (Zachariya) invoked his Lord, saying: "O my Lord! Grant me from You, a good offspring. You are indeed the All-Hearer of invocation."
4 النساء 9	وَلْيَخْشَ الَّذِينَ لَوْ تَرَكُوا مِنْ خَلْفِهِمْ ذُرِّيَّةً ضِعَافًا خَافُوا عَلَيْهِمْ فَلْيَتَّقُوا اللَّهَ وَلْيَقُولُوا قَوْلًا سَدِيدًا
H&K	And let those (executors and guardians) have the same fear in their minds as they would have for their own, if they had left weak offspring behind. So let them fear Allah and speak right words.
6 الأنعام 84	وَوَهَبْنَا لَهُ إِسْحَاقَ وَيَعْقُوبَ ۚ كُلًّا هَدَيْنَا ۚ وَنُوحًا هَدَيْنَا مِن قَبْلُ ۖ وَمِن ذُرِّيَّتِهِ دَاوُودَ وَسُلَيْمَانَ وَأَيُّوبَ وَيُوسُفَ وَمُوسَىٰ وَهَارُونَ ۚ وَكَذَٰلِكَ نَجْزِي الْمُحْسِنِينَ
H&K	And We bestowed upon him Ishaque (Isaac) and Ya'qub (Jacob), each of them We guided, and before him, We guided Nuh (Noah), and among his progeny Dawud (David), Sulaiman (Solomon), Ayub (Job), Yusuf (Joseph), Musa (Moses), and Harun (Aaron). Thus do We reward the good-doers.
6 الأنعام 87	وَمِنْ آبَائِهِمْ وَذُرِّيَّاتِهِمْ وَإِخْوَانِهِمْ ۖ وَاجْتَبَيْنَاهُمْ وَهَدَيْنَاهُمْ إِلَىٰ صِرَاطٍ مُّسْتَقِيمٍ
H&K	And also some of their fathers and their progeny and their brethren, We chose them, and We guided them to a Straight Path.
6 الأنعام 133	وَرَبُّكَ الْغَنِيُّ ذُو الرَّحْمَةِ ۚ إِن يَشَأْ يُذْهِبْكُمْ وَيَسْتَخْلِفْ مِن بَعْدِكُم مَّا يَشَاءُ كَمَا أَنشَأَكُم مِّن ذُرِّيَّةِ قَوْمٍ آخَرِينَ
H&K	And your Lord is Rich (Free of all wants), full of Mercy, if He will, He can destroy you, and in your place make whom He will as your successors, as He raised you from the seed of other people.
7 الأعراف 172	وَإِذْ أَخَذَ رَبُّكَ مِن بَنِي آدَمَ مِن ظُهُورِهِمْ ذُرِّيَّتَهُمْ وَأَشْهَدَهُمْ عَلَىٰ أَنفُسِهِمْ أَلَسْتُ بِرَبِّكُمْ ۖ قَالُوا بَلَىٰ ۛ شَهِدْنَا ۛ أَن تَقُولُوا يَوْمَ الْقِيَامَةِ إِنَّا كُنَّا عَنْ هَٰذَا غَافِلِينَ
H&K	And (remember) when your Lord brought forth from the Children of Adam, from their loins, their seed (or from Adam's loin his offspring) and made them testify as to themselves (saying): "Am I not your Lord?" They said: "Yes! We

	testify," lest you should say on the Day of Resurrection: "Verily, we have been unaware of this."
7 الأعراف 173	أَوْ تَقُولُوا إِنَّمَا أَشْرَكَ آبَاؤُنَا مِن قَبْلُ وَكُنَّا ذُرِّيَّةً مِّن بَعْدِهِمْ ۖ أَفَتُهْلِكُنَا بِمَا فَعَلَ الْمُبْطِلُونَ
H&K	Or lest you should say: "It was only our fathers aforetime who took others as partners in worship along with Allah, and we were (merely their) descendants after them; will You then destroy us because of the deeds of men who practised Al-Batil (i.e. polytheism and committing crimes and sins, invoking and worshipping others besides Allah)?" (Tafsir At-Tabari).
10 يونس 83	فَمَا آمَنَ لِمُوسَىٰ إِلَّا ذُرِّيَّةٌ مِّن قَوْمِهِ عَلَىٰ خَوْفٍ مِّن فِرْعَوْنَ وَمَلَئِهِمْ أَن يَفْتِنَهُمْ ۚ وَإِنَّ فِرْعَوْنَ لَعَالٍ فِي الْأَرْضِ وَإِنَّهُ لَمِنَ الْمُسْرِفِينَ
H&K	But none believed in Musa (Moses) except the offspring of his people, because of the fear of Fir'aun (Pharaoh) and his chiefs, lest they should persecute them; and verily, Fir'aun (Pharaoh) was arrogant tyrant on the earth, he was indeed one of the Musrifun (polytheists, sinners and transgressors, those who give up the truth and follow the evil, and commit all kinds of great sins).
13 الرعد 23	جَنَّاتُ عَدْنٍ يَدْخُلُونَهَا وَمَن صَلَحَ مِنْ آبَائِهِمْ وَأَزْوَاجِهِمْ وَذُرِّيَّاتِهِمْ ۖ وَالْمَلَائِكَةُ يَدْخُلُونَ عَلَيْهِم مِّن كُلِّ بَابٍ
H&K	'Adn (Eden) Paradise (everlasting Gardens), which they shall enter and (also) those who acted righteously from among their fathers, and their wives, and their offspring. And angels shall enter unto them from every gate (saying):
13 الرعد 38	وَلَقَدْ أَرْسَلْنَا رُسُلًا مِّن قَبْلِكَ وَجَعَلْنَا لَهُمْ أَزْوَاجًا وَذُرِّيَّةً ۚ وَمَا كَانَ لِرَسُولٍ أَن يَأْتِيَ بِآيَةٍ إِلَّا بِإِذْنِ اللَّهِ ۗ لِكُلِّ أَجَلٍ كِتَابٌ
H&K	And indeed We sent Messengers before you (O Muhammad SAW), and made for them wives and offspring. And it was not for a Messenger to bring a sign except by Allah's Leave. (For) each and every matter there is a Decree (from Allah).
14 ابراهيم 37	رَّبَّنَا إِنِّي أَسْكَنتُ مِن ذُرِّيَّتِي بِوَادٍ غَيْرِ ذِي زَرْعٍ عِندَ بَيْتِكَ الْمُحَرَّمِ رَبَّنَا لِيُقِيمُوا الصَّلَاةَ فَاجْعَلْ أَفْئِدَةً مِّنَ النَّاسِ تَهْوِي إِلَيْهِمْ وَارْزُقْهُم مِّنَ الثَّمَرَاتِ لَعَلَّهُمْ يَشْكُرُونَ
H&K	"O our Lord! I have made some of my offspring to dwell in an uncultivable valley by Your Sacred House (the Ka'bah at Makkah); in order, O our Lord, that they may perform As-Salat (Iqamat-as-Salat), so fill some hearts among

		men with love towards them, and (O Allah) provide them with fruits so that they may give thanks.
14 ابراهيم 40		رَبِّ اجْعَلْنِي مُقِيمَ الصَّلَاةِ وَمِن ذُرِّيَّتِي ۚ رَبَّنَا وَتَقَبَّلْ دُعَاءِ
H&K		"O my Lord! Make me one who performs As-Salat (Iqamat-as-Salat), and (also) from my offspring, our Lord! And accept my invocation.
17 الإسراء 3		ذُرِّيَّةَ مَنْ حَمَلْنَا مَعَ نُوحٍ ۚ إِنَّهُ كَانَ عَبْدًا شَكُورًا
H&K		"O offspring of those whom We carried (in the ship) with Nuh (Noah)! Verily, he was a grateful slave."
17 الإسراء 62		قَالَ أَرَأَيْتَكَ هَٰذَا الَّذِي كَرَّمْتَ عَلَيَّ لَئِنْ أَخَّرْتَنِ إِلَىٰ يَوْمِ الْقِيَامَةِ لَأَحْتَنِكَنَّ ذُرِّيَّتَهُ إِلَّا قَلِيلًا
H&K		[Iblis (Satan)] said: "See? This one whom You have honoured above me, if You give me respite (keep me alive) to the Day of Resurrection, I will surely seize and mislead his offspring (by sending them astray) all but a few!"
18 الكهف 50		وَإِذْ قُلْنَا لِلْمَلَائِكَةِ اسْجُدُوا لِآدَمَ فَسَجَدُوا إِلَّا إِبْلِيسَ كَانَ مِنَ الْجِنِّ فَفَسَقَ عَنْ أَمْرِ رَبِّهِ ۗ أَفَتَتَّخِذُونَهُ وَذُرِّيَّتَهُ أَوْلِيَاءَ مِن دُونِي وَهُمْ لَكُمْ عَدُوٌّ ۚ بِئْسَ لِلظَّالِمِينَ بَدَلًا
H&K		And (remember) when We said to the angels; "Prostrate to Adam." So they prostrated except Iblis (Satan). He was one of the jinns; he disobeyed the Command of his Lord. Will you then take him (Iblis) and his offspring as protectors and helpers rather than Me while they are enemies to you? What an evil is the exchange for the Zalimun (polytheists, and wrong-doers, etc).
19 مريم 58		أُولَٰئِكَ الَّذِينَ أَنْعَمَ اللَّهُ عَلَيْهِم مِّنَ النَّبِيِّينَ مِن ذُرِّيَّةِ آدَمَ وَمِمَّنْ حَمَلْنَا مَعَ نُوحٍ وَمِن ذُرِّيَّةِ إِبْرَاهِيمَ وَإِسْرَائِيلَ وَمِمَّنْ هَدَيْنَا وَاجْتَبَيْنَا ۚ إِذَا تُتْلَىٰ عَلَيْهِمْ آيَاتُ الرَّحْمَٰنِ خَرُّوا سُجَّدًا وَبُكِيًّا ۩
H&K		Those were they unto whom Allah bestowed His Grace from among the Prophets, of the offspring of Adam, and of those whom We carried (in the ship) with Nuh (Noah), and of the offspring of Ibrahim (Abraham) and Israel and from among those whom We guided and chose. When the Verses of the Most Beneficent (Allah) were recited unto them, they fell down prostrating and weeping.
25 الفرقان		وَالَّذِينَ يَقُولُونَ رَبَّنَا هَبْ لَنَا مِنْ أَزْوَاجِنَا وَذُرِّيَّاتِنَا قُرَّةَ أَعْيُنٍ وَاجْعَلْنَا لِلْمُتَّقِينَ إِمَامًا

74	
H&K	And those who say: "Our Lord! Bestow on us from our wives and our offspring who will be the comfort of our eyes, and make us leaders for the Muttaqun" (pious - see V. 2:2 and the footnote of V. 3:164)."
29 العنكبوت 27	وَوَهَبْنَا لَهُ إِسْحَاقَ وَيَعْقُوبَ وَجَعَلْنَا فِي ذُرِّيَّتِهِ النُّبُوَّةَ وَالْكِتَابَ وَآتَيْنَاهُ أَجْرَهُ فِي الدُّنْيَا ۖ وَإِنَّهُ فِي الْآخِرَةِ لَمِنَ الصَّالِحِينَ
H&K	And We bestowed on him [Ibrahim (Abraham)], Ishaque (Isaac) and Ya'qub (Jacob), and ordained among his offspring Prophethood and the Book [i.e. the Taurat (Torah) (to Musa - Moses), the Injeel (Gospel) (to 'Iesa - Jesus), the Quran (to Muhammad SAW), all from the offspring of Ibrahim (Abraham)], and We granted him his reward in this world, and verily, in the Hereafter he is indeed among the righteous.
36 يس 41	وَآيَةٌ لَهُمْ أَنَّا حَمَلْنَا ذُرِّيَّتَهُمْ فِي الْفُلْكِ الْمَشْحُونِ
H&K	And an Ayah (sign) for them is that We bore their offspring in the laden ship [of Nuh (Noah)].
37 الصافات 77	وَجَعَلْنَا ذُرِّيَّتَهُ هُمُ الْبَاقِينَ
H&K	And, his progeny, them We made the survivors (i.e. Shem, Ham and Japheth).
37 الصافات 113	وَبَارَكْنَا عَلَيْهِ وَعَلَىٰ إِسْحَاقَ ۚ وَمِن ذُرِّيَّتِهِمَا مُحْسِنٌ وَظَالِمٌ لِنَفْسِهِ مُبِينٌ
H&K	We blessed him and Ishaque (Isaac), and of their progeny are (some) that do right, and some that plainly wrong themselves.
40 غافر 8	رَبَّنَا وَأَدْخِلْهُمْ جَنَّاتِ عَدْنٍ الَّتِي وَعَدْتَهُمْ وَمَن صَلَحَ مِنْ آبَائِهِمْ وَأَزْوَاجِهِمْ وَذُرِّيَّاتِهِمْ ۚ إِنَّكَ أَنتَ الْعَزِيزُ الْحَكِيمُ
H&K	"Our Lord! And make them enter the 'Adn (Eden) Paradise (everlasting Gardens) which you have promised them, and to the righteous among their fathers, their wives, and their offspring! Verily, You are the All-Mighty, the All-Wise.

46 الأحقاف 15	وَوَصَّيْنَا الْإِنسَانَ بِوَالِدَيْهِ إِحْسَانًا ۖ حَمَلَتْهُ أُمُّهُ كُرْهًا وَوَضَعَتْهُ كُرْهًا ۖ وَحَمْلُهُ وَفِصَالُهُ ثَلَاثُونَ شَهْرًا ۚ حَتَّىٰ إِذَا بَلَغَ أَشُدَّهُ وَبَلَغَ أَرْبَعِينَ سَنَةً قَالَ رَبِّ أَوْزِعْنِي أَنْ أَشْكُرَ نِعْمَتَكَ الَّتِي أَنْعَمْتَ عَلَيَّ وَعَلَىٰ وَالِدَيَّ وَأَنْ أَعْمَلَ صَالِحًا تَرْضَاهُ وَأَصْلِحْ لِي فِي ذُرِّيَّتِي ۖ إِنِّي تُبْتُ إِلَيْكَ وَإِنِّي مِنَ الْمُسْلِمِينَ	
H&K	And We have enjoined on man to be dutiful and kind to his parents. His mother bears him with hardship and she brings him forth with hardship, and the bearing of him, and the weaning of him is thirty (30) months, till when he attains full strength and reaches forty years, he says: "My Lord! Grant me the power and ability that I may be grateful for Your Favour which You have bestowed upon me and upon my parents, and that I may do righteous good deeds, such as please You, and make my off-spring good. Truly, I have turned to You in repentance, and truly, I am one of the Muslims (submitting to Your Will)."	
52 الطور 21	وَالَّذِينَ آمَنُوا وَاتَّبَعَتْهُمْ ذُرِّيَّتُهُم بِإِيمَانٍ أَلْحَقْنَا بِهِمْ ذُرِّيَّتَهُمْ وَمَا أَلَتْنَاهُم مِّنْ عَمَلِهِم مِّن شَيْءٍ ۚ كُلُّ امْرِئٍ بِمَا كَسَبَ رَهِينٌ	
H&K	And those who believe and whose offspring follow them in Faith, to them shall We join their offspring, and We shall not decrease the reward of their deeds in anything. Every person is a pledge for that which he has earned.	
57 الحديد 26	وَلَقَدْ أَرْسَلْنَا نُوحًا وَإِبْرَاهِيمَ وَجَعَلْنَا فِي ذُرِّيَّتِهِمَا النُّبُوَّةَ وَالْكِتَابَ ۖ فَمِنْهُم مُّهْتَدٍ ۖ وَكَثِيرٌ مِّنْهُمْ فَاسِقُونَ	
H&K	And indeed, We sent Nuh (Noah) and Ibrahim (Abraham), and placed in their offspring Prophethood and Scripture, and among them there is he who is guided, but many of them are Fasiqun (rebellious, disobedient to Allah).	

		خِطْبَةِ النِّسَاءِ
	2 البقرة 235	وَلَا جُنَاحَ عَلَيْكُمْ فِيمَا عَرَّضْتُم بِهِ مِنْ خِطْبَةِ النِّسَاءِ أَوْ أَكْنَنتُمْ فِى أَنفُسِكُمْ ۚ عَلِمَ اللَّهُ أَنَّكُمْ سَتَذْكُرُونَهُنَّ وَلَٰكِن لَّا تُوَاعِدُوهُنَّ سِرًّا إِلَّا أَن تَقُولُوا قَوْلًا مَّعْرُوفًا ۚ وَلَا تَعْزِمُوا عُقْدَةَ النِّكَاحِ حَتَّىٰ يَبْلُغَ الْكِتَابُ أَجَلَهُ ۚ وَاعْلَمُوا أَنَّ اللَّهَ يَعْلَمُ مَا فِى أَنفُسِكُمْ فَاحْذَرُوهُ ۚ وَاعْلَمُوا أَنَّ اللَّهَ غَفُورٌ حَلِيمٌ
	Sahih	There is no blame upon you for that to which you [indirectly] allude concerning a proposal to women or for what you conceal within yourselves. Allah knows that you will have them in mind. But do not promise them secretly except for saying a proper saying. And do not determine to undertake a marriage contract until the decreed period reaches its end. And know that Allah knows what is within yourselves, so beware of Him. And know that Allah is Forgiving and Forbearing
	236	لَّا جُنَاحَ عَلَيْكُمْ إِن طَلَّقْتُمُ النِّسَاءَ مَا لَمْ تَمَسُّوهُنَّ أَوْ تَفْرِضُوا لَهُنَّ فَرِيضَةً ۚ وَمَتِّعُوهُنَّ عَلَى الْمُوسِعِ قَدَرُهُ وَعَلَى الْمُقْتِرِ قَدَرُهُ مَتَاعًا بِالْمَعْرُوفِ ۖ حَقًّا عَلَى الْمُحْسِنِينَ
	Sahih	There is no blame upon you if you divorce women you have not touched nor specified for them an obligation. But give them [a gift of] compensation - the wealthy according to his capability and the poor according to his capability - a provision according to what is acceptable, a duty upon the doers of good
	237	وَإِن طَلَّقْتُمُوهُنَّ مِن قَبْلِ أَن تَمَسُّوهُنَّ وَقَدْ فَرَضْتُمْ لَهُنَّ فَرِيضَةً فَنِصْفُ مَا فَرَضْتُمْ إِلَّا أَن يَعْفُونَ أَوْ يَعْفُوَ الَّذِى بِيَدِهِ عُقْدَةُ النِّكَاحِ ۚ وَأَن تَعْفُوا أَقْرَبُ لِلتَّقْوَىٰ ۚ وَلَا تَنسَوُا الْفَضْلَ بَيْنَكُمْ ۚ إِنَّ اللَّهَ بِمَا تَعْمَلُونَ بَصِيرٌ
	Sahih	And if you divorce them before you have touched them and you have already specified for them an obligation, then [give] half of what you specified - unless they forego the right or the one in whose hand is the marriage contract foregoes it. And to forego it is nearer to righteousness. And do not forget graciousness between you. Indeed Allah, of whatever you do, is Seeing
	24 النور 33	وَلْيَسْتَعْفِفِ الَّذِينَ لَا يَجِدُونَ نِكَاحًا حَتَّىٰ يُغْنِيَهُمُ اللَّهُ مِن فَضْلِهِ ۗ وَالَّذِينَ يَبْتَغُونَ الْكِتَابَ مِمَّا مَلَكَتْ أَيْمَانُكُمْ فَكَاتِبُوهُمْ إِنْ عَلِمْتُمْ فِيهِمْ خَيْرًا ۖ وَآتُوهُم مِّن مَّالِ اللَّهِ الَّذِى آتَاكُمْ ۚ وَلَا تُكْرِهُوا فَتَيَاتِكُمْ عَلَى الْبِغَاءِ إِنْ أَرَدْنَ تَحَصُّنًا لِّتَبْتَغُوا عَرَضَ الْحَيَاةِ الدُّنْيَا ۚ وَمَن يُكْرِههُّنَّ فَإِنَّ اللَّهَ مِن بَعْدِ إِكْرَاهِهِنَّ غَفُورٌ رَّحِيمٌ
		And let those who find not the financial means for marriage keep themselves chaste, until Allah enriches them of His Bounty. And such of your slaves as

	seek a writing (of emancipation), give them such writing, if you know that they are good and trustworthy. And give them something yourselves out of the wealth of Allah which He has bestowed upon you. And force not your maids to prostitution, if they desire chastity, in order that you may make a gain in the (perishable) goods of this worldly life. But if anyone compels them (to prostitution), then after such compulsion, Allah is Oft-Forgiving, Most Merciful (to those women, i.e. He will forgive them because they have been forced to do this evil action unwillingly).
	يُظَاهِرُونَ
33 الأحزاب 4	ما جَعَلَ اللَّهُ لِرَجُلٍ مِن قَلْبَيْنِ فِى جَوْفِهِ ۚ وَما جَعَلَ أَزْواجَكُمُ اللّٰٓئى تُظٰهِرونَ مِنهُنَّ أُمَّهٰتِكُم ۚ وَما جَعَلَ أَدعِياءَكُم أَبناءَكُم ۚ ذٰلِكُم قَولُكُم بِأَفْواهِكُم ۖ وَاللَّهُ يَقولُ الحَقَّ وَهُوَ يَهدِى السَّبيلَ
Sahih	Allah has not made for a man two hearts in his interior. And He has not made your wives whom you declare unlawful your mothers. And he has not made your adopted sons your [true] sons. That is [merely] your saying by your mouths, but Allah says the truth, and He guides to the [right] way.
58 المجادلة 2	الَّذينَ يُظٰهِرونَ مِنكُم مِن نِسائِهِم ما هُنَّ أُمَّهٰتِهِم ۖ إِن أُمَّهٰتُهُم إِلَّا الّٰٓئى وَلَدنَهُم ۚ وَإِنَّهُم لَيَقولونَ مُنكَرًا مِنَ القَولِ وَزورًا ۚ وَإِنَّ اللَّهَ لَعَفُوٌّ غَفورٌ
Sahih	Those who pronounce thihar among you [to separate] from their wives - they are not [consequently] their mothers. Their mothers are none but those who gave birth to them. And indeed, they are saying an objectionable statement and a falsehood. But indeed, Allah is Pardoning and Forgiving.
H&K	Those among you who make their wives unlawful (Az-Zihar) to them by saying to them "You are like my mother's back." They cannot be their mothers. None can be their mothers except those who gave them birth. And verily, they utter an ill word and a lie. And verily, Allah is Oft-Pardoning, Oft-Forgiving.
58 المجادلة 3	وَالَّذينَ يُظٰهِرونَ مِن نِسائِهِم ثُمَّ يَعودونَ لِما قالوا فَتَحريرُ رَقَبَةٍ مِن قَبلِ أَن يَتَماسّا ۚ ذٰلِكُم توعَظونَ بِهِ ۚ وَاللَّهُ بِما تَعمَلونَ خَبيرٌ
Sahih	And those who pronounce thihar from their wives and then [wish to] go back on what they said - then [there must be] the freeing of a slave before they touch one another. That is what you are admonished thereby; and Allah is Acquainted with what you do.

فَمَن لَّمْ يَجِدْ فَصِيَامُ شَهْرَيْنِ مُتَتَابِعَيْنِ مِن قَبْلِ أَن يَتَمَاسَّا ۚ فَمَن لَّمْ يَسْتَطِعْ فَإِطْعَامُ سِتِّينَ مِسْكِينًا ۚ ذَٰلِكَ لِتُؤْمِنُوا بِاللَّهِ وَرَسُولِهِ ۚ وَتِلْكَ حُدُودُ اللَّهِ ۗ وَلِلْكَافِرِينَ عَذَابٌ أَلِيمٌ	58 المجادلة 4
Sahih	And he who does not find [a slave] - then a fast for two months consecutively before they touch one another; and he who is unable - then the feeding of sixty poor persons. That is for you to believe [completely] in Allah and His Messenger; and those are the limits [set by] Allah. And for the disbelievers is a painful punishment.

DIVORCE الطلاق

وَالْمُطَلَّقَاتُ يَتَرَبَّصْنَ بِأَنفُسِهِنَّ ثَلَاثَةَ قُرُوءٍ ۚ وَلَا يَحِلُّ لَهُنَّ أَن يَكْتُمْنَ مَا خَلَقَ اللَّهُ فِي أَرْحَامِهِنَّ إِن كُنَّ يُؤْمِنَّ بِاللَّهِ وَالْيَوْمِ الْآخِرِ ۚ وَبُعُولَتُهُنَّ أَحَقُّ بِرَدِّهِنَّ فِي ذَٰلِكَ إِنْ أَرَادُوا إِصْلَاحًا ۚ وَلَهُنَّ مِثْلُ الَّذِي عَلَيْهِنَّ بِالْمَعْرُوفِ ۚ وَلِلرِّجَالِ عَلَيْهِنَّ دَرَجَةٌ ۗ وَاللَّهُ عَزِيزٌ حَكِيمٌ	2 البقرة 228
Sahih	Divorced women remain in waiting for three periods, and it is not lawful for them to conceal what Allah has created in their wombs if they believe in Allah and the Last Day. And their husbands have more right to take them back in this [period] if they want reconciliation. And due to the wives is similar to what is expected of them, according to what is reasonable. But the men have a degree over them [in responsibility and authority]. And Allah is Exalted in Might and Wise.
H&K	And divorced women shall wait (as regards their marriage) for three menstrual periods, and it is not lawful for them to conceal what Allah has created in their wombs, if they believe in Allah and the Last Day. And their husbands have the better right to take them back in that period, if they wish for reconciliation. And they (women) have rights (over their husbands as regards living expenses, etc.) similar (to those of their husbands) over them (as regards obedience and respect, etc.) to what is reasonable, but men have a degree (of responsibility) over them. And Allah is All-Mighty, All-Wise.
فَإِن طَلَّقَهَا فَلَا تَحِلُّ لَهُ مِن بَعْدُ حَتَّىٰ تَنكِحَ زَوْجًا غَيْرَهُ ۗ فَإِن طَلَّقَهَا فَلَا جُنَاحَ عَلَيْهِمَا أَن يَتَرَاجَعَا إِن ظَنَّا أَن يُقِيمَا حُدُودَ اللَّهِ ۗ وَتِلْكَ حُدُودُ اللَّهِ يُبَيِّنُهَا لِقَوْمٍ يَعْلَمُونَ	2 البقرة 230
Sahih	And if he has divorced her [for the third time], then she is not lawful to him afterward until [after] she marries a husband other than him. And if the latter husband divorces her [or dies], there is no blame upon the woman and her former husband for returning to each other if they think that they can keep

		[within] the limits of Allah. These are the limits of Allah, which He makes clear to a people who know
	H&K	And if he has divorced her (the third time), then she is not lawful unto him thereafter until she has married another husband. Then, if the other husband divorces her, it is no sin on both of them that they reunite, provided they feel that they can keep the limits ordained by Allah. These are the limits of Allah, which He makes plain for the people who have knowledge.
2 البقرة 231		وَإِذَا طَلَّقْتُمُ النِّسَاءَ فَبَلَغْنَ أَجَلَهُنَّ فَأَمْسِكُوهُنَّ بِمَعْرُوفٍ أَوْ سَرِّحُوهُنَّ بِمَعْرُوفٍ ۚ وَلَا تُمْسِكُوهُنَّ ضِرَارًا لِّتَعْتَدُوا ۚ وَمَن يَفْعَلْ ذَٰلِكَ فَقَدْ ظَلَمَ نَفْسَهُ ۚ وَلَا تَتَّخِذُوا آيَاتِ اللَّهِ هُزُوًا ۚ وَاذْكُرُوا نِعْمَتَ اللَّهِ عَلَيْكُمْ وَمَا أَنزَلَ عَلَيْكُم مِّنَ الْكِتَابِ وَالْحِكْمَةِ يَعِظُكُم بِهِ ۚ وَاتَّقُوا اللَّهَ وَاعْلَمُوا أَنَّ اللَّهَ بِكُلِّ شَيْءٍ عَلِيمٌ
	Sahih	And when you divorce women and they have [nearly] fulfilled their term, either retain them according to acceptable terms or release them according to acceptable terms, and do not keep them, intending harm, to transgress [against them]. And whoever does that has certainly wronged himself. And do not take the verses of Allah in jest. And remember the favor of Allah upon you and what has been revealed to you of the Book and wisdom by which He instructs you. And fear Allah and know that Allah is Knowing of all things
2 البقرة 232		وَإِذَا طَلَّقْتُمُ النِّسَاءَ فَبَلَغْنَ أَجَلَهُنَّ فَلَا تَعْضُلُوهُنَّ أَن يَنكِحْنَ أَزْوَاجَهُنَّ إِذَا تَرَاضَوْا بَيْنَهُم بِالْمَعْرُوفِ ۗ ذَٰلِكَ يُوعَظُ بِهِ مَن كَانَ مِنكُمْ يُؤْمِنُ بِاللَّهِ وَالْيَوْمِ الْآخِرِ ۗ ذَٰلِكُمْ أَزْكَىٰ لَكُمْ وَأَطْهَرُ ۗ وَاللَّهُ يَعْلَمُ وَأَنتُمْ لَا تَعْلَمُونَ
	Sahih	And when you divorce women and they have fulfilled their term, do not prevent them from remarrying their [former] husbands if they agree among themselves on an acceptable basis. That is instructed to whoever of you believes in Allah and the Last Day. That is better for you and purer, and Allah knows and you know not.
	H&K	And when you have divorced women and they have fulfilled the term of their prescribed period, do not prevent them from marrying their (former) husbands, if they mutually agree on reasonable basis. This (instruction) is an admonition for him among you who believes in Allah and the Last Day. That is more virtuous and purer for you. Allah knows and you know not.
2 البقرة 236		لَّا جُنَاحَ عَلَيْكُمْ إِن طَلَّقْتُمُ النِّسَاءَ مَا لَمْ تَمَسُّوهُنَّ أَوْ تَفْرِضُوا لَهُنَّ فَرِيضَةً ۚ وَمَتِّعُوهُنَّ عَلَى الْمُوسِعِ قَدَرُهُ وَعَلَى الْمُقْتِرِ قَدَرُهُ مَتَاعًا بِالْمَعْرُوفِ ۖ حَقًّا عَلَى الْمُحْسِنِينَ

Sahih		There is no blame upon you if you divorce women you have not touched nor specified for them an obligation. But give them [a gift of] compensation - the wealthy according to his capability and the poor according to his capability - a provision according to what is acceptable, a duty upon the doers of good
2 البقرة 237	وَإِن طَلَّقْتُمُوهُنَّ مِن قَبْلِ أَن تَمَسُّوهُنَّ وَقَدْ فَرَضْتُمْ لَهُنَّ فَرِيضَةً فَنِصْفُ مَا فَرَضْتُمْ إِلَّا أَن يَعْفُونَ أَوْ يَعْفُوَ الَّذِي بِيَدِهِ عُقْدَةُ النِّكَاحِ ۚ وَأَن تَعْفُوا أَقْرَبُ لِلتَّقْوَىٰ ۚ وَلَا تَنسَوُا الْفَضْلَ بَيْنَكُمْ ۚ إِنَّ اللَّهَ بِمَا تَعْمَلُونَ بَصِيرٌ	
Sahih		And if you divorce them before you have touched them and you have already specified for them an obligation, then [give] half of what you specified - unless they forego the right or the one in whose hand is the marriage contract foregoes it. And to forego it is nearer to righteousness. And do not forget graciousness between you. Indeed Allah, of whatever you do, is Seeing
2 البقرة 241	وَلِلْمُطَلَّقَاتِ مَتَاعٌ بِالْمَعْرُوفِ ۖ حَقًّا عَلَى الْمُتَّقِينَ	
Sahih		And for divorced women is a provision according to what is acceptable - a duty upon the righteous
33 الأحزاب 49	يَا أَيُّهَا الَّذِينَ آمَنُوا إِذَا نَكَحْتُمُ الْمُؤْمِنَاتِ ثُمَّ طَلَّقْتُمُوهُنَّ مِن قَبْلِ أَن تَمَسُّوهُنَّ فَمَا لَكُمْ عَلَيْهِنَّ مِنْ عِدَّةٍ تَعْتَدُّونَهَا ۖ فَمَتِّعُوهُنَّ وَسَرِّحُوهُنَّ سَرَاحًا جَمِيلًا	
Sahih		O You who have believed, when you marry believing women and then divorce them before you have touched them, then there is not for you any waiting period to count concerning them. So provide for them and give them a gracious release
65 الطلاق 1	يَا أَيُّهَا النَّبِيُّ إِذَا طَلَّقْتُمُ النِّسَاءَ فَطَلِّقُوهُنَّ لِعِدَّتِهِنَّ وَأَحْصُوا الْعِدَّةَ ۖ وَاتَّقُوا اللَّهَ رَبَّكُمْ ۖ لَا تُخْرِجُوهُنَّ مِن بُيُوتِهِنَّ وَلَا يَخْرُجْنَ إِلَّا أَن يَأْتِينَ بِفَاحِشَةٍ مُّبَيِّنَةٍ ۚ وَتِلْكَ حُدُودُ اللَّهِ ۚ وَمَن يَتَعَدَّ حُدُودَ اللَّهِ فَقَدْ ظَلَمَ نَفْسَهُ ۚ لَا تَدْرِي لَعَلَّ اللَّهَ يُحْدِثُ بَعْدَ ذَٰلِكَ أَمْرًا	
Sahih		O Prophet, when you [Muslims] divorce women, divorce them for [the commencement of] their waiting period and keep count of the waiting period, and fear Allah, your Lord. Do not turn them out of their [husbands'] houses, nor should they [themselves] leave [during that period] unless they are committing a clear immorality. And those are the limits [set by] Allah. And whoever transgresses the limits of Allah has certainly wronged himself. You know not; perhaps Allah will bring about after that a [different] matter

H&K	O Prophet (SAW)! When you divorce women, divorce them at their 'Iddah (prescribed periods), and count (accurately) their 'Iddah (periods). And fear Allah your Lord (O Muslims), and turn them not out of their (husband's) homes, nor shall they (themselves) leave, except in case they are guilty of some open illegal sexual intercourse. And those are the set limits of Allah. And whosoever transgresses the set limits of Allah, then indeed he has wronged himself. You (the one who divorces his wife) know not, it may be that Allah will afterward bring some new thing to pass (i.e. to return her back to you if that was the first or second divorce).
66 التحريم 5	عَسَىٰ رَبُّهُ إِن طَلَّقَكُنَّ أَن يُبْدِلَهُ أَزْوَاجًا خَيْرًا مِّنكُنَّ مُسْلِمَاتٍ مُّؤْمِنَاتٍ قَانِتَاتٍ تَائِبَاتٍ عَابِدَاتٍ سَائِحَاتٍ ثَيِّبَاتٍ وَأَبْكَارًا
	Perhaps his Lord, if he divorced you [all], would substitute for him wives better than you - submitting [to Allah], believing, devoutly obedient, repentant, worshipping, and traveling - [ones] previously married and virgins
	الشَّهْرَ الْحَرَامَ
2 البقرة 194	الشَّهْرُ الْحَرَامُ بِالشَّهْرِ الْحَرَامِ وَالْحُرُمَاتُ قِصَاصٌ ۚ فَمَنِ اعْتَدَىٰ عَلَيْكُمْ فَاعْتَدُوا عَلَيْهِ بِمِثْلِ مَا اعْتَدَىٰ عَلَيْكُمْ ۚ وَاتَّقُوا اللَّهَ وَاعْلَمُوا أَنَّ اللَّهَ مَعَ الْمُتَّقِينَ
	[Fighting in] the sacred month is for [aggression committed in] the sacred month, and for [all] violations is legal retribution. So whoever has assaulted you, then assault him in the same way that he has assaulted you. And fear Allah and know that Allah is with those who fear Him
217	يَسْأَلُونَكَ عَنِ الشَّهْرِ الْحَرَامِ قِتَالٍ فِيهِ ۖ قُلْ قِتَالٌ فِيهِ كَبِيرٌ ۖ وَصَدٌّ عَن سَبِيلِ اللَّهِ وَكُفْرٌ بِهِ وَالْمَسْجِدِ الْحَرَامِ وَإِخْرَاجُ أَهْلِهِ مِنْهُ أَكْبَرُ عِندَ اللَّهِ ۚ وَالْفِتْنَةُ أَكْبَرُ مِنَ الْقَتْلِ ۗ وَلَا يَزَالُونَ يُقَاتِلُونَكُمْ حَتَّىٰ يَرُدُّوكُمْ عَن دِينِكُمْ إِنِ اسْتَطَاعُوا ۚ وَمَن يَرْتَدِدْ مِنكُمْ عَن دِينِهِ فَيَمُتْ وَهُوَ كَافِرٌ فَأُولَٰئِكَ حَبِطَتْ أَعْمَالُهُمْ فِي الدُّنْيَا وَالْآخِرَةِ ۖ وَأُولَٰئِكَ أَصْحَابُ النَّارِ ۖ هُمْ فِيهَا خَالِدُونَ
	They ask you about the sacred month - about fighting therein. Say, "Fighting therein is great [sin], but averting [people] from the way of Allah and disbelief in Him and [preventing access to] al-Masjid al-Haram and the expulsion of its people therefrom are greater [evil] in the sight of Allah. And fitnah is greater than killing." And they will continue to fight you until they turn you back from

		your religion if they are able. And whoever of you reverts from his religion [to disbelief] and dies while he is a disbeliever - for those, their deeds have become worthless in this world and the Hereafter, and those are the companions of the Fire, they will abide therein eternally
المائدة 5	2	يَا أَيُّهَا الَّذِينَ آمَنُوا لَا تُحِلُّوا شَعَائِرَ اللَّهِ وَلَا **الشَّهْرَ الْحَرَامَ** وَلَا الْهَدْيَ وَلَا الْقَلَائِدَ وَلَا آمِّينَ الْبَيْتَ الْحَرَامَ يَبْتَغُونَ فَضْلًا مِن رَّبِّهِمْ وَرِضْوَانًا ۚ وَإِذَا حَلَلْتُمْ فَاصْطَادُوا ۚ وَلَا يَجْرِمَنَّكُمْ شَنَآنُ قَوْمٍ أَن صَدُّوكُمْ عَنِ الْمَسْجِدِ الْحَرَامِ أَن تَعْتَدُوا ۘ وَتَعَاوَنُوا عَلَى الْبِرِّ وَالتَّقْوَىٰ ۖ وَلَا تَعَاوَنُوا عَلَى الْإِثْمِ وَالْعُدْوَانِ ۚ وَاتَّقُوا اللَّهَ ۖ إِنَّ اللَّهَ شَدِيدُ الْعِقَابِ
		O you who have believed, do not violate the rites of Allah or [the sanctity of] the sacred month or [neglect the marking of] the sacrificial animals and garlanding [them] or [violate the safety of] those coming to the Sacred House seeking bounty from their Lord and [His] approval. But when you come out of ihram, then [you may] hunt. And do not let the hatred of a people for having obstructed you from al-Masjid al-Haram lead you to transgress. And cooperate in righteousness and piety, but do not cooperate in sin and aggression. And fear Allah; indeed, Allah is severe in penalty
	97	۞ جَعَلَ اللَّهُ الْكَعْبَةَ الْبَيْتَ الْحَرَامَ قِيَامًا لِّلنَّاسِ **وَالشَّهْرَ الْحَرَامَ** وَالْهَدْيَ وَالْقَلَائِدَ ۚ ذَٰلِكَ لِتَعْلَمُوا أَنَّ اللَّهَ يَعْلَمُ مَا فِي السَّمَاوَاتِ وَمَا فِي الْأَرْضِ وَأَنَّ اللَّهَ بِكُلِّ شَيْءٍ عَلِيمٌ
		Allah has made the Ka'bah, the Sacred House, standing for the people and [has sanctified] the sacred months and the sacrificial animals and the garlands [by which they are identified]. That is so you may know that Allah knows what is in the heavens and what is in the earth and that Allah is Knowing of all things.
		حُرُمٌ
المائدة 5	1	يَا أَيُّهَا الَّذِينَ آمَنُوا أَوْفُوا بِالْعُقُودِ ۚ أُحِلَّتْ لَكُم بَهِيمَةُ الْأَنْعَامِ إِلَّا مَا يُتْلَىٰ عَلَيْكُمْ غَيْرَ مُحِلِّي الصَّيْدِ وَأَنتُمْ **حُرُمٌ** ۗ إِنَّ اللَّهَ يَحْكُمُ مَا يُرِيدُ
		O you who have believed, fulfill [all] contracts. Lawful for you are the animals of grazing livestock except for that which is recited to you [in this Qur'an] -

		hunting not being permitted while you are in the state of ihram. Indeed, Allah ordains what He intends.
	95	يَٰٓأَيُّهَا ٱلَّذِينَ ءَامَنُوا۟ لَا تَقْتُلُوا۟ ٱلصَّيْدَ وَأَنتُمْ حُرُمٌ ۚ وَمَن قَتَلَهُۥ مِنكُم مُّتَعَمِّدًا فَجَزَآءٌ مِّثْلُ مَا قَتَلَ مِنَ ٱلنَّعَمِ يَحْكُمُ بِهِۦ ذَوَا عَدْلٍ مِّنكُمْ هَدْيًۢا بَٰلِغَ ٱلْكَعْبَةِ أَوْ كَفَّٰرَةٌ طَعَامُ مَسَٰكِينَ أَوْ عَدْلُ ذَٰلِكَ صِيَامًا لِّيَذُوقَ وَبَالَ أَمْرِهِۦ ۗ عَفَا ٱللَّهُ عَمَّا سَلَفَ ۚ وَمَنْ عَادَ فَيَنتَقِمُ ٱللَّهُ مِنْهُ ۗ وَٱللَّهُ عَزِيزٌ ذُو ٱنتِقَامٍ
		O you who have believed, do not kill game while you are in the state of ihram. And whoever of you kills it intentionally - the penalty is an equivalent from sacrificial animals to what he killed, as judged by two just men among you as an offering [to Allah] delivered to the Ka'bah, or an expiation: the feeding of needy people or the equivalent of that in fasting, that he may taste the consequence of his deed. Allah has pardoned what is past; but whoever returns [to violation], then Allah will take retribution from him. And Allah is Exalted in Might and Owner of Retribution
9 التوبة	5	فَإِذَا ٱنسَلَخَ ٱلْأَشْهُرُ ٱلْحُرُمُ فَٱقْتُلُوا۟ ٱلْمُشْرِكِينَ حَيْثُ وَجَدتُّمُوهُمْ وَخُذُوهُمْ وَٱحْصُرُوهُمْ وَٱقْعُدُوا۟ لَهُمْ كُلَّ مَرْصَدٍ ۚ فَإِن تَابُوا۟ وَأَقَامُوا۟ ٱلصَّلَوٰةَ وَءَاتَوُا۟ ٱلزَّكَوٰةَ فَخَلُّوا۟ سَبِيلَهُمْ ۚ إِنَّ ٱللَّهَ غَفُورٌ رَّحِيمٌ
		And when the sacred months have passed, then kill the polytheists wherever you find them and capture them and besiege them and sit in wait for them at every place of ambush. But if they should repent, establish prayer, and give zakah, let them [go] on their way. Indeed, Allah is Forgiving and Merciful.
9 التوبة	36	إِنَّ عِدَّةَ ٱلشُّهُورِ عِندَ ٱللَّهِ ٱثْنَا عَشَرَ شَهْرًا فِى كِتَٰبِ ٱللَّهِ يَوْمَ خَلَقَ ٱلسَّمَٰوَٰتِ وَٱلْأَرْضَ مِنْهَآ أَرْبَعَةٌ حُرُمٌ ۚ ذَٰلِكَ ٱلدِّينُ ٱلْقَيِّمُ ۚ فَلَا تَظْلِمُوا۟ فِيهِنَّ أَنفُسَكُمْ ۚ وَقَٰتِلُوا۟ ٱلْمُشْرِكِينَ كَآفَّةً كَمَا يُقَٰتِلُونَكُمْ كَآفَّةً ۚ وَٱعْلَمُوٓا۟ أَنَّ ٱللَّهَ مَعَ ٱلْمُتَّقِينَ
		Indeed, the number of months with Allah is twelve [lunar] months in the register of Allah [from] the day He created the heavens and the earth; of these, four are sacred. That is the correct religion, so do not wrong yourselves during them. And fight against the disbelievers collectively as they fight against you collectively. And know that Allah is with the righteous [who fear Him]
16 النحل	115	إِنَّمَا حَرَّمَ عَلَيْكُمُ ٱلْمَيْتَةَ وَٱلدَّمَ وَلَحْمَ ٱلْخِنزِيرِ وَمَآ أُهِلَّ لِغَيْرِ ٱللَّهِ بِهِۦ ۖ فَمَنِ ٱضْطُرَّ غَيْرَ بَاغٍ وَلَا عَادٍ فَإِنَّ ٱللَّهَ غَفُورٌ رَّحِيمٌ
		He has only forbidden to you dead animals, blood, the flesh of swine, and that which has been dedicated to other than Allah. But whoever is forced [by

		necessity], neither desiring [it] nor transgressing [its limit] - then indeed, Allah is Forgiving and Merciful
66 التحريم 1	يَا أَيُّهَا النَّبِيُّ لِمَ تُحَرِّمُ مَا أَحَلَّ اللَّهُ لَكَ ۖ تَبْتَغِي مَرْضَاتَ أَزْوَاجِكَ ۚ وَاللَّهُ غَفُورٌ رَحِيمٌ	
4 النساء 13	تِلْكَ حُدُودُ اللَّهِ ۚ وَمَن يُطِعِ اللَّهَ وَرَسُولَهُ يُدْخِلْهُ جَنَّاتٍ تَجْرِي مِن تَحْتِهَا الْأَنْهَارُ خَالِدِينَ فِيهَا ۚ وَذَٰلِكَ الْفَوْزُ الْعَظِيمُ	
4 النساء 14	وَمَن يَعْصِ اللَّهَ وَرَسُولَهُ وَيَتَعَدَّ حُدُودَهُ يُدْخِلْهُ نَارًا خَالِدًا فِيهَا وَلَهُ عَذَابٌ مُّهِينٌ	
4 النساء 176	يَسْتَفْتُونَكَ قُلِ اللَّهُ يُفْتِيكُمْ فِي الْكَلَالَةِ ۚ إِنِ امْرُؤٌ هَلَكَ لَيْسَ لَهُ وَلَدٌ وَلَهُ أُخْتٌ فَلَهَا نِصْفُ مَا تَرَكَ ۚ وَهُوَ يَرِثُهَا إِن لَّمْ يَكُن لَّهَا وَلَدٌ ۚ فَإِن كَانَتَا اثْنَتَيْنِ فَلَهُمَا الثُّلُثَانِ مِمَّا تَرَكَ ۚ وَإِن كَانُوا إِخْوَةً رِّجَالًا وَنِسَاءً فَلِلذَّكَرِ مِثْلُ حَظِّ الْأُنثَيَيْنِ ۗ يُبَيِّنُ اللَّهُ لَكُمْ أَن تَضِلُّوا ۗ وَاللَّهُ بِكُلِّ شَيْءٍ عَلِيمٌ	
5 المائدة 106	يَا أَيُّهَا الَّذِينَ آمَنُوا شَهَادَةُ بَيْنِكُمْ إِذَا حَضَرَ أَحَدَكُمُ الْمَوْتُ حِينَ الْوَصِيَّةِ اثْنَانِ ذَوَا عَدْلٍ مِّنكُمْ أَوْ آخَرَانِ مِنْ غَيْرِكُمْ إِنْ أَنتُمْ ضَرَبْتُمْ فِي الْأَرْضِ فَأَصَابَتْكُم مُّصِيبَةُ الْمَوْتِ ۚ تَحْبِسُونَهُمَا مِن بَعْدِ الصَّلَاةِ فَيُقْسِمَانِ بِاللَّهِ إِنِ ارْتَبْتُمْ لَا نَشْتَرِي بِهِ ثَمَنًا وَلَوْ كَانَ ذَا قُرْبَىٰ ۙ وَلَا نَكْتُمُ شَهَادَةَ اللَّهِ إِنَّا إِذًا لَّمِنَ الْآثِمِينَ	
	O you who have believed, testimony [should be taken] among you when death approaches one of you at the time of bequest - [that of] two just men from among you or two others from outside if you are traveling through the land and the disaster of death should strike you. Detain them after the prayer and let them both swear by Allah if you doubt [their testimony, saying], "We will not exchange our oath for a price, even if he should be a near relative, and we will not withhold the testimony of Allah. Indeed, we would then be of the sinful."	
107	فَإِنْ عُثِرَ عَلَىٰ أَنَّهُمَا اسْتَحَقَّا إِثْمًا فَآخَرَانِ يَقُومَانِ مَقَامَهُمَا مِنَ الَّذِينَ اسْتَحَقَّ عَلَيْهِمُ الْأَوْلَيَانِ فَيُقْسِمَانِ بِاللَّهِ لَشَهَادَتُنَا أَحَقُّ مِن شَهَادَتِهِمَا وَمَا اعْتَدَيْنَا إِنَّا إِذًا لَّمِنَ الظَّالِمِينَ	
108	ذَٰلِكَ أَدْنَىٰ أَن يَأْتُوا بِالشَّهَادَةِ عَلَىٰ وَجْهِهَا أَوْ يَخَافُوا أَن تُرَدَّ أَيْمَانٌ بَعْدَ أَيْمَانِهِمْ ۗ وَاتَّقُوا اللَّهَ وَاسْمَعُوا ۗ وَاللَّهُ لَا يَهْدِي الْقَوْمَ الْفَاسِقِينَ	

	Heritage/Inheritance ميراث
3 آل عمران 180	وَلَا يَحْسَبَنَّ الَّذِينَ يَبْخَلُونَ بِمَا آتَاهُمُ اللَّهُ مِن فَضْلِهِ هُوَ خَيْرًا لَّهُم ۖ بَلْ هُوَ شَرٌّ لَّهُمْ ۖ سَيُطَوَّقُونَ مَا بَخِلُوا بِهِ يَوْمَ الْقِيَامَةِ ۗ وَلِلَّهِ مِيرَاثُ السَّمَاوَاتِ وَالْأَرْضِ ۗ وَاللَّهُ بِمَا تَعْمَلُونَ خَبِيرٌ
Sahih	And let not those who [greedily] withhold what Allah has given them of His bounty ever think that it is better for them. Rather, it is worse for them. Their necks will be encircled by what they withheld on the Day of Resurrection. And to Allah belongs the heritage of the heavens and the earth. And Allah, with what you do, is [fully] Acquainted
57 الحديد 10	وَمَا لَكُمْ أَلَّا تُنفِقُوا فِي سَبِيلِ اللَّهِ وَلِلَّهِ مِيرَاثُ السَّمَاوَاتِ وَالْأَرْضِ ۚ لَا يَسْتَوِي مِنكُم مَّنْ أَنفَقَ مِن قَبْلِ الْفَتْحِ وَقَاتَلَ ۚ أُولَٰئِكَ أَعْظَمُ دَرَجَةً مِّنَ الَّذِينَ أَنفَقُوا مِن بَعْدُ وَقَاتَلُوا ۚ وَكُلًّا وَعَدَ اللَّهُ الْحُسْنَىٰ ۚ وَاللَّهُ بِمَا تَعْمَلُونَ خَبِيرٌ
Sahih	And why do you not spend in the cause of Allah while to Allah belongs the heritage of the heavens and the earth? Not equal among you are those who spent before the conquest [of Makkah] and fought [and those who did so after it]. Those are greater in degree than they who spent afterwards and fought. But to all Allah has promised the best [reward]. And Allah, with what you do, is Acquainted
	His/ heirs/Inherit ورث
4 النساء 11	يُوصِيكُمُ اللَّهُ فِي أَوْلَادِكُمْ ۖ لِلذَّكَرِ مِثْلُ حَظِّ الْأُنثَيَيْنِ ۚ فَإِن كُنَّ نِسَاءً فَوْقَ اثْنَتَيْنِ فَلَهُنَّ ثُلُثَا مَا تَرَكَ ۖ وَإِن كَانَتْ وَاحِدَةً فَلَهَا النِّصْفُ ۚ وَلِأَبَوَيْهِ لِكُلِّ وَاحِدٍ مِّنْهُمَا السُّدُسُ مِمَّا تَرَكَ إِن كَانَ لَهُ وَلَدٌ ۚ فَإِن لَّمْ يَكُن لَّهُ وَلَدٌ وَوَرِثَهُ أَبَوَاهُ فَلِأُمِّهِ الثُّلُثُ ۚ فَإِن كَانَ لَهُ إِخْوَةٌ فَلِأُمِّهِ السُّدُسُ ۚ مِن بَعْدِ وَصِيَّةٍ يُوصِي بِهَا أَوْ دَيْنٍ ۗ آبَاؤُكُمْ وَأَبْنَاؤُكُمْ لَا تَدْرُونَ أَيُّهُمْ أَقْرَبُ لَكُمْ نَفْعًا ۚ فَرِيضَةً مِّنَ اللَّهِ ۗ إِنَّ اللَّهَ كَانَ عَلِيمًا حَكِيمًا
Sahih	Allah instructs you concerning your children: for the male, what is equal to the share of two females. But if there are [only] daughters, two or more, for them is two thirds of one's estate. And if there is only one, for her is half. And for

		one's parents, to each one of them is a sixth of his estate if he left children. But if he had no children and the parents [alone] inherit from him, then for his mother is one third. And if he had brothers [or sisters], for his mother is a sixth, after any bequest he [may have] made or debt. Your parents or your children - you know not which of them are nearest to you in benefit. [These shares are] an obligation [imposed] by Allah. Indeed, Allah is ever Knowing and Wise.
12 *P142	۞ وَلَكُمْ نِصْفُ مَا تَرَكَ أَزْوَاجُكُمْ إِن لَّمْ يَكُن لَّهُنَّ وَلَدٌ ۚ فَإِن كَانَ لَهُنَّ وَلَدٌ فَلَكُمُ الرُّبُعُ مِمَّا تَرَكْنَ ۚ مِن بَعْدِ وَصِيَّةٍ يُوصِينَ بِهَا أَوْ دَيْنٍ ۚ وَلَهُنَّ الرُّبُعُ مِمَّا تَرَكْتُمْ إِن لَّمْ يَكُن لَّكُمْ وَلَدٌ ۚ فَإِن كَانَ لَكُمْ وَلَدٌ فَلَهُنَّ الثُّمُنُ مِمَّا تَرَكْتُم ۚ مِّن بَعْدِ وَصِيَّةٍ تُوصُونَ بِهَا أَوْ دَيْنٍ ۗ وَإِن كَانَ رَجُلٌ يُورَثُ كَلَالَةً أَوِ امْرَأَةٌ وَلَهُ أَخٌ أَوْ أُخْتٌ فَلِكُلِّ وَاحِدٍ مِّنْهُمَا السُّدُسُ ۚ فَإِن كَانُوا أَكْثَرَ مِن ذَٰلِكَ فَهُمْ شُرَكَاءُ فِي الثُّلُثِ ۚ مِن بَعْدِ وَصِيَّةٍ يُوصَىٰ بِهَا أَوْ دَيْنٍ غَيْرَ مُضَارٍّ ۚ وَصِيَّةً مِّنَ اللَّهِ ۗ وَاللَّهُ عَلِيمٌ حَلِيمٌ	
Sahih	And for you is half of what your wives leave if they have no child. But if they have a child, for you is one fourth of what they leave, after any bequest they [may have] made or debt. And for the wives is one fourth if you leave no child. But if you leave a child, then for them is an eighth of what you leave, after any bequest you [may have] made or debt. And if a man or woman leaves neither ascendants nor descendants but has a brother or a sister, then for each one of them is a sixth. But if they are more than two, they share a third, after any bequest which was made or debt, as long as there is no detriment [caused]. [This is] an ordinance from Allah, and Allah is Knowing and Forbearing	
7 الأعراف 43	وَنَزَعْنَا مَا فِي صُدُورِهِم مِّنْ غِلٍّ تَجْرِي مِن تَحْتِهِمُ الْأَنْهَارُ ۖ وَقَالُوا الْحَمْدُ لِلَّهِ الَّذِي هَدَانَا لِهَٰذَا وَمَا كُنَّا لِنَهْتَدِيَ لَوْلَا أَنْ هَدَانَا اللَّهُ ۖ لَقَدْ جَاءَتْ رُسُلُ رَبِّنَا بِالْحَقِّ ۖ وَنُودُوا أَن تِلْكُمُ الْجَنَّةُ أُورِثْتُمُوهَا بِمَا كُنتُمْ تَعْمَلُونَ	
128	قَالَ مُوسَىٰ لِقَوْمِهِ اسْتَعِينُوا بِاللَّهِ وَاصْبِرُوا ۖ إِنَّ الْأَرْضَ لِلَّهِ يُورِثُهَا مَن يَشَاءُ مِنْ عِبَادِهِ ۖ وَالْعَاقِبَةُ لِلْمُتَّقِينَ	
137	وَأَوْرَثْنَا الْقَوْمَ الَّذِينَ كَانُوا يُسْتَضْعَفُونَ مَشَارِقَ الْأَرْضِ وَمَغَارِبَهَا الَّتِي بَارَكْنَا فِيهَا ۖ وَتَمَّتْ كَلِمَتُ رَبِّكَ الْحُسْنَىٰ عَلَىٰ بَنِي إِسْرَائِيلَ بِمَا صَبَرُوا ۖ وَدَمَّرْنَا مَا كَانَ يَصْنَعُ فِرْعَوْنُ وَقَوْمُهُ وَمَا كَانُوا يَعْرِشُونَ	

169	فَخَلَفَ مِن بَعْدِهِمْ خَلْفٌ وَرِثُوا الْكِتَابَ يَأْخُذُونَ عَرَضَ هَٰذَا الْأَدْنَىٰ وَيَقُولُونَ سَيُغْفَرُ لَنَا وَإِن يَأْتِهِمْ عَرَضٌ مِّثْلُهُ يَأْخُذُوهُ ۚ أَلَمْ يُؤْخَذْ عَلَيْهِم مِّيثَاقُ الْكِتَابِ أَن لَّا يَقُولُوا عَلَى اللَّهِ إِلَّا الْحَقَّ وَدَرَسُوا مَا فِيهِ ۗ وَالدَّارُ الْآخِرَةُ خَيْرٌ لِّلَّذِينَ يَتَّقُونَ ۗ أَفَلَا تَعْقِلُونَ
19 مريم 63	تِلْكَ الْجَنَّةُ الَّتِي نُورِثُ مِنْ عِبَادِنَا مَن كَانَ تَقِيًّا
26 الشعراء 59	كَذَٰلِكَ ۖ وَأَوْرَثْنَاهَا بَنِي إِسْرَائِيلَ
85	وَاجْعَلْنِي مِن وَرَثَةِ جَنَّةِ النَّعِيمِ
27 النمل 16	وَوَرِثَ سُلَيْمَانُ دَاوُودَ ۖ وَقَالَ يَا أَيُّهَا النَّاسُ عُلِّمْنَا مَنطِقَ الطَّيْرِ وَأُوتِينَا مِن كُلِّ شَيْءٍ ۖ إِنَّ هَٰذَا لَهُوَ الْفَضْلُ الْمُبِينُ
33 الأحزاب 27	وَأَوْرَثَكُمْ أَرْضَهُمْ وَدِيَارَهُمْ وَأَمْوَالَهُمْ وَأَرْضًا لَّمْ تَطَئُوهَا ۚ وَكَانَ اللَّهُ عَلَىٰ كُلِّ شَيْءٍ قَدِيرًا
Sahih	And He caused you to inherit their land and their homes and their properties and a land which you have not trodden. And ever is Allah, over all things, competent
35 فاطر 32	ثُمَّ أَوْرَثْنَا الْكِتَابَ الَّذِينَ اصْطَفَيْنَا مِنْ عِبَادِنَا ۖ فَمِنْهُمْ ظَالِمٌ لِّنَفْسِهِ وَمِنْهُم مُّقْتَصِدٌ وَمِنْهُمْ سَابِقٌ بِالْخَيْرَاتِ بِإِذْنِ اللَّهِ ۚ ذَٰلِكَ هُوَ الْفَضْلُ الْكَبِيرُ
39 الزمر 74	وَقَالُوا الْحَمْدُ لِلَّهِ الَّذِي صَدَقَنَا وَعْدَهُ وَأَوْرَثَنَا الْأَرْضَ نَتَبَوَّأُ مِنَ الْجَنَّةِ حَيْثُ نَشَاءُ ۖ فَنِعْمَ أَجْرُ الْعَامِلِينَ
Sahih	And they will say, "Praise to Allah, who has fulfilled for us His promise and made us inherit the earth [so] we may settle in Paradise wherever we will. And excellent is the reward of [righteous] workers."

40 غافر 53		وَلَقَدْ آتَيْنَا مُوسَى الْهُدَىٰ وَأَوْرَثْنَا بَنِي إِسْرَائِيلَ الْكِتَابَ
42 الشورى 14		وَمَا تَفَرَّقُوا إِلَّا مِن بَعْدِ مَا جَاءَهُمُ الْعِلْمُ بَغْيًا بَيْنَهُمْ ۚ وَلَوْلَا كَلِمَةٌ سَبَقَتْ مِن رَّبِّكَ إِلَىٰ أَجَلٍ مُّسَمًّى لَّقُضِيَ بَيْنَهُمْ ۚ وَإِنَّ الَّذِينَ أُورِثُوا الْكِتَابَ مِن بَعْدِهِمْ لَفِي شَكٍّ مِّنْهُ مُرِيبٍ
Sahih	And they did not become divided until after knowledge had come to them - out of jealous animosity between themselves. And if not for a word that preceded from your Lord [postponing the penalty] until a specified time, it would have been concluded between them. And indeed, those who were granted inheritance of the Scripture after them are, concerning it, in disquieting doubt	
43 الزخرف 72		وَتِلْكَ الْجَنَّةُ الَّتِي أُورِثْتُمُوهَا بِمَا كُنتُمْ تَعْمَلُونَ
44 الدخان 28		كَذَٰلِكَ ۖ وَأَوْرَثْنَاهَا قَوْمًا آخَرِينَ

وارث Heir

2 البقرة 233		۞ وَالْوَالِدَاتُ يُرْضِعْنَ أَوْلَادَهُنَّ حَوْلَيْنِ كَامِلَيْنِ ۖ لِمَنْ أَرَادَ أَن يُتِمَّ الرَّضَاعَةَ ۚ وَعَلَى الْمَوْلُودِ لَهُ رِزْقُهُنَّ وَكِسْوَتُهُنَّ بِالْمَعْرُوفِ ۚ لَا تُكَلَّفُ نَفْسٌ إِلَّا وُسْعَهَا ۚ لَا تُضَارَّ وَالِدَةٌ بِوَلَدِهَا وَلَا مَوْلُودٌ لَّهُ بِوَلَدِهِ ۚ وَعَلَى الْوَارِثِ مِثْلُ ذَٰلِكَ ۗ فَإِنْ أَرَادَا فِصَالًا عَن تَرَاضٍ مِّنْهُمَا وَتَشَاوُرٍ فَلَا جُنَاحَ عَلَيْهِمَا ۗ وَإِنْ أَرَدتُّمْ أَن تَسْتَرْضِعُوا أَوْلَادَكُمْ فَلَا جُنَاحَ عَلَيْكُمْ إِذَا سَلَّمْتُم مَّا آتَيْتُم بِالْمَعْرُوفِ ۗ وَاتَّقُوا اللَّهَ وَاعْلَمُوا أَنَّ اللَّهَ بِمَا تَعْمَلُونَ بَصِيرٌ
Sahih	Mothers may breastfeed their children two complete years for whoever wishes to complete the nursing [period]. Upon the father is the mothers' provision and their clothing according to what is acceptable. No person is charged with more than his capacity. No mother should be harmed through her child, and no father through his child. And upon the [father's] heir is [a duty] like that [of the father]. And if they both desire weaning through mutual consent from both of	

	them and consultation, there is no blame upon either of them. And if you wish to have your children nursed by a substitute, there is no blame upon you as long as you give payment according to what is acceptable. And fear Allah and know that Allah is Seeing of what you do
15 الحجر 23	وَإِنَّا لَنَحْنُ نُحْيِي وَنُمِيتُ وَنَحْنُ الْوَارِثُونَ
21 الأنبياء 89	وَزَكَرِيَّا إِذْ نَادَىٰ رَبَّهُ رَبِّ لَا تَذَرْنِي فَرْدًا وَأَنتَ خَيْرُ الْوَارِثِينَ
Sahih	And [mention] Zechariah, when he called to his Lord, "My Lord, do not leave me alone [with no heir], while you are the best of inheritors."
23 المؤمنون 10	أُولَٰئِكَ هُمُ الْوَارِثُونَ
28 القصص 5	وَنُرِيدُ أَن نَّمُنَّ عَلَى الَّذِينَ اسْتُضْعِفُوا فِي الْأَرْضِ وَنَجْعَلَهُمْ أَئِمَّةً وَنَجْعَلَهُمُ الْوَارِثِينَ
Sahih	And We wanted to confer favor upon those who were oppressed in the land and make them leaders and make them inheritors
58	وَكَمْ أَهْلَكْنَا مِن قَرْيَةٍ بَطِرَتْ مَعِيشَتَهَا ۖ فَتِلْكَ مَسَاكِنُهُمْ لَمْ تُسْكَن مِّن بَعْدِهِمْ إِلَّا قَلِيلًا ۖ وَكُنَّا نَحْنُ الْوَارِثِينَ

يرث Inherit

4 النساء 176	يَسْتَفْتُونَكَ قُلِ اللَّهُ يُفْتِيكُمْ فِي الْكَلَالَةِ ۚ إِنِ امْرُؤٌ هَلَكَ لَيْسَ لَهُ وَلَدٌ وَلَهُ أُخْتٌ فَلَهَا نِصْفُ مَا تَرَكَ ۚ وَهُوَ يَرِثُهَا إِن لَّمْ يَكُن لَّهَا وَلَدٌ ۚ فَإِن كَانَتَا اثْنَتَيْنِ فَلَهُمَا الثُّلُثَانِ مِمَّا تَرَكَ ۚ وَإِن كَانُوا إِخْوَةً رِّجَالًا وَنِسَاءً فَلِلذَّكَرِ مِثْلُ حَظِّ الْأُنثَيَيْنِ ۗ يُبَيِّنُ اللَّهُ لَكُمْ أَن تَضِلُّوا ۗ وَاللَّهُ بِكُلِّ شَيْءٍ عَلِيمٌ
Sahih	They request from you a [legal] ruling. Say, "Allah gives you a ruling concerning one having neither descendants nor ascendants [as heirs]." If a man dies, leaving no child but [only] a sister, she will have half of what he left. And he inherits from her if she [dies and] has no child. But if there are two sisters [or more], they will have two-thirds of what he left. If there are both brothers and sisters, the male will have the share of two females. Allah makes clear to you [His law], lest you go astray. And Allah is Knowing of all things.

7 الأعراف 100	أَوَلَمْ يَهْدِ لِلَّذِينَ يَرِثُونَ الْأَرْضَ مِن بَعْدِ أَهْلِهَا أَن لَّوْ نَشَاءُ أَصَبْنَاهُم بِذُنُوبِهِمْ ۚ وَنَطْبَعُ عَلَىٰ قُلُوبِهِمْ فَهُمْ لَا يَسْمَعُونَ
19 مريم 6	يَرِثُنِي وَيَرِثُ مِنْ آلِ يَعْقُوبَ ۖ وَاجْعَلْهُ رَبِّ رَضِيًّا
Sahih	Who will inherit me and inherit from the family of Jacob. And make him, my Lord, pleasing [to You]."
21 الأنبياء 105	وَلَقَدْ كَتَبْنَا فِي الزَّبُورِ مِن بَعْدِ الذِّكْرِ أَنَّ الْأَرْضَ يَرِثُهَا عِبَادِيَ الصَّالِحُونَ
23 المؤمنون 11	الَّذِينَ يَرِثُونَ الْفِرْدَوْسَ هُمْ فِيهَا خَالِدُونَ

we/Inherit نرث

19 مريم 40	إِنَّا نَحْنُ نَرِثُ الْأَرْضَ وَمَنْ عَلَيْهَا وَإِلَيْنَا يُرْجَعُونَ
Sahih	Indeed, it is We who will inherit the earth and whoever is on it, and to Us they will be returned
80	وَنَرِثُهُ مَا يَقُولُ وَيَأْتِينَا فَرْدًا

to inherit ترث

4 النساء 19	يَا أَيُّهَا الَّذِينَ آمَنُوا لَا يَحِلُّ لَكُمْ أَن تَرِثُوا النِّسَاءَ كَرْهًا ۖ وَلَا تَعْضُلُوهُنَّ لِتَذْهَبُوا بِبَعْضِ مَا آتَيْتُمُوهُنَّ إِلَّا أَن يَأْتِينَ بِفَاحِشَةٍ مُّبَيِّنَةٍ ۚ وَعَاشِرُوهُنَّ بِالْمَعْرُوفِ ۚ فَإِن كَرِهْتُمُوهُنَّ فَعَسَىٰ أَن تَكْرَهُوا شَيْئًا وَيَجْعَلَ اللَّهُ فِيهِ خَيْرًا كَثِيرًا
Sahih	O you who have believed, it is not lawful for you to inherit women by compulsion. And do not make difficulties for them in order to take [back] part of what you gave them unless they commit a clear immorality. And live with them in kindness. For if you dislike them - perhaps you dislike a thing and Allah makes therein much good

4 النساء 12 ** J	ولكم نصف ما ترك أزواجكم إن لم يكن لهن ولد «منكم أو من غيركم» «فإن كان لهن ولد» فلكم الربع مما تركن من بعد وصية يوصين بها أو دين» وألحق بالولد في ذلك ولد الابن بالإجماع «ولهن» أي الزوجات تعددن أو لا «الربع مما تركتم إن لم يكن لكم ولد فإن كان لكم ولد» منهن أو من غيرهن «فلهن الثمن مما تركتم من بعد وصية توصون بها أو دين» وولد الابن في ذلك كالولد إجماعا «وإن كان رجل يورث» صفة والخبر «كلالة» أي لا والد له ولا ولد «أو امرأة» تورث كلالة «وله» أي للمورث كلالة «أخ أو أخت» أي من أم وقرأ به ابن مسعود وغيره «فلكل واحد منهما السدس» مما ترك «فإن كانوا» أي الإخوة والأخوات من الأم «أكثر من ذلك» أي من واحد «فهم شركاء في الثلث» يستوي فيه ذكرهم وأنثاهم «من بعد وصية يوصي بها أو دين غير مُضارّ» حال من ضمير يوصي أي غير مدخل الضرر على الورثة بأن يوصي بأكثر من الثلث «وصيةً» مصدر مؤكد ليوصيكم «من الله والله عليم» بما دبره لخلقه من الفرائض «حليم» بتأخير العقوبة عمن خالفه، وخصت السنة توريث من ذكر بمن ليس فيه مانع من قتل أو اختلاف دين أو رقٌ.	
4 النساء 12 ** H&K	In that which your wives leave, your share is a half if they have no child; but if they leave a child, you get a fourth of that which they leave after payment of legacies that they may have bequeathed or debts. In that which you leave, their (your wives) share is a fourth if you leave no child; but if you leave a child, they get an eighth of that which you leave after payment of legacies that you may have bequeathed or debts. If the man or woman whose inheritance is in question has left neither ascendants nor descendants, but has left a brother or a sister, each one of the two gets a sixth; but if more than two, they share in a third; after payment of lagacies he (or she) may have bequeathed or debts, so that no loss is caused (to anyone). This is a Commandment from Allah; and Allah is Ever All-Knowing, Most-Forbearing.	
	حجابا

hidden **barrier** | |
| 17 الإسراء 45 | وَإِذَا قَرَأْتَ الْقُرْآنَ جَعَلْنَا بَيْنَكَ وَبَيْنَ الَّذِينَ لَا يُؤْمِنُونَ بِالْآخِرَةِ حِجَابًا مَّسْتُورًا | |

143

H&K	And when you (Muhammad SAW) recite the Quran, We put between you and those who believe not in the Hereafter, an invisible veil (or screen their hearts, so they hear or understand it not).
19 مريم 17	فَاتَّخَذَتْ مِن دُونِهِمْ حِجَابًا فَأَرْسَلْنَا إِلَيْهَا رُوحَنَا فَتَمَثَّلَ لَهَا بَشَرًا سَوِيًّا
H&K	She placed a screen (to screen herself) from them; then We sent to her Our Ruh [angel Jibrael (Gabriel)], and he appeared before her in the form of a man in all respects.

جَلَابِيبِهِنَّ

33 الأحزاب 59	يَا أَيُّهَا النَّبِيُّ قُل لِّأَزْوَاجِكَ وَبَنَاتِكَ وَنِسَاءِ الْمُؤْمِنِينَ يُدْنِينَ عَلَيْهِنَّ مِن جَلَابِيبِهِنَّ ۚ ذَٰلِكَ أَدْنَىٰ أَن يُعْرَفْنَ فَلَا يُؤْذَيْنَ ۗ وَكَانَ اللَّهُ غَفُورًا رَّحِيمًا
Sahih	O Prophet, tell your wives and your daughters and the women of the believers to bring down over themselves [part] of their outer garments. That is more suitable that they will be known and not be abused. And ever is Allah Forgiving and Merciful.
P	O Prophet! Tell thy wives and thy daughters and the women of the believers to draw their cloaks close round them (when they go abroad). That will be better, so that they may be recognised and not annoyed. Allah is ever Forgiving, Merciful.
H&K	O Prophet! Tell your wives and your daughters and the women of the believers to draw their cloaks (veils) all over their bodies (i.e. screen themselves completely except the eyes or one eye to see the way). That will be better, that they should be known (as free respectable women) so as not to be annoyed. And Allah is Ever OftForgiving, Most Merciful.
J	يا أيها النبي قل لأزواجك وبناتك ونساء المؤمنين يدنين عليهن من جلابيبهن » جمع جلباب » وهي الملاءة التي تشتمل بها المرأة، أي يرخين بعضها على الوجوه إذا خرجن لحاجتهن إلا عينا واحدة «ذلك أدنى» أقرب إلى «أن يعرفن» بأنهن حرائر «فلا يؤذين» بالتعرض لهن بخلاف الإماء فلا يغطين وجوههن، فكان المنافقون يتعرضون لهم «وكان الله غفورا» لما سلف منهن من ترك الستر «رحيما» بهن إذ سترهن.

4 النساء 19	يَا أَيُّهَا الَّذِينَ آمَنُوا لَا يَحِلُّ لَكُمْ أَن تَرِثُوا النِّسَاءَ كَرْهًا ۖ وَلَا تَعْضُلُوهُنَّ لِتَذْهَبُوا بِبَعْضِ مَا آتَيْتُمُوهُنَّ إِلَّا أَن يَأْتِينَ بِفَاحِشَةٍ مُّبَيِّنَةٍ ۚ وَعَاشِرُوهُنَّ بِالْمَعْرُوفِ ۚ فَإِن كَرِهْتُمُوهُنَّ فَعَسَىٰ أَن تَكْرَهُوا شَيْئًا وَيَجْعَلَ اللَّهُ فِيهِ خَيْرًا كَثِيرًا
	O you who have believed, it is not lawful for you to inherit women by compulsion. And do not make difficulties for them in order to take [back] part of what you gave them unless they commit a clear immorality. And live with them in kindness. For if you dislike them - perhaps you dislike a thing and Allah makes therein much good.
22	وَلَا تَنكِحُوا مَا نَكَحَ آبَاؤُكُم مِّنَ النِّسَاءِ إِلَّا مَا قَدْ سَلَفَ ۚ إِنَّهُ كَانَ فَاحِشَةً وَمَقْتًا وَسَاءَ سَبِيلًا
	And do not marry those [women] whom your fathers married, except what has already occurred. Indeed, it was an immorality and hateful [to Allah] and was evil as a way.
24	وَالْمُحْصَنَاتُ مِنَ النِّسَاءِ إِلَّا مَا مَلَكَتْ أَيْمَانُكُمْ ۖ كِتَابَ اللَّهِ عَلَيْكُمْ ۚ وَأُحِلَّ لَكُم مَّا وَرَاءَ ذَٰلِكُمْ أَن تَبْتَغُوا بِأَمْوَالِكُم مُّحْصِنِينَ غَيْرَ مُسَافِحِينَ ۚ فَمَا اسْتَمْتَعْتُم بِهِ مِنْهُنَّ فَآتُوهُنَّ أُجُورَهُنَّ فَرِيضَةً ۚ وَلَا جُنَاحَ عَلَيْكُمْ فِيمَا تَرَاضَيْتُم بِهِ مِن بَعْدِ الْفَرِيضَةِ ۚ إِنَّ اللَّهَ كَانَ عَلِيمًا حَكِيمًا
	And [also prohibited to you are all] married women except those your right hands possess. [This is] the decree of Allah upon you. And lawful to you are [all others] beyond these, [provided] that you seek them [in marriage] with [gifts from] your property, desiring chastity, not unlawful sexual intercourse. So for whatever you enjoy [of marriage] from them, give them their due compensation as an obligation. And there is no blame upon you for what you mutually agree to beyond the obligation. Indeed, Allah is ever Knowing and Wise.
32	وَلَا تَتَمَنَّوْا مَا فَضَّلَ اللَّهُ بِهِ بَعْضَكُمْ عَلَىٰ بَعْضٍ ۚ لِّلرِّجَالِ نَصِيبٌ مِّمَّا اكْتَسَبُوا ۖ وَلِلنِّسَاءِ نَصِيبٌ مِّمَّا اكْتَسَبْنَ ۚ وَاسْأَلُوا اللَّهَ مِن فَضْلِهِ ۗ إِنَّ اللَّهَ كَانَ بِكُلِّ شَيْءٍ عَلِيمًا
	And do not wish for that by which Allah has made some of you exceed others. For men is a share of what they have earned, and for women is a share of what they have earned. And ask Allah of his bounty. Indeed Allah is ever, of all things, Knowing.

34	الرِّجَالُ قَوَّامُونَ عَلَى النِّسَاءِ بِمَا فَضَّلَ اللَّهُ بَعْضَهُمْ عَلَى بَعْضٍ وَبِمَا أَنفَقُوا مِنْ أَمْوَالِهِمْ ۚ فَالصَّالِحَاتُ قَانِتَاتٌ حَافِظَاتٌ لِّلْغَيْبِ بِمَا حَفِظَ اللَّهُ ۚ وَاللَّاتِي تَخَافُونَ نُشُوزَهُنَّ فَعِظُوهُنَّ وَاهْجُرُوهُنَّ فِي الْمَضَاجِعِ وَاضْرِبُوهُنَّ ۖ فَإِنْ أَطَعْنَكُمْ فَلَا تَبْغُوا عَلَيْهِنَّ سَبِيلًا ۗ إِنَّ اللَّهَ كَانَ عَلِيًّا كَبِيرًا
Sahih	Men are in charge of women by [right of] what Allah has given one over the other and what they spend [for maintenance] from their wealth. So righteous women are devoutly obedient, guarding in [the husband's] absence what Allah would have them guard. But those [wives] from whom you fear arrogance - [first] advise them; [then if they persist], forsake them in bed; and [finally], strike them. But if they obey you [once more], seek no means against them. Indeed, Allah is ever Exalted and Grand.
P	Men are in charge of women, because Allah hath made the one of them to excel the other, and because they spend of their property (for the support of women). So good women are the obedient, guarding in secret that which Allah hath guarded. As for those from whom ye fear rebellion, admonish them and banish them to beds apart, and scourge them. Then if they obey you, seek not a way against them. Lo! Allah is ever High, Exalted, Great.
H&K	Men are the protectors and maintainers of women, because Allah has made one of them to excel the other, and because they spend (to support them) from their means. Therefore the righteous women are devoutly obedient (to Allah and to their husbands), and guard in the husband's absence what Allah orders them to guard (e.g. their chastity, their husband's property, etc.). As to those women on whose part you see ill-conduct, admonish them (first), (next), refuse to share their beds, (and last) beat them (lightly, if it is useful), but if they return to obedience, seek not against them means (of annoyance). Surely, Allah is Ever Most High, Most Great.
J	«الرجال قوّامون» مسلطون «على النساء» يؤدبونهن ويأخذون على أيديهن «بما فضّل الله بعضهم على بعض» أي بتفضيله لهم عليهن بالعلم والعقل والولاية وغير ذلك «وبما أنفقوا» عليهن «من أموالهم فالصالحات» منهن «قانتات» مطيعات لأزواجهن «حافظات للغيب» أي لفروجهن وغيرها في غيبة أزواجهن «بما حفظ» لهن «الله» حيث أوصى عليهن الأزواج «واللاتي تخافون نشوزهن» عصيانهن لكم بأن ظهرت أماراته «فعظوهن» فخوّفوهن الله «واهجروهن في المضاجع» اعتزلوا إلى فراش آخر إن أظهرن النشوز «واضربوهن» ضربا غير

		مبرح إن لم يرجعن بالهجران «فإن أطعنكم» فيما يراد منهن «فلا تبغوا» تطلبوا «عليهن سبيلا» طريقا إلى ضربهن ظلما «إن الله كان عليا كبيرا» فاحذروه أن يعاقبكم إن ظلمتموهن.
4 النساء 129		وَلَن تَسْتَطِيعُوا أَن تَعْدِلُوا بَيْنَ النِّسَاءِ وَلَوْ حَرَصْتُمْ ۖ فَلَا تَمِيلُوا كُلَّ الْمَيْلِ فَتَذَرُوهَا كَالْمُعَلَّقَةِ ۚ وَإِن تُصْلِحُوا وَتَتَّقُوا فَإِنَّ اللَّهَ كَانَ غَفُورًا رَّحِيمًا
	Sahih	And you will never be able to be equal [in feeling] between wives, even if you should strive [to do so]. So do not incline completely [toward one] and leave another hanging. And if you amend [your affairs] and fear Allah – then indeed, Allah is ever Forgiving and Merciful.
	P	Ye will not be able to deal equally between (your) wives, however much ye wish (to do so). But turn not altogether away (from one), leaving her as in suspense. If ye do good and keep from evil, lo! Allah is ever Forgiving, Merciful
	H&K	You will never be able to do perfect justice between wives even if it is your ardent desire, so do not incline too much to one of them (by giving her more of your time and provision) so as to leave the other hanging (i.e. neither divorced nor married). And if you do justice, and do all that is right and fear Allah by keeping away from all that is wrong, then Allah is Ever Oft-Forgiving, Most Merciful
	J	«ولن تستطيعوا أن تعدلوا» تسووا «بين النساء» في المحبة «ولو حرصتم» على ذلك «فلا تميلوا كل الميل» إلى التي تحبوها في القسم والنفقة «فتذروها» أي تتركوا الممال عنها «كالمعلَّقة» التي لا هي أيم ولا هي ذات بعل «وإن تصلحوا» بالعدل في القسم «وتتقوا» الجور «فإن الله كان غفورا» لما في قلبكم من الميل «رحيما» بكم في ذلك.
4 النساء 3		وَإِنْ خِفْتُمْ أَلَّا تُقْسِطُوا فِي الْيَتَامَىٰ فَانكِحُوا مَا طَابَ لَكُم مِّنَ النِّسَاءِ مَثْنَىٰ وَثُلَاثَ وَرُبَاعَ ۖ فَإِنْ خِفْتُمْ أَلَّا تَعْدِلُوا فَوَاحِدَةً أَوْ مَا مَلَكَتْ أَيْمَانُكُمْ ۚ ذَٰلِكَ أَدْنَىٰ أَلَّا تَعُولُوا
	Sahih	And if you fear that you will not deal justly with the orphan girls, then marry those that please you of [other] women, two or three or four. But if you fear that you will not be just, then [marry only] one or those your right hand possesses. That is more suitable that you may not incline [to injustice
	P	And if ye fear that ye will not deal fairly by the orphans, marry of the women, who seem good to you, two or three or four; and if ye fear that ye cannot do justice (to so many) then one (only) or (the captives) that your right hands possess. Thus it is more likely that ye will not do injustice

H&K	And if you fear that you shall not be able to deal justly with the orphan-girls, then marry (other) women of your choice, two or three, or four but if you fear that you shall not be able to deal justly (with them), then only one or (the captives and the slaves) that your right hands possess. That is nearer to prevent you from doing injustice
J	«وإن خفتم أ» ن «لا تُقسطوا» تعدلوا «في اليتامى» فتحرجتم من أمرهم فخافوا أيضا أن لا تعدلوا بين النساء إذا نكحتموهن «فانكحوا» تزوجوا «ما» بمعنى من «طاب لكم من النساء مثنى وثلاث ورباع» أي اثنتين وثلاثا وأربعا ولا تزيدوا على ذلك «فإن خفتم أ» ن «لا تعدلوا» فيهن بالنفقة والقسم؟ «فواحدةً» انكحوها «أو» اقتصروا على «ما ملكت أيمانكم» من الإماء إذ ليس لهن من الحقوق ما للزوجات «ذلك» أي نكاح الأربع فقط أو الواحدة أو التسرِّي «أدنى» أقرب إلى «ألا تعولوا» تجوروا.
4 النساء 176	يَسْتَفْتُونَكَ قُلِ اللَّهُ يُفْتِيكُمْ فِي الْكَلَالَةِ ۚ إِنِ امْرُؤٌ هَلَكَ لَيْسَ لَهُ وَلَدٌ وَلَهُ أُخْتٌ فَلَهَا نِصْفُ مَا تَرَكَ ۚ وَهُوَ يَرِثُهَا إِن لَّمْ يَكُن لَّهَا وَلَدٌ ۚ فَإِن كَانَتَا اثْنَتَيْنِ فَلَهُمَا الثُّلُثَانِ مِمَّا تَرَكَ ۚ وَإِن كَانُوا إِخْوَةً رِّجَالًا وَنِسَاءً فَلِلذَّكَرِ مِثْلُ حَظِّ الْأُنثَيَيْنِ ۗ يُبَيِّنُ اللَّهُ لَكُمْ أَن تَضِلُّوا ۗ وَاللَّهُ بِكُلِّ شَيْءٍ عَلِيمٌ
	They request from you a [legal] ruling. Say, "Allah gives you a ruling concerning one having neither descendants nor ascendants [as heirs]." If a man dies, leaving no child but [only] a sister, she will have half of what he left. And he inherits from her if she [dies and] has no child. But if there are two sisters [or more], they will have two-thirds of what he left. If there are both brothers and sisters, the male will have the share of two females. Allah makes clear to you [His law], lest you go astray. And Allah is Knowing of all things.
5 المائدة 6	يَا أَيُّهَا الَّذِينَ آمَنُوا إِذَا قُمْتُمْ إِلَى الصَّلَاةِ فَاغْسِلُوا وُجُوهَكُمْ وَأَيْدِيَكُمْ إِلَى الْمَرَافِقِ وَامْسَحُوا بِرُءُوسِكُمْ وَأَرْجُلَكُمْ إِلَى الْكَعْبَيْنِ ۚ وَإِن كُنتُمْ جُنُبًا فَاطَّهَّرُوا ۚ وَإِن كُنتُم مَّرْضَىٰ أَوْ عَلَىٰ سَفَرٍ أَوْ جَاءَ أَحَدٌ مِّنكُم مِّنَ الْغَائِطِ أَوْ لَامَسْتُمُ النِّسَاءَ فَلَمْ تَجِدُوا مَاءً فَتَيَمَّمُوا صَعِيدًا طَيِّبًا فَامْسَحُوا بِوُجُوهِكُمْ وَأَيْدِيكُم مِّنْهُ ۚ مَا يُرِيدُ اللَّهُ لِيَجْعَلَ عَلَيْكُم مِّنْ حَرَجٍ وَلَٰكِن يُرِيدُ لِيُطَهِّرَكُمْ وَلِيُتِمَّ نِعْمَتَهُ عَلَيْكُمْ لَعَلَّكُمْ تَشْكُرُونَ
	O you who have believed, when you rise to [perform] prayer, wash your faces and your forearms to the elbows and wipe over your heads and wash your feet to the ankles. And if you are in a state of janabah, then purify yourselves. But

	if you are ill or on a journey or one of you comes from the place of relieving himself or you have contacted women and do not find water, then seek clean earth and wipe over your faces and hands with it. Allah does not intend to make difficulty for you, but He intends to purify you and complete His favor upon you that you may be grateful.
7 الأعراف 81	إِنَّكُمْ لَتَأْتُونَ الرِّجَالَ شَهْوَةً مِّن دُونِ النِّسَاءِ ۚ بَلْ أَنتُمْ قَوْمٌ مُّسْرِفُونَ
	Indeed, you approach men with desire, instead of women. Rather, you are a transgressing people."
127	وَقَالَ الْمَلَأُ مِن قَوْمِ فِرْعَوْنَ أَتَذَرُ مُوسَىٰ وَقَوْمَهُ لِيُفْسِدُوا فِي الْأَرْضِ وَيَذَرَكَ وَآلِهَتَكَ ۚ قَالَ سَنُقَتِّلُ أَبْنَاءَهُمْ وَنَسْتَحْيِي نِسَاءَهُمْ وَإِنَّا فَوْقَهُمْ قَاهِرُونَ
	And the eminent among the people of Pharaoh said," Will you leave Moses and his people to cause corruption in the land and abandon you and your gods?" [Pharaoh] said, "We will kill their sons and keep their women alive; and indeed, we are subjugators over them."
141	وَإِذْ أَنجَيْنَاكُم مِّنْ آلِ فِرْعَوْنَ يَسُومُونَكُمْ سُوءَ الْعَذَابِ ۖ يُقَتِّلُونَ أَبْنَاءَكُمْ وَيَسْتَحْيُونَ نِسَاءَكُمْ ۚ وَفِي ذَٰلِكُم بَلَاءٌ مِّن رَّبِّكُمْ عَظِيمٌ
	And [recall, O Children of Israel], when We saved you from the people of Pharaoh, [who were] afflicting you with the worst torment - killing your sons and keeping your women alive. And in that was a great trial from your Lord.
14 ابراهيم 6	وَإِذْ قَالَ مُوسَىٰ لِقَوْمِهِ اذْكُرُوا نِعْمَةَ اللَّهِ عَلَيْكُمْ إِذْ أَنجَاكُم مِّنْ آلِ فِرْعَوْنَ يَسُومُونَكُمْ سُوءَ الْعَذَابِ وَيُذَبِّحُونَ أَبْنَاءَكُمْ وَيَسْتَحْيُونَ نِسَاءَكُمْ ۚ وَفِي ذَٰلِكُم بَلَاءٌ مِّن رَّبِّكُمْ عَظِيمٌ
	And [recall, O Children of Israel], when Moses said to His people, "Remember the favor of Allah upon you when He saved you from the people of Pharaoh, who were afflicting you with the worst torment and were slaughtering your [newborn] sons and keeping your females alive. And in that was a great trial from your Lord.
24 النور 31	وَقُل لِّلْمُؤْمِنَاتِ يَغْضُضْنَ مِنْ أَبْصَارِهِنَّ وَيَحْفَظْنَ فُرُوجَهُنَّ وَلَا يُبْدِينَ زِينَتَهُنَّ إِلَّا مَا ظَهَرَ مِنْهَا ۖ وَلْيَضْرِبْنَ بِخُمُرِهِنَّ عَلَىٰ جُيُوبِهِنَّ ۖ وَلَا يُبْدِينَ زِينَتَهُنَّ إِلَّا لِبُعُولَتِهِنَّ أَوْ آبَائِهِنَّ أَوْ آبَاءِ بُعُولَتِهِنَّ أَوْ أَبْنَائِهِنَّ أَوْ أَبْنَاءِ بُعُولَتِهِنَّ أَوْ إِخْوَانِهِنَّ أَوْ بَنِي إِخْوَانِهِنَّ أَوْ بَنِي أَخَوَاتِهِنَّ أَوْ نِسَائِهِنَّ أَوْ مَا مَلَكَتْ أَيْمَانُهُنَّ أَوِ التَّابِعِينَ غَيْرِ أُولِي الْإِرْبَةِ مِنَ الرِّجَالِ أَوِ الطِّفْلِ الَّذِينَ لَمْ يَظْهَرُوا عَلَىٰ

	عَوْرَاتِ النِّسَاءِ ۖ وَلَا يَضْرِبْنَ بِأَرْجُلِهِنَّ لِيُعْلَمَ مَا يُخْفِينَ مِن زِينَتِهِنَّ ۚ وَتُوبُوا إِلَى اللَّهِ جَمِيعًا أَيُّهَ الْمُؤْمِنُونَ لَعَلَّكُمْ تُفْلِحُونَ
Sahih	And tell the believing women to reduce [some] of their vision and guard their private parts and not expose their adornment except that which [necessarily] appears thereof and to wrap [a portion of] their headcovers over their chests and not expose their adornment except to their husbands, their fathers, their husbands' fathers, their sons, their husbands' sons, their brothers, their brothers' sons, their sisters' sons, their women, that which their right hands possess, or those male attendants having no physical desire, or children who are not yet aware of the private aspects of women. And let them not stamp their feet to make known what they conceal of their adornment. And turn to Allah in repentance, all of you, O believers, that you might succeed.
P	And tell the believing women to lower their gaze and be modest, and to display of their adornment only that which is apparent, and to draw their veils over their bosoms, and not to reveal their adornment save to their own husbands or fathers or husbands' fathers, or their sons or their husbands' sons, or their brothers or their brothers' sons or sisters' sons, or their women, or their slaves, or male attendants who lack vigour, or children who know naught of women's nakedness. And let them not stamp their feet so as to reveal what they hide of their adornment. And turn unto Allah together, O believers, in order that ye may succeed
H&K	And tell the believing women to lower their gaze (from looking at forbidden things), and protect their private parts (from illegal sexual acts, etc.) and not to show off their adornment except only that which is apparent (like palms of hands or one eye or both eyes for necessity to see the way, or outer dress like veil, gloves, head-cover, apron, etc.), and to draw their veils all over Juyubihinna (i.e. their bodies, faces, necks and bosoms, etc.) and not to reveal their adornment except to their husbands, their fathers, their husband's fathers, their sons, their husband's sons, their brothers or their brother's sons, or their sister's sons, or their (Muslim) women (i.e. their sisters in Islam), or the (female) slaves whom their right hands possess, or old male servants who lack vigour, or small children who have no sense of the shame of sex. And let them not stamp their feet so as to reveal what they hide of their adornment. And all of you beg Allah to forgive you all, O believers, that you may be successful
J	وقل للمؤمنات يغضضن من أبصارهنّ» عما لا يحل لهنّ نظره «ويحفظن فروجهنّ» » عما لا يحل لهنّ فعله بها «ولا يبدين» يُظهرن «زينتهن إلا ما ظهر منها» وهو الوجه والكفان فيجوز نظره لأجني إن لم يخف فتنة في أحد وجهين، والثاني يحرم لأنه مظنة الفتنة، ورجح حسما للباب «وليضربن بخمرهنَّ على جيوبهنَّ» أي يسترن الرؤوس

	والأعناق والصدور بالمقانع «ولا يبدين زينتهنّ» الخفية، وهي ما عدا الوجه والكفين «إلا لبعولتهن» جمع بعل: أي زوج «أو آبائهن أو آباء بعولتهن أو أبنائهن أو أبناء بعولتهن أو إخوانهن أو بني إخوانهن أو بني أخواتهن أو نسائهن أو ما ملكت أيمانهن» فيجوز لهم نظره إلا ما بين السرة والركبة فيحرم نظره لغير الأزواج وخرج بنسائهن الكافرات فلا يجوز للمسلمات الكشف لهنّ وشمل ما ملكت أيمانهنّ العبيد «أو التابعين» في فضول الطعام «غير» بالجر صفة والنصب استثناء «أولي الإربة» أصحاب الحاجة إلى النساء «من الرجال» بأن لم ينتشر ذكر كل «أو الطفل» بمعنى الأطفال «الذين لم يظهروا» يطلعوا «على عورات النساء» للجماع فيجوز أن يبدين لهم ما عدا ما بين السرة والركبة «ولا يضربن بأرجلهن ليعلم ما يخفين من زينتهن» من خلخال يتقعقع «وتوبوا إلى الله جميعا أيها المؤمنون» مما وقع لكم من النظر الممنوع منه ومن غيره «لعلكم تفلحون» تنجون من ذلك لقبول التوبة منه وفي الآية تغليب الذكور على الإناث	
24 النور 60	وَالْقَوَاعِدُ مِنَ النِّسَاءِ اللَّاتِي لَا يَرْجُونَ نِكَاحًا فَلَيْسَ عَلَيْهِنَّ جُنَاحٌ أَن يَضَعْنَ ثِيَابَهُنَّ غَيْرَ مُتَبَرِّجَاتٍ بِزِينَةٍ ۖ وَأَن يَسْتَعْفِفْنَ خَيْرٌ لَّهُنَّ ۗ وَاللَّهُ سَمِيعٌ عَلِيمٌ	
	And women of post-menstrual age who have no desire for marriage - there is no blame upon them for putting aside their outer garments [but] not displaying adornment. But to modestly refrain [from that] is better for them. And Allah is Hearing and Knowing.	
27 النمل 55	أَئِنَّكُمْ لَتَأْتُونَ الرِّجَالَ شَهْوَةً مِّن دُونِ النِّسَاءِ ۚ بَلْ أَنتُمْ قَوْمٌ تَجْهَلُونَ	
	Do you indeed approach men with desire instead of women? Rather, you are a people behaving ignorantly."	
28 القصص 4	إِنَّ فِرْعَوْنَ عَلَا فِي الْأَرْضِ وَجَعَلَ أَهْلَهَا شِيَعًا يَسْتَضْعِفُ طَائِفَةً مِّنْهُمْ يُذَبِّحُ أَبْنَاءَهُمْ وَيَسْتَحْيِي نِسَاءَهُمْ ۚ إِنَّهُ كَانَ مِنَ الْمُفْسِدِينَ	

		Indeed, Pharaoh exalted himself in the land and made its people into factions, oppressing a sector among them, slaughtering their [newborn] sons and keeping their females alive. Indeed, he was of the corrupters.
33 الأحزاب 30		يَا نِسَاءَ النَّبِيِّ مَن يَأْتِ مِنكُنَّ بِفَاحِشَةٍ مُّبَيِّنَةٍ يُضَاعَفْ لَهَا الْعَذَابُ ضِعْفَيْنِ ۚ وَكَانَ ذَٰلِكَ عَلَى اللَّهِ يَسِيرًا
		O wives of the Prophet, whoever of you should commit a clear immorality - for her the punishment would be doubled two fold, and ever is that, for Allah, easy.
32		يَا نِسَاءَ النَّبِيِّ لَسْتُنَّ كَأَحَدٍ مِّنَ النِّسَاءِ ۚ إِنِ اتَّقَيْتُنَّ فَلَا تَخْضَعْنَ بِالْقَوْلِ فَيَطْمَعَ الَّذِي فِي قَلْبِهِ مَرَضٌ وَقُلْنَ قَوْلًا مَّعْرُوفًا
		O wives of the Prophet, you are not like anyone among women. If you fear Allah, then do not be soft in speech [to men], lest he in whose heart is disease should covet, but speak with appropriate speech.
52		لَّا يَحِلُّ لَكَ النِّسَاءُ مِن بَعْدُ وَلَا أَن تَبَدَّلَ بِهِنَّ مِنْ أَزْوَاجٍ وَلَوْ أَعْجَبَكَ حُسْنُهُنَّ إِلَّا مَا مَلَكَتْ يَمِينُكَ ۗ وَكَانَ اللَّهُ عَلَىٰ كُلِّ شَيْءٍ رَّقِيبًا
		Not lawful to you, [O Muhammad], are [any additional] women after [this], nor [is it] for you to exchange them for [other] wives, even if their beauty were to please you, except what your right hand possesses. And ever is Allah, over all things, an Observer.
4 النساء 25		وَمَن لَّمْ يَسْتَطِعْ مِنكُمْ طَوْلًا أَن يَنكِحَ الْمُحْصَنَاتِ الْمُؤْمِنَاتِ فَمِن مَّا مَلَكَتْ أَيْمَانُكُم مِّن فَتَيَاتِكُمُ الْمُؤْمِنَاتِ ۚ وَاللَّهُ أَعْلَمُ بِإِيمَانِكُم ۚ بَعْضُكُم مِّن بَعْضٍ ۚ فَانكِحُوهُنَّ بِإِذْنِ أَهْلِهِنَّ وَآتُوهُنَّ أُجُورَهُنَّ بِالْمَعْرُوفِ مُحْصَنَاتٍ غَيْرَ مُسَافِحَاتٍ وَلَا مُتَّخِذَاتِ أَخْدَانٍ ۚ فَإِذَا أُحْصِنَّ فَإِنْ أَتَيْنَ بِفَاحِشَةٍ فَعَلَيْهِنَّ نِصْفُ مَا عَلَى الْمُحْصَنَاتِ مِنَ الْعَذَابِ ۚ ذَٰلِكَ لِمَنْ خَشِيَ الْعَنَتَ مِنكُمْ ۚ وَأَن تَصْبِرُوا خَيْرٌ لَّكُمْ ۗ وَاللَّهُ غَفُورٌ رَّحِيمٌ
	H&K	And whoever of you have not the means wherewith to wed free, believing women, they may wed believing girls from among those (captives and slaves) whom your right hands possess, and Allah has full knowledge about your Faith, you are one from another. Wed them with the permission of their own folk (guardians, Auliya' or masters) and give them their Mahr according to what is reasonable; they (the above said captive and slave-girls) should be chaste, not adulterous, nor taking boy-friends. And after they have been taken in wedlock, if they commit illegal sexual intercourse, their punishment is half

	that for free (unmarried) women. This is for him among you who is afraid of being harmed in his religion or in his body; but it is better for you that you practise self-restraint, and Allah is Oft-Forgiving, Most Merciful.
P	And whoso is not able to afford to marry free, believing women, let them marry from the believing maids whom your right hands possess. Allah knoweth best (concerning) your faith. Ye (proceed) one from another; so wed them by permission of their folk, and give unto them their portions in kindness, they being honest, not debauched nor of loose conduct. And if when they are honourably married they commit lewdness they shall incur the half of the punishment (prescribed) for free women (in that case). This is for him among you who feareth to commit sin. But to have patience would be better for you. Allah is Forgiving, Merciful.
J	(ومن لم يستطع منكم طولا) أي غنى لـ (أن ينكح المحصنات) الحرائر (المؤمنات) هو جري على الغالب فلا مفهوم له (فمن ما ملكت أيمانكم) ينكح (من فتياتكم المؤمنات والله أعلم بإيمانكم) فاكتفوا بظاهره وكِلوا السرائر إليه فإنه العالم بتفضيلها ورب أمة تفضل حرة فيه وهذا تأنيس بنكاح الإماء (بعضكم من بعض) أي أنتم وهن سواء في الدين فلا تستنكفوا من نكاحهن (فانكحوهن بإذن أهلهن) مواليهن (وآتوهن) أعطوهن. (أجورهن) مهورهن (بالمعروف) من غير مطل ونقص (محصنات) عفائف حال (غير مسافحات) زانيات جهرا (ولا متخذات أخذان) أخلاء يزنون بهن سرا (فإذا أحصن) زوجن وفي قراءة بالبناء للفاعل تزوجن (فإن أتين بفاحشة) زنا (فعليهن نصف ما على المحصنات) الحرائر الأبكار إذا زنين (من العذاب) الحد فيجلدن خمسين ويغربن نصف سنة ويقاس عليهن العبيد ولم يجعل الإحصان شرطا لوجوب الحد لإفادة أنه لا رجم عليهن أصلا (ذلك) أي نكاح المملوكات عند عدم الطول (لمن خشي) (العنت) الزنا وأصله المشقة سمي به الزنا لأنه سببها بالحد في الدنيا والعقوبة في الآخرة (منكم) بخلاف من لا يخافه من الأحرار فلا يحل له نكاحها وكذا من استطاع طول حرة وعليه الشافعي وخرج بقوله "" من فتياتكم المؤمنات "" الكافرات: فلا يحل له نكاحها ولو عدل وخاف (وأن تصبروا) عن نكاح المملوكات (خير لكم) لئلا يصير الولد رقيقا (والله غفور رحيم) بالتوسعة في ذلك

	تَنكِحَ marries
2 البقرة 221	وَلَا تَنكِحُوا الْمُشْرِكَاتِ حَتَّىٰ يُؤْمِنَّ ۚ وَلَأَمَةٌ مُّؤْمِنَةٌ خَيْرٌ مِّن مُّشْرِكَةٍ وَلَوْ أَعْجَبَتْكُمْ ۗ وَلَا تُنكِحُوا الْمُشْرِكِينَ حَتَّىٰ يُؤْمِنُوا ۚ وَلَعَبْدٌ مُّؤْمِنٌ خَيْرٌ مِّن مُّشْرِكٍ وَلَوْ أَعْجَبَكُمْ ۗ أُولَٰئِكَ يَدْعُونَ إِلَى النَّارِ ۖ وَاللَّهُ يَدْعُو إِلَى الْجَنَّةِ وَالْمَغْفِرَةِ بِإِذْنِهِ ۖ وَيُبَيِّنُ آيَاتِهِ لِلنَّاسِ لَعَلَّهُمْ يَتَذَكَّرُونَ
Sahih	And do not marry polytheistic women until they believe. And a believing slave woman is better than a polytheist, even though she might please you. And do not marry polytheistic men [to your women] until they believe. And a believing slave is better than a polytheist, even though he might please you. Those invite [you] to the Fire, but Allah invites to Paradise and to forgiveness, by His permission. And He makes clear His verses to the people that perhaps they may remember.
P	Wed not idolatresses till they believe; for lo! a believing bondwoman is better than an idolatress though she please you; and give not your daughters in marriage to idolaters till they believe, for lo! a believing slave is better than an idolater though he please you. These invite unto the Fire, and Allah inviteth unto the Garden, and unto forgiveness by His grace, and expoundeth His revelations to mankind that haply they may remember.
H&K	And do not marry Al-Mushrikat (idolatresses, etc.) till they believe (worship Allah Alone). And indeed a slave woman who believes is better than a (free) Mushrikah (idolatress, etc.), even though she pleases you. And give not (your daughters) in marriage to Al-Mushrikun till they believe (in Allah Alone) and verily, a believing slave is better than a (free) Mushrik (idolater, etc.), even though he pleases you. Those (Al-Mushrikun) invite you to the Fire, but Allah invites (you) to Paradise and Forgiveness by His Leave, and makes His Ayat (proofs, evidences, verses, lessons, signs, revelations, etc.) clear to mankind that they may remember.
J	«ولا تنكحوا» تتزوجوا أيها المسلمون «المشركات» أي الكافرات «حتى يؤمنَّ ولأمة مؤمنة خير من مشركة» حرة لأن سبب نزولها العيب على من تزوج أمة وترغيبه في نكاح حرة مشركة «ولو أعجبتكم» لجمالها ومالها وهذا مخصوص بغير الكتابيات بآية (والمحصنات من الذين أوتوا الكتاب) «ولا تُنكحوا» تُزوجوا «المشركين» أي الكفار المؤمنات «حتى يؤمنوا ولعبد مؤمن خير من مشرك ولو أعجبكم» لماله وجماله «أولئك» أي أهل الشرك «يدعون إلى النار» بدعائهم إلى العمل الموجب لها فلا تليق مناكحتهم «والله يدعو» على لسان رسله «إلى الجنة والمغفرة» أي

	العمل الموجب لهما «بإذنه» بإرادته فتجب إجابته بتزويج أوليائه «ويبين آياته للناس لعلهم يتذكرون» يتعظون
2 البقرة 230	فَإِن طَلَّقَهَا فَلَا تَحِلُّ لَهُ مِن بَعْدُ حَتَّىٰ تَنكِحَ زَوْجًا غَيْرَهُ ۗ فَإِن طَلَّقَهَا فَلَا جُنَاحَ عَلَيْهِمَا أَن يَتَرَاجَعَا إِن ظَنَّا أَن يُقِيمَا حُدُودَ اللَّهِ ۗ وَتِلْكَ حُدُودُ اللَّهِ يُبَيِّنُهَا لِقَوْمٍ يَعْلَمُونَ
P	And if he hath divorced her (the third time), then she is not lawful unto him thereafter until she hath wedded another husband. Then if he (the other husband) divorce her it is no sin for both of them that they come together again if they consider that they are able to observe the limits of Allah. These are the limits of Allah. He manifesteth them for people who have knowledge.
H&K	And if he has divorced her (the third time), then she is not lawful unto him thereafter until she has married another husband. Then, if the other husband divorces her, it is no sin on both of them that they reunite, provided they feel that they can keep the limits ordained by Allah. These are the limits of Allah, which He makes plain for the people who have knowledge
J	فإن طلقها» الزوج بعد الثنتين «فلا تحل له من بعد» بعد الطلقة الثالثة «حتى تنكح» تتزوج «زوجا غيره» ويطأها كما في الحديث رواه الشيخان «فإن طلقها» أي الزوج الثاني «فلا جناح عليهما» أي الزوجة والزوج الأول «أن يتراجعا» إلى النكاح بعد انقضاء العدة «إن ظنا أن يقيما حدود الله وتلك» المذكورات «حدود الله يُبَيِّنها لقوم يعلمون» يتدبرون.
4 النساء 127	وَيَسْتَفْتُونَكَ فِي النِّسَاءِ ۖ قُلِ اللَّهُ يُفْتِيكُمْ فِيهِنَّ وَمَا يُتْلَىٰ عَلَيْكُمْ فِي الْكِتَابِ فِي يَتَامَى النِّسَاءِ اللَّاتِي لَا تُؤْتُونَهُنَّ مَا كُتِبَ لَهُنَّ وَتَرْغَبُونَ أَن تَنكِحُوهُنَّ وَالْمُسْتَضْعَفِينَ مِنَ الْوِلْدَانِ وَأَن تَقُومُوا لِلْيَتَامَىٰ بِالْقِسْطِ ۚ وَمَا تَفْعَلُوا مِنْ خَيْرٍ فَإِنَّ اللَّهَ كَانَ بِهِ عَلِيمًا
P	They consult thee concerning women. Say: Allah giveth you decree concerning them, and the Scripture which hath been recited unto you (giveth decree), concerning female orphans and those unto whom ye give not that which is ordained for them though ye desire to marry them, and (concerning) the weak among children, and that ye should deal justly with orphans. Whatever good ye do, lo! Allah is ever Aware of it.
H&K	They ask your legal instruction concerning women, say: Allah instructs you about them, and about what is recited unto you in the Book concerning the orphan girls whom you give not the prescribed portions (as regards Mahr and inheritance) and yet whom you desire to marry, and (concerning) the children who are weak and oppressed, and that you stand firm for justice to orphans. And whatever good you do, Allah is Ever All-Aware of it.

	ويستفتونك» يطلبون منك الفتوى «في» شأن «النساء» وميراثهن «قل» لهم «الله يفتيكم» فيهن وما يتلى عليكم في الكتاب» القرآن من آية الميراث ويفتيكم أيضا «في يتامى النساء اللاتي لا تؤتوهن ما كتب» فرض «لهن» من الميراث «وترغبون» أيها الأولياء عن «أن تنكحوهن» لدمامتهن وتعضلوهن أن يتزوجن طمعا في ميراثهن أي يفتيكم أن لا تفعلوا ذلك «و» في «المستضعفين» الصغار «ومن الولدان» أن تعطوهم حقوقهم «و» يأمركم «أن تقوموا لليتامى بالقسط» بالعدل في الميراث والمهر «وما تفعلوا من خير فإن الله كان به عليما» فيجازيكم به.
33 الأحزاب 50	يَا أَيُّهَا النَّبِيُّ إِنَّا أَحْلَلْنَا لَكَ أَزْوَاجَكَ اللَّاتِي آتَيْتَ أُجُورَهُنَّ وَمَا مَلَكَتْ يَمِينُكَ مِمَّا أَفَاءَ اللَّهُ عَلَيْكَ وَبَنَاتِ عَمِّكَ وَبَنَاتِ عَمَّاتِكَ وَبَنَاتِ خَالِكَ وَبَنَاتِ خَالَاتِكَ اللَّاتِي هَاجَرْنَ مَعَكَ وَامْرَأَةً مُؤْمِنَةً إِنْ وَهَبَتْ نَفْسَهَا لِلنَّبِيِّ إِنْ أَرَادَ النَّبِيُّ أَنْ يَسْتَنْكِحَهَا خَالِصَةً لَكَ مِنْ دُونِ الْمُؤْمِنِينَ ۗ قَدْ عَلِمْنَا مَا فَرَضْنَا عَلَيْهِمْ فِي أَزْوَاجِهِمْ وَمَا مَلَكَتْ أَيْمَانُهُمْ لِكَيْلَا يَكُونَ عَلَيْكَ حَرَجٌ ۗ وَكَانَ اللَّهُ غَفُورًا رَحِيمًا
H&K	O Prophet (Muhammad SAW)! Verily, We have made lawful to you your wives, to whom you have paid their Mahr (bridal money given by the husband to his wife at the time of marriage), and those (captives or slaves) whom your right hand possesses - whom Allah has given to you, and the daughters of your 'Amm (paternal uncles) and the daughters of your 'Ammah (paternal aunts) and the daughters of your Khal (maternal uncles) and the daughters of your Khalah (maternal aunts) who migrated (from Makkah) with you, and a believing woman if she offers herself to the Prophet, and the Prophet wishes to marry her; a privilege for you only, not for the (rest of) the believers. Indeed We know what We have enjoined upon them about their wives and those (captives or slaves) whom their right hands possess, - in order that there should be no difficulty on you. And Allah is Ever OftForgiving, Most Merciful.
P	O Prophet! Lo! We have made lawful unto thee thy wives unto whom thou hast paid their dowries, and those whom thy right hand possesseth of those whom Allah hath given thee as spoils of war, and the daughters of thine uncle on the father's side and the daughters of thine aunts on the father's side, and the daughters of thine uncle on the mother's side and the daughters of thine aunts on the mother's side who emigrated with thee, and a believing woman if she give herself unto the Prophet and the Prophet desire to ask her in marriage - a privilege for thee only, not for the (rest of) believers - We are Aware of that which We enjoined upon them concerning their wives and those whom their right hands possess - that thou mayst be free from blame, for Allah is ever Forgiving, Merciful.

J	يا أيها النبي إنا أحللنا لك أزواجك اللاتي آتيت أجورهن «مهورهن» «وما ملكت يمينك مما أفاء الله عليك» من الكفار بالسبي كصفية وجويرية «وبنات عمك وبنات عماتك وبنات خالك وبنات خالاتك اللاتي هاجرن معك» بخلاف من لم يهاجرن «وامرأةً مؤمنة إن وهبت نفسها للنبي إن أراد النبي أن يستنكحها» يطلب نكاحها بغير صداق «خالصة لك من دون المؤمنين» النكاح بلفظ الهبة من غير صداق «قد علمنا ما فرضنا عليهم» أي المؤمنين «في أزواجهم» من الأحكام بأن لا يزيدوا على أربع نسوة ولا يتزوجوا إلا بوليٍّ وشهود ومهر «و» في «ما ملكت أيمانهم» من الإماء بشراء وغيره بأن تكون الأمة ممن تحل لمالكها كالكتابية بخلاف المجوسية والوثنية وأن تستبرأ قبل الوطء «لكيلا» متعلق بما قبل ذلك «يكون عليك حرج» ضيق في النكاح «وكان الله غفوراً» فيما يعسر التحرز عنه «رحيماً» بالتوسعة في ذلك.
33 الأحزاب 53	يَا أَيُّهَا الَّذِينَ آمَنُوا لَا تَدْخُلُوا بُيُوتَ النَّبِيِّ إِلَّا أَن يُؤْذَنَ لَكُمْ إِلَىٰ طَعَامٍ غَيْرَ نَاظِرِينَ إِنَاهُ وَلَٰكِنْ إِذَا دُعِيتُمْ فَادْخُلُوا فَإِذَا طَعِمْتُمْ فَانتَشِرُوا وَلَا مُسْتَأْنِسِينَ لِحَدِيثٍ ۚ إِنَّ ذَٰلِكُمْ كَانَ يُؤْذِي النَّبِيَّ فَيَسْتَحْيِي مِنكُمْ ۖ وَاللَّهُ لَا يَسْتَحْيِي مِنَ الْحَقِّ ۚ وَإِذَا سَأَلْتُمُوهُنَّ مَتَاعًا فَاسْأَلُوهُنَّ مِن وَرَاءِ ==حِجَابٍ== ۚ ذَٰلِكُمْ أَطْهَرُ لِقُلُوبِكُمْ وَقُلُوبِهِنَّ ۚ وَمَا كَانَ لَكُمْ أَن تُؤْذُوا رَسُولَ اللَّهِ وَلَا أَن ==تَنكِحُوا== أَزْوَاجَهُ مِن بَعْدِهِ أَبَدًا ۚ إِنَّ ذَٰلِكُمْ كَانَ عِندَ اللَّهِ عَظِيمًا
H&K	O you who believe! Enter not the Prophet's houses, except when leave is given to you for a meal, (and then) not (so early as) to wait for its preparation. But when you are invited, enter, and when you have taken your meal, disperse, without sitting for a talk. Verily, such (behaviour) annoys the Prophet, and he is shy of (asking) you (to go), but Allah is not shy of (telling you) the truth. And when you ask (his wives) for anything you want, ask them from behind a screen, that is purer for your hearts and for their hearts. And it is not (right) for you that you should annoy Allah's Messenger, nor that you should ever marry his wives after him (his death). Verily! With Allah that shall be an enormity.
60 الممتحنة 10	يَا أَيُّهَا الَّذِينَ آمَنُوا إِذَا جَاءَكُمُ الْمُؤْمِنَاتُ مُهَاجِرَاتٍ فَامْتَحِنُوهُنَّ ۖ اللَّهُ أَعْلَمُ بِإِيمَانِهِنَّ ۖ فَإِنْ عَلِمْتُمُوهُنَّ مُؤْمِنَاتٍ فَلَا تَرْجِعُوهُنَّ إِلَى الْكُفَّارِ ۖ لَا هُنَّ حِلٌّ لَّهُمْ وَلَا هُمْ يَحِلُّونَ لَهُنَّ ۖ وَآتُوهُم مَّا أَنفَقُوا ۚ وَلَا جُنَاحَ عَلَيْكُمْ أَن ==تَنكِحُوهُنَّ== إِذَا آتَيْتُمُوهُنَّ أُجُورَهُنَّ ۚ وَلَا تُمْسِكُوا بِعِصَمِ الْكَوَافِرِ وَاسْأَلُوا مَا أَنفَقْتُمْ وَلْيَسْأَلُوا مَا أَنفَقُوا ۚ ذَٰلِكُمْ حُكْمُ اللَّهِ ۖ يَحْكُمُ بَيْنَكُمْ ۚ وَاللَّهُ عَلِيمٌ حَكِيمٌ
H&K	O you who believe! When believing women come to you as emigrants, examine them, Allah knows best as to their Faith, then if you ascertain that they are true believers, send them not back to the disbelievers, they are not

	lawful (wives) for the disbelievers nor are the disbelievers lawful (husbands) for them. But give the disbelievers that (amount of money) which they have spent [as their Mahr] to them. And there will be no sin on you to marry them if you have paid their Mahr to them. Likewise hold not the disbelieving women as wives, and ask for (the return of) that which you have spent (as Mahr) and let them (the disbelievers, etc.) ask back for that which they have spent. That is the Judgement of Allah. He judges between you. And Allah is All-Knowing, All-Wise.
24 النور 31	وَقُل لِّلْمُؤْمِنَاتِ يَغْضُضْنَ مِنْ أَبْصَارِهِنَّ وَيَحْفَظْنَ فُرُوجَهُنَّ وَلَا يُبْدِينَ زِينَتَهُنَّ إِلَّا مَا ظَهَرَ مِنْهَا ۖ وَلْيَضْرِبْنَ بِخُمُرِهِنَّ عَلَىٰ جُيُوبِهِنَّ ۖ وَلَا يُبْدِينَ زِينَتَهُنَّ إِلَّا لِبُعُولَتِهِنَّ أَوْ آبَائِهِنَّ أَوْ آبَاءِ بُعُولَتِهِنَّ أَوْ أَبْنَائِهِنَّ أَوْ أَبْنَاءِ بُعُولَتِهِنَّ أَوْ إِخْوَانِهِنَّ أَوْ بَنِي إِخْوَانِهِنَّ أَوْ بَنِي أَخَوَاتِهِنَّ أَوْ نِسَائِهِنَّ أَوْ مَا مَلَكَتْ أَيْمَانُهُنَّ أَوِ التَّابِعِينَ غَيْرِ أُولِي الْإِرْبَةِ مِنَ الرِّجَالِ أَوِ الطِّفْلِ الَّذِينَ لَمْ يَظْهَرُوا عَلَىٰ عَوْرَاتِ النِّسَاءِ ۖ وَلَا يَضْرِبْنَ بِأَرْجُلِهِنَّ لِيُعْلَمَ مَا يُخْفِينَ مِن زِينَتِهِنَّ ۚ وَتُوبُوا إِلَى اللَّهِ جَمِيعًا أَيُّهَ الْمُؤْمِنُونَ لَعَلَّكُمْ تُفْلِحُونَ
	جَيْبِكَ put your hand into the **opening of your garment [at the breast]**
27 النمل 12	وَأَدْخِلْ يَدَكَ فِي جَيْبِكَ تَخْرُجْ بَيْضَاءَ مِنْ غَيْرِ سُوءٍ ۖ فِي تِسْعِ آيَاتٍ إِلَىٰ فِرْعَوْنَ وَقَوْمِهِ ۚ إِنَّهُمْ كَانُوا قَوْمًا فَاسِقِينَ
H&K	"And put your hand into your bosom, it will come forth white without hurt. (These are) among the nine signs (you will take) to Fir'aun (Pharaoh) and his people, they are a people who are the Fasiqun (rebellious, disobedient to Allah).

28 القصص 32	اسْلُكْ يَدَكَ فِي جَيْبِكَ تَخْرُجْ بَيْضَاءَ مِنْ غَيْرِ سُوءٍ وَاضْمُمْ إِلَيْكَ جَنَاحَكَ مِنَ الرَّهْبِ ۖ فَذَانِكَ بُرْهَانَانِ مِن رَّبِّكَ إِلَىٰ فِرْعَوْنَ وَمَلَئِهِ ۚ إِنَّهُمْ كَانُوا قَوْمًا فَاسِقِينَ
H&K	"Put your hand in your bosom, it will come forth white without a disease, and draw your hand close to your side to be free from fear (that which you suffered from the snake, and also by that your hand will return to its original state). these are two Burhan (signs, miracles, evidences, proofs) from your Lord to Fir'aun (Pharaoh) and his chiefs. Verily, they are the people who are Fasiqun (rebellious, disobedient to Allah).

حَرَامٌ / حَرَامًا

[some] lawful and [some] **unlawful**

10 يونس 59	قُلْ أَرَأَيْتُم مَّا أَنزَلَ اللَّهُ لَكُم مِّن رِّزْقٍ فَجَعَلْتُم مِّنْهُ حَرَامًا وَحَلَالًا قُلْ آللَّهُ أَذِنَ لَكُمْ ۖ أَمْ عَلَى اللَّهِ تَفْتَرُونَ
H&K	Say (O Muhammad SAW to these polytheists): "Tell me, what provision Allah has sent down to you! And you have made of it lawful and unlawful." Say (O Muhammad SAW): "Has Allah permitted you (to do so), or do you invent a lie against Allah?"
16 النحل 116	وَلَا تَقُولُوا لِمَا تَصِفُ أَلْسِنَتُكُمُ الْكَذِبَ هَٰذَا حَلَالٌ وَهَٰذَا حَرَامٌ لِّتَفْتَرُوا عَلَى اللَّهِ الْكَذِبَ ۚ إِنَّ الَّذِينَ يَفْتَرُونَ عَلَى اللَّهِ الْكَذِبَ لَا يُفْلِحُونَ
H&K	And say not concerning that which your tongues put forth falsely: "This is lawful and this is forbidden," so as to invent lies against Allah. Verily, those who invent lies against Allah will never prosper.
21 الأنبياء 95	وَحَرَامٌ عَلَىٰ قَرْيَةٍ أَهْلَكْنَاهَا أَنَّهُمْ لَا يَرْجِعُونَ
H&K	And a ban is laid on every town (population) which We have destroyed that they shall not return (to this world again, nor repent to Us).

Patient	صابر
2 البقرة 153	يَا أَيُّهَا الَّذِينَ آمَنُوا اسْتَعِينُوا بِالصَّبْرِ وَالصَّلَاةِ ۚ إِنَّ اللَّهَ مَعَ **الصَّابِرِينَ**
H&K	O you who believe! Seek help in patience and As-Salat (the prayer). Truly! Allah is with As-Sabirin (the patient ones, etc.).
155	وَلَنَبْلُوَنَّكُم بِشَيْءٍ مِّنَ الْخَوْفِ وَالْجُوعِ وَنَقْصٍ مِّنَ الْأَمْوَالِ وَالْأَنفُسِ وَالثَّمَرَاتِ ۗ وَبَشِّرِ **الصَّابِرِينَ**
H&K	And certainly, We shall test you with something of fear, hunger, loss of wealth, lives and fruits, but give glad tidings to As-Sabirin (the patient ones, etc.).
177	۞ لَّيْسَ الْبِرَّ أَن تُوَلُّوا وُجُوهَكُمْ قِبَلَ الْمَشْرِقِ وَالْمَغْرِبِ وَلَٰكِنَّ الْبِرَّ مَنْ آمَنَ بِاللَّهِ وَالْيَوْمِ الْآخِرِ وَالْمَلَائِكَةِ وَالْكِتَابِ وَالنَّبِيِّينَ وَآتَى الْمَالَ عَلَىٰ حُبِّهِ ذَوِي الْقُرْبَىٰ وَالْيَتَامَىٰ وَالْمَسَاكِينَ وَابْنَ السَّبِيلِ وَالسَّائِلِينَ وَفِي الرِّقَابِ وَأَقَامَ الصَّلَاةَ وَآتَى الزَّكَاةَ وَالْمُوفُونَ بِعَهْدِهِمْ إِذَا عَاهَدُوا ۖ **وَالصَّابِرِينَ** فِي الْبَأْسَاءِ وَالضَّرَّاءِ وَحِينَ الْبَأْسِ ۗ أُولَٰئِكَ الَّذِينَ صَدَقُوا ۖ وَأُولَٰئِكَ هُمُ الْمُتَّقُونَ
H&K	It is not Al-Birr (piety, righteousness, and each and every act of obedience to Allah, etc.) that you turn your faces towards east and (or) west (in prayers); but Al-Birr is (the quality of) the one who believes in Allah, the Last Day, the Angels, the Book, the Prophets and gives his wealth, in spite of love for it, to the kinsfolk, to the orphans, and to Al-Masakin (the poor), and to the wayfarer, and to those who ask, and to set slaves free, performs As-Salat (Iqamat-as-Salat), and gives the Zakat, and who fulfill their covenant when they make it, and who are As-Sabirin (the patient ones, etc.) in extreme poverty and ailment (disease) and at the time of fighting (during the battles). Such are the people of the truth and they are Al-Muttaqun (pious - see V. 2:2).
249	فَلَمَّا فَصَلَ طَالُوتُ بِالْجُنُودِ قَالَ إِنَّ اللَّهَ مُبْتَلِيكُم بِنَهَرٍ فَمَن شَرِبَ مِنْهُ فَلَيْسَ مِنِّي وَمَن لَّمْ يَطْعَمْهُ فَإِنَّهُ مِنِّي إِلَّا مَنِ اغْتَرَفَ غُرْفَةً بِيَدِهِ ۚ فَشَرِبُوا مِنْهُ إِلَّا قَلِيلًا مِّنْهُمْ ۚ فَلَمَّا جَاوَزَهُ هُوَ وَالَّذِينَ آمَنُوا مَعَهُ قَالُوا لَا طَاقَةَ لَنَا الْيَوْمَ بِجَالُوتَ وَجُنُودِهِ ۚ قَالَ الَّذِينَ يَظُنُّونَ أَنَّهُم مُّلَاقُو اللَّهِ كَم مِّن فِئَةٍ قَلِيلَةٍ غَلَبَتْ فِئَةً كَثِيرَةً بِإِذْنِ اللَّهِ ۗ وَاللَّهُ مَعَ **الصَّابِرِينَ**
H&K	Then when Talut (Saul) set out with the army, he said: "Verily! Allah will try you by a river. So whoever drinks thereof, he is not of me, and whoever tastes it not, he is of me, except him who takes (thereof) in the hollow of his hand." Yet, they drank thereof, all, except a few of them. So when he had crossed it (the river), he and those who believed with him, they said: "We have no power

		this day against Jalut (Goliath) and his hosts." But those who knew with certainty that they were to meet their Lord, said: "How often a small group overcame a mighty host by Allah's Leave?" And Allah is with As-Sabirin (the patient ones, etc.).
3 آل عمران 17		الصَّابِرِينَ وَالصَّادِقِينَ وَالْقَانِتِينَ وَالْمُنفِقِينَ وَالْمُسْتَغْفِرِينَ بِالْأَسْحَارِ
	H&K	(They are) those who are patient ones, those who are true (in Faith, words, and deeds), and obedient with sincere devotion in worship to Allah. Those who spend [give the Zakat and alms in the Way of Allah] and those who pray and beg Allah's Pardon in the last hours of the night.
142		أَمْ حَسِبْتُمْ أَن تَدْخُلُوا الْجَنَّةَ وَلَمَّا يَعْلَمِ اللَّهُ الَّذِينَ جَاهَدُوا مِنكُمْ وَيَعْلَمَ الصَّابِرِينَ
	H&K	Do you think that you will enter Paradise before Allah tests those of you who fought (in His Cause) and (also) tests those who are As-Sabirin (the patient ones, etc.)?
146		وَكَأَيِّن مِّن نَّبِيٍّ قَاتَلَ مَعَهُ رِبِّيُّونَ كَثِيرٌ فَمَا وَهَنُوا لِمَا أَصَابَهُمْ فِي سَبِيلِ اللَّهِ وَمَا ضَعُفُوا وَمَا اسْتَكَانُوا ۗ وَاللَّهُ يُحِبُّ الصَّابِرِينَ
	H&K	And many a Prophet (i.e. many from amongst the Prophets) fought (in Allah's Cause) and along with him (fought) large bands of religious learned men. But they never lost heart for that which did befall them in Allah's Way, nor did they weaken nor degrade themselves. And Allah loves As-Sabirin (the patient ones, etc.).
200		يَا أَيُّهَا الَّذِينَ آمَنُوا اصْبِرُوا وَصَابِرُوا وَرَابِطُوا وَاتَّقُوا اللَّهَ لَعَلَّكُمْ تُفْلِحُونَ
	H&K	O you who believe! Endure and be more patient (than your enemy), and guard your territory by stationing army units permanently at the places from where the enemy can attack you, and fear Allah, so that you may be successful.
8 الأنفال 46		وَأَطِيعُوا اللَّهَ وَرَسُولَهُ وَلَا تَنَازَعُوا فَتَفْشَلُوا وَتَذْهَبَ رِيحُكُمْ ۖ وَاصْبِرُوا ۚ إِنَّ اللَّهَ مَعَ الصَّابِرِينَ
	H&K	And obey Allah and His Messenger, and do not dispute (with one another) lest you lose courage and your strength depart, and be patient. Surely, Allah is with those who are As-Sabirin (the patient ones, etc.).
65		يَا أَيُّهَا النَّبِيُّ حَرِّضِ الْمُؤْمِنِينَ عَلَى الْقِتَالِ ۚ إِن يَكُن مِّنكُمْ عِشْرُونَ صَابِرُونَ يَغْلِبُوا مِائَتَيْنِ ۚ وَإِن يَكُن مِّنكُم مِّائَةٌ يَغْلِبُوا أَلْفًا مِّنَ الَّذِينَ كَفَرُوا بِأَنَّهُمْ قَوْمٌ لَّا يَفْقَهُونَ

H&K	O Prophet (Muhammad SAW)! Urge the believers to fight. If there are twenty steadfast persons amongst you, they will overcome two hundred, and if there be a hundred steadfast persons they will overcome a thousand of those who disbelieve, because they (the disbelievers) are people who do not understand.
66	الْآنَ خَفَّفَ اللَّهُ عَنكُمْ وَعَلِمَ أَنَّ فِيكُمْ ضَعْفًا ۚ فَإِن يَكُن مِّنكُم مِّائَةٌ **صَابِرَةٌ** يَغْلِبُوا مِائَتَيْنِ ۚ وَإِن يَكُن مِّنكُمْ أَلْفٌ يَغْلِبُوا أَلْفَيْنِ بِإِذْنِ اللَّهِ ۗ وَاللَّهُ مَعَ **الصَّابِرِينَ**
H&K	Now Allah has lightened your (task), for He knows that there is weakness in you. So if there are of you a hundred steadfast persons, they shall overcome two hundred, and if there are a thousand of you, they shall overcome two thousand with the Leave of Allah. And Allah is with As-Sabirin (the patient ones, etc.).
16 النحل 126	وَإِنْ عَاقَبْتُمْ فَعَاقِبُوا بِمِثْلِ مَا عُوقِبْتُم بِهِ ۖ وَلَئِن صَبَرْتُمْ لَهُوَ خَيْرٌ لِّلصَّابِرِينَ
H&K	And if you punish (your enemy, O you believers in the Oneness of Allah), then punish them with the like of that with which you were afflicted. But if you endure patiently, verily, it is better for As-Sabirin (the patient ones, etc.).
18 الكهف 69	قَالَ سَتَجِدُنِي إِن شَاءَ اللَّهُ **صَابِرًا** وَلَا أَعْصِي لَكَ أَمْرًا
H&K	Musa (Moses) said: "If Allah will, you will find me patient, and I will not disobey you in aught."
21 الأنبياء 85	وَإِسْمَاعِيلَ وَإِدْرِيسَ وَذَا الْكِفْلِ ۖ كُلٌّ مِّنَ **الصَّابِرِينَ**
H&K	And (remember) Isma'il (Ishmael), and Idris (Enoch) and Dhul-Kifl (Isaiah), all were from among As-Sabirin (the patient ones, etc.).
22 الحج 35	الَّذِينَ إِذَا ذُكِرَ اللَّهُ وَجِلَتْ قُلُوبُهُمْ **وَالصَّابِرِينَ** عَلَىٰ مَا أَصَابَهُمْ وَالْمُقِيمِي الصَّلَاةِ وَمِمَّا رَزَقْنَاهُمْ يُنفِقُونَ
H&K	Whose hearts are filled with fear when Allah is mentioned; who patiently bear whatever may befall them (of calamities); and who perform As-Salat (Iqamat-as-Salat), and who spend (in Allah's Cause) out of what We have provided them.
28 القصص 80	وَقَالَ الَّذِينَ أُوتُوا الْعِلْمَ وَيْلَكُمْ ثَوَابُ اللَّهِ خَيْرٌ لِّمَنْ آمَنَ وَعَمِلَ صَالِحًا وَلَا يُلَقَّاهَا إِلَّا **الصَّابِرُونَ**

H&K	But those who had been given (religious) knowledge said: "Woe to you! The Reward of Allah (in the Hereafter) is better for those who believe and do righteous good deeds, and this none shall attain except those who are patient (in following the truth)."
33 الأحزاب 35	إِنَّ الْمُسْلِمِينَ وَالْمُسْلِمَاتِ وَالْمُؤْمِنِينَ وَالْمُؤْمِنَاتِ وَالْقَانِتِينَ وَالْقَانِتَاتِ وَالصَّادِقِينَ وَالصَّادِقَاتِ وَ**الصَّابِرِينَ وَالصَّابِرَاتِ** وَالْخَاشِعِينَ وَالْخَاشِعَاتِ وَالْمُتَصَدِّقِينَ وَالْمُتَصَدِّقَاتِ وَالصَّائِمِينَ وَالصَّائِمَاتِ وَالْحَافِظِينَ فُرُوجَهُمْ وَالْحَافِظَاتِ وَالذَّاكِرِينَ اللَّهَ كَثِيرًا وَالذَّاكِرَاتِ أَعَدَّ اللَّهُ لَهُم مَّغْفِرَةً وَأَجْرًا عَظِيمًا
H&K	Verily, the Muslims (those who submit to Allah in Islam) men and women, the believers men and women (who believe in Islamic Monotheism), the men and the women who are obedient (to Allah), the men and women who are truthful (in their speech and deeds), the men and the women who are patient (in performing all the duties which Allah has ordered and in abstaining from all that Allah has forbidden), the men and the women who are humble (before their Lord Allah), the men and the women who give Sadaqat (i.e. Zakat, and alms, etc.), the men and the women who observe Saum (fast) (the obligatory fasting during the month of Ramadan, and the optional Nawafil fasting), the men and the women who guard their chastity (from illegal sexual acts) and the men and the women who remember Allah much with their hearts and tongues (while sitting, standing, lying, etc. for more than 300 times extra over the remembrance of Allah during the five compulsory congregational prayers) or praying extra additional Nawafil prayers of night in the last part of night, etc.) Allah has prepared for them forgiveness and a great reward (i.e. Paradise).
37 الصافات 102	فَلَمَّا بَلَغَ مَعَهُ السَّعْيَ قَالَ يَا بُنَيَّ إِنِّي أَرَى فِي الْمَنَامِ أَنِّي أَذْبَحُكَ فَانظُرْ مَاذَا تَرَى ۚ قَالَ يَا أَبَتِ افْعَلْ مَا تُؤْمَرُ ۖ سَتَجِدُنِي إِن شَاءَ اللَّهُ مِنَ **الصَّابِرِينَ**
H&K	And, when he (his son) was old enough to walk with him, he said: "O my son! I have seen in a dream that I am slaughtering you (offer you in sacrifice to Allah), so look what you think!" He said: "O my father! Do that which you are commanded, Insha' Allah (if Allah will), you shall find me of As-Sabirin (the patient ones, etc.)."
38 ص 44	وَخُذْ بِيَدِكَ ضِغْثًا فَاضْرِب بِّهِ وَلَا تَحْنَثْ ۗ إِنَّا وَجَدْنَاهُ **صَابِرًا** ۚ نِّعْمَ الْعَبْدُ ۖ إِنَّهُ أَوَّابٌ
H&K	"And take in your hand a bundle of thin grass and strike therewith (your wife), and break not your oath. Truly! We found him patient. How excellent (a) slave! Verily, he was ever oft-returning in repentance (to Us)!"

39 الزمر 10	قُلْ يَا عِبَادِ الَّذِينَ آمَنُوا اتَّقُوا رَبَّكُمْ ۚ لِلَّذِينَ أَحْسَنُوا فِي هَٰذِهِ الدُّنْيَا حَسَنَةٌ ۗ وَأَرْضُ اللَّهِ وَاسِعَةٌ ۗ إِنَّمَا يُوَفَّى **الصَّابِرُونَ** أَجْرَهُم بِغَيْرِ حِسَابٍ
H&K	Say (O Muhammad SAW): "O My slaves who believe (in the Oneness of Allah Islamic Monotheism), be afraid of your Lord (Allah) and keep your duty to Him. Good is (the reward) for those who do good in this world, and Allah's earth is spacious (so if you cannot worship Allah at a place, then go to another)! Only those who are patient shall receive their rewards in full, without reckoning."
47 محمد 31	وَلَنَبْلُوَنَّكُمْ حَتَّىٰ نَعْلَمَ الْمُجَاهِدِينَ مِنكُمْ **وَالصَّابِرِينَ** وَنَبْلُوَ أَخْبَارَكُمْ
H&K	And surely, We shall try you till We test those who strive hard (for the Cause of Allah) and the patient ones, and We shall test your facts (i.e. the one who is a liar, and the one who is truthful).
	صبر
2 البقرة 45	وَاسْتَعِينُوا **بِالصَّبْرِ** وَالصَّلَاةِ ۚ وَإِنَّهَا لَكَبِيرَةٌ إِلَّا عَلَى الْخَاشِعِينَ
H&K	And seek help in patience and As-Salat (the prayer) and truly it is extremely heavy and hard except for Al-Khashi'un [i.e. the true believers in Allah - those who obey Allah with full submission, fear much from His Punishment, and believe in His Promise (Paradise, etc.) and in His Warnings (Hell, etc.)].
61	وَإِذْ قُلْتُمْ يَا مُوسَىٰ لَن **نَّصْبِرَ** عَلَىٰ طَعَامٍ وَاحِدٍ فَادْعُ لَنَا رَبَّكَ يُخْرِجْ لَنَا مِمَّا تُنبِتُ الْأَرْضُ مِن بَقْلِهَا وَقِثَّائِهَا وَفُومِهَا وَعَدَسِهَا وَبَصَلِهَا ۖ قَالَ أَتَسْتَبْدِلُونَ الَّذِي هُوَ أَدْنَىٰ بِالَّذِي هُوَ خَيْرٌ ۚ اهْبِطُوا مِصْرًا فَإِنَّ لَكُم مَّا سَأَلْتُمْ ۗ وَضُرِبَتْ عَلَيْهِمُ الذِّلَّةُ وَالْمَسْكَنَةُ وَبَاءُوا بِغَضَبٍ مِّنَ اللَّهِ ۗ ذَٰلِكَ بِأَنَّهُمْ كَانُوا يَكْفُرُونَ بِآيَاتِ اللَّهِ وَيَقْتُلُونَ النَّبِيِّينَ بِغَيْرِ الْحَقِّ ۗ ذَٰلِكَ بِمَا عَصَوا وَّكَانُوا يَعْتَدُونَ
H&K	And (remember) when you said, "O Musa (Moses)! We cannot endure one kind of food. So invoke your Lord for us to bring forth for us of what the earth grows, its herbs, its cucumbers, its Fum (wheat or garlic), its lentils and its onions." He said, "Would you exchange that which is better for that which is lower? Go you down to any town and you shall find what you want!" And they were covered with humiliation and misery, and they drew on themselves the Wrath of Allah. That was because they used to disbelieve the Ayat (proofs,

	evidences, verses, lessons, signs, revelations, etc.) of Allah and killed the Prophets wrongfully. That was because they disobeyed and used to transgress the bounds (in their disobedience to Allah, i.e. commit crimes and sins).
153	يَا أَيُّهَا الَّذِينَ آمَنُوا اسْتَعِينُوا **بِالصَّبْرِ** وَالصَّلَاةِ ۚ إِنَّ اللَّهَ مَعَ **الصَّابِرِينَ**
H&K	O you who believe! Seek help in patience and As-Salat (the prayer). Truly! Allah is with As-Sabirin (the patient ones, etc.).
175	أُولَٰئِكَ الَّذِينَ اشْتَرَوُا الضَّلَالَةَ بِالْهُدَىٰ وَالْعَذَابَ بِالْمَغْفِرَةِ ۚ فَمَا **أَصْبَرَهُمْ** عَلَى النَّارِ
H&K	Those are they who have purchased error at the price of Guidance, and torment at the price of Forgiveness. So how bold they are (for evil deeds which will push them) to the Fire.
250	وَلَمَّا بَرَزُوا لِجَالُوتَ وَجُنُودِهِ قَالُوا رَبَّنَا أَفْرِغْ عَلَيْنَا صَبْرًا وَثَبِّتْ أَقْدَامَنَا وَانْصُرْنَا عَلَى الْقَوْمِ الْكَافِرِينَ
H&K	And when they advanced to meet Jalut (Goliath) and his forces, they invoked: "Our Lord! Pour forth on us patience and make us victorious over the disbelieving people."
3 آل عمران 120	إِنْ تَمْسَسْكُمْ حَسَنَةٌ تَسُؤْهُمْ وَإِنْ تُصِبْكُمْ سَيِّئَةٌ يَفْرَحُوا بِهَا ۖ وَإِنْ **تَصْبِرُوا** وَتَتَّقُوا لَا يَضُرُّكُمْ كَيْدُهُمْ شَيْئًا ۗ إِنَّ اللَّهَ بِمَا يَعْمَلُونَ مُحِيطٌ
H&K	If a good befalls you, it grieves them, but if some evil overtakes you, they rejoice at it. But if you remain patient and become Al-Muttaqun (the pious - see V. 2:2), not the least harm will their cunning do to you. Surely, Allah surrounds all that they do.
125	بَلَىٰ ۚ إِنْ **تَصْبِرُوا** وَتَتَّقُوا وَيَأْتُوكُمْ مِنْ فَوْرِهِمْ هَٰذَا يُمْدِدْكُمْ رَبُّكُمْ بِخَمْسَةِ آلَافٍ مِنَ الْمَلَائِكَةِ مُسَوِّمِينَ
H&K	"Yes, if you hold on to patience and piety, and the enemy comes rushing at you; your Lord will help you with five thousand angels having marks (of distinction)."
186	۞ لَتُبْلَوُنَّ فِي أَمْوَالِكُمْ وَأَنْفُسِكُمْ وَلَتَسْمَعُنَّ مِنَ الَّذِينَ أُوتُوا الْكِتَابَ مِنْ قَبْلِكُمْ وَمِنَ الَّذِينَ أَشْرَكُوا أَذًى كَثِيرًا ۚ وَإِنْ **تَصْبِرُوا** وَتَتَّقُوا فَإِنَّ ذَٰلِكَ مِنْ عَزْمِ الْأُمُورِ
H&K	You shall certainly be tried and tested in your wealth and properties and in your personal selves, and you shall certainly hear much that will grieve you from those who received the Scripture before you (Jews and Christians) and from those who ascribe partners to Allah, but if you persevere patiently, and

	become Al-Muttaqun (the pious - see V. 2:2) then verily, that will be a determining factor in all affairs, and that is from the great matters, [which you must hold on with all your efforts].
200	يَا أَيُّهَا الَّذِينَ آمَنُوا **اصْبِرُوا** وَ**صَابِرُوا** وَرَابِطُوا وَاتَّقُوا اللَّهَ لَعَلَّكُمْ تُفْلِحُونَ
H&K	O you who believe! Endure and be more patient (than your enemy), and guard your territory by stationing army units permanently at the places from where the enemy can attack you, and fear Allah, so that you may be successful.
4 النساء 25	وَمَن لَّمْ يَسْتَطِعْ مِنكُمْ طَوْلًا أَن يَنكِحَ الْمُحْصَنَاتِ الْمُؤْمِنَاتِ فَمِن مَّا مَلَكَتْ أَيْمَانُكُم مِّن فَتَيَاتِكُمُ الْمُؤْمِنَاتِ ۚ وَاللَّهُ أَعْلَمُ بِإِيمَانِكُم ۚ بَعْضُكُم مِّن بَعْضٍ ۚ فَانكِحُوهُنَّ بِإِذْنِ أَهْلِهِنَّ وَآتُوهُنَّ أُجُورَهُنَّ بِالْمَعْرُوفِ مُحْصَنَاتٍ غَيْرَ مُسَافِحَاتٍ وَلَا مُتَّخِذَاتِ أَخْدَانٍ ۚ فَإِذَا أُحْصِنَّ فَإِنْ أَتَيْنَ بِفَاحِشَةٍ فَعَلَيْهِنَّ نِصْفُ مَا عَلَى الْمُحْصَنَاتِ مِنَ الْعَذَابِ ۚ ذَٰلِكَ لِمَنْ خَشِيَ الْعَنَتَ مِنكُمْ ۚ وَأَن **تَصْبِرُوا** خَيْرٌ لَّكُمْ ۗ وَاللَّهُ غَفُورٌ رَّحِيمٌ
H&K	And whoever of you have not the means wherewith to wed free, believing women, they may wed believing girls from among those (captives and slaves) whom your right hands possess, and Allah has full knowledge about your Faith, you are one from another. Wed them with the permission of their own folk (guardians, Auliya' or masters) and give them their Mahr according to what is reasonable; they (the above said captive and slave-girls) should be chaste, not adulterous, nor taking boy-friends. And after they have been taken in wedlock, if they commit illegal sexual intercourse, their punishment is half that for free (unmarried) women. This is for him among you who is afraid of being harmed in his religion or in his body; but it is better for you that you practise self-restraint, and Allah is Oft-Forgiving, Most Merciful.
6 الأنعام 34	وَلَقَدْ كُذِّبَتْ رُسُلٌ مِّن قَبْلِكَ **فَصَبَرُوا** عَلَىٰ مَا كُذِّبُوا وَأُوذُوا حَتَّىٰ أَتَاهُمْ نَصْرُنَا ۚ وَلَا مُبَدِّلَ لِكَلِمَاتِ اللَّهِ ۚ وَلَقَدْ جَاءَكَ مِن نَّبَإِ الْمُرْسَلِينَ
H&K	Verily, (many) Messengers were denied before you (O Muhammad SAW), but with patience they bore the denial, and they were hurt, till Our Help reached them, and none can alter the Words (Decisions) of Allah. Surely there has reached you the information (news) about the Messengers (before you).
7 الأعراف 87	وَإِن كَانَ طَائِفَةٌ مِّنكُمْ آمَنُوا بِالَّذِي أُرْسِلْتُ بِهِ وَطَائِفَةٌ لَّمْ يُؤْمِنُوا **فَاصْبِرُوا** حَتَّىٰ يَحْكُمَ اللَّهُ بَيْنَنَا ۚ وَهُوَ خَيْرُ الْحَاكِمِينَ

H&K	"And if there is a party of you who believes in that with which I have been sent and a party who do not believe, so be patient until Allah judges between us, and He is the Best of judges."
126	وَمَا تَنقِمُ مِنَّا إِلَّا أَنْ آمَنَّا بِآيَاتِ رَبِّنَا لَمَّا جَاءَتْنَا ۚ رَبَّنَا أَفْرِغْ عَلَيْنَا **صَبْرًا** وَتَوَفَّنَا مُسْلِمِينَ
H&K	"And you take vengeance on us only because we believed in the Ayat (proofs, evidences, lessons, signs, etc.) of our Lord when they reached us! Our Lord! pour out on us patience, and cause us to die as Muslims."
128	قَالَ مُوسَىٰ لِقَوْمِهِ اسْتَعِينُوا بِاللَّهِ **وَاصْبِرُوا** ۖ إِنَّ الْأَرْضَ لِلَّهِ يُورِثُهَا مَن يَشَاءُ مِنْ عِبَادِهِ ۖ وَالْعَاقِبَةُ لِلْمُتَّقِينَ
H&K	Musa (Moses) said to his people: "Seek help in Allah and be patient. Verily, the earth is Allah's. He gives it as a heritage to whom He will of His slaves, and the (blessed) end is for the Muttaqun (pious - see V. 2:2)."
137	وَأَوْرَثْنَا الْقَوْمَ الَّذِينَ كَانُوا يُسْتَضْعَفُونَ مَشَارِقَ الْأَرْضِ وَمَغَارِبَهَا الَّتِي بَارَكْنَا فِيهَا ۖ وَتَمَّتْ كَلِمَتُ رَبِّكَ الْحُسْنَىٰ عَلَىٰ بَنِي إِسْرَائِيلَ بِمَا **صَبَرُوا** ۖ وَدَمَّرْنَا مَا كَانَ يَصْنَعُ فِرْعَوْنُ وَقَوْمُهُ وَمَا كَانُوا يَعْرِشُونَ
H&K	And We made the people who were considered weak to inherit the eastern parts of the land and the western parts thereof which We have blessed. And the fair Word of your Lord was fulfilled for the Children of Israel, because of their endurance. And We destroyed completely all the great works and buildings which Fir'aun (Pharaoh) and his people erected.
8 الأنفال 46	وَأَطِيعُوا اللَّهَ وَرَسُولَهُ وَلَا تَنَازَعُوا فَتَفْشَلُوا وَتَذْهَبَ رِيحُكُمْ ۖ **وَاصْبِرُوا** ۚ إِنَّ اللَّهَ مَعَ الصَّابِرِينَ
H&K	And obey Allah and His Messenger, and do not dispute (with one another) lest you lose courage and your strength depart, and be patient. Surely, Allah is with those who are As-Sabirin (the patient ones, etc.).
10 يونس 109	وَاتَّبِعْ مَا يُوحَىٰ إِلَيْكَ **وَاصْبِرْ** حَتَّىٰ يَحْكُمَ اللَّهُ ۚ وَهُوَ خَيْرُ الْحَاكِمِينَ
H&K	And (O Muhammad SAW), follow the inspiration sent unto you, and be patient till Allah gives judgement. And He is the Best of judges.

11 هود 11	إِلَّا الَّذِينَ صَبَرُوا وَعَمِلُوا الصَّالِحَاتِ أُولَٰئِكَ لَهُم مَّغْفِرَةٌ وَأَجْرٌ كَبِيرٌ	
	H&K	Except those who show patience and do righteous good deeds, those: theirs will be forgiveness and a great reward (Paradise).
49	تِلْكَ مِنْ أَنبَاءِ الْغَيْبِ نُوحِيهَا إِلَيْكَ ۖ مَا كُنتَ تَعْلَمُهَا أَنتَ وَلَا قَوْمُكَ مِن قَبْلِ هَٰذَا ۖ فَاصْبِرْ ۖ إِنَّ الْعَاقِبَةَ لِلْمُتَّقِينَ	
	H&K	This is of the news of the unseen which We reveal unto you (O Muhammad SAW), neither you nor your people knew them before this. So be patient. Surely, the (good) end is for the Muttaqun (pious - see V. 2:2)
115	وَاصْبِرْ فَإِنَّ اللَّهَ لَا يُضِيعُ أَجْرَ الْمُحْسِنِينَ	
	H&K	And be patient; verily, Allah loses not the reward of the good-doers.
12 يوسف 18	وَجَاءُوا عَلَىٰ قَمِيصِهِ بِدَمٍ كَذِبٍ ۚ قَالَ بَلْ سَوَّلَتْ لَكُمْ أَنفُسُكُمْ أَمْرًا ۖ فَصَبْرٌ جَمِيلٌ ۖ وَاللَّهُ الْمُسْتَعَانُ عَلَىٰ مَا تَصِفُونَ	
	H&K	And they brought his shirt stained with false blood. He said: "Nay, but your ownselves have made up a tale. So (for me) patience is most fitting. And it is Allah (Alone) Whose help can be sought against that which you assert."
83	قَالَ بَلْ سَوَّلَتْ لَكُمْ أَنفُسُكُمْ أَمْرًا ۖ فَصَبْرٌ جَمِيلٌ ۖ عَسَى اللَّهُ أَن يَأْتِيَنِي بِهِمْ جَمِيعًا ۚ إِنَّهُ هُوَ الْعَلِيمُ الْحَكِيمُ	
	H&K	He [Ya'qub (Jacob)] said: "Nay, but your ownselves have beguiled you into something. So patience is most fitting (for me). May be Allah will bring them (back) all to me. Truly He! only He is All-Knowing, All-Wise."
90	قَالُوا أَإِنَّكَ لَأَنتَ يُوسُفُ ۖ قَالَ أَنَا يُوسُفُ وَهَٰذَا أَخِي ۖ قَدْ مَنَّ اللَّهُ عَلَيْنَا ۚ إِنَّهُ مَن يَتَّقِ وَيَصْبِرْ فَإِنَّ اللَّهَ لَا يُضِيعُ أَجْرَ الْمُحْسِنِينَ	
	H&K	They said: "Are you indeed Yusuf (Joseph)?" He said: "I am Yusuf (Joseph), and this is my brother (Benjamin). Allah has indeed been gracious to us. Verily, he who fears Allah with obedience to Him (by abstaining from sins and evil deeds, and by performing righteous good deeds), and is patient, then

		surely, Allah makes not the reward of the Muhsinun (good-doers - see V. 2:112) to be lost."
13 الرعد 22		وَالَّذِينَ **صَبَرُوا** ابْتِغَاءَ وَجْهِ رَبِّهِمْ وَأَقَامُوا الصَّلَاةَ وَأَنفَقُوا مِمَّا رَزَقْنَاهُمْ سِرًّا وَعَلَانِيَةً وَيَدْرَءُونَ بِالْحَسَنَةِ السَّيِّئَةَ أُولَٰئِكَ لَهُمْ عُقْبَى الدَّارِ
	H&K	And those who remain patient, seeking their Lord's Countenance, perform As-Salat (Iqamat-as-Salat), and spend out of that which We have bestowed on them, secretly and openly, and defend evil with good, for such there is a good end;
24		سَلَامٌ عَلَيْكُم بِمَا **صَبَرْتُمْ** ۚ فَنِعْمَ عُقْبَى الدَّارِ
	H&K	"Salamun 'Alaikum (peace be upon you) for that you persevered in patience! Excellent indeed is the final home!"
14 ابراهيم 12		وَمَا لَنَا أَلَّا نَتَوَكَّلَ عَلَى اللَّهِ وَقَدْ هَدَانَا سُبُلَنَا ۚ **وَلَنَصْبِرَنَّ** عَلَىٰ مَا آذَيْتُمُونَا ۚ وَعَلَى اللَّهِ فَلْيَتَوَكَّلِ الْمُتَوَكِّلُونَ
	H&K	"And why should we not put our trust in Allah while He indeed has guided us our ways. And we shall certainly bear with patience all the hurt you may cause us, and in Allah (Alone) let those who trust, put their trust."
21		وَبَرَزُوا لِلَّهِ جَمِيعًا فَقَالَ الضُّعَفَاءُ لِلَّذِينَ اسْتَكْبَرُوا إِنَّا كُنَّا لَكُمْ تَبَعًا فَهَلْ أَنتُم مُّغْنُونَ عَنَّا مِنْ عَذَابِ اللَّهِ مِن شَيْءٍ ۚ قَالُوا لَوْ هَدَانَا اللَّهُ لَهَدَيْنَاكُمْ ۖ سَوَاءٌ عَلَيْنَا أَجَزِعْنَا أَمْ **صَبَرْنَا** مَا لَنَا مِن مَّحِيصٍ
	H&K	And they all shall appear before Allah (on the Day of Resurrection) then the weak will say to those who were arrogant (chiefs): "Verily, we were following you; can you avail us anything from Allah's Torment?" They will say: "Had Allah guided us, we would have guided you. It makes no difference to us (now) whether we rage, or bear (these torments) with patience, there is no place of refuge for us."
16 النحل 42		الَّذِينَ **صَبَرُوا** وَعَلَىٰ رَبِّهِمْ يَتَوَكَّلُونَ
	H&K	(They are) those who remained patient (in this world for Allah's sake), and put their trust in their Lord (Allah Alone).
96		مَا عِندَكُمْ يَنفَدُ ۖ وَمَا عِندَ اللَّهِ بَاقٍ ۗ وَلَنَجْزِيَنَّ الَّذِينَ **صَبَرُوا** أَجْرَهُم بِأَحْسَنِ مَا كَانُوا يَعْمَلُونَ

H&K	Whatever is with you, will be exhausted, and whatever with Allah (of good deeds) will remain. And those who are patient, We will certainly pay them a reward in proportion to the best of what they used to do.
110	ثُمَّ إِنَّ رَبَّكَ لِلَّذِينَ هَاجَرُوا مِن بَعْدِ مَا فُتِنُوا ثُمَّ جَاهَدُوا وَصَبَرُوا إِنَّ رَبَّكَ مِن بَعْدِهَا لَغَفُورٌ رَّحِيمٌ
H&K	Then, verily! Your Lord for those who emigrated after they had been put to trials and thereafter strove hard and fought (for the Cause of Allah) and were patient, verily, your Lord afterward is, Oft-Forgiving, Most Merciful.
126	وَإِنْ عَاقَبْتُمْ فَعَاقِبُوا بِمِثْلِ مَا عُوقِبْتُم بِهِ ۖ وَلَئِن صَبَرْتُمْ لَهُوَ خَيْرٌ لِّلصَّابِرِينَ
H&K	And if you punish (your enemy, O you believers in the Oneness of Allah), then punish them with the like of that with which you were afflicted. But if you endure patiently, verily, it is better for As-Sabirin (the patient ones, etc.).
127	وَاصْبِرْ وَمَا صَبْرُكَ إِلَّا بِاللَّهِ ۚ وَلَا تَحْزَنْ عَلَيْهِمْ وَلَا تَكُ فِي ضَيْقٍ مِّمَّا يَمْكُرُونَ
H&K	And endure you patiently (O Muhammad SAW), your patience is not but from Allah. And grieve not over them (polytheists and pagans, etc.), and be not distressed because of what they plot.
18 الكهف 28	وَاصْبِرْ نَفْسَكَ مَعَ الَّذِينَ يَدْعُونَ رَبَّهُم بِالْغَدَاةِ وَالْعَشِيِّ يُرِيدُونَ وَجْهَهُ ۖ وَلَا تَعْدُ عَيْنَاكَ عَنْهُمْ تُرِيدُ زِينَةَ الْحَيَاةِ الدُّنْيَا ۖ وَلَا تُطِعْ مَنْ أَغْفَلْنَا قَلْبَهُ عَن ذِكْرِنَا وَاتَّبَعَ هَوَاهُ وَكَانَ أَمْرُهُ فُرُطًا
H&K	And keep yourself (O Muhammad SAW) patiently with those who call on their Lord (i.e. your companions who remember their Lord with glorification, praising in prayers, etc., and other righteous deeds, etc.) morning and afternoon, seeking His Face, and let not your eyes overlook them, desiring the pomp and glitter of the life of the world; and obey not him whose heart We have made heedless of Our Remembrance, one who follows his own lusts and whose affair (deeds) has been lost.
67	قَالَ إِنَّكَ لَن تَسْتَطِيعَ مَعِيَ صَبْرًا
H&K	He (Khidr) said: "Verily! You will not be able to have patience with me!
68	وَكَيْفَ تَصْبِرُ عَلَىٰ مَا لَمْ تُحِطْ بِهِ خُبْرًا
H&K	"And how can you have patience about a thing which you know not?"

72		قَالَ أَلَمْ أَقُلْ إِنَّكَ لَن تَسْتَطِيعَ مَعِيَ صَبْرًا
	H&K	He (Khidr) said: "Did I not tell you, that you would not be able to have patience with me?"
75		۞ قَالَ أَلَمْ أَقُل لَّكَ إِنَّكَ لَن تَسْتَطِيعَ مَعِيَ صَبْرًا
	H&K	(Khidr) said: "Did I not tell you that you can have no patience with me?"
78		قَالَ هَٰذَا فِرَاقُ بَيْنِي وَبَيْنِكَ ۚ سَأُنَبِّئُكَ بِتَأْوِيلِ مَا لَمْ تَسْتَطِع عَّلَيْهِ صَبْرًا
	H&K	(Khidr) said: "This is the parting between me and you, I will tell you the interpretation of (those) things over which you were unable to hold patience.
82		وَأَمَّا الْجِدَارُ فَكَانَ لِغُلَامَيْنِ يَتِيمَيْنِ فِي الْمَدِينَةِ وَكَانَ تَحْتَهُ كَنزٌ لَّهُمَا وَكَانَ أَبُوهُمَا صَالِحًا فَأَرَادَ رَبُّكَ أَن يَبْلُغَا أَشُدَّهُمَا وَيَسْتَخْرِجَا كَنزَهُمَا رَحْمَةً مِّن رَّبِّكَ ۚ وَمَا فَعَلْتُهُ عَنْ أَمْرِي ۚ ذَٰلِكَ تَأْوِيلُ مَا لَمْ تَسْطِع عَّلَيْهِ صَبْرًا
	H&K	"And as for the wall, it belonged to two orphan boys in the town; and there was under it a treasure belonging to them; and their father was a righteous man, and your Lord intended that they should attain their age of full strength and take out their treasure as a mercy from your Lord. And I did it not of my own accord. That is the interpretation of those (things) over which you could not hold patience."
20 طه 130		فَاصْبِرْ عَلَىٰ مَا يَقُولُونَ وَسَبِّحْ بِحَمْدِ رَبِّكَ قَبْلَ طُلُوعِ الشَّمْسِ وَقَبْلَ غُرُوبِهَا ۖ وَمِنْ آنَاءِ اللَّيْلِ فَسَبِّحْ وَأَطْرَافَ النَّهَارِ لَعَلَّكَ تَرْضَىٰ
	H&K	So bear patiently (O Muhammad SAW) what they say, and glorify the praises of your Lord before the rising of the sun, and before its setting, and during some of the hours of the night, and at the sides of the day (an indication for the five compulsory congregational prayers), that you may become pleased with the reward which Allah shall give you.
23 المؤمنون 111		إِنِّي جَزَيْتُهُمُ الْيَوْمَ بِمَا صَبَرُوا أَنَّهُمْ هُمُ الْفَائِزُونَ
	H&K	Verily! I have rewarded them this Day for their patience, they are indeed the ones that are successful.

25 الفرقان 20		وَمَا أَرْسَلْنَا قَبْلَكَ مِنَ الْمُرْسَلِينَ إِلَّا إِنَّهُمْ لَيَأْكُلُونَ الطَّعَامَ وَيَمْشُونَ فِي الْأَسْوَاقِ ۗ وَجَعَلْنَا بَعْضَكُمْ لِبَعْضٍ فِتْنَةً **أَتَصْبِرُونَ** ۗ وَكَانَ رَبُّكَ بَصِيرًا
	H&K	And We never sent before you (O Muhammad SAW) any of the Messengers but verily, they ate food and walked in the markets. And We have made some of you as a trial for others: will you have patience? And your Lord is Ever All-Seer (of everything).
42		إِنْ كَادَ لَيُضِلُّنَا عَنْ آلِهَتِنَا لَوْلَا أَنْ **صَبَرْنَا** عَلَيْهَا ۚ وَسَوْفَ يَعْلَمُونَ حِينَ يَرَوْنَ الْعَذَابَ مَنْ أَضَلُّ سَبِيلًا
	H&K	"He would have nearly misled us from our aliha (gods), had it not been that we were patient and constant in their worship!" And they will know when they see the torment, who it is that is most astray from the (Right) Path!
75		أُولَٰئِكَ يُجْزَوْنَ الْغُرْفَةَ بِمَا **صَبَرُوا** وَيُلَقَّوْنَ فِيهَا تَحِيَّةً وَسَلَامًا
	H&K	Those will be rewarded with the highest place (in Paradise) because of their patience. Therein they shall be met with greetings and the word of peace and respect.
28 القصص 54		أُولَٰئِكَ يُؤْتَوْنَ أَجْرَهُمْ مَرَّتَيْنِ بِمَا **صَبَرُوا** وَيَدْرَءُونَ بِالْحَسَنَةِ السَّيِّئَةَ وَمِمَّا رَزَقْنَاهُمْ يُنْفِقُونَ
	H&K	These will be given their reward twice over, because they are patient, and repel evil with good, and spend (in charity) out of what We have provided them.
29 العنكبوت 59		الَّذِينَ **صَبَرُوا** وَعَلَىٰ رَبِّهِمْ يَتَوَكَّلُونَ
	H&K	Those who are patient, and put their trust (only) in their Lord (Allah).
30 الروم 60		**فَاصْبِرْ** إِنَّ وَعْدَ اللَّهِ حَقٌّ ۖ وَلَا يَسْتَخِفَّنَّكَ الَّذِينَ لَا يُوقِنُونَ
	H&K	So be patient (O Muhammad SAW). Verily, the Promise of Allah is true, and let not those who have no certainty of faith, discourage you from conveying Allah's Message (which you are obliged to convey)

31 لقمان 17	يَا بُنَيَّ أَقِمِ الصَّلَاةَ وَأْمُرْ بِالْمَعْرُوفِ وَانْهَ عَنِ الْمُنكَرِ **وَاصْبِرْ** عَلَىٰ مَا أَصَابَكَ ۖ إِنَّ ذَٰلِكَ مِنْ عَزْمِ الْأُمُورِ
H&K	"O my son! Aqim-is-Salat (perform As-Salat), enjoin (people) for Al-Ma'ruf (Islamic Monotheism and all that is good), and forbid (people) from Al-Munkar (i.e. disbelief in the Oneness of Allah, polytheism of all kinds and all that is evil and bad), and bear with patience whatever befall you. Verily! These are some of the important commandments ordered by Allah with no exemption.
32 السجدة 24	وَجَعَلْنَا مِنْهُمْ أَئِمَّةً يَهْدُونَ بِأَمْرِنَا لَمَّا **صَبَرُوا** ۖ وَكَانُوا بِآيَاتِنَا يُوقِنُونَ
H&K	And We made from among them (Children of Israel), leaders, giving guidance under Our Command, when they were patient and used to believe with certainty in Our Ayat (proofs, evidences, verses, lessons, signs, revelations, etc.).
38 ص 6	وَانطَلَقَ الْمَلَأُ مِنْهُمْ أَنِ امْشُوا **وَاصْبِرُوا** عَلَىٰ آلِهَتِكُمْ ۖ إِنَّ هَٰذَا لَشَيْءٌ يُرَادُ
H&K	And the leaders among them went about (saying): "Go on, and remain constant to your aliha (gods)! Verily, This is a thing designed (against you)!
17	**اصْبِرْ** عَلَىٰ مَا يَقُولُونَ وَاذْكُرْ عَبْدَنَا دَاوُودَ ذَا الْأَيْدِ ۖ إِنَّهُ أَوَّابٌ
H&K	Be patient (O Muhammad SAW) of what they say, and remember Our slave Dawud (David), endued with power. Verily, he was ever oft-returning in all matters and in repentance (toward Allah).
40 غافر 55	**فَاصْبِرْ** إِنَّ وَعْدَ اللَّهِ حَقٌّ وَاسْتَغْفِرْ لِذَنبِكَ وَسَبِّحْ بِحَمْدِ رَبِّكَ بِالْعَشِيِّ وَالْإِبْكَارِ
H&K	So be patient (O Muhammad SAW). Verily, the Promise of Allah is true, and ask forgiveness for your fault, and glorify the praises of your Lord in the Ashi (i.e. the time period after the midnoon till sunset) and in the Ibkar (i.e. the time period from early morning or sunrise till before midnoon) [it is said that, that means the five compulsory congregational Salat (prayers) or the 'Asr and Fajr prayers].

77	فَاصْبِرْ إِنَّ وَعْدَ اللَّهِ حَقٌّ ۚ فَإِمَّا نُرِيَنَّكَ بَعْضَ الَّذِي نَعِدُهُمْ أَوْ نَتَوَفَّيَنَّكَ فَإِلَيْنَا يُرْجَعُونَ
H&K	So be patient (O Muhammad SAW), verily, the Promise of Allah is true, and whether We show you (O Muhammad SAW in this world) some part of what We have promised them, or We cause you to die, then it is to Us they all shall be returned.
41 فصلت 24	فَإِن يَصْبِرُوا فَالنَّارُ مَثْوًى لَّهُمْ ۖ وَإِن يَسْتَعْتِبُوا فَمَا هُم مِّنَ الْمُعْتَبِينَ
H&K	Then, if they have patience, yet the Fire will be a home for them, and if they beg for to be excused, yet they are not of those who will ever be excused.
42 الشورى 43	وَلَمَن صَبَرَ وَغَفَرَ إِنَّ ذَٰلِكَ لَمِنْ عَزْمِ الْأُمُورِ
H&K	And verily, whosoever shows patience and forgives that would truly be from the things recommended by Allah.
46 الأحقاف 35	فَاصْبِرْ كَمَا صَبَرَ أُولُو الْعَزْمِ مِنَ الرُّسُلِ وَلَا تَسْتَعْجِل لَّهُمْ ۚ كَأَنَّهُمْ يَوْمَ يَرَوْنَ مَا يُوعَدُونَ لَمْ يَلْبَثُوا إِلَّا سَاعَةً مِّن نَّهَارٍ ۚ بَلَاغٌ ۚ فَهَلْ يُهْلَكُ إِلَّا الْقَوْمُ الْفَاسِقُونَ
H&K	Therefore be patient (O Muhammad SAW) as did the Messengers of strong will and be in no haste about them (disbelievers). On the Day when they will see that (torment) with which they are promised (i.e. threatened, it will be) as if they had not stayed more than an hour in a single day. (O mankind! This Quran is sufficient as) a clear Message (or proclamation to save yourself from destruction). But shall any be destroyed except the people who are Al-Fasiqun (the rebellious, disobedient to Allah).
49 الحجرات 5	وَلَوْ أَنَّهُمْ صَبَرُوا حَتَّىٰ تَخْرُجَ إِلَيْهِمْ لَكَانَ خَيْرًا لَّهُمْ ۚ وَاللَّهُ غَفُورٌ رَّحِيمٌ
H&K	And if they had patience till you could come out to them, it would have been better for them. And Allah is Oft-Forgiving, Most Merciful.
50 ق 39	فَاصْبِرْ عَلَىٰ مَا يَقُولُونَ وَسَبِّحْ بِحَمْدِ رَبِّكَ قَبْلَ طُلُوعِ الشَّمْسِ وَقَبْلَ الْغُرُوبِ

H&K	So bear with patience (O Muhammad SAW) all that they say, and glorify the Praises of your Lord, before the rising of the sun and before (its) setting (i.e. the Fajr, Zuhr, and 'Asr prayers).	
52 الطور 16		اصْلَوْهَا فَاصْبِرُوا أَوْ لَا تَصْبِرُوا سَوَاءٌ عَلَيْكُمْ ۖ إِنَّمَا تُجْزَوْنَ مَا كُنتُمْ تَعْمَلُونَ
H&K	Taste you therein its heat, and whether you are patient of it or impatient of it, it is all the same. You are only being requited for what you used to do.	
48		وَاصْبِرْ لِحُكْمِ رَبِّكَ فَإِنَّكَ بِأَعْيُنِنَا ۖ وَسَبِّحْ بِحَمْدِ رَبِّكَ حِينَ تَقُومُ
H&K	So wait patiently (O Muhammad SAW) for the Decision of your Lord, for verily, you are under Our Eyes, and glorify the Praises of your Lord when you get up from sleep.	
68 القلم 48		فَاصْبِرْ لِحُكْمِ رَبِّكَ وَلَا تَكُن كَصَاحِبِ الْحُوتِ إِذْ نَادَىٰ وَهُوَ مَكْظُومٌ
H&K	So wait with patience for the Decision of your Lord, and be not like the Companion of the Fish, when he cried out (to Us) while he was in deep sorrow. (See the Quran, Verse 21:87).	
70 المعارج 5		فَاصْبِرْ صَبْرًا جَمِيلًا
H&K	So be patient (O Muhammad SAW), with a good patience.	
73 المزمل 10		وَاصْبِرْ عَلَىٰ مَا يَقُولُونَ وَاهْجُرْهُمْ هَجْرًا جَمِيلًا
H&K	And be patient (O Muhammad SAW) with what they say, and keep away from them in a good way.	
74 المدثر 7		وَلِرَبِّكَ فَاصْبِرْ

H&K	And be patient for the sake of your Lord (i.e. perform your duty to Allah)!
76 الانسان 12	وَجَزَاهُم بِمَا صَبَرُوا جَنَّةً وَحَرِيرًا
H&K	And their recompense shall be Paradise, and silken garments, because they were patient.
24	فَاصْبِرْ لِحُكْمِ رَبِّكَ وَلَا تُطِعْ مِنْهُمْ آثِمًا أَوْ كَفُورًا
H&K	Therefore be patient (O Muhammad SAW) and submit to the Command of your Lord (Allah, by doing your duty to Him and by conveying His Message to mankind), and obey neither a sinner nor a disbeliever among them.
90 البلد 17	ثُمَّ كَانَ مِنَ الَّذِينَ آمَنُوا وَتَوَاصَوْا بِالصَّبْرِ وَتَوَاصَوْا بِالْمَرْحَمَةِ
H&K	Then he became one of those who believed, and recommended one another to perseverance and patience, and (also) recommended one another to pity and compassion.
103 العصر 3	إِلَّا الَّذِينَ آمَنُوا وَعَمِلُوا الصَّالِحَاتِ وَتَوَاصَوْا بِالْحَقِّ وَتَوَاصَوْا بِالصَّبْرِ
H&K	Except those who believe (in Islamic Monotheism) and do righteous good deeds, and recommend one another to the truth (i.e. order one another to perform all kinds of good deeds (Al-Ma'ruf) which Allah has ordained, and abstain from all kinds of sins and evil deeds (Al-Munkar) which Allah has forbidden), and recommend one another to patience (for the sufferings, harms, and injuries which one may encounter in Allah's Cause during preaching His religion of Islamic Monotheism or Jihad, etc.).

	الْإِيمَانِ
2 البقرة 93	وَإِذْ أَخَذْنَا مِيثَاقَكُمْ وَرَفَعْنَا فَوْقَكُمُ الطُّورَ خُذُوا مَا آتَيْنَاكُم بِقُوَّةٍ وَاسْمَعُوا ۖ قَالُوا سَمِعْنَا وَعَصَيْنَا وَأُشْرِبُوا فِي قُلُوبِهِمُ الْعِجْلَ بِكُفْرِهِمْ ۚ قُلْ بِئْسَمَا يَأْمُرُكُم بِهِ إِيمَانُكُمْ إِن كُنتُم مُّؤْمِنِينَ
H&K	And (remember) when We took your covenant and We raised above you the Mount (saying), "Hold firmly to what We have given you and hear (Our Word). They said, "We have heard and disobeyed." And their hearts absorbed (the worship of) the calf because of their disbelief. Say: "Worst indeed is that which your faith enjoins on you if you are believers."
2 البقرة 108	أَمْ تُرِيدُونَ أَن تَسْأَلُوا رَسُولَكُمْ كَمَا سُئِلَ مُوسَىٰ مِن قَبْلُ ۗ وَمَن يَتَبَدَّلِ الْكُفْرَ بِالْإِيمَانِ فَقَدْ ضَلَّ سَوَاءَ السَّبِيلِ
H&K	Or do you want to ask your Messenger (Muhammad Peace be upon him) as Musa (Moses) was asked before (i.e. show us openly our Lord?) And he who changes Faith for disbelief, verily, he has gone astray from the right way.
109	وَدَّ كَثِيرٌ مِّنْ أَهْلِ الْكِتَابِ لَوْ يَرُدُّونَكُم مِّن بَعْدِ إِيمَانِكُمْ كُفَّارًا حَسَدًا مِّنْ عِندِ أَنفُسِهِم مِّن بَعْدِ مَا تَبَيَّنَ لَهُمُ الْحَقُّ ۖ فَاعْفُوا وَاصْفَحُوا حَتَّىٰ يَأْتِيَ اللَّهُ بِأَمْرِهِ ۗ إِنَّ اللَّهَ عَلَىٰ كُلِّ شَيْءٍ قَدِيرٌ
H&K	Many of the people of the Scripture (Jews and Christians) wish that if they could turn you away as disbelievers after you have believed, out of envy from their ownselves, even, after the truth (that Muhammad Peace be upon him is Allah's Messenger) has become manifest unto them. But forgive and overlook, till Allah brings His Command. Verily, Allah is Able to do all things.
143	وَكَذَٰلِكَ جَعَلْنَاكُمْ أُمَّةً وَسَطًا لِّتَكُونُوا شُهَدَاءَ عَلَى النَّاسِ وَيَكُونَ الرَّسُولُ عَلَيْكُمْ شَهِيدًا ۗ وَمَا جَعَلْنَا الْقِبْلَةَ الَّتِي كُنتَ عَلَيْهَا إِلَّا لِنَعْلَمَ مَن يَتَّبِعُ الرَّسُولَ مِمَّن يَنقَلِبُ عَلَىٰ عَقِبَيْهِ ۚ وَإِن كَانَتْ لَكَبِيرَةً إِلَّا عَلَى الَّذِينَ هَدَى اللَّهُ ۗ وَمَا كَانَ اللَّهُ لِيُضِيعَ إِيمَانَكُمْ ۚ إِنَّ اللَّهَ بِالنَّاسِ لَرَءُوفٌ رَّحِيمٌ
H&K	Thus We have made you [true Muslims - real believers of Islamic Monotheism, true followers of Prophet Muhammad SAW and his Sunnah (legal ways)], a Wasat (just) (and the best) nation, that you be witnesses over mankind and the Messenger (Muhammad SAW) be a witness over you. And We made the Qiblah (prayer direction towards Jerusalem) which you used to face, only to test those who followed the Messenger (Muhammad SAW) from those who would turn on their heels (i.e. disobey the Messenger). Indeed it was great (heavy) except for those whom Allah guided. And Allah would never make your faith (prayers) to be lost (i.e. your prayers offered towards

		Jerusalem). Truly, Allah is full of kindness, the Most Merciful towards mankind.
3 آل عمران 86		كَيْفَ يَهْدِي اللَّهُ قَوْمًا كَفَرُوا بَعْدَ **إِيمَانِهِمْ** وَشَهِدُوا أَنَّ الرَّسُولَ حَقٌّ وَجَاءَهُمُ الْبَيِّنَاتُ ۚ وَاللَّهُ لَا يَهْدِي الْقَوْمَ الظَّالِمِينَ
H&K		How shall Allah guide a people who disbelieved after their belief and after they bore witness that the Messenger (Muhammad SAW) is true and after clear proofs had come unto them? And Allah guides not the people who are Zalimun (polytheists and wrong-doers).
3 آل عمران 90		إِنَّ الَّذِينَ كَفَرُوا بَعْدَ **إِيمَانِهِمْ** ثُمَّ ازْدَادُوا كُفْرًا لَّن تُقْبَلَ تَوْبَتُهُمْ وَأُولَٰئِكَ هُمُ الضَّالُّونَ
H&K		Verily, those who disbelieved after their Belief and then went on increasing in their disbelief (i.e. disbelief in the Quran and in Prophet Muhammad SAW) - never will their repentance be accepted [because they repent only by their tongues and not from their hearts]. And they are those who are astray.
3 آل عمران 100		يَا أَيُّهَا الَّذِينَ آمَنُوا إِن تُطِيعُوا فَرِيقًا مِّنَ الَّذِينَ أُوتُوا الْكِتَابَ يَرُدُّوكُم بَعْدَ **إِيمَانِكُمْ** كَافِرِينَ
H&K		O you who believe! If you obey a group of those who were given the Scripture (Jews and Christians), they would (indeed) render you disbelievers after you have believed!
3 آل عمران 106		يَوْمَ تَبْيَضُّ وُجُوهٌ وَتَسْوَدُّ وُجُوهٌ ۚ فَأَمَّا الَّذِينَ اسْوَدَّتْ وُجُوهُهُمْ أَكَفَرْتُم بَعْدَ **إِيمَانِكُمْ** فَذُوقُوا الْعَذَابَ بِمَا كُنتُمْ تَكْفُرُونَ
H&K		On the Day (i.e. the Day of Resurrection) when some faces will become white and some faces will become black; as for those whose faces will become black (to them will be said): "Did you reject Faith after accepting it? Then taste the torment (in Hell) for rejecting Faith."
167		وَلِيَعْلَمَ الَّذِينَ نَافَقُوا ۚ وَقِيلَ لَهُمْ تَعَالَوْا قَاتِلُوا فِي سَبِيلِ اللَّهِ أَوِ ادْفَعُوا ۖ قَالُوا لَوْ نَعْلَمُ قِتَالًا لَّاتَّبَعْنَاكُمْ ۗ هُمْ لِلْكُفْرِ يَوْمَئِذٍ أَقْرَبُ مِنْهُمْ **لِلْإِيمَانِ** ۚ يَقُولُونَ بِأَفْوَاهِهِم مَّا لَيْسَ فِي قُلُوبِهِمْ ۗ وَاللَّهُ أَعْلَمُ بِمَا يَكْتُمُونَ
H&K		And that He might test the hypocrites, it was said to them: "Come, fight in the Way of Allah or (at least) defend yourselves." They said: "Had we known that fighting will take place, we would certainly have followed you." They were

	that day, nearer to disbelief than to Faith, saying with their mouths what was not in their hearts. And Allah has full knowledge of what they conceal.
173	الَّذِينَ قَالَ لَهُمُ النَّاسُ إِنَّ النَّاسَ قَدْ جَمَعُوا لَكُمْ فَاخْشَوْهُمْ فَزَادَهُمْ إِيمَانًا وَقَالُوا حَسْبُنَا اللَّهُ وَنِعْمَ الْوَكِيلُ
H&K	Those (i.e. believers) unto whom the people (hypocrites) said, "Verily, the people (pagans) have gathered against you (a great army), therefore, fear them." But it (only) increased them in Faith, and they said: "Allah (Alone) is Sufficient for us, and He is the Best Disposer of affairs (for us)."
3 آل عمران 177	إِنَّ الَّذِينَ اشْتَرَوُا الْكُفْرَ بِالْإِيمَانِ لَن يَضُرُّوا اللَّهَ شَيْئًا وَلَهُمْ عَذَابٌ أَلِيمٌ
H&K	Verily, those who purchase disbelief at the price of Faith, not the least harm will they do to Allah. For them, there is a painful torment.
193	رَّبَّنَا إِنَّنَا سَمِعْنَا مُنَادِيًا يُنَادِي لِلْإِيمَانِ أَنْ آمِنُوا بِرَبِّكُمْ فَآمَنَّا ۚ رَبَّنَا فَاغْفِرْ لَنَا ذُنُوبَنَا وَكَفِّرْ عَنَّا سَيِّئَاتِنَا وَتَوَفَّنَا مَعَ الْأَبْرَارِ
H&K	"Our Lord! Verily, we have heard the call of one (Muhammad SAW) calling to Faith: 'Believe in your Lord,' and we have believed. Our Lord! Forgive us our sins and remit from us our evil deeds, and make us die in the state of righteousness along with Al-Abrar (those who are obedient to Allah and follow strictly His Orders).
5 المائدة 5	الْيَوْمَ أُحِلَّ لَكُمُ الطَّيِّبَاتُ ۖ وَطَعَامُ الَّذِينَ أُوتُوا الْكِتَابَ حِلٌّ لَّكُمْ وَطَعَامُكُمْ حِلٌّ لَّهُمْ ۖ وَالْمُحْصَنَاتُ مِنَ الْمُؤْمِنَاتِ وَالْمُحْصَنَاتُ مِنَ الَّذِينَ أُوتُوا الْكِتَابَ مِن قَبْلِكُمْ إِذَا آتَيْتُمُوهُنَّ أُجُورَهُنَّ مُحْصِنِينَ غَيْرَ مُسَافِحِينَ وَلَا مُتَّخِذِي أَخْدَانٍ ۗ وَمَن يَكْفُرْ بِالْإِيمَانِ فَقَدْ حَبِطَ عَمَلُهُ وَهُوَ فِي الْآخِرَةِ مِنَ الْخَاسِرِينَ
H&K	Made lawful to you this day are At-Tayyibat [all kinds of Halal (lawful) foods, which Allah has made lawful (meat of slaughtered eatable animals, etc., milk products, fats, vegetables and fruits, etc.). The food (slaughtered cattle, eatable animals, etc.) of the people of the Scripture (Jews and Christians) is lawful to you and yours is lawful to them. (Lawful to you in marriage) are chaste women from the believers and chaste women from those who were given the Scripture (Jews and Christians) before your time, when you have given their due Mahr (bridal money given by the husband to his wife at the time of marriage), desiring chastity (i.e. taking them in legal wedlock) not committing illegal sexual intercourse, nor taking them as girl-friends. And whosoever

	disbelieves in the Oneness of Allah and in all the other Articles of Faith [i.e. His (Allah's), Angels, His Holy Books, His Messengers, the Day of Resurrection and Al-Qadar (Divine Preordainments)], then fruitless is his work, and in the Hereafter he will be among the losers.
6 الأنعام 82	الَّذِينَ آمَنُوا وَلَمْ يَلْبِسُوا إِيمَانَهُم بِظُلْمٍ أُولَٰئِكَ لَهُمُ الْأَمْنُ وَهُم مُّهْتَدُونَ
H&K	It is those who believe (in the Oneness of Allah and worship none but Him Alone) and confuse not their belief with Zulm (wrong i.e. by worshipping others besides Allah), for them (only) there is security and they are the guided.
158	هَلْ يَنظُرُونَ إِلَّا أَن تَأْتِيَهُمُ الْمَلَائِكَةُ أَوْ يَأْتِيَ رَبُّكَ أَوْ يَأْتِيَ بَعْضُ آيَاتِ رَبِّكَ ۗ يَوْمَ يَأْتِي بَعْضُ آيَاتِ رَبِّكَ لَا يَنفَعُ نَفْسًا إِيمَانُهَا لَمْ تَكُنْ آمَنَتْ مِن قَبْلُ أَوْ كَسَبَتْ فِي إِيمَانِهَا خَيْرًا ۗ قُلِ انتَظِرُوا إِنَّا مُنتَظِرُونَ
H&K	Do they then wait for anything other than that the angels should come to them, or that your Lord should come, or that some of the Signs of your Lord should come (i.e. portents of the Hour e.g., arising of the sun from the west)! The day that some of the Signs of your Lord do come, no good will it do to a person to believe then, if he believed not before, nor earned good (by performing deeds of righteousness) through his Faith. Say: "Wait you! we (too) are waiting."
8 الأنفال 2	إِنَّمَا الْمُؤْمِنُونَ الَّذِينَ إِذَا ذُكِرَ اللَّهُ وَجِلَتْ قُلُوبُهُمْ وَإِذَا تُلِيَتْ عَلَيْهِمْ آيَاتُهُ زَادَتْهُمْ إِيمَانًا وَعَلَىٰ رَبِّهِمْ يَتَوَكَّلُونَ
H&K	The believers are only those who, when Allah is mentioned, feel a fear in their hearts and when His Verses (this Quran) are recited unto them, they (i.e. the Verses) increase their Faith; and they put their trust in their Lord (Alone);
9 التوبة 23	يَا أَيُّهَا الَّذِينَ آمَنُوا لَا تَتَّخِذُوا آبَاءَكُمْ وَإِخْوَانَكُمْ أَوْلِيَاءَ إِنِ اسْتَحَبُّوا الْكُفْرَ عَلَى الْإِيمَانِ ۚ وَمَن يَتَوَلَّهُم مِّنكُمْ فَأُولَٰئِكَ هُمُ الظَّالِمُونَ
H&K	O you who believe! Take not for Auliya' (supporters and helpers) your fathers and your brothers if they prefer disbelief to Belief. And whoever of you does so, then he is one of the Zalimun (wrong-doers, etc.).
66	لَا تَعْتَذِرُوا قَدْ كَفَرْتُم بَعْدَ إِيمَانِكُمْ ۚ إِن نَّعْفُ عَن طَائِفَةٍ مِّنكُمْ نُعَذِّبْ طَائِفَةً بِأَنَّهُمْ كَانُوا مُجْرِمِينَ

H&K	Make no excuse; you have disbelieved after you had believed. If We pardon some of you, We will punish others amongst you because they were Mujrimun (disbelievers, polytheists, sinners, criminals, etc.).
124	وَإِذَا مَا أُنزِلَتْ سُورَةٌ فَمِنْهُم مَّن يَقُولُ أَيُّكُمْ زَادَتْهُ هَٰذِهِ إِيمَانًا ۚ فَأَمَّا الَّذِينَ آمَنُوا فَزَادَتْهُمْ إِيمَانًا وَهُمْ يَسْتَبْشِرُونَ
H&K	And whenever there comes down a Surah (chapter from the Quran), some of them (hypocrites) say: "Which of you has had his Faith increased by it?" As for those who believe, it has increased their Faith, and they rejoice.
10 يونس 9	إِنَّ الَّذِينَ آمَنُوا وَعَمِلُوا الصَّالِحَاتِ يَهْدِيهِمْ رَبُّهُم بِإِيمَانِهِمْ ۖ تَجْرِي مِن تَحْتِهِمُ الْأَنْهَارُ فِي جَنَّاتِ النَّعِيمِ
H&K	Verily, those who believe [in the Oneness of Allah along with the six articles of Faith, i.e. to believe in Allah, His Angels, His Books, His Messengers, Day of Resurrection, and Al-Qadar (Divine Preordainments) - Islamic Monotheism], and do deeds of righteousness, their Lord will guide them through their Faith; under them will flow rivers in the Gardens of delight (Paradise).
98	فَلَوْلَا كَانَتْ قَرْيَةٌ آمَنَتْ فَنَفَعَهَا إِيمَانُهَا إِلَّا قَوْمَ يُونُسَ لَمَّا آمَنُوا كَشَفْنَا عَنْهُمْ عَذَابَ الْخِزْيِ فِي الْحَيَاةِ الدُّنْيَا وَمَتَّعْنَاهُمْ إِلَىٰ حِينٍ
H&K	Was there any town (community) that believed (after seeing the punishment), and its Faith (at that moment) saved it (from the punishment)? (The answer is none,) - except the people of Yunus (Jonah); when they believed, We removed from them the torment of disgrace in the life of the (present) world, and permitted them to enjoy for a while.
16 النحل 106	مَن كَفَرَ بِاللَّهِ مِن بَعْدِ إِيمَانِهِ إِلَّا مَنْ أُكْرِهَ وَقَلْبُهُ مُطْمَئِنٌّ بِالْإِيمَانِ وَلَٰكِن مَّن شَرَحَ بِالْكُفْرِ صَدْرًا فَعَلَيْهِمْ غَضَبٌ مِّنَ اللَّهِ وَلَهُمْ عَذَابٌ عَظِيمٌ
H&K	Whoever disbelieved in Allah after his belief, except him who is forced thereto and whose heart is at rest with Faith but such as open their breasts to disbelief, on them is wrath from Allah, and theirs will be a great torment.
30 الروم 56	وَقَالَ الَّذِينَ أُوتُوا الْعِلْمَ وَالْإِيمَانَ لَقَدْ لَبِثْتُمْ فِي كِتَابِ اللَّهِ إِلَىٰ يَوْمِ الْبَعْثِ ۖ فَهَٰذَا يَوْمُ الْبَعْثِ وَلَٰكِنَّكُمْ كُنتُمْ لَا تَعْلَمُونَ

H&K	And those who have been bestowed with knowledge and faith will say: "Indeed you have stayed according to the Decree of Allah, until the Day of Resurrection, so this is the Day of Resurrection, but you knew not."
32 السجدة 29	قُلْ يَوْمَ الْفَتْحِ لَا يَنفَعُ الَّذِينَ كَفَرُوا إِيمَانُهُمْ وَلَا هُمْ يُنظَرُونَ
H&K	Say: "On the Day of Al-Fath (Decision), no profit will it be to those who disbelieve if they (then) believe! Nor will they be granted a respite."
33 الأحزاب 22	وَلَمَّا رَأَى الْمُؤْمِنُونَ الْأَحْزَابَ قَالُوا هَٰذَا مَا وَعَدَنَا اللَّهُ وَرَسُولُهُ وَصَدَقَ اللَّهُ وَرَسُولُهُ ۚ وَمَا زَادَهُمْ إِلَّا إِيمَانًا وَتَسْلِيمًا
H&K	And when the believers saw AlAhzab (the Confederates), they said: "This is what Allah and His Messenger (Muhammad SAW) had promised us, and Allah and His Messenger (Muhammad SAW) had spoken the truth, and it only added to their faith and to their submissiveness (to Allah).
40 غافر 10	إِنَّ الَّذِينَ كَفَرُوا يُنَادَوْنَ لَمَقْتُ اللَّهِ أَكْبَرُ مِن مَّقْتِكُمْ أَنفُسَكُمْ إِذْ تُدْعَوْنَ إِلَى الْإِيمَانِ فَتَكْفُرُونَ
H&K	Those who disbelieve will be addressed (at the time of entering into the Fire): "Allah's aversion was greater towards you (in the worldly life when you used to reject the Faith) than your aversion towards one another (now in the Fire of Hell, as you are now enemies to one another), when you were called to the Faith but you used to refuse."
28	وَقَالَ رَجُلٌ مُّؤْمِنٌ مِّنْ آلِ فِرْعَوْنَ يَكْتُمُ إِيمَانَهُ أَتَقْتُلُونَ رَجُلًا أَن يَقُولَ رَبِّيَ اللَّهُ وَقَدْ جَاءَكُم بِالْبَيِّنَاتِ مِن رَّبِّكُمْ ۖ وَإِن يَكُ كَاذِبًا فَعَلَيْهِ كَذِبُهُ ۖ وَإِن يَكُ صَادِقًا يُصِبْكُم بَعْضُ الَّذِي يَعِدُكُمْ ۖ إِنَّ اللَّهَ لَا يَهْدِي مَنْ هُوَ مُسْرِفٌ كَذَّابٌ
H&K	And a believing man of Fir'aun's (Pharaoh) family, who hid his faith said: "Would you kill a man because he says: My Lord is Allah, and he has come to you with clear signs (proofs) from your Lord? And if he is a liar, upon him will be (the sin of) his lie; but if he is telling the truth, then some of that (calamity) wherewith he threatens you will befall on you." Verily, Allah guides not one who is a Musrif (a polytheist, or a murderer who shed blood without a right, or those who commit great sins, oppressor, transgressor), a liar!

85	فَلَمْ يَكُ يَنفَعُهُمْ إِيمَانُهُمْ لَمَّا رَأَوْا بَأْسَنَا ۖ سُنَّتَ اللَّهِ الَّتِي قَدْ خَلَتْ فِي عِبَادِهِ ۖ وَخَسِرَ هُنَالِكَ الْكَافِرُونَ
H&K	Then their Faith (in Islamic Monotheism) could not avail them when they saw Our punishment. (Like) this has been the way of Allah in dealing with His slaves. And there the disbelievers lost utterly (when Our Torment covered them).
42 الشورى 52	وَكَذَٰلِكَ أَوْحَيْنَا إِلَيْكَ رُوحًا مِّنْ أَمْرِنَا ۚ مَا كُنتَ تَدْرِي مَا الْكِتَابُ وَلَا الْإِيمَانُ وَلَٰكِن جَعَلْنَاهُ نُورًا نَّهْدِي بِهِ مَن نَّشَاءُ مِنْ عِبَادِنَا ۚ وَإِنَّكَ لَتَهْدِي إِلَىٰ صِرَاطٍ مُّسْتَقِيمٍ
H&K	And thus We have sent to you (O Muhammad SAW) Ruhan (an Inspiration, and a Mercy) of Our Command. You knew not what is the Book, nor what is Faith? But We have made it (this Quran) a light wherewith We guide whosoever of Our slaves We will. And verily, you (O Muhammad SAW) are indeed guiding (mankind) to the Straight Path (i.e. Allah's religion of Islamic Monotheism).
48 الفتح 4	هُوَ الَّذِي أَنزَلَ السَّكِينَةَ فِي قُلُوبِ الْمُؤْمِنِينَ لِيَزْدَادُوا إِيمَانًا مَّعَ إِيمَانِهِمْ ۗ وَلِلَّهِ جُنُودُ السَّمَاوَاتِ وَالْأَرْضِ ۚ وَكَانَ اللَّهُ عَلِيمًا حَكِيمًا
H&K	He it is Who sent down As-Sakinah (calmness and tranquillity) into the hearts of the believers, that they may grow more in Faith along with their (present) Faith. And to Allah belong the hosts of the heavens and the earth, and Allah is Ever All-Knower, All-Wise.
49 الحجرات 7	وَاعْلَمُوا أَنَّ فِيكُمْ رَسُولَ اللَّهِ ۚ لَوْ يُطِيعُكُمْ فِي كَثِيرٍ مِّنَ الْأَمْرِ لَعَنِتُّمْ وَلَٰكِنَّ اللَّهَ حَبَّبَ إِلَيْكُمُ الْإِيمَانَ وَزَيَّنَهُ فِي قُلُوبِكُمْ وَكَرَّهَ إِلَيْكُمُ الْكُفْرَ وَالْفُسُوقَ وَالْعِصْيَانَ ۚ أُولَٰئِكَ هُمُ الرَّاشِدُونَ
H&K	And know that, among you there is the Messenger of Allah (SAW). If he were to obey you (i.e. follow your opinions and desires) in much of the matter, you would surely be in trouble, but Allah has endeared the Faith to you and has beautified it in your hearts, and has made disbelief, wickedness and disobedience (to Allah and His Messenger SAW) hateful to you. These! They are the rightly guided ones,

49 الحجرات 11	يَا أَيُّهَا الَّذِينَ آمَنُوا لَا يَسْخَرْ قَوْمٌ مِّن قَوْمٍ عَسَىٰ أَن يَكُونُوا خَيْرًا مِّنْهُمْ وَلَا نِسَاءٌ مِّن نِّسَاءٍ عَسَىٰ أَن يَكُنَّ خَيْرًا مِّنْهُنَّ ۖ وَلَا تَلْمِزُوا أَنفُسَكُمْ وَلَا تَنَابَزُوا بِالْأَلْقَابِ ۖ بِئْسَ الِاسْمُ الْفُسُوقُ بَعْدَ **الْإِيمَانِ** ۚ وَمَن لَّمْ يَتُبْ فَأُولَٰئِكَ هُمُ الظَّالِمُونَ	
H&K	O you who believe! Let not a group scoff at another group, it may be that the latter are better than the former; nor let (some) women scoff at other women, it may be that the latter are better than the former, nor defame one another, nor insult one another by nicknames. How bad is it, to insult one's brother after having Faith [i.e. to call your Muslim brother (a faithful believer) as: "O sinner", or "O wicked", etc.]. And whosoever does not repent, then such are indeed Zalimun (wrong-doers, etc.).	
49 الحجرات 14	۞ قَالَتِ الْأَعْرَابُ آمَنَّا ۖ قُل لَّمْ تُؤْمِنُوا وَلَٰكِن قُولُوا أَسْلَمْنَا وَلَمَّا يَدْخُلِ **الْإِيمَانُ** فِي قُلُوبِكُمْ ۖ وَإِن تُطِيعُوا اللَّهَ وَرَسُولَهُ لَا يَلِتْكُم مِّنْ أَعْمَالِكُمْ شَيْئًا ۚ إِنَّ اللَّهَ غَفُورٌ رَّحِيمٌ	
H&K	The bedouins say: "We believe." Say: "You believe not but you only say, 'We have surrendered (in Islam),' for Faith has not yet entered your hearts. But if you obey Allah and His Messenger (SAW), He will not decrease anything in reward for your deeds. Verily, Allah is Oft-Forgiving, Most Merciful."	
17	يَمُنُّونَ عَلَيْكَ أَنْ أَسْلَمُوا ۖ قُل لَّا تَمُنُّوا عَلَيَّ إِسْلَامَكُم ۖ بَلِ اللَّهُ يَمُنُّ عَلَيْكُمْ أَنْ هَدَاكُمْ **لِلْإِيمَانِ** إِن كُنتُمْ صَادِقِينَ	
H&K	They regard as favour upon you (O Muhammad SAW) that they have embraced Islam. Say: "Count not your Islam as a favour upon me. Nay, but Allah has conferred a favour upon you, that He has guided you to the Faith, if you indeed are true.	
52 الطور 21	وَالَّذِينَ آمَنُوا وَاتَّبَعَتْهُمْ ذُرِّيَّتُهُم **بِإِيمَانٍ** أَلْحَقْنَا بِهِمْ ذُرِّيَّتَهُمْ وَمَا أَلَتْنَاهُم مِّنْ عَمَلِهِم مِّن شَيْءٍ ۚ كُلُّ امْرِئٍ بِمَا كَسَبَ رَهِينٌ	
H&K	And those who believe and whose offspring follow them in Faith, to them shall We join their offspring, and We shall not decrease the reward of their deeds in anything. Every person is a pledge for that which he has earned.	
58 المجادلة 22	لَا تَجِدُ قَوْمًا يُؤْمِنُونَ بِاللَّهِ وَالْيَوْمِ الْآخِرِ يُوَادُّونَ مَنْ حَادَّ اللَّهَ وَرَسُولَهُ وَلَوْ كَانُوا آبَاءَهُمْ أَوْ أَبْنَاءَهُمْ أَوْ إِخْوَانَهُمْ أَوْ عَشِيرَتَهُمْ ۚ أُولَٰئِكَ كَتَبَ فِي قُلُوبِهِمُ **الْإِيمَانَ** وَأَيَّدَهُم بِرُوحٍ مِّنْهُ ۖ وَيُدْخِلُهُمْ جَنَّاتٍ تَجْرِي	

		مِن تَحْتِهَا الْأَنْهَارُ خَالِدِينَ فِيهَا ۚ رَضِيَ اللَّهُ عَنْهُمْ وَرَضُوا عَنْهُ ۚ أُولَٰئِكَ حِزْبُ اللَّهِ ۚ أَلَا إِنَّ حِزْبَ اللَّهِ هُمُ الْمُفْلِحُونَ
H&K		You (O Muhammad SAW) will not find any people who believe in Allah and the Last Day, making friendship with those who oppose Allah and His Messenger (Muhammad SAW), even though they were their fathers, or their sons, or their brothers, or their kindred (people). For such He has written Faith in their hearts, and strengthened them with Ruh (proofs, light and true guidance) from Himself. And We will admit them to Gardens (Paradise) under which rivers flow, to dwell therein (forever). Allah is pleased with them, and they with Him. They are the Party of Allah. Verily, it is the Party of Allah that will be the successful.
59 الحشر 9		وَالَّذِينَ تَبَوَّءُوا الدَّارَ **وَالْإِيمَانَ** مِن قَبْلِهِمْ يُحِبُّونَ مَنْ هَاجَرَ إِلَيْهِمْ وَلَا يَجِدُونَ فِي صُدُورِهِمْ حَاجَةً مِّمَّا أُوتُوا وَيُؤْثِرُونَ عَلَىٰ أَنفُسِهِمْ وَلَوْ كَانَ بِهِمْ خَصَاصَةٌ ۚ وَمَن يُوقَ شُحَّ نَفْسِهِ فَأُولَٰئِكَ هُمُ الْمُفْلِحُونَ
H&K		And those who, before them, had homes (in Al-Madinah) and had adopted the Faith, love those who emigrate to them, and have no jealousy in their breasts for that which they have been given (from the booty of Bani An-Nadir), and give them (emigrants) preference over themselves, even though they were in need of that. And whosoever is saved from his own covetousness, such are they who will be the successful.
10		وَالَّذِينَ جَاءُوا مِن بَعْدِهِمْ يَقُولُونَ رَبَّنَا اغْفِرْ لَنَا وَلِإِخْوَانِنَا الَّذِينَ سَبَقُونَا **بِالْإِيمَانِ** وَلَا تَجْعَلْ فِي قُلُوبِنَا غِلًّا لِّلَّذِينَ آمَنُوا رَبَّنَا إِنَّكَ رَءُوفٌ رَّحِيمٌ
H&K		And those who came after them say: "Our Lord! Forgive us and our brethren who have preceded us in Faith, and put not in our hearts any hatred against those who have believed. Our Lord! You are indeed full of kindness, Most Merciful.
60 الممتحنة 10		يَا أَيُّهَا الَّذِينَ آمَنُوا إِذَا جَاءَكُمُ الْمُؤْمِنَاتُ مُهَاجِرَاتٍ فَامْتَحِنُوهُنَّ ۖ اللَّهُ أَعْلَمُ **بِإِيمَانِهِنَّ** ۖ فَإِنْ عَلِمْتُمُوهُنَّ مُؤْمِنَاتٍ فَلَا تَرْجِعُوهُنَّ إِلَى الْكُفَّارِ ۖ لَا هُنَّ حِلٌّ لَّهُمْ وَلَا هُمْ يَحِلُّونَ لَهُنَّ ۖ وَآتُوهُم مَّا أَنفَقُوا ۚ وَلَا جُنَاحَ عَلَيْكُمْ أَن تَنكِحُوهُنَّ إِذَا آتَيْتُمُوهُنَّ أُجُورَهُنَّ ۚ وَلَا تُمْسِكُوا بِعِصَمِ الْكَوَافِرِ وَاسْأَلُوا مَا أَنفَقْتُمْ وَلْيَسْأَلُوا مَا أَنفَقُوا ۚ ذَٰلِكُمْ حُكْمُ اللَّهِ ۖ يَحْكُمُ بَيْنَكُمْ ۚ وَاللَّهُ عَلِيمٌ حَكِيمٌ
H&K		O you who believe! When believing women come to you as emigrants, examine them, Allah knows best as to their Faith, then if you ascertain that they are true believers, send them not back to the disbelievers, they are not lawful (wives) for the disbelievers nor are the disbelievers lawful (husbands) for them. But give the disbelievers that (amount of money) which they have spent [as their Mahr] to them. And there will be no sin on you to marry them if

	you have paid their Mahr to them. Likewise hold not the disbelieving women as wives, and ask for (the return of) that which you have spent (as Mahr) and let them (the disbelievers, etc.) ask back for that which they have spent. That is the Judgement of Allah. He judges between you. And Allah is All-Knowing, All-Wise.
74 المدثر 31	وَمَا جَعَلْنَا أَصْحَابَ النَّارِ إِلَّا مَلَائِكَةً ۙ وَمَا جَعَلْنَا عِدَّتَهُمْ إِلَّا فِتْنَةً لِّلَّذِينَ كَفَرُوا لِيَسْتَيْقِنَ الَّذِينَ أُوتُوا الْكِتَابَ وَيَزْدَادَ الَّذِينَ آمَنُوا إِيمَانًا ۙ وَلَا يَرْتَابَ الَّذِينَ أُوتُوا الْكِتَابَ وَالْمُؤْمِنُونَ ۙ وَلِيَقُولَ الَّذِينَ فِي قُلُوبِهِم مَّرَضٌ وَالْكَافِرُونَ مَاذَا أَرَادَ اللَّهُ بِهَٰذَا مَثَلًا ۚ كَذَٰلِكَ يُضِلُّ اللَّهُ مَن يَشَاءُ وَيَهْدِي مَن يَشَاءُ ۚ وَمَا يَعْلَمُ جُنُودَ رَبِّكَ إِلَّا هُوَ ۚ وَمَا هِيَ إِلَّا ذِكْرَىٰ لِلْبَشَرِ
H&K	And We have set none but angels as guardians of the Fire, and We have fixed their number (19) only as a trial for the disbelievers, in order that the people of the Scripture (Jews and Christians) may arrive at a certainty [that this Quran is the truth as it agrees with their Books i.e. their number (19) is written in the Taurat (Torah) and the Injeel (Gospel)] and the believers may increase in Faith (as this Quran is the truth) and that no doubts may be left for the people of the Scripture and the believers, and that those in whose hearts is a disease (of hypocrisy) and the disbelievers may say: "What Allah intends by this (curious) example?" Thus Allah leads astray whom He wills and guides whom He wills. And none can know the hosts of your Lord but He. And this (Hell) is nothing else than a (warning) reminder to mankind.

أَيْمَانِكُمْ/ أَيْمَانَكُمْ/الْأَيْمَانَ

2 البقرة 224	وَلَا تَجْعَلُوا اللَّهَ عُرْضَةً لِّأَيْمَانِكُمْ أَن تَبَرُّوا وَتَتَّقُوا وَتُصْلِحُوا بَيْنَ النَّاسِ ۗ وَاللَّهُ سَمِيعٌ عَلِيمٌ
H&K	And make not Allah's (Name) an excuse in your oaths against your doing good and acting piously, and making peace among mankind. And Allah is All-Hearer, All-Knower (i.e. do not swear much and if you have sworn against doing something good then give an expiation for the oath and do good).
225	لَّا يُؤَاخِذُكُمُ اللَّهُ بِاللَّغْوِ فِي أَيْمَانِكُمْ وَلَٰكِن يُؤَاخِذُكُم بِمَا كَسَبَتْ قُلُوبُكُمْ ۗ وَاللَّهُ غَفُورٌ حَلِيمٌ
H&K	Allah will not call you to account for that which is unintentional in your oaths, but He will call you to account for that which your hearts have earned. And Allah is Oft-Forgiving, Most-Forbearing.
3 آل عمران 77	إِنَّ الَّذِينَ يَشْتَرُونَ بِعَهْدِ اللَّهِ وَأَيْمَانِهِمْ ثَمَنًا قَلِيلًا أُولَٰئِكَ لَا خَلَاقَ لَهُمْ فِي الْآخِرَةِ وَلَا يُكَلِّمُهُمُ اللَّهُ وَلَا يَنظُرُ إِلَيْهِمْ يَوْمَ الْقِيَامَةِ وَلَا يُزَكِّيهِمْ وَلَهُمْ عَذَابٌ أَلِيمٌ

	H&K	Verily, those who purchase a small gain at the cost of Allah's Covenant and their oaths, they shall have no portion in the Hereafter (Paradise). Neither will Allah speak to them, nor look at them on the Day of Resurrection, nor will He purify them, and they shall have a painful torment.
4 النساء 3	*	وَإِنْ خِفْتُمْ أَلَّا تُقْسِطُوا فِي الْيَتَامَىٰ فَانكِحُوا مَا طَابَ لَكُم مِّنَ النِّسَاءِ مَثْنَىٰ وَثُلَاثَ وَرُبَاعَ ۖ فَإِنْ خِفْتُمْ أَلَّا تَعْدِلُوا فَوَاحِدَةً أَوْ مَا مَلَكَتْ أَيْمَانُكُمْ ۚ ذَٰلِكَ أَدْنَىٰ أَلَّا تَعُولُوا
	H&K	And if you fear that you shall not be able to deal justly with the orphan-girls, then marry (other) women of your choice, two or three, or four but if you fear that you shall not be able to deal justly (with them), then only one or (the captives and the slaves) that your **right hands possess**. That is nearer to prevent you from doing injustice.
24	*	۞ وَالْمُحْصَنَاتُ مِنَ النِّسَاءِ إِلَّا مَا مَلَكَتْ أَيْمَانُكُمْ ۖ كِتَابَ اللَّهِ عَلَيْكُمْ ۚ وَأُحِلَّ لَكُم مَّا وَرَاءَ ذَٰلِكُمْ أَن تَبْتَغُوا بِأَمْوَالِكُم مُّحْصِنِينَ غَيْرَ مُسَافِحِينَ ۚ فَمَا اسْتَمْتَعْتُم بِهِ مِنْهُنَّ فَآتُوهُنَّ أُجُورَهُنَّ فَرِيضَةً ۚ وَلَا جُنَاحَ عَلَيْكُمْ فِيمَا تَرَاضَيْتُم بِهِ مِن بَعْدِ الْفَرِيضَةِ ۚ إِنَّ اللَّهَ كَانَ عَلِيمًا حَكِيمًا
	H&K	Also (forbidden are) women already married, except those (captives and slaves) whom **your right hands possess**. Thus has Allah ordained for you. All others are lawful, provided you seek (them in marriage) with Mahr (bridal money given by the husband to his wife at the time of marriage) from your property, desiring chastity, not committing illegal sexual intercourse, so with those of whom you have enjoyed sexual relations, give them their Mahr as prescribed; but if after a Mahr is prescribed, you agree mutually (to give more), there is no sin on you. Surely, Allah is Ever All-Knowing, All-Wise.
25	*	وَمَن لَّمْ يَسْتَطِعْ مِنكُمْ طَوْلًا أَن يَنكِحَ الْمُحْصَنَاتِ الْمُؤْمِنَاتِ فَمِن مَّا مَلَكَتْ أَيْمَانُكُم مِّن فَتَيَاتِكُمُ الْمُؤْمِنَاتِ ۚ وَاللَّهُ أَعْلَمُ بِإِيمَانِكُم ۚ بَعْضُكُم مِّن بَعْضٍ ۚ فَانكِحُوهُنَّ بِإِذْنِ أَهْلِهِنَّ وَآتُوهُنَّ أُجُورَهُنَّ بِالْمَعْرُوفِ مُحْصَنَاتٍ غَيْرَ مُسَافِحَاتٍ وَلَا مُتَّخِذَاتِ أَخْدَانٍ ۚ فَإِذَا أُحْصِنَّ فَإِنْ أَتَيْنَ بِفَاحِشَةٍ فَعَلَيْهِنَّ نِصْفُ مَا عَلَى الْمُحْصَنَاتِ مِنَ الْعَذَابِ ۚ ذَٰلِكَ لِمَنْ خَشِيَ الْعَنَتَ مِنكُمْ ۚ وَأَن تَصْبِرُوا خَيْرٌ لَّكُمْ ۗ وَاللَّهُ غَفُورٌ رَّحِيمٌ
	H&K	And whoever of you have not the means wherewith to wed free, believing women, they may wed believing girls from among those (captives and slaves) whom **your right hands possess**, and Allah has full knowledge about your Faith, you are one from another. Wed them with the permission of their own folk (guardians, Auliya' or masters) and give them their Mahr according to what is reasonable; they (the above said captive and slave-girls) should be chaste, not adulterous, nor taking boy-friends. And after they have been taken in wedlock, if they commit illegal sexual intercourse, their punishment is half that for free (unmarried) women. This is for him among you who is afraid of

		being harmed in his religion or in his body; but it is better for you that you practise self-restraint, and Allah is Oft-Forgiving, Most Merciful.
	33	وَلِكُلٍّ جَعَلْنَا مَوَالِيَ مِمَّا تَرَكَ الْوَالِدَانِ وَالْأَقْرَبُونَ ۚ وَالَّذِينَ عَقَدَتْ **أَيْمَانُكُمْ** فَآتُوهُمْ نَصِيبَهُمْ ۚ إِنَّ اللَّهَ كَانَ عَلَىٰ كُلِّ شَيْءٍ شَهِيدًا
	H&K	And to everyone, We have appointed heirs of that (property) left by parents and relatives. To those also with whom you have made a pledge (brotherhood), give them their due portion (by Wasiya - wills, etc.). Truly, Allah is Ever a Witness over all things.
	36 *	۞ وَاعْبُدُوا اللَّهَ وَلَا تُشْرِكُوا بِهِ شَيْئًا ۖ وَبِالْوَالِدَيْنِ إِحْسَانًا وَبِذِي الْقُرْبَىٰ وَالْيَتَامَىٰ وَالْمَسَاكِينِ وَالْجَارِ ذِي الْقُرْبَىٰ وَالْجَارِ الْجُنُبِ وَالصَّاحِبِ بِالْجَنْبِ وَابْنِ السَّبِيلِ وَمَا مَلَكَتْ **أَيْمَانُكُمْ** ۗ إِنَّ اللَّهَ لَا يُحِبُّ مَن كَانَ مُخْتَالًا فَخُورًا
	H&K	Worship Allah and join none with Him in worship, and do good to parents, kinsfolk, orphans, Al-Masakin (the poor), the neighbour who is near of kin, the neighbour who is a stranger, the companion by your side, the wayfarer (you meet), and those (slaves) whom your right hands possess. Verily, Allah does not like such as are proud and boastful;
5 المائدة	53	وَيَقُولُ الَّذِينَ آمَنُوا أَهَٰؤُلَاءِ الَّذِينَ أَقْسَمُوا بِاللَّهِ جَهْدَ **أَيْمَانِهِمْ** ۙ إِنَّهُمْ لَمَعَكُمْ ۚ حَبِطَتْ أَعْمَالُهُمْ فَأَصْبَحُوا خَاسِرِينَ
	H&K	And those who believe will say: "Are these the men (hypocrites) who swore their strongest oaths by Allah that they were with you (Muslims)?" All that they did has been in vain (because of their hypocrisy), and they have become the losers.
5 المائدة	89	لَا يُؤَاخِذُكُمُ اللَّهُ بِاللَّغْوِ فِي **أَيْمَانِكُمْ** وَلَٰكِن يُؤَاخِذُكُم بِمَا عَقَّدتُّمُ **الْأَيْمَانَ** ۖ فَكَفَّارَتُهُ إِطْعَامُ عَشَرَةِ مَسَاكِينَ مِنْ أَوْسَطِ مَا تُطْعِمُونَ أَهْلِيكُمْ أَوْ كِسْوَتُهُمْ أَوْ تَحْرِيرُ رَقَبَةٍ ۖ فَمَن لَّمْ يَجِدْ فَصِيَامُ ثَلَاثَةِ أَيَّامٍ ۚ ذَٰلِكَ كَفَّارَةُ **أَيْمَانِكُمْ** إِذَا حَلَفْتُمْ ۚ وَاحْفَظُوا **أَيْمَانَكُمْ** ۚ كَذَٰلِكَ يُبَيِّنُ اللَّهُ لَكُمْ آيَاتِهِ لَعَلَّكُمْ تَشْكُرُونَ
	H&K	Allah will not punish you for what is unintentional in your oaths, but He will punish you for your deliberate oaths; for its expiation (a deliberate oath) feed ten Masakin (poor persons), on a scale of the average of that with which you feed your own families; or clothe them; or manumit a slave. But whosoever cannot afford (that), then he should fast for three days. That is the expiation for the oaths when you have sworn. And protect your oaths (i.e. do not swear much). Thus Allah make clear to you His Ayat (proofs, evidences, verses, lessons, signs, revelations, etc.) that you may be grateful.

108	ذَٰلِكَ أَدْنَىٰ أَن يَأْتُوا بِالشَّهَادَةِ عَلَىٰ وَجْهِهَا أَوْ يَخَافُوا أَن تُرَدَّ **أَيْمَانٌ** بَعْدَ **أَيْمَانِهِمْ** ۗ وَاتَّقُوا اللَّهَ وَاسْمَعُوا ۗ وَاللَّهُ لَا يَهْدِي الْقَوْمَ الْفَاسِقِينَ
H&K	That should make it closer (to the fact) that their testimony would be in its true nature and shape (and thus accepted), or else they would fear that (other) oaths would be admitted after their oaths. And fear Allah and listen (with obedience to Him). And Allah guides not the people who are Al-Fasiqun (the rebellious and disobedient).
6 الأنعام 109	وَأَقْسَمُوا بِاللَّهِ جَهْدَ **أَيْمَانِهِمْ** لَئِن جَاءَتْهُمْ آيَةٌ لَّيُؤْمِنُنَّ بِهَا ۚ قُلْ إِنَّمَا الْآيَاتُ عِندَ اللَّهِ ۖ وَمَا يُشْعِرُكُمْ أَنَّهَا إِذَا جَاءَتْ لَا يُؤْمِنُونَ
H&K	And they swear their strongest oaths by Allah, that if there came to them a sign, they would surely believe therein. Say: "Signs are but with Allah and what will make you (Muslims) perceive that (even) if it (the sign) came, they will not believe?"
7 الأعراف 17 *	ثُمَّ لَآتِيَنَّهُم مِّن بَيْنِ أَيْدِيهِمْ وَمِنْ خَلْفِهِمْ وَعَنْ **أَيْمَانِهِمْ** وَعَن شَمَائِلِهِمْ ۖ وَلَا تَجِدُ أَكْثَرَهُمْ شَاكِرِينَ
H&K	Then I will come to them from before them and behind them, from their right and from their left, and You will not find most of them as thankful ones (i.e. they will not be dutiful to You)."
9 التوبة 12	وَإِن نَّكَثُوا **أَيْمَانَهُم** مِّن بَعْدِ عَهْدِهِمْ وَطَعَنُوا فِي دِينِكُمْ فَقَاتِلُوا أَئِمَّةَ الْكُفْرِ ۙ إِنَّهُمْ لَا **أَيْمَانَ** لَهُمْ لَعَلَّهُمْ يَنتَهُونَ
H&K	But if they violate their oaths after their covenant, and attack your religion with disapproval and criticism then fight (you) the leaders of disbelief (chiefs of Quraish - pagans of Makkah) - for surely their oaths are nothing to them - so that they may stop (evil actions).
13	أَلَا تُقَاتِلُونَ قَوْمًا نَّكَثُوا **أَيْمَانَهُمْ** وَهَمُّوا بِإِخْرَاجِ الرَّسُولِ وَهُم بَدَءُوكُمْ أَوَّلَ مَرَّةٍ ۚ أَتَخْشَوْنَهُمْ ۚ فَاللَّهُ أَحَقُّ أَن تَخْشَوْهُ إِن كُنتُم مُّؤْمِنِينَ
H&K	Will you not fight a people who have violated their oaths (pagans of Makkah) and intended to expel the Messenger, while they did attack you first? Do you fear them? Allah has more right that you should fear Him, if you are believers.

16 النحل 38		وَأَقْسَمُوا بِاللَّهِ جَهْدَ **أَيْمَانِهِمْ** لَا يَبْعَثُ اللَّهُ مَن يَمُوتُ ۚ بَلَىٰ وَعْدًا عَلَيْهِ حَقًّا وَلَٰكِنَّ أَكْثَرَ النَّاسِ لَا يَعْلَمُونَ
	H&K	And they swear by Allah their strongest oaths, that Allah will not raise up him who dies. Yes, (He will raise them up), a promise (binding) upon Him in truth, but most of mankind know not.
71	*	وَاللَّهُ فَضَّلَ بَعْضَكُمْ عَلَىٰ بَعْضٍ فِي الرِّزْقِ ۚ فَمَا الَّذِينَ فُضِّلُوا بِرَادِّي رِزْقِهِمْ عَلَىٰ مَا مَلَكَتْ **أَيْمَانُهُمْ** فَهُمْ فِيهِ سَوَاءٌ ۚ أَفَبِنِعْمَةِ اللَّهِ يَجْحَدُونَ
	H&K	And Allah has preferred some of you above others in wealth and properties. Then, those who are preferred will by no means hand over their wealth and properties to those (slaves) whom their right hands possess, so that they may be equal with them in respect thereof. Do they then deny the Favour of Allah?
16 النحل 91		وَأَوْفُوا بِعَهْدِ اللَّهِ إِذَا عَاهَدتُّمْ وَلَا تَنقُضُوا **الْأَيْمَانَ** بَعْدَ تَوْكِيدِهَا وَقَدْ جَعَلْتُمُ اللَّهَ عَلَيْكُمْ كَفِيلًا ۚ إِنَّ اللَّهَ يَعْلَمُ مَا تَفْعَلُونَ
	H&K	And fulfill the Covenant of Allah (Bai'a: pledge for Islam) when you have covenanted, and break not the oaths after you have confirmed them, and indeed you have appointed Allah your surety. Verily! Allah knows what you do.
92		وَلَا تَكُونُوا كَالَّتِي نَقَضَتْ غَزْلَهَا مِن بَعْدِ قُوَّةٍ أَنكَاثًا تَتَّخِذُونَ **أَيْمَانَكُمْ** دَخَلًا بَيْنَكُمْ أَن تَكُونَ أُمَّةٌ هِيَ أَرْبَىٰ مِنْ أُمَّةٍ ۚ إِنَّمَا يَبْلُوكُمُ اللَّهُ بِهِ ۚ وَلَيُبَيِّنَنَّ لَكُمْ يَوْمَ الْقِيَامَةِ مَا كُنتُمْ فِيهِ تَخْتَلِفُونَ
	H&K	And be not like her who undoes the thread which she has spun after it has become strong, by taking your oaths a means of deception among yourselves, lest a nation may be more numerous than another nation. Allah only tests you by this [i.e. who obeys Allah and fulfills Allah's Covenant and who disobeys Allah and breaks Allah's Covenant]. And on the Day of Resurrection, He will certainly make clear to you that wherein you used to differ [i.e. a believer confesses and believes in the Oneness of Allah and in the Prophethood of Prophet Muhammad SAW which the disbeliever denies it and that was their difference amongst them in the life of this world].
94		وَلَا تَتَّخِذُوا **أَيْمَانَكُمْ** دَخَلًا بَيْنَكُمْ فَتَزِلَّ قَدَمٌ بَعْدَ ثُبُوتِهَا وَتَذُوقُوا السُّوءَ بِمَا صَدَدتُّمْ عَن سَبِيلِ اللَّهِ ۖ وَلَكُمْ عَذَابٌ عَظِيمٌ
	H&K	And make not your oaths, a means of deception among yourselves, lest a foot may slip after being firmly planted, and you may have to taste the evil (punishment in this world) of having hindered (men) from the Path of Allah

	(i.e. Belief in the Oneness of Allah and His Messenger, Muhammad SAW), and yours will be a great torment (i.e. the Fire of Hell in the Hereafter).
23 المؤمنون 6 *	إِلَّا عَلَىٰ أَزْوَاجِهِمْ أَوْ مَا مَلَكَتْ أَيْمَانُهُمْ فَإِنَّهُمْ غَيْرُ مَلُومِينَ
H&K	Except from their wives or (the captives and slaves) that their right hands possess, for then, they are free from blame;
24 النور 31 *	وَقُل لِّلْمُؤْمِنَاتِ يَغْضُضْنَ مِنْ أَبْصَارِهِنَّ وَيَحْفَظْنَ فُرُوجَهُنَّ وَلَا يُبْدِينَ زِينَتَهُنَّ إِلَّا مَا ظَهَرَ مِنْهَا ۖ وَلْيَضْرِبْنَ بِخُمُرِهِنَّ عَلَىٰ جُيُوبِهِنَّ ۖ وَلَا يُبْدِينَ زِينَتَهُنَّ إِلَّا لِبُعُولَتِهِنَّ أَوْ آبَائِهِنَّ أَوْ آبَاءِ بُعُولَتِهِنَّ أَوْ أَبْنَائِهِنَّ أَوْ أَبْنَاءِ بُعُولَتِهِنَّ أَوْ إِخْوَانِهِنَّ أَوْ بَنِي إِخْوَانِهِنَّ أَوْ بَنِي أَخَوَاتِهِنَّ أَوْ نِسَائِهِنَّ أَوْ مَا مَلَكَتْ أَيْمَانُهُنَّ أَوِ التَّابِعِينَ غَيْرِ أُولِي الْإِرْبَةِ مِنَ الرِّجَالِ أَوِ الطِّفْلِ الَّذِينَ لَمْ يَظْهَرُوا عَلَىٰ عَوْرَاتِ النِّسَاءِ ۖ وَلَا يَضْرِبْنَ بِأَرْجُلِهِنَّ لِيُعْلَمَ مَا يُخْفِينَ مِن زِينَتِهِنَّ ۚ وَتُوبُوا إِلَى اللَّهِ جَمِيعًا أَيُّهَ الْمُؤْمِنُونَ لَعَلَّكُمْ تُفْلِحُونَ
H&K	And tell the believing women to lower their gaze (from looking at forbidden things), and protect their private parts (from illegal sexual acts, etc.) and not to show off their adornment except only that which is apparent (like palms of hands or one eye or both eyes for necessity to see the way, or outer dress like veil, gloves, head-cover, apron, etc.), and to draw their veils all over Juyubihinna (i.e. their bodies, faces, necks and bosoms, etc.) and not to reveal their adornment except to their husbands, their fathers, their husband's fathers, their sons, their husband's sons, their brothers or their brother's sons, or their sister's sons, or their (Muslim) women (i.e. their sisters in Islam), or the (female) slaves whom their right hands possess, or old male servants who lack vigour, or small children who have no sense of the shame of sex. And let them not stamp their feet so as to reveal what they hide of their adornment. And all of you beg Allah to forgive you all, O believers, that you may be successful.
24 النور 33	وَلْيَسْتَعْفِفِ الَّذِينَ لَا يَجِدُونَ نِكَاحًا حَتَّىٰ يُغْنِيَهُمُ اللَّهُ مِن فَضْلِهِ ۗ وَالَّذِينَ يَبْتَغُونَ الْكِتَابَ مِمَّا مَلَكَتْ أَيْمَانُكُمْ فَكَاتِبُوهُمْ إِنْ عَلِمْتُمْ فِيهِمْ خَيْرًا ۖ وَآتُوهُم مِّن مَّالِ اللَّهِ الَّذِي آتَاكُمْ ۚ وَلَا تُكْرِهُوا فَتَيَاتِكُمْ عَلَى الْبِغَاءِ إِنْ أَرَدْنَ تَحَصُّنًا لِّتَبْتَغُوا عَرَضَ الْحَيَاةِ الدُّنْيَا ۚ وَمَن يُكْرِههُّنَّ فَإِنَّ اللَّهَ مِن بَعْدِ إِكْرَاهِهِنَّ غَفُورٌ رَّحِيمٌ
H&K	And let those who find not the financial means for marriage keep themselves chaste, until Allah enriches them of His Bounty. And such of your slaves as seek a writing (of emancipation), give them such writing, if you know that they are good and trustworthy. And give them something yourselves out of the wealth of Allah which He has bestowed upon you. And force not your maids to prostitution, if they desire chastity, in order that you may make a gain in the (perishable) goods of this worldly life. But if anyone compels them (to prostitution), then after such compulsion, Allah is Oft-Forgiving, Most

	Merciful (to those women, i.e. He will forgive them because they have been forced to do this evil action unwillingly).
24 النور 53	۞ وَأَقْسَمُوا بِاللَّهِ جَهْدَ أَيْمَانِهِمْ لَئِنْ أَمَرْتَهُمْ لَيَخْرُجُنَّ ۖ قُل لَّا تُقْسِمُوا ۖ طَاعَةٌ مَّعْرُوفَةٌ ۚ إِنَّ اللَّهَ خَبِيرٌ بِمَا تَعْمَلُونَ
H&K	They swear by Allah their strongest oaths, that if only you would order them, they would leave (their homes for fighting in Allah's Cause). Say: "Swear you not; (this) obedience (of yours) is known (to be false). Verily, Allah knows well what you do."
58 *	يَا أَيُّهَا الَّذِينَ آمَنُوا لِيَسْتَأْذِنكُمُ الَّذِينَ مَلَكَتْ أَيْمَانُكُمْ وَالَّذِينَ لَمْ يَبْلُغُوا الْحُلُمَ مِنكُمْ ثَلَاثَ مَرَّاتٍ ۚ مِّن قَبْلِ صَلَاةِ الْفَجْرِ وَحِينَ تَضَعُونَ ثِيَابَكُم مِّنَ الظَّهِيرَةِ وَمِن بَعْدِ صَلَاةِ الْعِشَاءِ ۚ ثَلَاثُ عَوْرَاتٍ لَّكُمْ ۚ لَيْسَ عَلَيْكُمْ وَلَا عَلَيْهِمْ جُنَاحٌ بَعْدَهُنَّ ۚ طَوَّافُونَ عَلَيْكُم بَعْضُكُمْ عَلَىٰ بَعْضٍ ۚ كَذَٰلِكَ يُبَيِّنُ اللَّهُ لَكُمُ الْآيَاتِ ۗ وَاللَّهُ عَلِيمٌ حَكِيمٌ
H&K	O you who believe! Let your legal slaves and slave-girls, and those among you who have not come to the age of puberty ask your permission (before they come to your presence) on three occasions; before Fajr (morning) prayer, and while you put off your clothes for the noonday (rest), and after the 'Isha' (late-night) prayer. (These) three times are of privacy for you, other than these times there is no sin on you or on them to move about, attending (helping) you each other. Thus Allah makes clear the Ayat (the Verses of this Quran, showing proofs for the legal aspects of permission for visits, etc.) to you. And Allah is All-Knowing, All-Wise.
30 الروم 28 *	ضَرَبَ لَكُم مَّثَلًا مِّنْ أَنفُسِكُمْ ۖ هَل لَّكُم مِّن مَّا مَلَكَتْ أَيْمَانُكُم مِّن شُرَكَاءَ فِي مَا رَزَقْنَاكُمْ فَأَنتُمْ فِيهِ سَوَاءٌ تَخَافُونَهُمْ كَخِيفَتِكُمْ أَنفُسَكُمْ ۚ كَذَٰلِكَ نُفَصِّلُ الْآيَاتِ لِقَوْمٍ يَعْقِلُونَ
H&K	He sets forth for you a parable from your ownselves, - Do you have partners among those whom your right hands possess (i.e. your slaves) to share as equals in the wealth We have bestowed on you? Whom you fear as you fear each other? Thus do We explain the signs in detail to a people who have sense.
33 الأحزاب 50 *	يَا أَيُّهَا النَّبِيُّ إِنَّا أَحْلَلْنَا لَكَ أَزْوَاجَكَ اللَّاتِي آتَيْتَ أُجُورَهُنَّ وَمَا مَلَكَتْ يَمِينُكَ مِمَّا أَفَاءَ اللَّهُ عَلَيْكَ وَبَنَاتِ عَمِّكَ وَبَنَاتِ عَمَّاتِكَ وَبَنَاتِ خَالِكَ وَبَنَاتِ خَالَاتِكَ اللَّاتِي هَاجَرْنَ مَعَكَ وَامْرَأَةً مُّؤْمِنَةً إِن وَهَبَتْ نَفْسَهَا لِلنَّبِيِّ إِنْ أَرَادَ النَّبِيُّ أَن يَسْتَنكِحَهَا خَالِصَةً لَّكَ مِن دُونِ الْمُؤْمِنِينَ ۗ قَدْ عَلِمْنَا مَا فَرَضْنَا عَلَيْهِمْ فِي أَزْوَاجِهِمْ وَمَا مَلَكَتْ أَيْمَانُهُمْ لِكَيْلَا يَكُونَ عَلَيْكَ حَرَجٌ ۗ وَكَانَ اللَّهُ غَفُورًا رَّحِيمًا
H&K	O Prophet (Muhammad SAW)! Verily, We have made lawful to you your wives, to whom you have paid their Mahr (bridal money given by the husband to his wife at the time of marriage), and those (captives or slaves) whom your right hand possesses - whom Allah has given to you, and the daughters of your

	'Amm (paternal uncles) and the daughters of your 'Ammah (paternal aunts) and the daughters of your Khal (maternal uncles) and the daughters of your Khalah (maternal aunts) who migrated (from Makkah) with you, and a believing woman if she offers herself to the Prophet, and the Prophet wishes to marry her; a privilege for you only, not for the (rest of) the believers. Indeed We know what We have enjoined upon them about their wives and those (captives or slaves) **whom their right hands possess**, - in order that there should be no difficulty on you. And Allah is Ever OftForgiving, Most Merciful.
55 *	لَا جُنَاحَ عَلَيْهِنَّ فِي آبَائِهِنَّ وَلَا أَبْنَائِهِنَّ وَلَا إِخْوَانِهِنَّ وَلَا أَبْنَاءِ إِخْوَانِهِنَّ وَلَا أَبْنَاءِ أَخَوَاتِهِنَّ وَلَا نِسَائِهِنَّ وَلَا مَا مَلَكَتْ **أَيْمَانُهُنَّ** ۗ وَاتَّقِينَ اللَّهَ ۚ إِنَّ اللَّهَ كَانَ عَلَىٰ كُلِّ شَيْءٍ شَهِيدًا
H&K	It is no sin on them (the Prophet's wives, if they appear unveiled) before their fathers, or their sons, or their brothers, or their brother's sons, or the sons of their sisters, or their own (believing) women, or their (female) slaves, and keep your duty to Allah. Verily, Allah is Ever AllWitness over everything.
35 فاطر 42	وَأَقْسَمُوا بِاللَّهِ جَهْدَ **أَيْمَانِهِمْ** لَئِنْ جَاءَهُمْ نَذِيرٌ لَيَكُونُنَّ أَهْدَىٰ مِنْ إِحْدَى الْأُمَمِ ۖ فَلَمَّا جَاءَهُمْ نَذِيرٌ مَا زَادَهُمْ إِلَّا نُفُورًا
H&K	And they swore by Allah their most binding oath, that if a warner came to them, they would be more guided than any of the nations (before them), yet when a warner (Muhammad SAW) came to them, it increased in them nothing but flight (from the truth),
57 الحديد 12 *	يَوْمَ تَرَى الْمُؤْمِنِينَ وَالْمُؤْمِنَاتِ يَسْعَىٰ نُورُهُمْ بَيْنَ أَيْدِيهِمْ **وَبِأَيْمَانِهِمْ** بُشْرَاكُمُ الْيَوْمَ جَنَّاتٌ تَجْرِي مِنْ تَحْتِهَا الْأَنْهَارُ خَالِدِينَ فِيهَا ۚ ذَٰلِكَ هُوَ الْفَوْزُ الْعَظِيمُ
H&K	On the Day you shall see the believing men and the believing women their light running forward before them and by **their right hands**. Glad tidings for you this Day! Gardens under which rivers flow (Paradise), to dwell therein forever! Truly, this is the great success!
58 المجادلة 16	اتَّخَذُوا **أَيْمَانَهُمْ** جُنَّةً فَصَدُّوا عَنْ سَبِيلِ اللَّهِ فَلَهُمْ عَذَابٌ مُهِينٌ
H&K	They have made their oaths a screen (for their evil actions). Thus they hinder (men) from the Path of Allah, so they shall have a humiliating torment.
63 المنافقون 2	اتَّخَذُوا **أَيْمَانَهُمْ** جُنَّةً فَصَدُّوا عَنْ سَبِيلِ اللَّهِ ۚ إِنَّهُمْ سَاءَ مَا كَانُوا يَعْمَلُونَ
H&K	They have made their oaths a screen (for their hypocrisy). Thus they hinder (men) from the Path of Allah. Verily, evil is what they used to do.

قَدْ فَرَضَ اللَّهُ لَكُمْ تَحِلَّةَ أَيْمَانِكُمْ ۚ وَاللَّهُ مَوْلَاكُمْ ۖ وَهُوَ الْعَلِيمُ الْحَكِيمُ	66 التحريم 2	
Allah has already ordained for you (O men), the dissolution of your oaths. And Allah is your Maula (Lord, or Master, or Protector, etc.) and He is the All-Knower, the All-Wise.	H&K	
يَا أَيُّهَا الَّذِينَ آمَنُوا تُوبُوا إِلَى اللَّهِ تَوْبَةً نَّصُوحًا عَسَىٰ رَبُّكُمْ أَن يُكَفِّرَ عَنكُمْ سَيِّئَاتِكُمْ وَيُدْخِلَكُمْ جَنَّاتٍ تَجْرِي مِن تَحْتِهَا الْأَنْهَارُ يَوْمَ لَا يُخْزِي اللَّهُ النَّبِيَّ وَالَّذِينَ آمَنُوا مَعَهُ ۖ نُورُهُمْ يَسْعَىٰ بَيْنَ أَيْدِيهِمْ وَبِأَيْمَانِهِمْ يَقُولُونَ رَبَّنَا أَتْمِمْ لَنَا نُورَنَا وَاغْفِرْ لَنَا ۖ إِنَّكَ عَلَىٰ كُلِّ شَيْءٍ قَدِيرٌ	66 التحريم 8 *	
O you who believe! Turn to Allah with sincere repentance! It may be that your Lord will remit from you your sins, and admit you into Gardens under which rivers flow (Paradise) the Day that Allah will not disgrace the Prophet (Muhammad SAW) and those who believe with him, their Light will run forward before them and with (their Records Books of deeds) **in their right** hands they will say: "Our Lord! Keep perfect our Light for us [and do not put it off till we cross over the Sirat (a slippery bridge over the Hell) safely] and grant us forgiveness. Verily, You are Able to do all things."	H&K	
أَمْ لَكُمْ أَيْمَانٌ عَلَيْنَا بَالِغَةٌ إِلَىٰ يَوْمِ الْقِيَامَةِ ۙ إِنَّ لَكُمْ لَمَا تَحْكُمُونَ	68 القلم 39	
Or you have oaths from Us, reaching to the Day of Resurrection that yours will be what you judge.	H&K	
إِلَّا عَلَىٰ أَزْوَاجِهِمْ أَوْ مَا مَلَكَتْ أَيْمَانُهُمْ فَإِنَّهُمْ غَيْرُ مَلُومِينَ	70 المعارج 30 *	
Except with their wives and the (women slaves and captives) whom **their right** hands possess, for (then) they are not to be blamed,	H&K	

	Similar Meaning/Tashabuh	آيات قريبة المعنى – تشابه
	✧	
2 البقرة 6		إِنَّ الَّذِينَ كَفَرُوا **سَوَاءٌ عَلَيْهِمْ أَأَنذَرْتَهُمْ أَمْ لَمْ تُنذِرْهُمْ لَا يُؤْمِنُونَ**
36 يس 10		**وَسَوَاءٌ عَلَيْهِمْ أَأَنذَرْتَهُمْ أَمْ لَمْ تُنذِرْهُمْ لَا يُؤْمِنُونَ**
	✧	
2 البقرة 27		الَّذِينَ يَنقُضُونَ عَهْدَ اللَّهِ مِن بَعْدِ مِيثَاقِهِ وَيَقْطَعُونَ مَا أَمَرَ اللَّهُ بِهِ أَن يُوصَلَ وَيُفْسِدُونَ فِي الْأَرْضِ ۚ أُولَٰئِكَ **هُمُ الْخَاسِرُونَ**
13 الرعد 25		وَالَّذِينَ يَنقُضُونَ عَهْدَ اللَّهِ مِن بَعْدِ مِيثَاقِهِ وَيَقْطَعُونَ مَا أَمَرَ اللَّهُ بِهِ أَن يُوصَلَ وَيُفْسِدُونَ فِي الْأَرْضِ ۙ أُولَٰئِكَ **لَهُمُ اللَّعْنَةُ وَلَهُمْ سُوءُ الدَّارِ**
	✧	
2 البقرة 62		إِنَّ الَّذِينَ آمَنُوا وَالَّذِينَ هَادُوا وَالنَّصَارَىٰ وَالصَّابِئِينَ مَنْ آمَنَ بِاللَّهِ وَالْيَوْمِ الْآخِرِ وَعَمِلَ صَالِحًا **فَلَهُمْ أَجْرُهُمْ عِندَ رَبِّهِمْ** وَلَا خَوْفٌ عَلَيْهِمْ وَلَا هُمْ يَحْزَنُونَ
5 المائدة 69		إِنَّ الَّذِينَ آمَنُوا وَالَّذِينَ هَادُوا وَالصَّابِئُونَ وَالنَّصَارَىٰ مَنْ آمَنَ بِاللَّهِ وَالْيَوْمِ الْآخِرِ وَعَمِلَ صَالِحًا فَلَا خَوْفٌ عَلَيْهِمْ وَلَا هُمْ يَحْزَنُونَ
	✧	
2 البقرة 48		وَاتَّقُوا يَوْمًا لَّا تَجْزِي نَفْسٌ عَن نَّفْسٍ شَيْئًا وَلَا يُقْبَلُ مِنْهَا **شَفَاعَةٌ** وَلَا يُؤْخَذُ مِنْهَا **عَدْلٌ** وَلَا هُمْ يُنصَرُونَ

123	وَاتَّقُوا يَوْمًا لَّا تَجْزِي نَفْسٌ عَن نَّفْسٍ شَيْئًا وَلَا يُقْبَلُ مِنْهَا عَدْلٌ وَلَا تَنفَعُهَا شَفَاعَةٌ وَلَا هُمْ يُنصَرُونَ	
	✦	
162	خَالِدِينَ فِيهَا ۖ لَا يُخَفَّفُ عَنْهُمُ الْعَذَابُ وَلَا هُمْ يُنظَرُونَ	2 البقرة
88	خَالِدِينَ فِيهَا لَا يُخَفَّفُ عَنْهُمُ الْعَذَابُ وَلَا هُمْ يُنظَرُونَ	3 آل عمران
	✦	
134	تِلْكَ أُمَّةٌ قَدْ خَلَتْ ۖ لَهَا مَا كَسَبَتْ وَلَكُم مَّا كَسَبْتُمْ ۖ وَلَا تُسْأَلُونَ عَمَّا كَانُوا يَعْمَلُونَ	2 البقرة
141	تِلْكَ أُمَّةٌ قَدْ خَلَتْ ۖ لَهَا مَا كَسَبَتْ وَلَكُم مَّا كَسَبْتُمْ ۖ وَلَا تُسْأَلُونَ عَمَّا كَانُوا يَعْمَلُونَ	
	✦	
80	إِنَّا كَذَلِكَ نَجْزِي الْمُحْسِنِينَ	37 الصافات
105	قَدْ صَدَّقْتَ الرُّؤْيَا ۚ إِنَّا كَذَلِكَ نَجْزِي الْمُحْسِنِينَ	
110	كَذَلِكَ نَجْزِي الْمُحْسِنِينَ	
121	إِنَّا كَذَلِكَ نَجْزِي الْمُحْسِنِينَ	
131	إِنَّا كَذَلِكَ نَجْزِي الْمُحْسِنِينَ	
34	لَهُم مَّا يَشَاءُونَ عِندَ رَبِّهِمْ ۚ ذَلِكَ جَزَاءُ الْمُحْسِنِينَ	39 الزمر
44	إِنَّا كَذَلِكَ نَجْزِي الْمُحْسِنِينَ	77 المرسلات

بحث في مفردات القرآن الكريم

النسخ في القران

ABROGATION

NASCH	
	الآية المنسوخة :
4 النساء 43	يَا أَيُّهَا الَّذِينَ آمَنُوا لَا تَقْرَبُوا الصَّلَاةَ وَأَنتُمْ سُكَارَىٰ حَتَّىٰ تَعْلَمُوا مَا تَقُولُونَ وَلَا جُنُبًا إِلَّا عَابِرِي سَبِيلٍ حَتَّىٰ تَغْتَسِلُوا ۚ وَإِن كُنتُم مَّرْضَىٰ أَوْ عَلَىٰ سَفَرٍ أَوْ جَاءَ أَحَدٌ مِّنكُم مِّنَ الْغَائِطِ أَوْ لَامَسْتُمُ النِّسَاءَ فَلَمْ تَجِدُوا مَاءً فَتَيَمَّمُوا صَعِيدًا طَيِّبًا فَامْسَحُوا بِوُجُوهِكُمْ وَأَيْدِيكُمْ ۗ إِنَّ اللَّهَ كَانَ عَفُوًّا غَفُورًا
H&K	O you who believe! Approach not As-Salat (the prayer) when you are in a drunken state until you know (the meaning) of what you utter, nor when you are in a state of Janaba, (i.e. in a state of sexual impurity and have not yet taken a bath) except when travelling on the road (without enough water, or just passing through a mosque), till you wash your whole body. And if you are ill, or on a journey, or one of you comes after answering the call of nature, or you have been in contact with women (by sexual relations) and you find no water, perform Tayammum with clean earth and rub therewith your faces and hands (Tayammum). Truly, Allah is Ever Oft-Pardoning, Oft-Forgiving
J	يا أيها الذين آمنوا لا تقربوا الصلاة» أي لا تصلوا «وأنتم سكارى» من الشراب لأن سبب نزولها صلاة جماعة في حال سكر «حتى تعلموا ما تقولون» بأن تصحوا «ولا جُنُبا» بإيلاج أو إنزال ونصبه على الحال وهو يطلق على المفرد وغيره «إلا عابري» مجتازي «سبيل» طريق أي مسافرين «حتى تغتسلوا» فلكم أن تصلوا واستثناء المسافر لأن له حكما آخر سيأتي وقيل المراد النهي عن قربان مواضع الصلاة أي المساجد إلا عبورها من غير مكث «وإن كنتم مرضى» مرضا يضره الماء «أو على سفر» أي مسافرين وأنتم جنب أو محدثون «أو جاء أحد منكم من الغائط» هو المكان المعَدُّ لقضاء الحاجة أي أحدث «أو لامستم النساء» وفي قراءة بلا ألف

	وكلاهما بمعنى اللمس هو الجَسُّ باليد قاله ابن عمر وعليه الشافعي وألحق به الجس بباقي البشرة وعن ابن عباس هو الجماع «فلم تجدوا ماءً» تتطهرون به للصلاة بعد الطلب والتفتيش وهو راجع إلى ما عدا المرضى «فتيمموا» اقصدوا بعد دخول الوقت «صعيدا طيبا» ترابا طاهرا فاضربوا به ضربتين «فامسحوا بوجوهكم وأيديكم» مع المرفقين منه ومسح يتعدى بنفسه وبالحرف «إن الله كان عفوا غفورا»
الآية الناسخة :	
5 المائدة 90	يَا أَيُّهَا الَّذِينَ آمَنُوا إِنَّمَا الْخَمْرُ وَالْمَيْسِرُ وَالْأَنصَابُ وَالْأَزْلَامُ رِجْسٌ مِّنْ عَمَلِ الشَّيْطَانِ فَاجْتَنِبُوهُ لَعَلَّكُمْ تُفْلِحُونَ
H&K	O you who believe! Intoxicants (all kinds of alcoholic drinks), gambling, Al-Ansab, and Al-Azlam (arrows for seeking luck or decision) are an abomination of Shaitan's (Satan) handiwork. So avoid (strictly all) that (abomination) in order that you may be successful.
J	يا أيها الذين آمنوا إنما الخمر» المسكر الذي يخامر العقل «والميسر» القمار «والأنصاب» الأصنام «والأزلام» قداح الاستقسام «رجس» خبيث مستقذر «من عمل الشيطان» الذي يزيّنه «فاجتنبوه» أي الرجس المعبر به عن هذه الأشياء أن تفعلوه «لعلكم تفلحون».
	✦
الآية المنسوخة :	
58 المجادلة 12	يَا أَيُّهَا الَّذِينَ آمَنُوا إِذَا نَاجَيْتُمُ الرَّسُولَ فَقَدِّمُوا بَيْنَ يَدَيْ نَجْوَاكُمْ صَدَقَةً ۚ ذَٰلِكَ خَيْرٌ لَّكُمْ وَأَطْهَرُ ۚ فَإِن لَّمْ تَجِدُوا فَإِنَّ اللَّهَ غَفُورٌ رَّحِيمٌ
H&K	O you who believe! When you (want to) consult the Messenger (Muhammad SAW) in private, spend something in charity before your private consultation. That will be better and purer for you. But if you find not (the means for it), then verily, Allah is Oft-Forgiving, Most Merciful.

		الآية الناسخة :
13		أَأَشْفَقْتُمْ أَن تُقَدِّمُوا بَيْنَ يَدَيْ نَجْوَاكُمْ صَدَقَاتٍ ۚ فَإِذْ لَمْ تَفْعَلُوا وَتَابَ اللَّهُ عَلَيْكُمْ فَأَقِيمُوا الصَّلَاةَ وَآتُوا الزَّكَاةَ وَأَطِيعُوا اللَّهَ وَرَسُولَهُ ۚ وَاللَّهُ خَبِيرٌ بِمَا تَعْمَلُونَ
	H&K	Are you afraid of spending in charity before your private consultation (with him)? If then you do it not, and Allah has forgiven you, then (at least) perform As-Salat (Iqamat-as-Salat) and give Zakat and obey Allah (i.e. do all what Allah and His Prophet SAW order you to do). And Allah is All-Aware of what you do.
		◈
		الآية المنسوخة :
73 المزمل 1+2+3		يَا أَيُّهَا الْمُزَّمِّلُ ﴿1﴾ قُمِ اللَّيْلَ إِلَّا قَلِيلًا ﴿2﴾ نِصْفَهُ أَوِ انقُصْ مِنْهُ قَلِيلًا ﴿3﴾
1	H&K	O you wrapped in garments (i.e. Prophet Muhammad SAW)!
2	H&K	Stand (to pray) all night, except a little.
3	H&K	Half of it, or a little less than that,
		الآية الناسخة :
73 المزمل 20		إِنَّ رَبَّكَ يَعْلَمُ أَنَّكَ تَقُومُ أَدْنَىٰ مِن ثُلُثَيِ اللَّيْلِ وَنِصْفَهُ وَثُلُثَهُ وَطَائِفَةٌ مِّنَ الَّذِينَ مَعَكَ ۚ وَاللَّهُ يُقَدِّرُ اللَّيْلَ وَالنَّهَارَ ۚ عَلِمَ أَن لَّن تُحْصُوهُ فَتَابَ عَلَيْكُمْ ۖ فَاقْرَءُوا مَا تَيَسَّرَ مِنَ الْقُرْآنِ ۚ عَلِمَ أَن سَيَكُونُ مِنكُم مَّرْضَىٰ ۙ وَآخَرُونَ يَضْرِبُونَ فِي الْأَرْضِ يَبْتَغُونَ مِن فَضْلِ اللَّهِ ۙ وَآخَرُونَ يُقَاتِلُونَ فِي سَبِيلِ اللَّهِ ۖ فَاقْرَءُوا مَا تَيَسَّرَ مِنْهُ ۚ وَأَقِيمُوا الصَّلَاةَ وَآتُوا الزَّكَاةَ وَأَقْرِضُوا اللَّهَ قَرْضًا حَسَنًا ۚ

		وَمَا تُقَدِّمُوا لِأَنفُسِكُم مِّنْ خَيْرٍ تَجِدُوهُ عِندَ اللَّهِ هُوَ خَيْرًا وَأَعْظَمَ أَجْرًا ۚ وَاسْتَغْفِرُوا اللَّهَ ۖ إِنَّ اللَّهَ غَفُورٌ رَّحِيمٌ
	H&K	Verily, your Lord knows that you do stand (to pray at night) a little less than two-thirds of the night, or half the night, or a third of the night, and so do a party of those with you, And Allah measures the night and the day. He knows that you are unable to pray the whole night, so He has turned to you (in mercy). So, recite you of the Quran as much as may be easy for you. He knows that there will be some among you sick, others travelling through the land, seeking of Allah's Bounty; yet others fighting in Allah's Cause. So recite as much of the Quran as may be easy (for you), and perform As-Salat (Iqamat-as-Salat) and give Zakat, and lend to Allah a goodly loan, and whatever good you send before you for yourselves, (i.e. Nawafil non-obligatory acts of worship: prayers, charity, fasting, Hajj and 'Umrah, etc.), you will certainly find it with Allah, better and greater in reward. And seek Forgiveness of Allah. Verily, Allah is Oft-Forgiving, Most-Merciful.
		✦

	الرِّبَا Interest	
2 البقرة 275	الَّذِينَ يَأْكُلُونَ الرِّبَا لَا يَقُومُونَ إِلَّا كَمَا يَقُومُ الَّذِي يَتَخَبَّطُهُ الشَّيْطَانُ مِنَ الْمَسِّ ۚ ذَٰلِكَ بِأَنَّهُمْ قَالُوا إِنَّمَا الْبَيْعُ مِثْلُ الرِّبَا ۗ وَأَحَلَّ اللَّهُ الْبَيْعَ وَحَرَّمَ الرِّبَا ۚ فَمَن جَاءَهُ مَوْعِظَةٌ مِّن رَّبِّهِ فَانتَهَىٰ فَلَهُ مَا سَلَفَ وَأَمْرُهُ إِلَى اللَّهِ ۖ وَمَنْ عَادَ فَأُولَٰئِكَ أَصْحَابُ النَّارِ ۖ هُمْ فِيهَا خَالِدُونَ	
Sahih	Those who consume interest cannot stand [on the Day of Resurrection] except as one stands who is being beaten by Satan into insanity. That is because they say, "Trade is [just] like interest." But Allah has permitted trade and has forbidden interest. So whoever has received an admonition from his Lord and desists may have what is past, and his affair rests with Allah. But whoever returns to [dealing in interest or usury] - those are the companions of the Fire; they will abide eternally therein	
H&K	Those who eat Riba (usury) will not stand (on the Day of Resurrection) except like the standing of a person beaten by Shaitan (Satan) leading him to insanity. That is because they say: "Trading is only like Riba (usury)," whereas Allah has permitted trading and forbidden Riba (usury). So whosoever receives an admonition from his Lord and stops eating Riba (usury) shall not be punished for the past; his case is for Allah (to judge); but whoever returns [to Riba (usury)], such are the dwellers of the Fire - they will abide therein.	
276	يَمْحَقُ اللَّهُ الرِّبَا وَيُرْبِي الصَّدَقَاتِ ۗ وَاللَّهُ لَا يُحِبُّ كُلَّ كَفَّارٍ أَثِيمٍ	
Sahih	Allah destroys interest and gives increase for charities. And Allah does not like every sinning disbeliever	
H&K	Allah will destroy Riba (usury) and will give increase for Sadaqat (deeds of charity, alms, etc.) And Allah likes not the disbelievers, sinners.	
278	يَا أَيُّهَا الَّذِينَ آمَنُوا اتَّقُوا اللَّهَ وَذَرُوا مَا بَقِيَ مِنَ الرِّبَا إِن كُنتُم مُّؤْمِنِينَ	
Sahih	O you who have believed, fear Allah and give up what remains [due to you] of interest, if you should be believers	
H&K	O you who believe! Be afraid of Allah and give up what remains (due to you) from Riba (usury) (from now onward), if you are (really) believers.	
279	فَإِن لَّمْ تَفْعَلُوا فَأْذَنُوا بِحَرْبٍ مِّنَ اللَّهِ وَرَسُولِهِ ۖ وَإِن تُبْتُمْ فَلَكُمْ رُءُوسُ أَمْوَالِكُمْ لَا تَظْلِمُونَ وَلَا تُظْلَمُونَ	

Sahih	And if you do not, then be informed of a war [against you] from Allah and His Messenger. But if you repent, you may have your principal - [thus] you do no wrong, nor are you wronged
H&K	And if you do not do it, then take a notice of war from Allah and His Messenger but if you repent, you shall have your capital sums. Deal not unjustly (by asking more than your capital sums), and you shall not be dealt with unjustly (by receiving less than your capital sums).
3 آل عمران 130	يَا أَيُّهَا الَّذِينَ آمَنُوا لَا تَأْكُلُوا الرِّبَا أَضْعَافًا مُّضَاعَفَةً ۖ وَاتَّقُوا اللَّهَ لَعَلَّكُمْ تُفْلِحُونَ
Sahih	O you who have believed, do not consume usury, doubled and multiplied, but fear Allah that you may be successful
H&K	And if you do not do it, then take a notice of war from Allah and His Messenger but if you repent, you shall have your capital sums. Deal not unjustly (by asking more than your capital sums), and you shall not be dealt with unjustly (by receiving less than your capital sums).
4 النساء 161	وَأَخْذِهِمُ الرِّبَا وَقَدْ نُهُوا عَنْهُ وَأَكْلِهِمْ أَمْوَالَ النَّاسِ بِالْبَاطِلِ ۚ وَأَعْتَدْنَا لِلْكَافِرِينَ مِنْهُمْ عَذَابًا أَلِيمًا
Sahih	And [for] their taking of usury while they had been forbidden from it, and their consuming of the people's wealth unjustly. And we have prepared for the disbelievers among them a painful punishment.
H&K	And their taking of Riba (usury) though they were forbidden from taking it and their devouring of men's substance wrongfully (bribery, etc.). And We have prepared for the disbelievers among them a painful torment.
30 الروم 39	وَمَا آتَيْتُم مِّن رِّبًا لِّيَرْبُوَ فِي أَمْوَالِ النَّاسِ فَلَا يَرْبُو عِندَ اللَّهِ ۖ وَمَا آتَيْتُم مِّن زَكَاةٍ تُرِيدُونَ وَجْهَ اللَّهِ فَأُولَٰئِكَ هُمُ الْمُضْعِفُونَ
Sahih	And whatever you give for interest to increase within the wealth of people will not increase with Allah. But what you give in zakah, desiring the countenance of Allah - those are the multipliers.
H&K	And that which you give in gift (to others), in order that it may increase (your wealth by expecting to get a better one in return) from other people's property, has no increase with Allah, but that which you give in Zakat seeking Allah's Countenance then those, they shall have manifold increase.

	شِفاءٌ Healing
10 يونس 57	يَا أَيُّهَا النَّاسُ قَدْ جَاءَتْكُم مَّوْعِظَةٌ مِّن رَّبِّكُمْ وَشِفاءٌ لِّمَا فِي الصُّدُورِ وَهُدًى وَرَحْمَةٌ لِّلْمُؤْمِنِينَ
Sahih	O mankind, there has to come to you instruction from your Lord and healing for what is in the breasts and guidance and mercy for the believers
H&K	O mankind! There has come to you a good advice from your Lord (i.e. the Quran, ordering all that is good and forbidding all that is evil), and a healing for that (disease of ignorance, doubt, hypocrisy and differences, etc.) in your breasts, - a guidance and a mercy (explaining lawful and unlawful things, etc.) for the believers.
16 النحل 69	ثُمَّ كُلِي مِن كُلِّ الثَّمَرَاتِ فَاسْلُكِي سُبُلَ رَبِّكِ ذُلُلًا ۚ يَخْرُجُ مِن بُطُونِهَا شَرَابٌ مُّخْتَلِفٌ أَلْوَانُهُ فِيهِ شِفاءٌ لِّلنَّاسِ ۗ إِنَّ فِي ذَٰلِكَ لَآيَةً لِّقَوْمٍ يَتَفَكَّرُونَ
Sahih	Then eat from all the fruits and follow the ways of your Lord laid down [for you]." There emerges from their bellies a drink, varying in colors, in which there is healing for people. Indeed in that is a sign for a people who give thought
H&K	"Then, eat of all fruits, and follow the ways of your Lord made easy (for you)." There comes forth from their bellies, a drink of varying colour wherein is healing for men. Verily, in this is indeed a sign for people who think.
J	ثم كلي من كل الثمرات فاسلكي» ادخلي «سبل ربك» طرقه في طلب المرعى «ذللا» جمع » ذلول حال من السبل أي مسخرة لك فلا تعسر عليك وإن توعرت ولا تضلي على العود منها وإن بعدت، وقيل من الضمير في اسلكي أي منقادة لما يراد منك «يخرج من بطونها شراب» هو العسل «مختلف ألوانه فيه شفاء للناس» من الأوجاع قيل لبعضها كما دل عليه تنكير شفاء أو لكلها بضميمته إلى غيره وبدونها بنيته وقد أمر به صلى الله عليه وسلم من استطلق عليه بطنه. رواه الشيخان «إن في ذلك لآية لقوم يتفكرون» في صنعه تعالى
17 الإسراء 82	وَنُنَزِّلُ مِنَ الْقُرْآنِ مَا هُوَ شِفاءٌ وَرَحْمَةٌ لِّلْمُؤْمِنِينَ ۙ وَلَا يَزِيدُ الظَّالِمِينَ إِلَّا خَسَارًا
Sahih	And We send down of the Qur'an that which is healing and mercy for the believers, but it does not increase the wrongdoers except in loss

P	And We reveal of the Qur'an that which is a healing and a mercy for believers though it increase the evil-doers in naught save ruin.
H&K	And We send down from the Quran that which is a healing and a mercy to those who believe (in Islamic Monotheism and act on it), and it increases the Zalimun (polytheists and wrong-doers) nothing but loss.
J	وننزل من» للبيان «القرآن ما هو شفاء» من الضلالة «ورحمة للمؤمنين» به «ولا يزيد» الظالمين» الكافرين «إلا خسارا» لكفرهم به.
26 الشعراء 80	وَإِذَا مَرِضْتُ فَهُوَ يَشْفِينِ
Sahih	And when I am ill, it is He who cures me
41 فصلت 44	وَلَوْ جَعَلْنَاهُ قُرْآنًا أَعْجَمِيًّا لَقَالُوا لَوْلَا فُصِّلَتْ آيَاتُهُ ۖ أَأَعْجَمِيٌّ وَعَرَبِيٌّ ۗ قُلْ هُوَ لِلَّذِينَ آمَنُوا هُدًى وَشِفَاءٌ ۖ وَالَّذِينَ لَا يُؤْمِنُونَ فِي آذَانِهِمْ وَقْرٌ وَهُوَ عَلَيْهِمْ عَمًى ۚ أُولَٰئِكَ يُنَادَوْنَ مِن مَّكَانٍ بَعِيدٍ
Sahih	And if We had made it a non-Arabic Qur'an, they would have said, "Why are its verses not explained in detail [in our language]? Is it a foreign [recitation] and an Arab [messenger]?" Say, "It is, for those who believe, a guidance and cure." And those who do not believe - in their ears is deafness, and it is upon them blindness. Those are being called from a distant place
p	And if We had appointed it a Lecture in a foreign tongue they would assuredly have said: If only its verses were expounded (so that we might understand)? What! A foreign tongue and an Arab? - Say unto them (O Muhammad): For those who believe it is a guidance and a healing; and as for those who disbelieve, there is a deafness in their ears, and it is blindness for them. Such are called to from afar.
H&K	And if We had sent this as a Quran in a foreign language other than Arabic, they would have said: "Why are not its Verses explained in detail (in our language)? What! (A Book) not in Arabic and (the Messenger) an Arab?" Say: "It is for those who believe, a guide and a healing. And as for those who disbelieve, there is heaviness (deafness) in their ears, and it (the Quran) is blindness for them. They are those who are called from a place far away (so they neither listen nor understand).
J	ولو جعلناه» أي الذكر «قرآناً أعجميا لقالوا لولا» هلا «فصلت» بينت «آياته» حتى نفهمها «أ» قرآن «اعجمي و» نبي «عربي» استفهام إنكار منهم بتحقيق الهمزة الثانية وقلبها ألفا بإشباع، ودونه «قل هو للذين آمنوا هدى» من الضلالة «وشفاء» من الجهل «والذين لا

| | | يؤمنون في آذانهم وقر» ثقل فلا يسمعونه «وهو عليهم عمى» فلا يفهمونه «أولئك ينادون من مكان بعيد» أي هم كالمنادى من مكان بعيد لا يسمع ولا يفهم ما ينادى به |

Features and Guide

ONE PAGE INDEX- MAIN INDEX.   P210
ONE PAGE INDEX- RELATIVES.   P211
TWO PAGE INDEX Other TOPICS   P 212+213
EIGHT PAGE VOCABULARY INDEX.   P214 – P221

One column contains Arabic Alfa-Bet letters.

Verse Translation: Sahih International- First 120 page.

        Hilali & Khan (H&K) from P120 till End

        Pickthal   (P)   few Verses only in second half

        Al-Jalalayn   (J) Arabic- Few Verses in second half

* **- Main index**, one page- **covers close relatives/family** members such as أَبَا أُمُّ

...الْأَوْلَادِ والد الْأَخ أُخْتَ خَالَاتِكُمْ أَزْوَاجِ امْرَأَةُ النِّسَاءَ أُنثَىٰ الذَّكَرُ ابن بنات Holy Quran verses included those Vocabularies were listed in the book with **English translation**.

* **- Relatives-** one page

* **- Topics** like: [blood] relationship, Engagement, Thihaar, Divorce, Sacred months,
   Will and Inheritance.   **See P211 Index**

* **- Secondary index** of 8 pages (3 columns each) **Topics/Vocabularies** /Pages relates to: Inheritance/Will / 58 6 يُوصِينَ وَصِيَّةٍ يُوصَىٰ/ 73 52 وَوَصَّيْنَا) (59 يَرِثُهَا ,وارث 6 /وَوَرِثَهُ) (70 الْوَصِيَّةُ , Divorce (107 فَطَلِّقُوهُنَّ /طَلَّقْتُمُ النِّسَاءَ/93 طَلَّقَكُنَّ/ 107 98 86 طَلَّقْتُمُ), Periods of/after.. 107 الْعِدَّةَ وَأَحْصُوا لِعِدَّتِهِنَّ) ( ) 4 الطلاق 65 أَشْهُرٍ ثَلَاثَةَ فَعِدَّتُهُنَّ,) Calala الْكَلَالَةِ59 58), أَرْضَعْنَكُمْ Women period 97 الْمَحِيضِ), Sick person 17 الْمَرِيضِ), Child feeding/period 32 تَسْتَرْضِعُوا 56 32 الرَّضَاعَةِ),

Engagement/Marriage خِطْبَةِ النِّسَاءِ 128 98), Women dress 7 لِبَاسَهُمَا), Hijab 17 بِخُمُرِهِنَّ),
See P211 for more
Witness 88 شُهَدَاءُ /فَشَهَادَةُ /شَهَادَاتٍ), Debt 58 6 دَيْنٍ), Baby 17 الطِّفْلِ), ... etc.

* **- Highlighted** specific words/part of a sentence in order to quickly find a word.

* – **Most Aya (Verse)** are translated into English, and for an extra knowledge/understanding one can use the **Sura (Chapter) Number and Name** to pick another translation free, for Arabic Al-Jalalayn can be a top choice- difficult though.

* - Two or three Scholar translations used for certain Verses.   **See P120-P205**

* – Very easy to navigate through the book as well as the Index, and therefore, it is of great importance to a wide type of people from **Schools, at Home, and to a professional personnel as well as Scholars, Libraries and Researchers.**

* – Arabic 28 letter Alpha Bet are inserted in the right- hand side column, good idea for which even Arab readers will find it essential.

* -The Arabic ال (the) is ignored during search.

*- This book is two books in one, having Family Members in Holy Quran as a base.

الحجرات 49 13	يَا أَيُّهَا النَّاسُ إِنَّا خَلَقْنَاكُم مِّن ذَكَرٍ وَأُنثَىٰ وَجَعَلْنَاكُمْ شُعُوبًا وَقَبَائِلَ لِتَعَارَفُوا ۚ إِنَّ أَكْرَمَكُمْ عِندَ اللَّهِ أَتْقَاكُمْ ۚ إِنَّ اللَّهَ عَلِيمٌ خَبِيرٌ
P110	O mankind, indeed We have created you from male and female and made you peoples and tribes that you may know one another. Indeed, the most noble of you in the sight of Allah is the most righteous of you. Indeed, Allah is Knowing and Acquainted.
Hadith	….O people. I have conveyed the Message, and have left you with something which, if you hold fast to it, you will never go astray: that is, the Book of God and the sunnah of His Prophet… Know for certain that every Muslim is a brother of another Muslim, and that all Muslims are brethren….. O people, your Lord is one and your father Adam is one. There is no virtue of an Arab over a foreigner, nor a foreigner over an Arab, and neither white over black nor black over white, except by righteousness. **Part of Farewell Sermon**

الكتب الصادره والمسجلة في المكتبة البريطانية

Books submitted to the British Library:

9781513646077 Paperback
Similar Meaning Quran Verses   with English Translation

9781513646084 Paperback
Similar Meaning Quran Verses   with Arabic Tafsir

9781513652382 Paperback
Family Members in Holy Quran Verses   with English Translation *

9781513652399 Paperback
Family Members in Holy Quran Verses   with Arabic Tafsir *

978-1-916566-00-2   Hardcover
03 May 2023
Family Members in Holy Quran Verses   with English Translation

----

ISBN: 9781513652405
Year: 2020
Format:/MicroSD/ CD *
Family Members in Holy Quran Verses Recitation (Digital-MP3) 10 HOURS by Hamza Muhammad Dakka

....

978-1-916566-064 Current book
 June 2023

Main Family Index			فهرس أفراد ألعائلة الرئيسي		
Headings	العناوين	Page صفحة	Headings	العناوين	Page صفحة
Father	أبا	5 12 19	Children/the/their/	أَوْلَادًا/الْأَوْلَادِ/أَوْلَادَهُنَّ/ أَوْلَادُهُم	66-69
Fathers	آباء	5-22	Father of	والد	69-74
Father of	أبو..	22-24	the Brother/his	الْأَخِ/ أَخِيهِ	75-77
My Father	أبي	24-29	Sister	أُخْتٌ/ الْأُخْتِ/ الْأُخْتَيْنِ	77-79
Son	ابن/ابناء/أَبْنَاءَكُمْ/أَبْنَاؤُكُمْ	29-43	your sisters	أَخَوَاتُكُمْ	79-80
the Sons	الْبَنُونَ	43	Brothers	إِخْوَانًا /إِخْوَانِهِمْ/ لِإِخْوَانِهِمْ	80-82
Sons	بَنِينَ	43-45	her Sister	أُخْتَهَا	82
Daughter	ابْنَتَ	45	our Brother	أَخَانَا	82-83
Daughters	بنات	45-48	Your Brothers/Mothers B+S	أَخَوَاتُكُمْ/ إِخْوَانَكُمْ/ أَخْوَالِكُمْ/ خَالَاتِكُمْ	83
Mother	أُمٌّ	48-49	your brothers	إِخْوَانَكُمْ	84-85
your Mother	أمك	49-50	Wives/Couples	أَزْوَاج	86-93
His/her Mother/s	فَلِأُمِّهِ/أُمُّهُ/أُمَّهَا/أُمَّهَاتُ	50-52	your Wives	أَزْوَاجِكُمْ	93-95
your Mothers	أُمَّهَاتُكُمْ	53-54	Woman (لامراته 60) Wife of امرأة امرات 62 108		47 58 90 96
their Mothers	أُمَّهَاتُهُمْ	55	the Females/Women	النِّسَاءَ	97-107
would I give birth?	أَأَلِدُ	55	few women	نِسْوَةٌ	108
his son	مَوْلُودٌ لَهُ	56	M/F	أُنْثَى/ الْأُنْثَى/ ذَكَرٍ/ الذَّكَرُ	108-111
Son...	/وَلَدٌ/وَلَدَ/وَلَدًا /مَوْلُودٌ/وَلَدِهِ/وَلَدَهُمْ الْوَلَدَانِ/ولدان	56-66	2 Males/F	الذَّكَرَيْنِ/الذَّكْرَانَ/ الْأُنْثَيَيْنِ	111-112
Son	وليدا	56	Husband	بُعُولَتِهِنَّ	112

RELATIVES		.. الْقُرْبَىٰ ... وَالْأَقْرَبُونَ .. أَقْرَبُ الْمُقَرَّبُونَ مَقْرَبَةٍ وَذِي	113-119
Who is a Relative		وَذِي الْقُرْبَىٰ	113
Whom are Relatives		ذَوِي الْقُرْبَىٰ	113
Near/close Neighbor		وَبِذِي الْقُرْبَىٰ / ذِي الْقُرْبَىٰ	114
The Relative		ذِي الْقُرْبَىٰ	114
Near Relatives		وَالْأَقْرَبِينَ/ الْأَقْرَبِينَ	114
Close Relatives		وَالْأَقْرَبُونَ	115
Those who are Relatives		أُولُو الْقُرْبَىٰ	115
Nearest		أَقْرَبُ	116
Near Relative		ذَا قُرْبَىٰ	116
The Relative		ذَا الْقُرْبَىٰ	117
And to the near Relatives		وَلِذِي الْقُرْبَىٰ	117
The Relative		ذِي الْقُرْبَىٰ	118
To the near /close Relatives		وَلِذِي الْقُرْبَىٰ	118
Relatives		أُولِي قُرْبَىٰ	118
Being Relative		الْقُرْبَىٰ	119
Brought near		الْمُقَرَّبُونَ	119
Near Relationship		مَقْرَبَةٍ	119
Barrier		حجابا	143 144
Partition		حِجَابٍ	90 157
their outer garments		جلابيبهن	47 91 106 144

[blood] relationship	Topics	الأَرْحَام	120-121
Offspring		ذُرِّيَّةٌ	122-127
proposal to women/Engagement		خِطْبَةِ النِّسَاءِ	128
pronounce thihar		(ظهار) يُظَاهِرُونَ	129
DIVORCE		الطلاق	130-132
Sacred Month		الشَّهْرَ الْحَرَامَ	133-134
in the state of ihram		حُرُمٌ	134-136
		حَرَامٌ/ حَرَامًا	159
WILL and INHERITANCE/ bequest		الوصيه والميراث	
Heritage /Inheritance		ميراث	137
His/ heirs/Inherit		ورث	137
Heir		وارث	140
Inherit		يرث	141
we/Inherit		نرث	142
to inherit		ترث	142
Abrogation		النسخ في القران	140
Women related general dress and other topics		ايات تخص لباس النساء وغيره	141
Barrier		حجابا	143 144
Cloaks/outer garments		جَلَابِيبِهِنَّ	144 106 91 47

Marries		تَنكِحَ	154
opening of your garment		جَيْبِكَ	158
Unlawful		حَرَامٌ/ حَرَامًا	159
Patient		صابر	160
Patience		صبر	164
Iman-Faith		الإِيمَانِ	177
Oaths/ right hands		أَيْمَانِكُمْ/ أَيْمَانَكُمْ/الأَيْمَانَ	186
Similar Meaning/Tashabuh		تشابه-أيات قريبة المعنى	195
Abrogation		النسخ في القران	197
Interest		الرِّبَا	201
Healing		شِفَاءٌ	203

Family Index (secondary)   فهرس أفراد العائلة الإضافي

أ	أ	أ	Alpha Bet
أَأَلِدُ 55	أَصْلَابِكُمْ 32 45	امرات 62 108	
أَبْصَارِهِنَّ 17	اضْرِبُوهُنَّ 101	امراة 46 58 90 96 / لامراته 60	
أَحْلَلْنَا 46	أَطْرَافِهَا 15	أَمْوَالٌ اقْتَرَفْتُمُوهَا 9	
أَحْصَنَتْ 39 45	أَطْهَرُ 46 86 90	الْإِنْسِ 79	
إِحْسَانًا 32 52 69 72	اعْتَصِمُوا 16 80	أَنصَارَ 34 42	
اخْفِضْ 88	إِعْرَاضًا 96	أَوْلِيَاءَ 7 9 18	
أَحْمَدُ 42	أُفٍّ 72 74	إِمْلَاقٍ 65	أ
أَدْعِيَاءَكُمْ 40	الْأَقْرَبُونَ 71/ وَالْأَقْرَبِينَ	أَنفَقْتُمْ/يُنفِقُونَ 30	ب
ادْعُوهُمْ 19	أَقْسَطُ 19	أَهْل 12 26 33 38 40 42 50 52 58 82 102	ت
أَرْضَعْنَكُمْ الرَّضَاعَةِ 32 / أَرْضِعِيهِ 49	آلِ يَعْقُوبَ 10	الْأَرْحَامِ 55 66 87 99 109 112	ث
أَزْوَاجًا 44 86 88 89 91 92 93	بِالْأَلْقَابِ 107	أُولِي الْإِرْبَةِ 17	ج
اسْتَحْيُوا 41	أُمَّةٍ 20		ح
اصْطَفَاكِ 98	امْرَأَ 15		خ

	ث	ت	ب
	الثُّلُثُ 6 58 75 الثُّلُثَانِ 59	تَرَكَ 6 58 59 70 71	بَايِعْهُنَّ /يُبَايِعْنَكَ 69
	ثَلَاثُونَ / ثَلَاثٍ 33 52 54 92 99	تُخْبَرُونَ 95	البَدْوِ 13
د	ثَمانية 54 87	تُحَرِّمْ 92	بَشَرٌ 14 16 33 57
ذ	الثَّوَابِ/ ثَوَابًا 43 109	تَرِثُوا 100	البِرَّ 30
ر		تَعْدِلُوا 71 99 102	بَصِيرًا /يُبْصِرُ 26
ز	ج	تَعْضُلُوهُنَّ 86 100	بِضَاعَتَنَا / بِضَاعَتَهُمْ 12
س		تُشْرِكَ 73	بُطُونٍ 53 54 87
ش	جَازٍ / يَجْزِي 62	تُظَاهِرُونَ /ظَاهِرَ 40 54 55	بُعُولَتِهِنَّ 17 / بَعْلِي 55
ص	جَلَابِيبِهِنَّ 106 144 47 91	تَغِيضُ الأَرْحَامُ 109	بُيُوتٍ 17
	جُنَاحٌ 17 19 105	تُقْسِطُوا 99	
	جَنَاحَكَ 88	تَنكِحُوهُنَّ 59	
	جُبًّا 101 103	فَتَيَمَّمُوا 101 103	
	جُيُوبِهِنَّ 17		

215

	د	خ	ح
	دَخَلْتُم 17 32	خِطْبَةِ النِّسَاءِ 98	حِجَابٍ 156 90 حجابا 143
	دُولَةً 42	بِخُمُرِهِنَّ 17	حُجُورِكُم 32
ض	دِيَارِنَا 30	خسر / خسروا 36 68	الْحُرُّ بِالْحُرِّ 75
ط	دِيَارِهِم 109	خير 11 12 18 25 30 43..	حَرَجٌ 17 47 89
ظ	الدِّين 11 16 19 33 67 84 85	الْخَيْل 98	حَرَصْتُم 102
ع	دَيْنٍ 6 58		حرم 7 14 34 65 68 87 111 112
غ	**ذ**		حَفَدَةً 44
ف	ذَا الْقُرْبَىٰ 38 40 / ذَوِي / ذِي 32 37 42 69		حَلَائِلُ 32
ق	ذُرِّيَّاتِهِم 7 13 20 / ذُرِّيَّةً 8 87		الْحَوْلِ 86
	ذَكَرٍ أَوْ أُنْثَىٰ 109 110		
	ذَكَرٍ وَأُنْثَىٰ 110		
	الذَّكَرَ وَالْأُنْثَىٰ 111		

ش	س	ر	
	سَبِيلٍ/ سَبِيلًا 101	رَبَائِبُكُمْ 32	
شُرَكَاءَ 43 / شُرَكَاؤُهُمْ 67 شَرِيكٌ 60 62	السِّجْنِ 13	رَجُلٌ 19 46 58 رِجَالِكُمْ/ الرِّجَالِ	
شَهْوَةً 103 105/ الشَّهَوَاتِ 43	السَّعْيَ 20	أَرْضَعْنَكُمْ 32 الرَّضَاعَةِ 32 56 تَسْتَرْضِعُوا	ك
شَهَادَاتٍ/ فَشَهَادَةُ/ شُهَدَاءُ 88	سَرِّحُوهُنَّ 97	وَفِي الرِّقَابِ وَالْغَارِمِينَ 30 38	ل
شِيَعًا 40	سَفَرٍ 103		م
شَيْخًا 5 55	سكارى 101	ز	ن
	سَوْءَةَ 77	الزَّكَاةَ 16 30 69 84 113	ه
		زَيْدٌ 89	و
		زين 17 43 67 69 89 105	ي
		زِينَتَهُنَّ 17	

ص	ط	ع	
الصَّالِحَاتِ 86 87 109 119	طَائِفَةً 40 42	عَاشِرُوهُنَّ 100	ا
الصَّاحِبِ 32	الطِّفْلِ 17	الْعَبْدُ 75	ب
الصَّدَقَاتُ 38 / صَدُقَاتِهِنَّ 99	طَلَّقْتُمُ 86 98 107 /طَلَّقْكُنَّ 93	عَجُوزٌ 55	ت
صَدِيقِكُمْ 17	طَلَّقْتُمُ النِّسَاءَ/ فَطَلِّقُوهُنَّ 107	عَوْرَاتٍ 17	ث
صَدِيقَةٌ 34		الْعِيرُ 13	ج
صبر 164 176 صابر 20/الصابرين 28 30 113 160 167 170	ظ	فَعِدَّتُهُنَّ ثَلَاثَةُ أَشْهُرٍ (الطلاق 4 65)	ح
ض	تُظَاهِرُونَ 40	لِعِدَّتِهِنَّ وَأَحْصُوا الْعِدَّةَ 107	خ
الضَّالِّينَ 27	ظِلَالٍ 91	عَدُوًّا 66	د
الضَّرَّاءِ 30	ظُلُمَاتٍ ثَلَاثٍ 54	عَشِيرَتُكُمْ 9 /عَشِيرَتَهُمْ 22 / عَشِيرَتَكَ 115	ذ
ضِرَارًا 97	الظَّنَّ 7 21	عَرَّضْتُمْ 98	ر
ضُرِبَ 41 /يَضْرِبْنَ 17/ اضْرِبُوهُنَّ 101/ ضَرَبْتُمْ 116		عُقْدَةَ النِّكَاحِ 98	ز
ضَلَالٍ 10 16 24 108			س
ضَيْفِي 46			ش

غ	ف	ق	ص
			ض
غَالِبٌ 60	فَاتَكُمْ 92	الْقِصَاصُ 75	ط
الْغَائِطِ 101 103	فِتْنَةٌ 66	بِالْقِسْطِ 58 71	ظ
الْغُلَامُ 14 لِغُلَامَيْنِ 14	فَتَاهَا 108	وَقَضَىٰ 72 قَضَىٰ 57 61 72 89	ع
غَنِمْتُم 37	فُرُوجَهُنَّ 17	الْقُرْبَىٰ 30 32 37 38 40 42 69	غ
الْأَغْنِيَاءِ 42/الْغَنِيُّ 60/ غَنِيًّا 71	فَرِيضَةً 6 38 98 100	الْقُرْبَىٰ وَالْيَتَامَىٰ وَالْمَسَاكِينِ 37 42	ف
	وَفِصَالُهُ 52	الْقُرُونُ 74	ق
		الْقَنَاطِيرِ الْمُقَنْطَرَةِ 43	ك
		قَوَّامُونَ 101	ل
		وَالْقَوَاعِدُ 105	م
		قَوْمٌ 94 104 105 107	ن
		الْقُرَىٰ 42 48 52	ه
			و
			ي

	م	م	ك
ا		الْمَالُ/ مال 30 43 44 45 61 63 مَالًا 60	
ب	وَمَغْفِرَةٌ 69	الْمَحِيضِ 97	الْكِبَرَ 72
ت	وَالْمُؤَلَّفَةِ قُلُوبُهُمْ 38	مَسَاكِنُ 9	الكتاب 7 29 30 33 35 36
ث	الْمُعَوِّقِينَ 81	مُبَشِّرًا 42	كُرْهًا 52
ج	مَوْلَاكُمْ 16 الْمَوْلَى/ مَوَالِيكُمْ 19 / مَوَالِيَ 71	أَحْصَنَّ 39 45/ مُسَافِحِينَ/ مَلَكَتْ الْمُحْصَنَاتُ مُحْصِنِينَ 100	الْكَلَالَةَ 59
ح	الْمَهْدِ وَكَهْلًا 35	مُحَمَّدٌ 5	الْكَيْلَ/ نَكْتَلْ 11 12
خ	مَلَكَتْ أَيْمَانُكُمْ 32 99 100	أَمْوَالَنَا 9 37 44 45 65 66 67 68 69 84 94 101 أَمْوَالُكُمْ	
د	مُطَهَّرَةٌ (أَزْوَاجٌ) 86 87	مَنَاسِكَكُمْ 6	
ذ		الْمِسْكِينَ 38 40	ل
ر		الْمُسْتَضْعَفِينَ 58 59 102	لِبَاسَهُمَا 7
ز		الْأَقْرَبِينَ/ الاقربون 30 70 71 114-116/الْمُقَرَّبِينَ 31 119	لطيف 13
س		الْمَلَأُ 16 36	لعن 31 35 79 لَعَنَتْ
ش		الْمَرِيضِ 17	
ص		مَلَكَتْ 17 19 32 47 88 90 93 99 100	

220

ض	ي	هـ	ن
ط			
ظ	لِلْيَتَامَىٰ../الْيَتَامَىٰ 37 42 84/ يَتَامَىٰ 59 102/ 99	هَاجَرْنَ 46	النَّاسِ 6 11 12 16 60
ع	يُغْنِي 12 15/ يَسْتَنْكِحَهَا 90/47	هَبْ 89	نِحْلَةً 99
غ	يُغْنِي/ يُبْصِرُ / يَسْمَعُ 15	هُدًى 7 21 34	نَفْسِي (نَفْسِكَ) 36 77
ف	يَغْضُضْنَ 17	هَلَكَ 59	تَنكِحُوا / نَكَحَ 6 أَنكِحَكَ 45/ نِكَاحًا 105
ق	يَتَوَفَّوْنَ 86	الْهَوَىٰ 71	نُشُوزًا 96 نُشُوزَهُنَّ 101
ك	يُدْنِينَ 47	و	نَصِيبٌ 71 99 101
ل	يُظَاهِرُونَ 40 54 55 63	وَوَرِثَهُ 6/ وَارِثٌ 56	وَنَسْتَحْيِي وَيَسْتَحْيُونَ 36
م	يُعْرَفْنَ فَلَا يُؤْذَيْنَ 47	وَوَصَّيْنَا 52 73/ يُوصَىٰ وَصِيَّةٍ يُوصِينَ 6 58 / الْوَصِيَّةُ 70	نِسَاءَ النَّبِيِّ 105 106
ن	يُعَمَّرُ مُعَمَّرٍ 91/ عُمُرِهِ يَنْقُصُ	وَضَعَتْهَا /وَضَعْتُهَا 108 تَضَعُ 110	الْكَيْلُ/ نَكْتَلْ 11 12
هـ	يَطْهُرْنَ/ تَطَهَّرْنَ/ الْمُتَطَهِّرِينَ 97	وَلِيًّا 15 58	
و	يَرِثُهَا 59	وَهْنٍ/ وَهْنًا 52	
ي		وَهَبَتْ 46	

SUMMARY

Research Quranic Topics is part continuation of Family Members in Holy Quran Verses book where Family Members was the main subject. In this extended book of 226 pages, I am researching Verses Specific Topics on:

Women, Sacred Months, Patience, Iman- Faith, and Interest.

All researched verses are accompanied by Sahih English translation up to P119. After that, from P120 to the end, the default English translation is Hilali & Khan. I have added one or two more different Scholar translations for certain Verses from P120 to the end in order to have better understanding and/or to clear any doubt.

Muslim women viewed in the west as having less rights than men. It is a false claim:

- Women been given half the men's amount of Inheritance because man/brother is the main supporter of the family in the absence of the father, noting that it is a duty for the brother to give /support sisters and mother even if they are married, and during the two Muslim Eids, brothers and/or the father <u>must give</u> the sisters/daughters some <u>money</u>- also to her/their children, to keep contact, and to help when needed, but there is NO similar requirement from female towards brothers. Also looking at Calala Verses, one could see that the daughter gets high share in this case.
- Women equal to men in ALL verses, both get same and equal good or bad deed.
- Given evidence/being a witness- God never said they are inferior to a man, but he asked for two of them as a substitute for the man IN CASE ONE FORGET SOMETHING, THE OTHER WILL REMIND HER, what a powerful chosen words, and who can deny that certain days per month a women witnessing a Will draft is likely to fall into this category of forgetting some details during such an important event. What God is telling us that men has the upper hand over women- they are strong no doubt, but also because of the extra Inheritance they can give/donate to charity, sisters or to a good cause. and therefore, earning a good dead.
- God created Muslim woman with above features, He is the one asking us to follow Islam, He did not tell us that women of other faiths are stronger or can never forget, at the same time He is asking us to believe in the TRUE other faiths before they started modifying the rules in order to suit their interest.
- Women dress and relating terms are highlighted as well as Engagement and Marriage plus all other terms in between, and the Divorce is explained.
- Sacred Months Verses are shown as well and relating rulings stressing how Islam cares for animals/birds and other creatures, not just as an advice or warning, but ACTUAL PENALTY, not only that, but the penalty itself serving

as holy issue by paying for the poor people in society, <u>slaughtering and giving the meat to poor people, or letting free a slave/servant.</u>

- Patience is a very important topic, all verses have same aim of withstanding whatever happened when we try our best to deal with an issue like a job, money, education etc, but once it comes from human we are given a clear instruction : <u>to do exactly same they done to you, but not initiate or exaggerate</u>, also if we decide not to respond and leave it for judgment day, then we have better and higher reward, God it telling us that he gave same ruling to Moses, which is : an eye for an eye and a tooth for a tooth.
- Iman is a major topic: The Messenger (Muhammad SAW) believes in what has been sent down to him from his Lord, and (so do) the believers. Each one believes in Allah, His Angels, His Books, and His Messengers. They say, "We make no distinction between one another of His Messengers"- 285 البقرة 2

آمَنَ الرَّسُولُ بِمَا أُنزِلَ إِلَيْهِ مِن رَّبِّهِ وَالْمُؤْمِنُونَ ۚ كُلٌّ آمَنَ بِاللَّهِ وَمَلَائِكَتِهِ وَكُتُبِهِ وَرُسُلِهِ لَا نُفَرِّقُ بَيْنَ أَحَدٍ مِّن رُّسُلِهِ ۚ وَقَالُوا سَمِعْنَا وَأَطَعْنَا ۖ غُفْرَانَكَ رَبَّنَا وَإِلَيْكَ الْمَصِيرُ

- Ayman has same letters but two different meaning in verses like: Oath and (the captives and the slaves) that your **right hands possess**
- Healing- Shifaa, is a small subject, but Honey is clearly mentioned as healing, also mentioned Quran as healing for Mumins.
- Interest topic is easily understood by all of us from practical point of view and the effect on private as well as on society.

Islam is dealing with relating problems through multiple ways:

We are encouraged to donate, lend- without interest, not to waste- food or other stuff, not to Gamble, and not to drink any alcohol.

* Not only that Islam is telling us that it is duty upon Muslim:

As-Sadaqat (here it means Zakat) are only for the Fuqara' (poor), and Al-Masakin (the poor) and those employed to collect (the funds); and for to attract the hearts of those who have been inclined (towards Islam); and to free the captives; and for those in debt; and for Allah's Cause (i.e. for Mujahidun - those fighting in the holy wars), and for the wayfarer (a traveller who is cut off from everything) a duty imposed by Allah-60 التوبة9

❈ إِنَّمَا الصَّدَقَاتُ لِلْفُقَرَاءِ وَالْمَسَاكِينِ وَالْعَامِلِينَ عَلَيْهَا وَالْمُؤَلَّفَةِ قُلُوبُهُمْ وَفِي الرِّقَابِ وَالْغَارِمِينَ وَفِي سَبِيلِ اللَّهِ وَابْنِ السَّبِيلِ ۖ فَرِيضَةً مِّنَ اللَّهِ ۗ وَاللَّهُ عَلِيمٌ حَكِيمٌ

AUTHOR

A retired United Kingdom qualified engineer with seven years research into the Holy Quran Verses, during which the 5 books below were written:

* Similar Meaning in Quran Verses- Tashabuh, (English translation and Arabic Tafsir).

* Family Members in Holy Quran Verses, (English translation and Arabic Tafsir).

* Family Members in Holy Quran Verses, (English translation May 2023) Hardcover.

  Also available Ebook and Paperback.

* Quran Vocabulary and Verse- (Part 1/2) Volume 1 will be printed same time as this book – paperback 500 page ((English translation).

furthermore, an Audio MP3 File was created on SD/MicroSD for same Family book verses- reciting most of the Verses- useful for people with difficult reading capability.

Born in the Holy Land, with the privilege having Arabic as mother tongue, plus Hebrew, English, and Turkish languages, but with a strange study syllabus of four years secondary school during which Quranic and Islamic (History) lessons were replaced by Hebrew literature and TORA- Bible.

First year in the secondary I studied in Roman Orthodox internal school in Nazareth, where after all restrictions, We were able, and been encouraged to -at least- read from an Arabic text book and loudly during our lunch/dinner in front of the dining priests, teaching staff and pupils and to be corrected for any mistakes, and in the following three years secondary school to be taught Arabic by a proud and patriotic Christian teacher who fluently mastered knowledge from Quran verses, and the strength and beauty of verses that led two of the students to divert their study from Scientific branch and to become Arabic teachers and Muslim preacher, but it took me until after retirement to follow suit having slowly stocked my shelves with Islamic books.

HAMZA MUHAMMAD DAKKA   حمزة محمد دقة

dakkahm@yahoo.co.uk